Writing Weimar

For R.C.O.

Writing Weimar

Critical Realism in
German Literature
1918–1933

DAVID MIDGLEY

OXFORD

UNIVERSITY PRESS

OXFORD

UNIVERSITY PRESS

Great Clarendon Street, Oxford OX2 6DP

Oxford University Press is a department of the University of Oxford.
It furthers the University's objective of excellence in research, scholarship,
and education by publishing worldwide in

Oxford New York

Athens Auckland Bangkok Bogotá Buenos Aires Calcutta
Cape Town Chennai Dar es Salaam Delhi Florence Hong Kong Istanbul
Karachi Kuala Lumpur Madrid Melbourne Mexico City Mumbai
Nairobi Paris São Paulo Singapore Taipei Tokyo Toronto Warsaw

and associated companies in Berlin Ibadan

Oxford is a registered trade mark of Oxford University Press
in the UK and certain other countries

Published in the United States
by Oxford University Press Inc., New York

© David Midgley 2000

The moral rights of the author have been asserted

Database right Oxford University Press (maker)

First published 2000

British Library Cataloguing in Publication Data

Data available

Library of Congress Cataloging in Publication Data
Midgley, David R., 1948–
Writing Weimar : critical realism in German literature, 1918–1933 / David Midgley.
Includes bibliographical references and index.
1. German literature—20th century—History and criticism. 2. Realism in literature. I.
Title.
PT405.M458 2000   830.9'00912—dc21   99-055510
ISBN 0-19-815179-9

3 5 7 9 10 8 6 4 2

Typeset by Best-set Typesetter Ltd., Hong Kong
Printed in Great Britain
on acid-free paper by
Biddles Ltd,
Guildford and King's Lynn

Preface

I have tried to write the sort of book that will interest specialist and non-specialist readers alike. The subject is a complex one, and I have had to look for ways to condense my presentation of it without allowing my account to become superficial. These considerations explain the policy I have adopted towards source references and footnotes.

For the benefit of those who may want (or need) an immediate sense of where my information comes from, I have made use of source references embedded in the text. But in order not to disrupt the flow overmuch for the general reader, I have tried to be discreet in my use of this method of referencing. The works of primary authors are referred to by short titles which should enable them to be easily identified in section A of my bibliography, and the titles of journals and magazines of the Weimar period are referred to by a system of abbreviations which is explained on p. ix. References to the secondary literature, which is listed in section B of my bibliography, use the Harvard method. The footnotes provide the original German version of quotations, and more generally they substantiate or elucidate points which are likely to be primarily of interest to specialist readers.

There is one other presentational point which I ought perhaps to explain here, although it is a well-established convention in German academic publications. I have used *double inverted commas* to represent true quotations, and *single inverted commas* for concepts or terms in conventional public usage (as well as for quotations within quotations). This was essential to my purpose in a book which aims precisely to clarify distinctions in the public use of a term like 'Sachlichkeit', for example, and which also has frequent cause to distinguish between authoritative statement and ironic allusion in the writings of the authors discussed.

I wish to record my gratitude to a number of colleagues for their support, encouragement, and advice during my work on this project. They are Christopher Innes (York, Ontario), Michael Minden (Cambridge), Hans-Harald Müller (Hamburg), Ritchie Robertson (Oxford), Ronald Speirs (Birmingham), Edward Timms (Sussex), and John White (King's College, London). At the same time, of course, none of them should be held accountable for what I have decided to put into the finished product.

I must also express my thanks to the Humanities Research Board of the British Academy for providing me with a term's funded leave in 1995 which enabled me to make significant progress on the book.

D. M.

Cambridge 1999

Contents

List of Illustrations   viii

List of Abbreviations   ix

Introduction: Writing under Weimar   1

1. 'Neue Sachlichkeit': The Career of an Idea   14

2. Poetry for Everyday Use?   57

3. The Theatre as Political Community   95

4. The Novel I: Representing the Times   141

5. The Novel II: Facing up to Disillusionment   189

6. Remembering the War   226

7. The City and the Country   260

8. Technology versus Humanity   304

Epilogue: Interpreting Weimar Culture   353

Bibliography   358

Index   379

List of Illustrations

Fig. 1 Max Beckmann, *The Night*, 1918–19   25
© DACS 2000. Kunstsammlung Nordrhein-Westfalen.
Photograph: Walter Klein.

Fig. 2 Rudolf Schlichter, *Portrait of Bertolt Brecht*, 1926   27
Städtische Galerie im Lenbachhaus, Munich.

Fig. 3 Christian Schad, *Portrait of Egon Erwin Kisch*, 1928   28
Hamburger Kunsthalle. Photograph: Elke Walford.

Fig. 4 Karl Völker, *Image of Industry*, 1923   30
Staatliche Galerie Moritzburg, Halle.

Fig. 5 George Grosz, *Pillars of Society*, 1926   190
By permission of the Estate of George Grosz Princeton,
NJ. Staatliche Museen Preußischer Kulturbesitz,
Nationalgalerie, Berlin. Photograph: Jörg P. Anders.

Fig. 6 Otto Dix, *This is how I looked as a soldier*, 1924   227
© DACS 2000. Galerie Nierendorf, Berlin.

Fig. 7 Gustav Wunderwald, *By the S-Bahn in Wedding*, 1927   271
Berliner Bank AG. Photograph: Angelika Weidling.

Fig. 8 John Heartfield, *Die Rationalisierung marschiert*, 1927   316
© DACS 2000. Akademie der Künste zu Berlin.

List of Abbreviations

The following abbreviations are used for references to the collected works of literary authors and to the titles of periodicals:

BFA	*Große kommentierte Berliner und Frankfurter Ausgabe* (Brecht)
GS	*Gesammelte Schriften*
GW	*Gesammelte Werke*
KWA	*Kommentierte Werkausgabe* (Broch)
L	*Die Linkskurve*
LW	*Die literarische Welt*
NB	*Die neue Bücherschau*
NM	*Der neue Merkur*
NR	*Die neue Rundschau*
Q	*Der Querschnitt.* Facsimile Querschnitt durch den Querschnitt 1921–1936, Frankfurt 1977
RF	*Die rote Fahne*
SW	*Sämtliche Werke*
TB	*Das Tage-Buch*
WA	*Werkausgabe*
WB	*Die Weltbühne*

Introduction
Writing under Weimar

The pedant registers a new epochal style. Life goes on . . .

Paul Hatvani (1921)[1]

The brief period of the Weimar Republic was a time of complex
transitions in German culture. The First World War and its aftermath had undermined traditional structures of authority, while
also leaving in their wake a powerful yearning in some quarters
for the security of those very structures. The vigour of economic
modernization in the mid-1920s, and the subsequent abrupt
impact of the Great Depression, lent a new urgency to debates
about the character of German society, about the status of particular social groups, and about how the role of technology in
society should be understood. And the political impact of the
mass movements of left and right—each motivated by its own
sense of an exclusive claim to inherit the future—presented a persistent challenge, not only to the insecure political authority of a
newly-fledged parliamentary democracy, but also to traditional
intellectual attitudes rooted in that distinctive German heritage
of Romanticism, classical humanism, and philosophical idealism. Literary writers of the time were faced with the problem of
having to reassess the nature and purpose of their writing in the
light of radically altered and inherently unstable circumstances.
The purpose of this book is to examine how the changing nature
of German society is critically reflected in the literature of the
Weimar period, and how changing perceptions of the function of
literature are reflected in literary texts.

In certain obvious senses, the experiences of transition present
themselves in literary writing in the form of issues. The

---

[1] Paul Hatvani's article "Zeitbild" appeared in the journal *Renaissance* in 1921,
and is quoted in the documentary anthologies by Best (p. 231) and Anz and Stark
(p. 106).

spectacular wave of war novels which appeared at the end of the 1920s was not just an expression of the need to recover the memory of the First World War; it was also associated with an ideological struggle for control over how the war and its outcome were interpreted. The collapse of imperial authority is reflected in the 'nihilistic' impulses to be found in the poetry of the period, as well as in the utopian thrust of its radical politics. And the experiences of deracination and disorientation engendered by social and economic upheaval become commonplace themes in the novels and plays of the period. But there are also important developments occurring in the formal practice of literary writing which are not so straightforwardly linked to social and political circumstances. When functional criteria are brought to bear on the writing of lyric poetry, then the consequence is not just a challenge to traditional assumptions about the expressive role of poetic language, but an expansion of the conventional understanding of what poetic writing can do. When major novelists confront the problems of depicting the historical experience of their time, they also raise fundamental questions about the nature of narrative representation which have significance both within the historical framework of the Weimar Republic and beyond it. And even within that most public of literary media, the theatre, the questions explored by writers of the time extend far beyond matters of theatrical representation and political orientation, and into the more difficult area of how theatrical performance can assist in the promotion of a critical, analytical awareness of the world.

In my subtitle I have used the term 'critical realism' as an initial indication of the emphasis I wish to place on my investigation of the literature of the Weimar period. I do so quite independently of the earlier uses of this formulation of which I am aware,[2] and I mean it to be understood quite literally. A turn towards realist depiction and towards realist assumptions about the expressive function of language was a general feature of German literature in the 1920s, by contrast with the visionary

---

[2] In Marxist literary criticism of the Stalinist period 'critical realism' was used to distinguish 'bourgeois' social criticism from what was to be expected of 'socialist realism': cf. Gleb Struve, *Geschichte der Sowjetliteratur* (Munich: Isar Verlag, 1958), 292; Georg Lukács, *The Meaning of Contemporary Realism* (London: Merlin Press, 1963), 93 ff. The term was also used in a general way to denote the characteristic interests of German academic philosophy during the 1920s: Ringer, 371.

aspirations and verbal experiments that had characterized the Expressionist movement of the previous decade. My particular focus within that general trend is on those writers who maintained a critical perspective on the social reality they were depicting, and especially on those whose works reflect a critical awareness of the means by which realist literary depiction is achieved. I should emphasize that this notion of critical realism does not provide convenient criteria for selecting a particular group of authors in preference to others: as Brecht was to note at a later date, in cultural history there are diverse lines of development which run through individual lives and individual works.[3] But I do believe that the distinctive heritage of German literary writing from the period 1918–33 is the product of a peculiar readiness on the part of the writers of that time to pose radical questions about social reality and about the role of literature in communicating the nature of that reality, and it is that cultural heritage that I have set out to describe. (Within the broad trend there were, to be sure, also instances of 'uncritical' realism, both in the sense of superficial reportage and in the sense of unquestioned partisanship; but then the issues raised by those kinds of writing were themselves the subject of critical reflection in the course of the debates of the time, and I have tried to bring out the implications of that particular critical reflection towards the end of Chapter 1.)

There were two considerations which initially suggested to me that a book of this kind was needed. One was the tendency for Weimar culture to be discussed as if all elements of it were contributing in one way or another to the political catastrophe which overtook Germany in 1933. The other was the tendency for German literary history to be presented in terms of a tidy sequence of epochal styles, each constituting a logical reaction against the preceding one.

During the decades which immediately followed the Second World War it was entirely understandable that historical analysis should have been dominated by the need to develop a full awareness of the cultural as well as the political and institutional factors which had provided favourable conditions for the rise to power of Adolf Hitler. And it remains the case that

[3] Bertolt Brecht, *Arbeitsjournal* (Frankfurt: Suhrkamp, 1974), i. 23.

understanding 'Weimar culture' in its fullest sense must include an awareness of those elements within the legislative, judicial, military, and educational institutions of the Republic which manifestly favoured the forces of nationalist restoration and reaction (Laqueur). A desperate cleaving to holistic conceptions of understanding has been identified as a characteristic feature of the academic profession under the Republic in particular (Ringer), and of the wider intellectual culture in general (Ziolkowski); and a sense that German intellectuals between the wars, across a wide range of ideological positions, were responding unhealthily to the processes of rationalization and specialization of inquiry which characterize the modern world has continued to prompt illuminating investigations of the thought of the Weimar period and its implications for our own time (Barnouw 1988; Bolz). But as far as the literary writing of the period is concerned, it is particularly unfortunate that what probably remains the most widely available general account of the subject in English, Peter Gay's *Weimar Culture: The Outsider as Insider* (originally published in 1969), contrives to present the writing of the period after 1925—i.e. after the election of Hindenburg as President—as if it had been totally dominated by the forces of kitsch, reaction, and infantile regression.

It is important, of course, that in any assessment of literary writing under the Weimar Republic we should retain a clear sense of what was either downright sinister or simply inept in the context of its time. But much of the writing I shall be discussing in the chapters that follow contributes something to the critical understanding of those very forces of kitsch, reaction, and regression that Gay highlights, even if it can be argued that it was politically ineffective in the circumstances of the day. Many of the authors in question had their works burned, or otherwise suppressed, in the course of the National Socialists' attempts to assert their particular holistic conception of what it meant to be German; and over recent decades much scholarly effort has been devoted to recovering an awareness of those works and interpreting them in their historical context. The volumes of essays in English respectively assembled by Keith Bullivant, Alan Bance, and Tony Phelan contain valuable contributions to the understanding of specific elements in the complex fabric of Weimar culture, and I have referred to these where appropriate. For points of detail I have also drawn on various publications by that great enthusiast of Weimar culture, John Willett. But I have two reservations about his most popular account of the subject, *The New Sobriety* of 1978. For one thing he is giving an account of (predominantly left-wing and avant-garde) culture in Germany between the Bolshevik Revolution of 1917 and the Nazi takeover of 1933 which is every bit as undifferentiated as Gay's is dismissive. For another, it is a book which flies under false colours. Willett's title is a restrictive, and therefore inescapably tendentious, translation of the term 'Neue Sachlichkeit'. That term has indeed been used as a general label for certain dominant tendencies in German culture during the 1920s, but as I show in Chapter 1, its precise meaning was itself the subject of intense controversy between the ideological camps *within* the culture of the Weimar period. This point takes us to the heart of the methodological problem which has bedevilled all attempts to achieve a coherent account of literary writing under the Republic.

A high priority for German literary scholars in the 1950s and early 1960s was to recover the Expressionist literature of the decade around the First World War from the neglect and misrepresentation it had suffered during the Nazi years. When they extended their inquiries into the period of the 1920s, the initial tendency was to look for a paradigm shift in literary style, away from the visionary and ecstatic qualities of Expressionism and towards a sober and objective realism that could be labelled 'Sachlichkeit' (Denkler 1968). The limitations of such stylistic criteria were swiftly identified: on the one hand it was recognized that the literary trends of the 1920s could not be understood without reference to the strong currents of radical politics in the period (Grimm and Hermand, 15–45), and on the other hand it was argued that the 'Sachlichkeit' which at first sight appeared to be a distinguishing feature of the culture of the 1920s needed to be understood in relation to longer-term developments in German culture (Kreuzer). The publication of Helmut Lethen's book *Neue Sachlichkeit* in 1970 had the effect of putting a sharper edge on this debate. Lethen was applying the label specifically to middle-class writers whom he saw as colluding in the generation of a cultural atmosphere favourable to

National Socialism, indeed he was interpreting 'Neue Sachlichkeit' as a cultural outlook which could be represented as a "class-specific substitute for socialism" (p. 32). Lethen, in other words, was viewing the literary realism of the Weimar period from a perspective which was typical of the Marxist intellectuals of the time—particularly Walter Benjamin and Ernst Bloch—and was judging it in the light of their pronounced sense of disappointment at the failure of German society to accomplish a revolutionary transformation in Marxist terms.[4] His approach was subsequently endorsed by Jost Hermand, who argued the case (in Bullivant (ed.)) for seeing an underlying unity of historical development within the diversity of Weimar culture (a diversity which he was simultaneously describing in the compendious volume he published with Frank Trommler in 1978). But elsewhere Lethen's book was rightly criticized for its relentlessly negative account of a literature which was still in the process of being rediscovered and reassessed (Prümm 1972). Other publications of the 1970s were at pains to emphasize the multiplicity of factors which made Weimar culture what it was, and indeed its openness to a wealth of cultural possibilities for the future, rather than any sense of a teleological impetus towards a final goal (Köhn; Rothe 1974).[5] Since that time much material from the Weimar period has become more easily accessible, as individual works have been reissued, periodicals reprinted, and anthologies of documents compiled (Kaes 1983; Kaes et al. 1994). This has perhaps made it easier to explore the complex cross-currents of literary and cultural activity under Weimar, but it has not necessarily made it easier to analyse them. The most pressing task for historical interpretation has become one of distinguishing patterns of actual cultural development among the welter of potentialities. As far as the meaning of the term 'Neue Sachlichkeit' is concerned, it was clearly established by the early 1980s that it could

---

[4] By comparison, the policy adopted by the East German Academy of the Arts for their official history of twentieth-century literature was more catholic in nature, even if they solved the problem of periodization by taking the dates of the Bolshevik Revolution and the defeat of Hitler as their defining reference points: see Hans Kaufmann, "Literaturgeschichte, Band 10", *Weimarer Beiträge*, 15 (1969), 453–78.

[5] Henri R. Paucker similarly emphasized the diversity of Weimar culture in the introduction to his Reclam anthology of 1974, even if he too resorted to 'Neue Sachlichkeit' as the general label for the literature of the period in his title.

not be taken to denote a distinct cultural epoch, let alone a coherent artistic movement; rather it should be understood as referring to certain cultural tendencies which were prevalent during the so-called stabilization phase of the Weimar Republic (1924–9), but which existed alongside other trends, and which were shared by authors of highly diverse political persuasions (Petersen). My own contribution to the understanding of the term has been to look behind the appearance of unity which the retrospective application of such a label inevitably suggests, and to ask how the word 'Sachlichkeit' was in fact used in the context of the cultural debates of the Weimar period. What I am trying to show in Chapter 1 is that the term 'Neue Sachlichkeit' masks a multiplicity of meanings which, in the particular circumstances of the mid-1920s in Germany, came to embrace such diverse phenomena as functional design and the resurgent vitalism of popular entertainment, social satire, and technological potential. I argue there that 'Neue Sachlichkeit' does not in itself constitute a serviceable category for cultural analysis, both because of the heterogeneity of the phenomena to which it refers, and because of the way the various ideological camps of around 1930 competed to invest the term with their respective varieties of cultural vision. In other words, the meaning of the term 'Neue Sachlichkeit' should be viewed as one field of tensions amongst others within the cultural debates of Weimar Germany, and if we are to advance our understanding of cultural developments in the Weimar period, then we need to differentiate among the varieties of tension which appear to coalesce in the discussions of that term.

As the immediate experience of the Nazi years has receded, it has become easier to distinguish between forces which contributed directly to the installation of Hitler's regime and the currents of cultural development which have significance in a wider time-frame. It has become apparent that 1933 is by no means such a clear watershed in cultural terms as it is politically, and that there are some strong elements of continuity running through from the Republic to the Third Reich (Schäfer 1981). Just as there are manifestations of high modernism in Weimar culture which can be traced back to the 1880s (Müller-Seidel), so too were the organizations of working-class culture in the 1920s operating within traditions established well before

the First World War (Davies; Guttsmann). In a longer-term perspective, then, the tensions of the Weimar period can be seen as
a peculiarly intensive phase in the adaptation of a pre-industrial
society to the consequences of industrialization (Mayer 1984).
The issues raised by the impact of technology, functional design,
and economic rationalization therefore need to be considered in
relation to cultural changes which had been in train since the
early nineteenth century (Segeberg 1987a; Großklaus and
Lämmert). Some of the specific features of literary writing under
Weimar would undoubtedly benefit from further investigation
in such longer-term perspectives, and in my epilogue I have
made a few suggestions about lines of inquiry which might
prove fruitful.

Two other recent publications need to be mentioned at this
point (even if they are a little tangential to my own concerns)
because they have made, or are likely to make, a strong impression on public perceptions of Weimar culture. One is Peter
Sloterdijk's *Critique of Cynical Reason*, which was a spectacular publishing success in Germany in the mid-1980s and
appeared in English translation in 1987. Sloterdijk's treatise was
mainly prompted by the manifestation of cynicism, and its association with entrenched social power, in the political and cultural life of the Federal Republic in the 1970s and 1980s; and
the critical positions he adopts are likely to feature prominently
in any future cultural history of that period. But he culled his
most striking examples of cynical utterance from writers of the
1920s. His book owed its notoriety in large part to the provocative resonances of the quotations he had compiled. But Sloterdijk was not concerned (as I am) to interpret those quotations
in the context of the literary works from which they are taken,
nor indeed the works in their historical context.

The other item in question is the latest book by Helmut
Lethen. In his various publications of the 1980s, Lethen developed a special interest in images of coldness as a distinctive
feature of the emotional and intellectual climate of the inter-
war period, and he has now gathered his findings together under
the title *Verhaltenslehren der Kälte: Lebensversuche zwischen
den Kriegen* (Behavioural Doctrines of Coldness: Experiments
in Living between the Wars). There are passages in that book

which describe with great clarity the conflicting nature of the social and cultural developments which took place in Germany after the First World War; and when he is presenting specific textual evidence Lethen gives a vivid picture of the cultural volte-face that occurred when German intellectuals repudiated the organic categories which had characterized discussions of German national identity under the Wilhelmine Empire and asserted in their place the values of scientific empiricism and Western civilization. When he speaks of the literature of the Weimar period conveying the sense of a humanity torn between the impulse to rational self-assertion and a posture of submission before external forces (p. 38) then, again, he is making a point which seems well worth pursuing. What makes his book as a whole unconvincing as an interpretation of cultural developments between the wars, however, is the artificial nature of the intellectual construction he imposes on them. He adopts the conceptual apparatus of a cultural anthropology which itself developed between the wars, even though he knows it to have been called into question by subsequent research (p. 30); and he does so because it provides him with a model of cultural transition which he can describe in the terms of (Freudian) individual psychology. His model is that of a transition from a 'guilt culture' to a 'shame culture', in which the mechanisms of internal conscience are replaced by those of social anxiety—even though he has to acknowledge that any such transition in Germany after 1918 at best took the form of unfulfilled projects (*Entwürfe*: p. 36). Those "projects", according to Lethen's argument, constitute a unified cultural development because they are collectively characterized by the cultivation of a "cold persona"—with the proviso that any manifestation of concern with human vulnerability in the literature can be accounted for as a form of 'magical thinking' (p. 38) and a Freudian 'return' of anxiety (pp. 11, 43, 245 ff.). There is, then, a reductive impulse running through Lethen's work from his 1970 book to the present day: in 1970 he was using the term 'Neue Sachlichkeit' to mean the defining attitude of a particular social class regardless of the variety of purposes pursued by the authors in question, and in 1994 he is using it to mean the defining mentality of a particular cultural phase regardless of the variety of social and intellectual perspectives to be found in individual works.[6]

What gives Weimar culture its distinctive character is not any single pattern of development, but the turbulence of a complex European society in a state of upheaval, and we find that turbulence reflected in the work of individual writers. The simple vitality of the new revue-style entertainments provokes agonized reflections on the part of sophisticated essayists and the defenders of an old ideal of self-cultivation. The radically analytical effects of dadaist montage and avant-garde narrative have their counterparts among more traditionalist novelists (such as Jakob Wassermann and Hermann Hesse) who are working to uphold or reconstruct the principles of integral personality. Alongside the ebullient populism of the new cabaret-style poetry there are powerful traditions of bucolic lyricism, reflective modernism, and hieratic elitism. And the recognition of the enormous potential of technology impinges on the thinking of the nationalist and racist right, as well as on that of the liberal and socialist left, and indeed of the vacillating 'unpolitical' figures in between. I have not attempted to give a comprehensive account of all these facets of Weimar literature in the chapters that follow. But I have looked for ways to evoke, not just the diversity of cultural impulses at work in the literature, but the dynamic interaction that occurs between those impulses in the circumstances of the time.

The solution I have adopted is to separate out a number of aspects of literary activity, each of which seems to me to constitute a relatively coherent element in the overall picture, but each of which offers possibilities for examining the interplay of tensions within a group of texts. When I discuss lyric poetry in Chapter 2, I try to show the range of poetic styles and attitudes that were being cultivated during the Weimar period, but I focus in particular on Brecht and the cabaret-style poets because of the manifest interest they show in the functions of public discourse, and because of the implications this carries for the long-

---

[6] For further critical comment on Lethen's work, see Wege (1994); also D. Midgley, "Vom Lebenswandel in der mechanisierten Gesellschaft: Zu neueren Tendenzen in der Theorisierung der kulturellen Entwicklung im Zeitraum der Weimarer Republik", in F. Möbius, N. Saul, and D. Steuer (eds.), *Schwellen: Exkursionen der Literaturwissenschaft* (Würzburg: Koenighausen und Neumann, 1999), 177–84.

term development of critical thinking about poetry. When I examine the ferment of theatrical activity in Chapter 3, I am considering the sense in which the work of particular figures relates to conceptions of political community and the potential for nurturing (self-)critical awareness of social relations through theatrical performance. In Chapter 4 I compare the best-known major novels of the period as attempts at large-scale narrative representation of the character of the times, and focus particularly on the methodological thinking which led Alfred Döblin and Robert Musil to adopt unconventional narrative techniques. I consider the attitude of disillusionment as a pervasive feature of Weimar culture in Chapter 5, but I do so in order to distinguish between the variety of forms that disillusionment took in practice, and with a particular eye for the positive use of disillusioning narrative structures as an instrument of enlightenment. Chapter 6 is devoted to the wave of war novels which set in at the end of the 1920s, and concentrates on particular examples which bring out the nature of the ideological struggle that was taking place over the retrospective interpretation of wartime experience. In Chapter 7 I describe the traditionally strong antagonism between stereotypical conceptions of urban and rural life, and the particular political significance with which it became invested under the circumstances of the Weimar Republic, but my main concern is to examine how the cultural tensions of the time are reflected in the depiction of Berlin on the one hand and provincial society on the other. Chapter 8, finally, explores the literary representation of technology in the period, because it is here above all that we can see an inherited literary discourse, which was hostile to mechanization, adapting to the changing circumstances of an industrial and mass culture, in which technology had to be recognized as a force that would shape the world of the future. What I am above all concerned to do there is to bring out the variety of perspectives from which the impact of technology was being interpreted, and to set those perspectives in relation to each other.

Readers who have a specialist knowledge of the field will undoubtedly have their own ideas about how such an account ought to have been organized. Some might wish to see more emphasis on working-class writing, or on the publications of the fascist right. Some might wish to see more specific attention given to women writers, or to the cultural contributions of the Jews. No doubt individual chapters could have been profitably devoted to the travel literature, or to the treatment of historical themes, or to the mavericks and mystics (such figures as Arnolt Bronnen and Franz Jung, or Ernst Barlach and Hans Henny Jahnn) whose works also cast interesting light on the character of German culture during the period in question. Others again might wonder why I have not found room to discuss the relationship between German and Austrian authors, or why my account frequently focuses on what was happening in Berlin as opposed to cultural activity elsewhere. Each of these responses has its own kind of legitimacy, and I have an answer to all of them.

My prime concern in this book has been to assess the significance of the critical perspectives and the critical techniques which come into prominence in German literature during the period of the Weimar Republic, those developments, in other words, which have in the past been (unsatisfactorily) subsumed under the notion of 'Neue Sachlichkeit'. Within my chapters as I have devised them I have found frequent opportunities to relate the works of individual figures to the familiar dimensions of German history between the wars, including the social trends, including the political and racial persecutions. While it would of course be possible to imagine additional chapters organized around other thematic complexes than those I have highlighted, it seemed to me that they would not add significantly to the quality of understanding achieved by examining the historical developments in the functions of literary writing during the Weimar period under the combination of headings I have selected. As for the place of Austrian authors in a study of this kind, the point I would make is this: the way the political map of Europe was redrawn after the First World War had the effect of separating German-speaking Austria from the other territories of the erstwhile Hapsburg Empire, and thus of re-emphasizing the distinctive identity of the German language-community as a whole. While it is true that the more conservative of Austrian authors—the Hofmannsthal of the Salzburg Festival, the Werfel of the *Barbara* novel of 1928—attached great importance to the notion of a distinctive Austrian cultural heritage, it is equally the case that others who hailed from various corners of the Hapsburg Empire—Broch from Vienna and Musil from Carinthia, Kisch from Prague, and Joseph Roth from Eastern Galicia—found their writing careers to be strongly linked in one way or another to the fate of the German Reich in the circumstances of the post-1918 world. In those circumstances it was Berlin rather than any other German-speaking city that became the main focal point for new cultural developments—and some of the repercussions of that refocusing of German cultural identity are explicitly addressed in Chapter 7.

In short, I have arranged this book in such a way that it gives as representative a picture as I am able to draw of the developments in German literary writing between 1918 and 1933. Each chapter explores a particular field of tensions within which writers of various ideological persuasions and social backgrounds were having to orientate themselves. And the first of those fields of tension to which I wish to turn my attention is the significance that became attached to the term 'Sachlichkeit' in the process of cultural reappraisal that followed the First World War.

'Neue Sachlichkeit': The Career of an Idea

What was this 'Neue Sachlichkeit'? Everything that was not so incorporeal [*unsachlich*] as the prophecy and missionary ardour that had gone before.

Ludwig Marcuse[1]

'Neue Sachlichkeit' is reactionary.

Bertolt Brecht (*BFA* 21, 356)

The Expressionist wave was breaking by 1920. Art critics were sensing that artistic experiment in 'pure' colour and abstract form had reached the limits of its possibilities (Anz and Stark, 98 f.). Kurt Pinthus presented his famous anthology of Expressionist poetry, *Menschheitsdämmerung*, as a monument to a bygone era. The "death" of Expressionism was proclaimed in articles by Ivan Goll and Paul Hatvani in the course of 1921 (Best, 225–34). And over the next few years the representative Expressionist dramatists were to turn from high pathos to comedy (Knobloch). The direction that cultural activity might take in the years to come became a matter of negotiation among the various perspectives from which the contemporary social and cultural world was being scrutinized. Only in the second half of the 1920s did the term 'Neue Sachlichkeit' come to be widely adopted as a label for the characteristic cultural trends of the time—and no sooner had these trends been so identified than they were subjected to criticism and rejection in their turn. The purpose of this chapter is to explore the reasons for the rise and subsequent fall in intellectual esteem that the notion of 'Neue Sachlichkeit' underwent during the period of the Weimar Republic, and to identify the precise connotations which the

[1] Ludwig Marcuse, *Mein zwanzigstes Jahrhundert* (Munich: Paul List, 1960), 90.

term came to carry in the context of the cultural debates of the time.

To speak of Expressionism itself as a unified movement is, of course, to impose an appearance of conceptual coherence on a phenomenon which was both dynamic and multifarious in character. The decade between 1910 and 1920 had seen a vibrant sequence of programmatic declarations and artistic experiments in which a rising generation had sought to break with the stagnant social and cultural atmosphere of a consolidated German Reich. Before the outbreak of war in 1914, poets and artists had evoked apocalyptic disruption out of a spirit of opposition to Wilhelmine complacency; and the Expressionist dramas which began to be staged in 1917 presented imagined outcomes to intensely fraught human experiences, including those of protracted mechanized warfare. Literary writers had experimented in radical ways with the expressive power of language and even sub-linguistic utterance ('bruitism'), and intellectuals had become increasingly concerned with the possibilities of radical political change. The title that Kurt Pinthus gave to his anthology of Expressionist poetry, *Menschheitsdämmerung*, points to the all-encompassing, indeed universalistic pretension of much of the poetry it contains, but also to the sense of profound cultural crisis articulated in that poetry: a 'twilight' of humanity which contains both the awareness of imminent demise and the intimation of a new dawning. By 1920, the Expressionist aspiration to give expression to the 'essences' beyond empirical experience was being challenged from radical as well as traditional positions, and the prophetic visions were being overtaken by a down-to-earth concern with social practicalities in a postrevolutionary world.

In Berlin the Dadaists were working at the total dissolution of the boundary between artistic creativity and political activity, elevating the inherent dynamism of the wartime avantgarde into a governing principle of being as they did so. The early exponents of Dada, intellectuals from various combatant nations who had been drawn together in neutral Switzerland by a common purpose of moral and cultural protest, gave voice to their outrage in ways which sought to shake off the constraints of their various national cultures, including the constraints of linguistic orthodoxy itself. Their deliberate affronts to inherited cultural assumptions carried an implication that creative effort was to be constantly directed at exciting a surge of emotive energy in the public mind. Chosen as a conscious emblem of the elusiveness of meaning, the term 'Dada' became a watchword for provocative artistic activity whose goal was no longer a 'finished' work of art, but art as a public manifestation. In 1927 a German magazine published the memoir in which Tristan Tzara recalled his greatest sense of achievement, on taking the Dada experience to Paris, as the moment when the audience at the Salle Gareau went "completely dada" (Ferber, 129)—although Tzara was also reproached by his former German associates with having turned Dada, in the relatively liberal and relaxed atmosphere of Paris, into a new kind of museum piece (Philipp, 27 f.). In the volatile political climate of Berlin in 1918–19, Dada cultivated a "satirical hyperrealism" (Raoul Hausmann) of which the best-known examples are the graphics and photo-montages of George Grosz and John Heartfield. Through various forms of public agitation—including the famous leafleting of a session of the National Assembly by the self-styled Oberdada, Johannes Baader—Dada intervened in the political life of the young Weimar Republic in a spirit of permanent subversion (Benson, 123–34, 163–8).

As a contemporary reviewer noted, Dada had initiated a critique of Expressionism at the precise moment when it was crystallizing into something "historical, typical, characteristic, final", which the avant-garde spirit was consciously striving to overcome in its turn (Benson, 1). But already in 1920, the essayist Rudolf Kayser was writing an epitaph for Expressionism from a more traditionalist perspective in the highbrow journal *Der neue Merkur* (The New Mercury). For Kayser, literary Expressionism denoted nothing more and nothing less than the chaos attending the dissolution of an entire cultural epoch, the epoch of Renaissance individualism. In its evocations of cosmic ecstasy and its invocations of abstract humanity, Expressionism represented for him a precipitate attempt to grasp at metaphysical truths by abandoning the realm of empirical realities. Expressionism, he argued, had not achieved the presentation of a human type, as earlier literary movements had done, but only of airy gestures, slogans, and poses (*Gebärden, Modeworte, Frisuren*). In Expressionism, European humanity had lost sight of the fundamental truth about its own specific brand of spirituality, namely that the spirit (*Geist*) consisted in the relationship of tension between the perceiving individual and the perceived object. The new direction which Kayser proposed for creative writing was a rehabilitation of "personality" in a spirit of liberal humanism, a principle which he was to champion in the ensuing years as editor of the *Neue Rundschau* (New Review), the house magazine of the S. Fischer Verlag, and which he described in 1920 as giving expression to the strength and creativity of "humanity in the flesh" (*NM* IV, 4, 248–58).

The repudiation of Expressionism that is most likely to be familiar to students of German literature is a statement by the then unknown Bertolt Brecht in the Augsburg newspaper of the Independent Socialist Party for which he was writing reviews in 1919. After reading an anthology of Expressionist dramas which included Toller's *Die Wandlung* (Transfiguration) and Kaiser's *Hölle Weg Erde* (Hell Way Earth), Brecht noted:

Flache Visionen, sofort zu vergessen. Kosmos dünn. Der Mensch als Objekt, Proklamation statt: als Mensch. Der abstrahierte Mensch, der Singular von Menschheit. Seine Sache liegt in schwachen Händen.

(*BFA* 21, 89: Shallow visions, instantly forgettable. Cosmos thin. Human beings as objects, as proclamations, instead of as human beings. The human being in the abstract, the singular of humanity. His cause lies in weak hands.)

Earlier the same year, Brecht had recorded a more sweeping critique of Expressionism as a movement, reacting against the starkness of its constraints and its frequent intellectual superficiality: just as in politics Germany had acquired a new parliament but lacked parliamentarians, so too in literature it was expressing delight in ideas—but no ideas (*BFA* 21, 49). He applied the same brand of polemical wordplay to the published plays of Expressionist writers: here was a "will to drama", but no drama, their texts appeared like displaced newspaper articles, mere expressions of editorial opinion (*BFA* 21, 89). In practice, the relationship between Brecht's own works and Expressionist drama is more subtle and more complex than these comments suggest. His earliest plays, *Baal* and *Trommeln in der Nacht* (Drums in the Night), contain provocative repudiations of fashionable public interest in Expressionist lyricism and revolutionary idealism. But as Ronald Speirs has argued (in Bance (ed.), 138 f.), in their deliberately anti-psychological portrayal of quasi-mythical figures, in their strong use of symbol, and in their scenic representations of the ecstatic experience of life's 'essences', these plays also display characteristic features of Expressionist drama. Moreover, by the late 1920s Brecht was proclaiming Georg Kaiser in particular as an important precursor to his own conception of a "theatre for a scientific age" because of the way Kaiser had pioneered the dramatization of ideas and analytical insights in his plays (BFA 21, 274 f.).[2]

As we shall see in later chapters, it was characteristic of Brecht that he engaged with the latest cultural trends of his time in order first to absorb and understand them and subsequently to transcend them. A more straightforward case of a literary writer reacting directly against Expressionism around 1920 is presented by Brecht's fellow Bavarian, Oskar Maria Graf. Graf came from a humble, though not impoverished background: his father had built a successful baker's business in the village of Berg on the Starnberger See, and he himself profited from the literary and cultural influences of nearby Munich. At the age of 17, however, he cut himself loose from his family and lived by means of casual employment until he could establish himself as a freelance writer in 1920. Politically he was closely associated with Munich's bohemian anarchist network, and in 1918 he was involved in subversive activity connected with the exposure of Germany's responsibility for precipitating the First World War (Bauer, 90 ff.; Lützeler 1986a, 55 ff.). The programme which Graf announced in 1920, in the wake of the brutal suppression of the revolutionary Räterepublik the previous year, and to which he effectively adhered in his subsequent writings, emphasizes a natural vitalism as the necessary antidote to the airy intellectualization of human problems. In the pages of his own ad hoc literary periodical, which bore the down-to-earth title *Die Bücherkiste* (The Book-Box), he called for a mode of narrative

---

[2] On the relationship between Brecht and Kaiser, see Schürer. On the relationship between Brecht's poetry and Expressionism, see Philip Thomson, "Sachlichkeit und Pathos: Brecht und der Expressionismus", in Bernd Hüppauf (ed.), *Expressionismus und Kulturkrise* (Heidelberg: Winter, 1983), 183–205.

writing which would convey the powerful unpredictability of events and personalities. "Nothing in the world," he insisted, "follows an ordered sequence." It was high time that writers went over to a purely factual account of events as they have occurred, abandoning the pursuit of elegant forms and preconceived conclusions, and leaving the task of explication to lawyers, professors, and specialists in ethical niceties. With a pointed thrust against the "preaching" of Expressionism, he calls for living, breathing human individuals to be given the opportunity to tell their own story in their own way: "Man lasse die Lebendigen reden und erzählen, nicht die Prediger." And his reason for arguing in this way is expressed in terms of casting off the illusions and intellectual pretensions of the recent past and achieving that sober, matter-of-fact outlook which is necessary in art, criticism, politics, and all other aspects of post-war life. He sums up that outlook in a single word: "Sachlichkeit".[3]

The word "sachlich" appears—fleetingly, as a seemingly inconsequential adjective—in Rudolf Kayser's essay, when he is describing his particular conception of the creative mission for the individual in making sense of the world around him (*NM* IV, 4, 257). In the 1922 version of Brecht's *Baal*, "Sachlichkeit" expresses an attitude of impassive practicality which happens, in its context, to be opposed to the anguish of a young woman whom Baal has violated (*BFA* 1, 98). In Graf's brief statement of 1920 it signifies the fundamental principle underlying a new literary programme; and in this sense, as a principle of sober observation, objective appraisal and the dispassionate presentation of empirical experience, "Sachlichkeit" more generally acquired the status of a guiding precept in the post-war years.

As early as July 1919 it had served the young essayist Harald Landry as a watchword in his exposition of political liberalism. In a spirit not far removed from that of Graf, Landry calls for a stripping away of literary pretentiousness, an "Entliterarisierung des Geistes" (*NM* III, 4, 266–74). For the literary critic Bernhard Diebold, writing in December 1921, an attitude of "Sachlichkeit" was to provide firm ground for establishing

---

[3] Oskar Maria Graf, "Gegen die Dichter von heute", *Die Bücherkiste*, 2 (1920–1), 5/6, 5.

new ideals (*NM* V, 9, 640). It is also implicitly the principle which underlies the critical style advocated by the prominent theatre critic Herbert Ihering in 1926, namely an elimination of cultured jargon and of stylistic nuance for its own sake, the clear open statement of opinion in a vocabulary which does not presuppose any special theoretical premisses (*LW* 2, 10, 1). When *Die literarische Welt* (The Literary World), the journal in which Ihering was writing, had first appeared the previous year, "Sachlichkeit" was precisely the quality that its editor, Willy Haas, promised to his readers, and the general character of *Die literarische Welt* makes it a prime example of the down-to-earth ethos he seems to have had in mind. Appearing weekly in newspaper format, rather than as a monthly brochure, it provided a forum for the frank exchange of unvarnished opinions in a spirit of editorial detachment, uniting within its pages, like the house of Ernst Rowohlt which published it, writers of highly disparate (and increasingly polarized) ideological orientations.

"Sachlichkeit" in a complementary sense—the sense of a breezy openness to the contemporary world—is what was offered by another new periodical publication of the 1920s, *Der Querschnitt* (The Cross-Section). It began in 1921 as a low-circulation bi-monthly newsletter, through which the art dealer Alfred Flechtheim informed his clients of new trends in the visual arts. From 1924, under the editorship of Hermann von Wedderkop, it became a high-profile glossy monthly aimed at a self-consciously up-to-date and up-market readership. Wedderkop's first editorial again promised "Sachlichkeit" and precision, a diet of hard facts in compensation for the hyper-literary character of Expressionism and the high-minded earnestness of the German intellectual tradition generally (*Q*, 13 f.; Ferber, 5 f.). There is transparent irony in his paradoxical description of *Der Querschnitt* as a "Magazin der aktuellen Ewigkeitswerte" (magazine of up-to-the-minute eternal values). In practice he proved adept at stimulating the appetites of readers with a judicious mixture of sensationalism and serious cultural comment. *Der Querschnitt* carried interviews with such celebrities as Mussolini or Rasputin's daughter alongside features on the latest furniture design or "Frei-Körper-Kultur" (i.e. naturism). It displayed photographs of well-dressed—or undressed—ladies

alongside articles by Europe's most prestigious authors. All elements of contemporary reality were grist to Wedderkop's mill,
and when it came to defining a contemporary role for the arts,
he argued in a leading article in July 1926 that they had the
option of either keeping abreast with current trends or falling
by the wayside: the stuff of contemporary aesthetics had to
be identical with that of the newspapers and the cinema, of
sport and technology (*Q*, XIX). The zest for life displayed
by the German public following the depredations of war and
the ensuing economic crisis led serious-minded writers to echo
Wedderkop's breezy appeal to a sense of modernity. Brecht was
far from alone in the mid-1920s in recognizing the theatrical
potential in popular taste, which was bringing up to 6,000
spectators nightly to revue-style entertainments in Berlin during
the 1925–6 season (*Q*, 55–8). In the pages of *Der Querschnitt*
we even find the poet Karl Wolfskehl (otherwise remembered as
a fastidious disciple of Stefan George) reporting from backstage
on the activities of the Tiller Girls (Ferber, 205). And earlier, in
December 1925, we find Walter Benjamin, in collaboration with
the theatre director Bernhard Reich, enthusing about a possible future model for the theatre which would harness both
the popular appeal of the revue and the technical potential of
modern engineering: it would be "the Wembley of stagecraft"
(Ferber, 33–7).

The combination of technological innovation with the robust
physicality of popular entertainment came to be widely discussed as an invasive 'Americanism'. To the highbrow critic
it was as if the American lifestyle was being imported into
Germany along with the capital investment upon which the
revival of the German economy after 1923 was largely dependent. Europeans appeared to be assimilating to an alien social
type characterized by rationality, matter-of-factness, and a high
pace of living (*NR* 39/I, 339).[4] In the realm of high culture, a
special symbolic importance came to be attached to Ernst
Křenek's opera *Jonny spielt auf* (Jonny's Big Moment) of 1927,

---

[4] Antipathy towards 'Americanism' was especially strong in the pages of *Die Tat*,
and in the writings of Hermann Keyserling and Adolf Halfeld (see Lethen 1970,
25). Halfeld's *Amerika und der Amerikanismus* (Jena: Diederichs, 1927), painted a
Spenglerian picture of 'soulless' civilization, and attracted a considerable following
(see P. Berg, 136 ff.).

in which the negro jazz musician Jonny 'triumphs' by dint of verve, vitality, and egoistic drive over a 'decadent' European culture (cf. Ermen, 825 f.). Optimistic interpreters of the vigorous new trends in popular entertainment, such as Siegfried Kracauer, saw them as evidence of a rational and 'democratic' cultural potential (*Ornament*, 53 f.). In the *Neue Rundschau* of 1928, on the other hand, Max Rychner—amongst others—speaks on behalf of a traditional liberal humanism which feels threatened by the mass culture and levelling-down of 'Americanism', by contrast with the differentiation and individualism he associates with Europe (*NR* 39/II, 225–35). A fashionable book on the culture of the chorus line, Fritz Giehse's *Girlkultur* of 1926, staunchly defended European tradition against the encroachment of mechanistic attitudes, and when the former Dadaist Richard Huelsenbeck reviewed it for *Die literarische Welt* he took the opportunity to denounce the whole American way of life for its morality of pervasive uniformity (*LW* 2, 16, 3). It was in provocative response to such traditionalist phobias that Brecht and Feuchtwanger took to mimicking the diction and ethos of a stereotyped Americanism in their publications of the 1920s, but their artistic exploitation of the cult did not rest there. The values of 'Americanism' are parodied and ironized in Feuchtwanger's *PEP* poems of 1928 (cf. Modick, 124 ff.); and Brecht constructs the ambience of an imaginary American boom-town in his *Mahagonny* opera of 1929 precisely in order to challenge both the underlying assumptions of consumer society and the entertainment industry as the ideological vehicle of those assumptions.

In a psychologically astute article published before the First World War, the essayist Robert Müller had pointed out that when Germans spoke of 'Americanism' they were in fact projecting onto an idealized national type qualities that were in truth characteristic of the modern German nation itself—and he named these as "Sachlichkeit", discipline, egoism, and a sense of reality.[5] Rudolf Kayser took up Müller's point in the *Vossische Zeitung* in 1925, observing that 'Americanism' was a slogan for processes of social transformation which were giving Europe its own cartels and skyscrapers, its own film industries and

---

[5] Robert Müller, "Kritik des Amerikanismus", *Die Schaubühne*, 10/1 (1914), 544.

technical innovations, as well as its own boxers, jazzbands, and theatrical spectacles (Kaes, 265). What was new and more radical about the post-war transformation, however, was its firm association with the rationalization and standardization of industrial production, and the implications this had for personal lifestyles. Production-line methods which had been pioneered in America before the war and developed with spectacular success by Henry Ford were eagerly imitated in Germany, where both management and workforce expected technical innovation to lead inexorably to improved living standards (Wulf). In the wake of Henry Ford's autobiography (published in German in 1923) a flood of publications presented industrial rationalization as the way forward to democracy and social stability through consumerism, a notion which was to be abruptly revealed as a political delusion with the onset of the Great Depression in 1929 (cf. Hermand and Trommler, 50 ff.). And in Germany's industrial heartland in particular, we find the ideals of rationalization and standardization taken not only as the basis for a new, 'revitalized' attitude to life, but as the very model for artistic activity. In the pages of *Der Scheinwerfer* (Headlight), which began publication in Essen in 1927, the mechanical requirements of production-line engineering become invested with 'organic' significance, and the image for artistic activity which is offered in the place of traditional aesthetic categories is that of the precision-drilled hole (Schütz and Vogt, 19–22). The author, writing under one of several pseudonyms, is Erik Reger, who went on to produce a powerful depiction of how economic power was wielded by German industrialists during the 1920s in his novel *Union der festen Hand* (Union of the Firm Hand, 1931); to judge by the criteria he applies in his other essays and reviews of the time, he was not being ironic.

The peculiar momentum of cultural redefinition in Germany after 1918 was leading to an intellectual fusion of seemingly disparate elements: revitalization and rationalization, mass enthusiasm and technological potential, physicality and sober contemplation. If this combination of associations came to cohere in public awareness as 'Neue Sachlichkeit', then that was due in large part—and in large part inadvertently—to an art exhibition assembled in 1925 by Georg Friedrich Hartlaub, the director of the Municipal Gallery in Mannheim. It has to be emphasized, in the specific context of the Mannheim exhibition and more generally, that the term 'Neue Sachlichkeit' was not intended to stand as an adequate classification for the whole of contemporary art. Another art expert who was involved with the exhibition as a consultant, Franz Roh, wrestled somewhat inconclusively with this problem of classification in a book published in the same year, and incorporated into his own title both the catch-all historical notion of 'Post-Expressionism' and a consciously tentative label for a more limited aspect of broad trends, namely 'Magical Realism' (Roh). (The latter term, incidentally, has been appropriated with some justification for the lyrical variety of nature poetry sustained through the 1920s by Oskar Loerke, Alfred Mombert, and others.[6]) The circular in which Hartlaub invited artists to participate in his 1925 exhibition makes it plain that he recognized modes of objective representational art as having persisted alongside the more abstract tendencies of the previous decade, as well as arising out of the reaction against Expressionist trends. His intention was, he explained, "to unite representative works by artists who, during the last ten years, have been neither impressionistically diffuse nor expressionistically abstract," and who "have displayed a strength of conviction in either remaining true to a sense of positive tangible reality, or in regaining that sense" (Schmied 1969, 7). Just as representational art had persisted through the previous decade alongside Expressionism, so too did a strong tradition of the abstract and fantastical persist through the 1920s, most notably in the work of Vassily Kandinsky.

Among the artists of the period whose works are most commonly remembered nowadays, Hartlaub's selection included

---

[6] Among literary scholars, Karl Holl was quick to apply Roh's term 'magischer Realismus' to literature because for him it was suggestive of a spiritualizing impetus that he felt to be at work in the poetry of Brecht, Bronnen, and Zech as well as Barlach and Kolbenheyer: "Der Wandel des deutschen Lebensgefühls im Spiegel der deutschen Kunst seit der Reichsgründung", *Deutsche Vierteljahresschrift*, 4 (1926), 562 f. More generally the term has tended to be favoured by scholars of a conservative persuasion who want to emphasize the virtues of concrete representation of experience as distinct from critical engagement with the social world: see, for example, Wilhelm Duwe, *Deutsche Dichtung des 20. Jahrhunderts* (Zurich: Orell Füssli, 1962), vol. i, 200 f.

Fig. 1. Max Beckmann *The Night*, 1918–19

Max Beckmann, who had developed a very personal idiom independently of the dominant movement of the preceding decade.[7] Beckmann's work of the post-war years reflected the experience of psychic horror and spent idealism in stark images imbued with a quasi-mythical potency, as in his famous evocation of brutality invading a domestic interior, *The Night* (Fig. 1). George Grosz, whose paintings and line-drawings of the early 1920s have served above all to fix the popular image of Weimar art as socially committed and aggressively tendentious (Fig. 5), was also included, as was Otto Dix, who cultivated a pose of unflinching confrontation in his self-portraits (Fig. 6) as well as

---

[7] In a programmatic note of 1918, Beckmann speaks of a "transzendente Sachlichkeit" rooted in the love of nature and humanity as the way forward beyond the hypertrophied mysticism (*Geschwulstmystik*) of the previous decade, and looks to Cézanne and Van Gogh, amongst others, as models (see Max Beckmann, *Die Realität der Träume in den Bildern* (Munich: Piper, 1990), 22).

in his provocative depictions of repugnant social realities. But Hartlaub's exhibition also showed examples of recent painting quite different in character from these, such as works by Georg Schrimpf depicting a pastel-shaded idyllic world peopled by doll-like women and children. Looking back on the 1920s, the art historian Wieland Schmied sees a variety of European influences at work in German post-Expressionist art. They include both the 'naive' style of Henri Rousseau and the 'neo-classical' phase of Picasso; the 'metaphysical painting' of the Italians Chirico and Carrà, as well as the mechanistic compositions of Fernand Léger and the neo-realism of other contemporary French painters (Schmied 1985, 37 f.; Willett 1978a, 111 ff.). The unifying feature, in the German context, is not so much a new style as a way of looking at things which—as we have already seen in statements by writers and critics—vehemently repudiates the theoretical, intellectual, holistic pretensions of Expressionism. "Gone was the gesture which can capture the world organically in a brush-stroke." (Schmied 1985, 39) In terms of the history of art, 'Neue Sachlichkeit' became a shorthand term for the variety of ways in which a rising generation of artists foreswore the confident personal visions and gestures of Expressionism and turned instead to constructing discrete images of a post-war reality they had experienced as profoundly fragmented.

In the Dada phase of 1919–20, collage had been developed as a *technique* for provocatively erasing the boundary between art and reality: in the works of Hannah Höch and Kurt Schwitters it became a medium for subtly deconstructing the cultural texture of modern life; and through John Heartfield especially, it gave rise to a witty and ingenious tradition of political poster-art (Fig. 8). In the art of 'Neue Sachlichkeit', collage became a *compositional* principle which advertises its mistrust of appearances even as it strives meticulously to record them (cf. Schmied 1985, 39). A portrait by Otto Dix or Rudolf Schlichter is typically stylized, giving special emphasis to particular features or physical objects as distinctive attributes of the person depicted. Schlichter's 1926 portrait of Brecht, for example, presents the 'trade-mark' image cultivated by Brecht at the time, giving prominence to the cigar and the leather jacket, while also capturing something of the suppressed sensibility of the young poet

Fig. 2. Rudolf Schlichter, *Portrait of Bertolt Brecht*, 1926

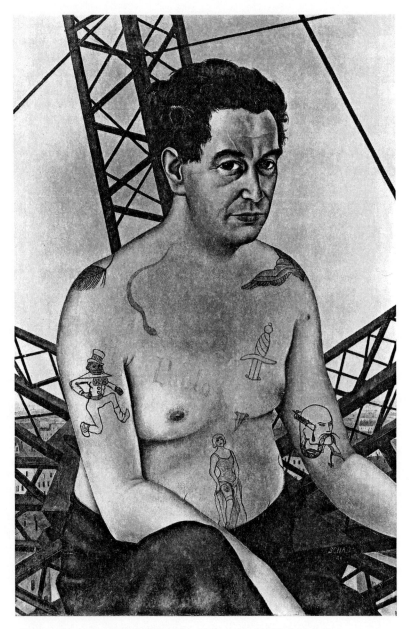

Fig. 3. Christian Schad, *Portrait of Egon Erwin Kisch*, 1928

in the facial features (Fig. 2). Often there is a certain archness
in the way that such compositions of the mid-1920s exhibit their
self-consciousness of how such images of celebrity status are
constructed. In the portraits of Christian Schad, who did not
exhibit in Mannheim, but did contribute to various subsequent
exhibitions of 'Neue Sachlichkeit', an eery stillness often results
from the clinical precision with which he presents detail that
is simultaneously suggestive of intimate knowledge and emotional detachment. Even his portrait of the self-styled "roving
reporter" Egon Erwin Kisch (Fig. 3)—which evokes the then
fashionable enthusiasm for technology by perching him on a
huge industrial crane, and which alludes to exotic adventure by
adorning his torso with tatoos—confers a certain brooding
isolation on the human subject. An earlier, more diagrammatic
representation of the world of industrial work by Karl Völker
(Fig. 4) evokes the alienation of the individual in a depersonalized landscape by incorporating into the composition that
"fixed stare" of the observer which Walter Benjamin was later
to identify as a characteristic of the satirical prose-writing of the
younger generation (as we shall see in Chapter 5). The more
naturalistic representations of Berlin street scenes by Gustav
Wunderwald are suggestive rather of the retreat of intimacy and
humanity from a landscape dominated by looming tenements
and overhead railway lines (Fig. 7), and in the hard-edged
verism of the later 1920s, the last vestiges of emotional involvement appear to have been drained from the world. The human
figures in works by Anton Räderscheidt exude a coldness which
seems to deny any possibility of interpersonal communication.
Franz Radziwill paints bleak urban landscapes in which the only
hint of human activity is a solitary passing aircraft. And Carl
Grossberg, a commercial artist by training, assiduously com-
poses a ghostly world of industrial machinery from which all
human content is banished (cf. Bertonati, 16–17).

With these last few examples we are touching on connotations of 'Sachlichkeit' which go beyond the intentions
that Hartlaub had expressed when he devised his Mannheim
exhibition, but which are essential to an understanding of the
reasons why his title, 'Neue Sachlichkeit', assumed central
importance in the wider cultural debates of the late 1920s. The
painting of the period embraced that sense of a need for sober,

Fig. 4. Karl Völker, *Image of Industry*, 1923

objective appraisal which we have seen articulated by writers and critics, and it captured the mood of radical scepticism and apprehension which followed the rapid collapse of political idealism in the post-war world. But beyond that, it reflected—albeit in a studiously despiritualized fashion—a new perception of the human environment which had taken hold since 1918, even if its origins go back considerably earlier.[8]

Ever since the turn of the century, architects and designers had been trying to harness the potential of industrial

[8] As the art historian Wieland Schmied has noted, the earliest documented use of the term 'Neue Sachlichkeit' appears to be in a programmatic statement on architectural design by Hermann Muthesius, one of the founders of the Werkbund, in 1900 (see Heizmann, 22).

production in the hope of bringing about a fruitful reconciliation between technology, aesthetic principle, and the need to humanize working and living conditions for large sections of the population. The organization through which they sought to realize these aims was the Werkbund, founded in 1907.[9] Their efforts received active support from the civic authorities in a number of cities after the First World War, and the resulting large-scale housing estates for urban workers helped to put the stamp of utilitarian rationality on the city landscape (Willett 1978a, 124–32; Lane, 87 ff.). Among the cultural institutions of the Weimar Republic it is probably the Bauhaus that is most commonly associated with a rigorously functional approach to the design of buildings and objects for household use, but there is an important distinction to be drawn between two historical phases in its operation. When Walter Gropius founded the Bauhaus at Weimar in 1919 it was a distinctly romantic project for the cultivation of integrated conceptions of creativity and of lifestyles generally; but in 1924 the Bauhaus moved to Dessau in order to cultivate closer links with manufacturing industry, and began to focus its efforts much more directly on design for mass production (Whitford, 136–64; Willett 1978a, 118–23). The Bauhaus presented several major exhibitions during the 1920s, but the event which probably did most to bring functional design to general public awareness during the Weimar period was an exhibition in Stuttgart in 1927, which was mounted under the aegis of the Werkbund, with strong leadership from the Bauhaus architect Mies van der Rohe. (The Werkbund had plans for a still more spectacular exhibition in Berlin in 1930—a "Weltbau-Ausstellung" indeed—but that project had to be deferred and reduced in scale under the impact of the Great Depression.)

The Stuttgart exhibition was an international affair, with architects from ten nations involved, but as the architectural historian Henry-Russell Hitchcock noted, it was regarded at the time as the sort of thing that only the Germans could have organized (Hitchcock, 195). What made it possible was a propitious combination of creative ambition, political will, and public finance. With the help of American loans under the Dawes Plan

[9] For an illuminating account of the achievements of the Werkbund, see Albrecht Wellmer, *The Persistence of Modernity* (Cambridge: Polity, 1991), 95–112.

of 1924, as well as funding from local taxes, the Stuttgart authorities were planning the construction of 1,600 new homes, and in these circumstances the leaders of the Werkbund were able to persuade them to earmark a portion of that budget for sixty-one dwellings to be designed by the leading innovative architects of the day, and to allocate them a site above the town on which to build them: the Weißenhof (Kirsch). As with Hartlaub's art exhibition, it is possible to discern significant differences in design concept among the contributors to the Weißenhof estate. The Bauhaus representatives were associated with universal principles and a clear differentiation of elements in the construction, while Hans Scharoun and the brothers Taut were still being described as Expressionists at the time because of the way they incorporated non-functional features—curved surfaces and rounded openings—into their structures. Those who espoused the most uncompromisingly utilitarian principles in 1927, such as Ludwig Hilbeseimer, are probably the least commonly remembered now. But the impression created by the Weißenhof estate as a whole was that of a pared-down functionalist approach to housing, characterized by flat rooves and box-like compartments (which was derided and treated with contempt during the Nazi years). Such design entered the public imagination as the epitome of 'Neue Sachlichkeit', as a cartoon in the magazine *UHU* in 1929 testifies (Lethen 1990, 120). Moreover, the architectural exhibition was accompanied by a sensational display of the latest household gadgets and interior design—wholly functional bathroom and kitchen equipment, vacuum cleaners, electric stoves, washing-machines and dish-washers—which evoked unprecedented possibilities for the transformation of domestic life. And the whole show was presented to the public as a purposeful offensive on behalf of a 'sachlich' approach to living: the poster which advertised it showed a traditionally ornate and cluttered bourgeois living-room crossed out by hand, with the question written underneath, "Wie wohnen?" (How should we live?) The implied answer, clearly, was "not like this!"

By this time, too, excited anticipation of the possible new developments that technology might bring to the arts was being focused on the theatre, and in particular on the exploits of Piscator. In the wake of Hartlaub's exhibition, we find the term "neue Sachlichkeit"—the newness of it reflected in the fact that the adjective is not yet capitalized—applied to Piscator's style of theatrical production as early as March 1926. The author in question, Leo Lania, was subsequently to become one of Piscator's closest associates. Lania had hailed an earlier Piscator production at the Berlin Volksbühne, with its innovatory use of slide projections, as a step on the road to a deromanticized conception of art, a theatrical equivalent of journalistic reportage, which brought the sober realities of the class struggle in factories, offices, and prisons onto the stage. Now, in Piscator's staging of Alfons Paquet's *Sturmflut* (Tidal Wave), the 'sachlich' presentation of political and social events was being enhanced by the scenic use of moving film. Lania enthusiastically welcomes this technical development as something which invests the theatre with a power to evoke the true agents of contemporary history: "the masses, the landscape, the epoch" (*LW* 2, 10, 3). Other theatre critics were to echo this strong association of Piscator's name with the notion of 'Neue Sachlichkeit' in the course of 1926 and 1927.[10] Lania's own chief contribution to Piscator's theatre was the playscript for a 1928 production about international competition for oil. The title was suggestive of the cynical exploitation of favourable market conditions: *Konjunktur*. With its presentation of international politics predominantly in the form of projected newspaper headlines, and its abandonment of the acting area to the technical paraphernalia of a developing oilfield, it was a venture which demonstrated the inherent constraints of a conception of theatre totally subordinated to the principle of documentation (Innes, 79 f., 85 f.). It was nevertheless symptomatic of what a positive programme of 'Sachlichkeit' had come to mean on the political left.

Konjunktur was criticized in the Communist Party journal *Die rote Fahne* (The Red Flag) for its burlesque treatment of momentous political issues (*RF*, 12 April 1928), but there was no lack of a positive echo within the Communist movement for

---

[10] Both Herbert Ihering (sympathetically) and Paul Fechter (unsympathetically) speak of Piscator as the champion of a new quality of 'Sachlichkeit' in September 1926 (Rühle 1967, 722, 727). Diebold also speaks of Piscator as the foremost exponent of 'Neue Sachlichkeit' in his very enthusiastic essay "Das Piscator-Drama" in the *Frankfurter Zeitung* of 20 Nov. 1927.

Lania's enthusiasm towards advanced theatrical technology as an innovatory factor in itself. When Piscator opened a new independent theatre, the Piscatorbühne, in September 1927, its development was closely followed in the pages of *Die rote Fahne*, not least because it promised to fulfil hopes for a politically committed "proletarian theatre". Piscator's choice of Toller's *Hoppla, wir leben!* (Hoppla! Such is Life) for his opening production was sternly criticized because the central figure of the drama, and thus the central issues, represented the problems of a disillusioned bourgeois idealist rather than anything that the Communist movement could recognize as the preoccupations of a genuine revolutionary (Brauneck 1973, 275–92). But one of the more fully argued contributions draws two kinds of distinction which are directly relevant to our present discussion. First, it is the exploitation of technical facilities that enables Piscator's production to triumph over the weaknesses of Toller's script and generally to transcend the limitations of the mere dialogue drama associated with the "bourgeois-private" theatre of the past; this opening-up of the realm of theatrical possibilities is seen, indeed, as "giving life to this age of technical high-performance" (*dieses Zeitalter der technischen Höchstleistungen*). Secondly, Toller's script is seen as having advanced technically over his earlier plays by virtue of his adoption of elements of reportage; this, indeed, is the respect in which his art is seen as having moved "closer to the proletariat" (*RF*, 7 September 1927). Even if the term 'Neue Sachlichkeit' is generally avoided by Communist critics— other than as a way of referring to fashionable "bourgeois" art exhibitions (*RF*, 1 January 1927)—there is clear evidence here that two important impulses associated with the wider use of the term are also playing a powerful role within Communist thinking about the arts in the mid-1920s. Technology is accorded high significance as a vehicle of social and ideological transformation, and the literary mode appropriate to proletarian interests is that of reportage.

Since 1924, *Die rote Fahne* had actively promoted the publication of reports from the workplace by "worker correspondents" as part of its programme of political education; such reports came to be thought of as an important element in the development of a specifically "proletarian" literature (Brauneck

1973, 29ff.; Schonauer, 126ff.; Berg (ed.), 35ff.). But in a broader publishing market, too, the feuilleton supplements of major daily newspapers and such leading weekly publications as *Die Weltbühne* and *Das Tage-Buch* responded to the perceived public demand for background information by encouraging young writers to cultivate the art of reportage. In the hands of skilful stylists—Egon Erwin Kisch, Siegfried Kracauer, Alfons Paquet, Joseph Roth, and others—reportage became a subtle literary genre which was both open to the substance of modern social life and also capable of bringing out the significance of events which ordinary journalism tended to reduce to anecdotal status (cf. Geisler, 3–15). And around 1930, techniques of documentary writing came to fulfil a creative function in the composition of novels which addressed the politically fraught subjects of the lost World War (Edlef Koeppen) and subsequent political machinations (Theodor Plievier, Erik Reger). Public discussions of the mid-1920s tend to indicate, however, that the criterion of 'factual content' in itself, of the 'de-literarization' of public discourse, far outweighed any other consideration in the assessment of the communicative effectiveness of reportage. Kisch chose deliberately to highlight the sensationalist aspect of his art with the title he gave to his first personal anthology of such compositions in 1924: *Der rasende Reporter* was a formula which evoked above all the boundlessly energetic pursuit of background information in obscure and frequently exotic circumstances. Evidence suggests that he was making a conscious bid for popular success with that title, and that he subsequently regretted the stereotyping of his public image which inevitably resulted. A careful reading of his preface to that first major publication shows rather that the emphasis he gives there to the claim of "unbiased" reporting of "sheer facts" reflects the same sense of a need to combat political lies and delusions in the post-war world which we earlier saw expressed by Graf and Landry (cf. Geisler, 57–60). The stereotypical expectation of reportage remained dominant, however, in the retrospective collection *Fazit* (Summary) published by Ernst Glaeser in 1929. Glaeser's professed criterion for selection—even if it is not totally borne out by the quite varied contents—is exclusively thematic. The quality he had looked for was sociological interest as opposed to aesthetic appeal—which was incidentally his pretext for excluding authors of right-wing persuasion (*Fazit*, 5–7).

When a reprint of *Fazit* was published in 1977, the volume was presented as *the* representative anthology of literary 'Neue Sachlichkeit' (*Fazit*, 317). There is clearly some justification for this claim: when *Fazit* first appeared it was hailed by Kurt Pinthus (the same Kurt Pinthus who had published the representative anthology of Expressionist poetry a decade earlier) as emblematic of the new style which he described as "manly" (*männlich*) and "scientific" (*wissenschaftlich*) in its approach (*TB* 10/I, 904; Kaes, 328–33). But by the same token, *Fazit* illustrates precisely the limitations of the term for the purposes of literary history. Glaeser's selection includes, in addition to samples of genuine reportage by Kisch, Roth, and Glaeser himself, a quite lyrical description of the gas industry by Alfons Paquet, some highly reflective reminiscences of encounters with French culture by Arnold Zweig, and some vigorous essays on contemporary cultural trends by Ihering, Kracauer, and Ossietzky. It also includes a witty assemblage of personal statistical information by Lion Feuchtwanger which effectively parodies the whole contemporary fascination with factual data. Glaeser's editorial insistence on the "sociological" dimension of his chosen texts was less a reflection of the actual accomplishments of these authors than of a programmatic erasure of the distinction between writing and documentation which Glaeser shared at this time with many writers on the radical left. Bernhard von Brentano, another contributor to *Fazit*, expressly equates the profession of writer with the tasks of comment and analysis traditionally denoted in German by the term *Publizist* (*WB* 25/II, 54 f.). In *Die neue Bücherschau* (New Book Review), the chief literary journal of the radical left between 1925 and 1929, reportage was held up as an exemplary technique of social investigation, again in pseudo-scientific terms. It was seen as achieving a "complete picture" by means of the minute examination of each square millimetre of a surface in turn (*NB* 4, 166–9). And Johannes R. Becher, the former Expressionist poet whose efforts as a literary organizer within the German Communist Party resulted in the foundation of a League of Proletarian-Revolutionary Writers (BPRS) in 1928, was equally unequivocal in the mid-1920s in his championing of reportage as *the* avant-garde literary medium of the moment (*NB* 6, 491–4; Kaes, 325–7). Like Leo Lania, Becher was also enthusiastic about the prospects for using advanced theatrical technology for the presentation of statistical information and the "economic topography" of bourgeois society, urging revolutionary writers to keep pace with the times by incorporating "skyscrapers, jazz, and the rhythms of machinery" into their works, even if they perceived many contemporary developments as symptoms of cultural decay (Nössig et al., 419 f.). Such blurring of distinctions between scientific and literary modes of perception was to attract criticism from within the Marxist camp in due course, as we shall see. But in 1929 it was already prompting Joseph Roth to give a jocular definition of 'Neue Sachlichkeit' as "a cross between a pilot, a Marxist and a reporter" (*LW* 5, 39, 3; *Werke* 3, 96).

In June 1926, prompted by the sense of an incipient new vogue, *Die literarische Welt* had canvassed the opinions of prominent authors on the question of whether literary writing (*Dichtung*) was being influenced by the new "Sachlichkeit" of reportage. The strong traditional association of 'reportage' with newspaper reporting led several respondents to comment archly that "Sachlichkeit" (in the sense of sober objectivity) was indeed a new phenomenon in the world of journalism, if indeed it was to be found there at all. The sharpest repudiations of any putative influence of reportage on literary writing came from two writers who, in their distinctive ways, certainly did not fail to keep abreast of the times: Alfred Döblin crisply expressed horror at the very idea that journalism could ever gain an influence over literature, while Ernst Toller anticipated an important element of the later criticism of 'Neue Sachlichkeit' by drawing a categorical distinction between literature as an activity which "formed" human values and relationships, and the "Sachlichkeit" that was appropriate to the examination of purely functional relations. Toller was to present himself as a leading exponent of documentary writing in its proper place with a volume on contemporary miscarriages of justice which appeared the following year, but here he voices deep suspicion of a pervasive *pose* of 'Sachlichkeit' which in fact betokens the *absence* of human identity: "Wer nichts *ist*, stelzt sachlich." (*LW* 2, 26, 3) An unequivocally positive response to the question comes from authors associated—like Oskar Maria Graf—with pre-war traditions of anarchist thought, Erich Mühsam and the poet Klabund, who are able to interpret it as signifying a model for literary activity which they had always sought to promote: the writer as an accomplished kind of agitator. George Grosz, in similar vein, points to the social exposés of Sinclair Lewis and Upton Sinclair as representing a new literary tradition that is every bit as legitimate as the "unworldly" (*weltfremd*) lyricism of earlier decades; and Max Hermann-Neiße makes a similar point with reference to the novels of Zola. The majority of responses are more guardedly differentiated in their assessment. Heinrich Mann refers to criteria of artistic quality by which both reportage and the novel may equally be measured; Bruno Frank, Emil Ludwig, and Ernst Weiß—with varying kinds of emphasis—acknowledge the need for contemporary narrative writing to be open to the subject-matter and the stylistic approach characteristic of reportage; and Max Brod, cleaving to a Schopenhauerian artistic ideal of "cognition independent of the will", finds the whole issue "very complicated" (ibid. 2–3).

Diffuse as these responses to a naively formulated question may be, they already serve to throw into relief the problematic nature of the relevance of 'Neue Sachlichkeit' to literary writing. For if, on the one hand, investigative 'Sachlichkeit' could be associated by many writers with a continuous programme of active social involvement, we also find the conservative Max Brod and the radical Ernst Toller apparently united here in their suspicion that contemporary trends are threatening the autonomy of art and its scope for independently fashioning human awareness. If such suspicions were to be voiced with increasing polemical acerbity around 1930, then this was due not only to underlying ideological differences between authors, but rather more to the sense of broader social developments which 'Neue Sachlichkeit' had come to signify in the meantime.

The vogueishness of the term 'Neue Sachlichkeit' had provided Carl Sternheim with the subject-matter for a comedy as early as 1926. The setting for his play *Die Schule von Uznach oder Neue Sachlichkeit* is an imaginary finishing school on Lake

Constance, where self-consciously emancipated young women of various nationalities have been sent from high bourgeois homes unable to restrain or contain them. In Uznach they follow a strenuous regime of demystification and rhythmic gymnastics with the ostensible goal of transcending all sentimentality through "dance awareness" (*Tanzerkenntnis*). The true purpose of this educational programme remains ambiguous, like much else in Sternheim's plays.[11] Uznach is conceived by its director as a "new Rhodes", a preparation for the leap into a new age, the precise ideal content of which has yet to be determined, and the implications of 'Neue Sachlichkeit' within the text remain equally vague. Sternheim pillories the fashionable attitudes of the leisured classes, here as elsewhere, portraying an atmosphere of vacuous generalities and cultivated ennui, and he captures something of the dominant trends of the mid-1920s when he allows the director's son, Klaus, to pose the pointed question of precisely *how* the educationist can hope to nurture a sense of independent-mindedness in a generation besotted by "technical nonsense". But the comic dimension of his play remains dependent upon elements of untranscended romantic cliché embodied in the relationship which Klaus strikes up with a naively chaste girl from provincial Germany: this relationship restores a sense of romance and drama to life—and rapidly prompts other members of the cast to recognize how much they had missed it.

The sense that 'Sachlichkeit' was coming to occupy a prominent position in public awareness beyond the ranks of the self-consciously fashionable, however, is confirmed for us from an unexpected source. In 1927 a young theologian, writing for a specialist journal, found himself obliged to distinguish explicitly between his own use of the term and that of contemporary common usage. What he was trying to define was a concept of morality based on the idea of doing something "for the sake of the cause" (*Sache*), and thus implicitly in the interests of a higher value. The connotation which he is anxious to bracket out is

---

[11] Among the secondary literature on Sternheim, see particularly Ansgar Hillach, "*Die Schule von Uznach* oder der Immoralist als neusachlicher Romantiker? Aufforderung, statt Etikettenschwindel Sternheim-Lektüre zu betreiben", in Wolfgang Wendler (ed.), *Carl Sternheim Materialienbuch* (Darmstadt: Luchterhand 1980), 133–58.

the one that prevails in the sphere of technology, where the "cause" or purpose of an action is predetermined by a purely practical goal (the "specifications") which is itself morally indifferent. In other words, vulgar functionalism again provides the background against which the theologian must present his argument.[12] By 1928 the pervasive use of 'Sachlichkeit' as a vogue term for the mood of the times had become enshrined in popular song—the title song, indeed, which Marcellus Schiffer and Mischa Spoliansky wrote for their revue *Es liegt in der Luft* (There's Something in the Air). Their text shows, once again, what a diffuse bundle of notions has now come to adhere to the term. The feeling that is "in the air" is associated with the humming of aeroplanes and airships, the crackle of electricity, and the mystique of wireless communication which has now been added to the technical marvels of moving film and the telephone. But the contemporary atmosphere of 'Sachlichkeit' is equally characterized by the elimination of sentimentality and the cliché image of emphatically functional architecture:

> Früher, das warn Zeiten . . .
> Starb das Vögelchen im Bauer,
> trug gleich die Familie Trauer!
> Heut ist eine andere Zeit.
> Triffst zum Beispiel du Herrn Koch,
> fragst du ihn voll Sachlichkeit:
> Was Herr Koch, Sie leben noch?
>
> Weg mit Schnörkel, Stuck und Schaden!
> Glatt baut man die Hausfassaden!
> Morgen baut man Häuser bloß,
> ganz und gar fassadenlos.
> Krempel sind wir überdrüssig.
> Viel zu viel ist überflüssig.
> Fort, die Möbel aus der Wohnung.
> Fort mit was nicht hingehört.
> Wir behaupten ohne Schonung,
> jeder Mensch, der da ist, stört.[13]

---

[12] Rudolf Hermann, "Die Sachlichkeit als ethischer Grundbegriff", *Zeitschrift für systematische Theologie*, 5 (1927–8), 2, 250–312 (260).

[13] Quoted in Mathias Eberle, "Otto Dix and 'Neue Sachlichkeit'", in Christos M. Joannides, Norman Rosenthal, Wieland Schmied (eds.), *German Art in the 20th Century* (London: Royal Academy of Arts, 1985), 452–4. Cf. also Willett 1978*a*, 111.

(In the past, those were the days . . . When the bird died in its cage the family went straight into mourning! Times have changed now. If you bump into Herr Koch you ask him quite objectively, "What Herr Koch, are you still alive?"
Cut your stucco and your losses! We're building houses with flat façades! Tomorrow we'll just build the houses, without any façades at all. We are sick of ornate trifles. Much too much is superfluous. Get rid of the furniture out of the flat. Get rid of everything that's out of place. We declare without mercy: if there's anybody there they're in the way.)

In this ostensible disdain for human fellow-feeling, as in much of the painting of 'Neue Sachlichkeit', there is an element of quizzical self-irony which implicitly acknowledges that the attitudes of mind that are apparently being celebrated in the song are in fact open to question. Such ironic posturing— which is familiar to us from Brecht's *Threepenny Opera* and will confront us in other writers of the time[14]—makes it doubly difficult to render in plain English what 'Sachlichkeit' had come to signify. When John Willett translates the first line of the Schiffer/Spoliansky refrain as "There's something in the air called objectivity", then the leaden flatness of the English term reveals one aspect of the problem: "objectivity" contains nothing of the sparkle of "electricity", with which it has to rhyme, nor anything of the quasi-erotic 'buzz' of modern urban life which the song also invokes alongside its allusions to culti- vated unsentimentality. Willett (1978a, 112) correctly explains the implications of a "neutral, sober, matter-of-fact approach" which links this particular brand of "objectivity" to functional and utilitarian values. What he does not tell us is that, in its context, the song lends erotic appeal to an ethos in which human relations tend to take on the character of commodity transactions. A contemporary account of the show described it as capturing what was "in the air" in Berlin at the time precisely because it was imbued with the values of a department store: "you have a look round, you buy or you don't buy, you pay or you don't pay, and at the end of the day it is as if nothing

[14] Reinhold Grimm draws attention to a prime example, namely Fritz von Unruh's play *Phaea* of 1930, which not only parodies the attitudes of 'Sachlichkeit', but is also patently written *for* the culture of 'Sachlichkeit' (Grimm and Hermand, 24 f.).

has happened, you take the goods back and exchange them" (Schrader and Schebera, 127). 1928, in fact, marks the point at which progressive writers and intellectuals begin to turn away from 'Neue Sachlichkeit', largely because of the association it had acquired with moral indifference and superficial commercialism.

The widespread repudiation of 'Sachlichkeit' as a literary vogue from 1928 onwards was initiated by writers and critics who had helped in one way or another to promote it in the first place. It was in the November of 1928 that the *Neue Rundschau* published a critical survey by Bernhard Diebold, which is palpably motivated by profound disappointment that literary writers were not achieving that sober depiction of contemporary reality for which Diebold and others had been calling around 1920. Instead of the artistic resolve to fashion an image (*Abbild*) of reality, Diebold sees all around him a frantic pandering to the public taste of a time that "has no time for art", and at best a "romanticization" of the factual and the technological which leaves only a sense of irreality in the reader. He dates the most promising recent attempts to fashion a proper sense of the real (*Wirklichkeitsgestaltung*) at 1923–4 with the productions of plays by Brecht (*Trommeln in der Nacht*) and Arnolt Bronnen (*Vatermord*), and the publication of Thomas Mann's *Der Zauberberg* (although in this last instance Diebold speaks disparagingly of the—implicitly unreal—"psychoanalysis" of the contemporary world). He sees novelists turning to a historical world of ready-made "facts", and dramatists losing themselves in frivolous self-irony; Brecht's audiences are limited to a "clique", and the avant-garde left are generally no more than "bonviveurs of technology" (*NR* 39/II, 550–61). It was an intemperate essay, published under an editorial disclaimer stressing that there were in fact a wide variety of ways in which a literary writer could achieve "internal relevance" to the contemporary world (*innere Aktualität*). In retrospect it is apparent that in 1928 a young generation of writers was still adjusting to a new sense of artistic purpose, and that the real heyday of social criticism in the novel was yet to come with works by Feuchtwanger and Fallada, Hermann Kesten and Irmgard Keun—to say nothing of the monumental prose works of Döblin, Musil, and Broch. In the theatre, too, it

was only around 1930 that Ödön von Horváth was to emerge
as a serious playwright who combines the intellectual play-
fulness of the modish Berlin theatre with elements of popular
tradition.

The earliest instance of an explicit critique of 'Neue Sachlichkeit' from an explicit Marxist perspective appears to stem
from the Hungarian exile Béla Balázs. In 1929, when Kurt
Pinthus hailed the sober prose style of the rising generation of
writers as a manifestation of "manliness", Balázs was quick
to publish a reply in *Die Weltbühne*, in which he argued that
a literature which prided itself on registering objective facts was
little more than a manifestation of resignation in the face of
the facts (*WB* 25/I, 969–71; Kaes, 333 f.). But already in the
previous year Balázs had criticized the trends associated with
'Neue Sachlichkeit' because they showed how contemporary
life was becoming commodified. Industrial rationalization was
reducing human beings to a mechanical role, he argued, and
the cult of 'Sachlichkeit' was merely an aesthetic reflection of
that process and a manifestation of the 'reification' of culture
under bourgeois capitalism. Literary authors were committing
intellectual suicide, he wrote, if they aligned themselves with the
view that literature had become redundant. What they ought to
be striving for was a mode of representation which would make
clear the historical significance (*Sinn*) of the facts (*WB* 24/II,
916–18).

Brecht's repudiation of 'Neue Sachlichkeit' as "reactionary"
(which is quoted at the head of this chapter) probably dates
from earlier still.[15] In February 1927, Brecht had struck an
ostentatious blow for utilitarian criteria by awarding the prize
in a poetry competition to the author of a raucously unpre-
tentious celebration of a champion racing cyclist (*LW* 3, 5, 1).
Privately, Brecht imagined a dialogue in which the author of that
poem, Hannes Küpper, argues against Brecht's theatrical experiments of the mid-1920s, and for a new, "sachlich" collectivism.

---

[15] The reference to Küpper "turning up" in this text suggests a recent personal
encounter. As we shall see in Chapter 2, there is evidence that Brecht knew Küpper
personally before the publication of Küpper's MacNamara poem in *Die literarische
Welt* in February 1927. It seems unlikely that Küpper would have waited until a
much later date to show Brecht the playscript that Brecht mentions (*BFA* 21, 354).
The dating of Brecht's "Neue Sachlichkeit" notes at 1929 (*BFA* 21, 738) therefore
seems to me implausible.

While he feels united with Küpper in opposition to the sentimental "Unsachlichkeit" of bourgeois taste in general, Brecht
has mixed feelings about the cultural implications of the "Sachlichkeit" which is already evident in the visual arts and which
is now taking hold in the theatre as well. It is a necessary development, and part of the ongoing dialectical transformation
of public attitudes to which his own theatrical activities are
attuned, but in itself it is not a development he welcomes (*BFA*
21, 352–6). Why does he call it reactionary? The clearest answer
is to be found in a poem which Brecht first published in a
carneval magazine in February 1928 (see *BFA* 11, 355), and
which invokes a spontaneously gathered crowd of intellectuals
"worshipping" an oil-tank. Parodying liturgical style in the
manner he had developed in his *Hauspostille* collection, Brecht
pillories the suppression of individual judgement which he fears
from a technocratically orientated collectivism:

> Du Häßlicher
> Du bist der Schönste!
> Tue uns Gewalt an
> Du Sachlicher!
> Lösche aus unser Ich!
> Mache uns kollektiv!
> Denn nicht wie wir wollen
> Sondern wie Du willst.

(*BFA* 11, 175: Thou ugly One | Thou art the most beauteous! | Do vio-
lence unto us | Thou 'sachlich' One! | Expunge our ego! | Make us col-
lective! | For—not as we will | But as Thou willt.)

Other intellectuals on the left undertake a similar reappraisal
in the course of the same year. Klaus Herrmann, who had enthusiastically welcomed the trend towards reportage in *Die neue
Bücherschau* in 1926, regrets in 1929 that authors who lack any
real literary talent are finding a ready market simply because
they reflect contemporary issues (*NB* 7, 649–53). In *Die literarische Welt* the prospects for a vigorous new literary revival
are generally regarded more optimistically, but expressions of
disillusionment are to be found there, too. In the first number
of 1929, Lion Feuchtwanger remarks that the cult of Americanism or "Anglo-Saxonism" is running out of control and
clouding the judgement of publishers, while Heinrich Mann

misses in contemporary writing that sense of passionate conviction that would lend drive and purpose to its insistent factuality (*LW* 5, 1, 3).[16] Heinrich Mann was to press his point home a year later when reviewing an anthology of new German fiction edited by Hermann Kesten, the literary adviser of the Kiepenheuer Verlag, entitled 24 *Neue deutsche Erzähler* (24 New German Storytellers). The collection displays some well-crafted prose from the young generation. There is puckish humour from F. C. Weiskopf, and a rather more sombre tale from Erich Kästner; there are chapters from Toller's autobiography, and from novels by Kesten, Joseph Roth, and Siegfried Kracauer; and perhaps the gem of the collection is Anna Seghers's imaginative psychological study of two political prisoners condemned to endure each other's company while assigned to the maintenance of a telegraph line through a desert, "Die Wellblech-Hütte" (The Corrugated-Iron Shack). What rather determines the character of the anthology, however, is a preponderance of anecdotes which clearly reflect important experiences of the post-war years—the political upheavals, cases of economic opportunism, persisting social injustice and psychic oppression—but which limit their presentation of such themes to the narration of verbal exchanges and surface events. In his foreword, Kesten invoked Heinrich Mann's own watchword about the need for the literary writer to be "useful" to the world in which he is living. In his review, Mann regretted the overwhelming limitation to an external narrative perspective—they were all "reporting", it was as if their "souls" were cowering behind a bulwark of "Sachlichkeit". Mann draws an unfavourable comparison with the Naturalism of forty years earlier, which had at least consisted, in Zola's well-known phrase, in the observation of the world "through a temperament"; it was again that lack of passionate conviction, the seeming absence of an independent and authoritative identity, that he condemned in the young generation of 1930 (*LW* 6, 14, 1–2).[17]

[16] Both Heinrich Mann and Willy Haas had criticized the attitudes of the young in more general terms in *Die literarische Welt* in 1928, and had drawn sharp protests in response: *LW* 4, 45, 1 and 48, 13; also 14/15 (Osterbeilage), 3.

[17] Naturalism had been the yardstick applied by Bernhard Diebold, too, in his fulminatory article of 1928; the comparison was resisted by Alfred Döblin, however, who saw contemporary literature—in the wake of Expressionism, and in the wake

Ödön von Horváth had been represented in Kesten's anthology with a sardonic little anecdote about sex and the constraints on political awareness, and privately recorded his indignation at Heinrich Mann's undifferentiated censure. If the postwar generation appeared unemotional, he pointed out, it was because they could no longer have any faith in psychological subtleties or sacrifices in the name of great causes: "An die Seele glauben wir nicht, weil wir an das 'Opfer' nicht glauben." (Krischke, 73 f.) In the novel *Der ewige Spießer* (perhaps best translated as "The Wandering Philistine") which Horváth published later the same year, it is possible to detect an element of revenge on Heinrich Mann in the satirical portrayal of the would-be democrat and hack writer Schmitz as a dionysian creature of mood who openly deprecates the "generation of 1902" (Midgley 1988, 27). But the textual history of the same work shows a subtle shift in Horváth's attitude to 'Sachlichkeit', too. In an early draft this term had been explicitly associated with the erotic pleasure which a modern young lady is able to derive from her own cool detachment (*GW* IV, 505); the final version develops the same material in a manner which highlights instead the contemporary pressures to extract commercial "productivity" from her natural sensuality (*GW* III, 244–61). What Horváth is showing us in this section of his published novel is a process by which human relations take on the quality of commodity transactions—as Béla Balázs had warned.

But the most telling, and the most emphatic public statement on the literary cult of 'Sachlichkeit' had already appeared in January 1930 in the form of a long essay by Joseph Roth in *Die literarische Welt*, calling a halt to the whole 'deliterarizing' trend: "Schluß mit der 'Neuen Sachlichkeit'". This intervention by Roth was especially significant because of his prominent association with what had come to be thought of as literary 'Neue Sachlichkeit'. Contributions from his pen had taken pride of place in both Glaeser's *Fazit* collection and in Kesten's *24 Neue Deutsche Erzähler*. He was known to have schooled

of the social and cultural rupture brought by the First World War—as wrestling with reality in ways which went beyond the imitative principle associated with German Naturalism (*LW* 8, 46, 6). On the complexities of Döblin's relationship with the trends associated with 'Neue Sachlichkeit', see Dieter Mayer, " 'Naturalismus, wie ich ihn meine.' Alfred Döblin und die Neue Sachlichkeit", *Literatur für Leser* (1987), 125–34.

himself in a style of detached, laconic observation as a regular writer of feuilleton articles for the *Frankfurter Zeitung* and other newspapers. His novel of 1927, *Die Flucht ohne Ende* (Never-Ending Flight), which gives a rich and poignant account of the rootlessness commonly experienced by the generation that had been through the First World War and its aftermath, had been pointedly described on the title-page as a "report" (*Bericht*). It had also carried a foreword which expressly denies that there is any element of invention in the text and encourages readers to view it not as "literature", but as a first-hand reconstruction of authentic personal experience—and reviewers had responded to it in precisely this spirit, as an important contribution to "documentary" literature.[18] By 1930, Roth clearly felt an urgent need to dissociate himself from the overwhelming trend towards reportage.

In "Schluß mit der 'Neuen Sachlichkeit'", Roth denounces the whole contemporary tendency to attach greater importance to the appearance of documentary authenticity than to the articulation of complex truths. It is a trend, he argues, which mindlessly values the raw material of reportage higher than the artistic presentation of it, and trusts the caption beneath a photograph rather than asking whether the photograph truly represents reality. He was alluding in particular to the momentous vogue for war novels which had set in following the spectacular success of Remarque's *Im Westen nichts Neues* (All Quiet on the Western Front) in 1929, and which had flooded the book market with the attempts of ungifted writers to tell 'what it was really like'. Roth exempts just two war novels from his blanket accusation of blinkered pseudo-authenticity: *Ginster* by Siegfried Kracauer and *Der Streit um den Sergeanten Grischa* (The Case of Sergeant Grischa) by Arnold Zweig. What was dangerous about 'Sachlichkeit' as a slogan, he argued, was the implication that the values and concerns of the present moment, as nurtured by commercial interests, should be allowed to supplant any deeper considerations of communicative purpose: "Die 'Sachlichkeit' beginnt, die 'Zweckmäßigkeit' zu ersetzen

---

[18] See Hans Natonek, "Dichtung als Dokument: Der Roman, nach dem man sich sehnt", *Neue Leipziger Zeitung*, 27 Nov. 1927; also the surveys of new prose-writing in *Die neue Bücherschau*, 5, 259 f. (Klaus Herrmann) and 6, 577 ff. (Hans Georg Brenner); and Kurt Pinthus' article in *Das Tage-Buch* of June 1929 (Kaes, 329).

und zu verdrängen. Schließlich bekommt sie den gefährlichsten Nebensinn, den der Zeitgemäßheit." (*LW* 5, 3, 3–4 and 4, 7–8; *Werke* 3, 153–64)

Joseph Roth has often been represented as turning away from a commitment to social criticism, and towards a kind of quietistic resignation, with the publication of his novel *Hiob* (Job) in 1930, or indeed towards nostalgia for the old order of Hapsburg Austria in *Radetzkymarsch* (1932). There is certainly an implicit anti-Marxist thrust in his essay "Schluß mit der 'Neuen Sachlichkeit'", and very soon afterwards we find him expressing broad approval for the patrician conservatism of Rudolf Borchardt (*LW* 6, 7, 1–2; *Werke* 3, 171–74). (Borchardt had issued his own counterblast to the trend that subordinated literary criteria to 'the needs of the times' in a speech of 1929, reversing the proposition and emphasizing instead the obligations of 'the times' towards literature: "Die Aufgaben der Zeit gegenüber der Literatur": Kaes, 500 ff.) But Roth had raised a fundamental question of literary aesthetics which the Marxist left also found itself compelled to address. Roth had expressed his sense of the specific task of the literary writer (as opposed to the newspaper reporter) using the same term as Bernhard Diebold: "Gestaltung". The implication of the term was the formation or fashioning of an image of reality which was—at least in aesthetic terms—complete. The same term is a keyword in Georg Lukács's criticism of contemporary trends in Marxist writing, in the pages of *Die Linkskurve* in 1932.

It was with the establishment of *Die Linkskurve* (The Leftward Curve) in 1929 that the committed Communist writers of the BPRS asserted their independence of 'bourgeois' publication outlets, dissociating themselves aggressively in the process from potential 'left liberal' sympathizers such as Döblin, Graf, Toller, and Tucholsky. (*Die Linkskurve* was funded partly from private sources and partly through the International Bureau for Revolutionary Literature in Moscow, and was forced to cease publication for financial reasons before the end of 1932: Gallas, 45, 70 f.). Before Lukács joined the editorial board in the summer of 1931, discussion of the criteria for literary criticism had centred on the documentation of factual details in amplification of a Marxist social analysis, and on the rejection of traditional (Kantian) thinking about the 'disinterestedness' of art (cf. Gallas, 91–118). The purpose of Lukács's initial intervention in June 1932 was to refute the notion that (subjective) ideological commitment, or "tendentiousness", is an adequate criterion for judging a work of literature, and to establish instead a standard of political commitment (*Parteilichkeit*) which consists in the adequate representation of objective historical developments in society (*L* 4, 6, 13–21). His open denunciation of the former position as "Trotskyist" makes it clear that he is in part consciously serving the interests of traditional and anti-modernist literary thinking, which was becoming consolidated in the Soviet Union at this time as Socialist Realism (cf. Gallas, 64–9); but his insistence on the self-assured authorial 'shaping' (*Gestaltung*) of social reality as a literary method that Marxists ought to share with classical nineteenth-century Realists such as Balzac and Tolstoy rests on his own special conception of the novel as a vehicle of historical awareness (Midgley 1988). We shall see in Chapter 4 how Lukács's *Theory of the Novel* (1920) relates to some of the more ambitious novels written during the Weimar Republic. Of more direct relevance in our present context is the fact that in subsequent articles Lukács delivered a sustained attack on the whole literary trend of reportage.

The occasion for Lukács's onslaught was the publication of a novel by Ernst Ottwalt, a Communist of middle-class origins and a collaborator of Brecht's, in which he satirized the injustices of the bureaucracy and legal system of the Weimar Republic under the title *Denn sie wissen, was sie tun* (For they know what they do). Lukács acknowledges the merits of the book, its systematic and energetic presentation of a politically important theme. His purpose, however, is to establish general criteria for creative writing, and much as he sympathizes with the motives which have driven politically engaged writers to adopt techniques of factual reportage and montage out of hostility towards the psychological emphasis of "bourgeois" novelists, he presents this development as a purely "mechanical" reaction to literary tradition (and an example of "petty-bourgeois radicalism") which lacks a secure awareness of the historical developments in which that tradition is rooted. What Lukács is arguing, in the light of his own extensive philosophical and sociological investigations, is that the total social reality of the modern age cannot be adequately represented through ostensibly objective documentary methods in literary writing, methods which can only lead to a product which is "pseudo-art" as well as "pseudo-science". Reportage, as a mode of writing, is unable to integrate either the subjective components in social processes or the subjective dimension of the narrative reconstruction of those processes, both of which are necessary to an adequate representation of the "typical forces" at work in society at a particular historical conjuncture. The particular ideological complexion of that subjective perspective is unimportant, as Lukács's reference to the examples of Balzac and Tolstoy is intended to illustrate; it is the integration of the subjective dimension into the "Gestaltung" of reality which is essential to Lukács's conception of the novel as a specific vehicle of communication. The weakness he discerns in the method of Ottwalt's novel is that the narrative perspective itself remains trapped within the machinery of judicial administration, and is therefore unable to convey any sense of the historical processes to which the depicted events belong. Generalizing this insight in terms of Marxist concepts, Lukács argues that literary reportage serves only to affirm characteristic features of capitalist society with its "fetishistic" attitude towards particular mechanisms in the overall historical development (L 4, 7, 23–30 and 8, 26–31).[19] The dogmatism with which Lukács consistently rejected modernist literary experiment was to open up a gulf between himself and other Marxist thinkers—Brecht, Benjamin, Adorno, Bloch—which appears unbridgeable in retrospect. As an exposition of the shortcomings of the literary outlook most closely associated with 'Neue Sachlichkeit', however, Lukács's essay "Reportage oder Gestaltung" stands unrivalled in its intellectual rigour (cf. Geisler, 88–96).

The other much-quoted Marxist critique of 'Neue Sachlichkeit' from the early 1930s, Walter Benjamin's "Linke Melancholie" (Left-Wing Melancholy) of 1931, acquires a special significance by virtue of the specific connection it makes to contemporary social developments. Benjamin is reviewing the

[19] Brauneck (1973, 53) argues, in defence of Ottwalt's approach, that he is writing for a *context* in which the subject of 'class justice' is being continuously discussed by a working-class readership.

third in a rapid sequence of volumes of poetry by Erich Kästner published between 1928 and 1932, and the central focus of his argument concerns the emergence of a particular socio-economic group in the mid-1920s, the bearers of the aspirations and moral attitudes that Kästner typically satirizes in his poems. Benjamin envisages them as young, upwardly mobile commercial agents without family responsibilities, looking for a quick financial return, and shameless in the display of their newly acquired economic power and status (limited as it may be in relation to society as a whole). Kästner's most comprehensive description of them is to be found in a poem called "Zeitgenossen haufenweise" (The Men of Today—Masses of 'em), which had appeared in *Die Weltbühne* in December 1928, and was included in his 1930 collection *Lärm im Spiegel* (A Rumpus in the Mirror). In outward appearance these men are as indistinguishable as mass-produced transfers, they exude the unrestrained confidence of those on whom the times have bestowed guaranteed affluence, they have a telephone where their heart should be, and it is electric light that burns in their souls:

> Sie wissen ganz genau, daß Kreise rund sind
> und Invalidenbeine nur aus Holz.
> Sie sprechen fließend, und aus diesem Grund sind
> sie Tag und Nacht—auch sonntags—auf sich stolz.
>
> In ihren Händen wird aus allem Ware.
> In ihrer Seele brennt elektrisch Licht.
> Sie messen auch das Unberechenbare.
> Was sich nicht zählen läßt, das gibt es nicht!

(They know for certain that circles are round, and that wooden legs are only wood. They speak unfalteringly, and for this reason they are proud of themselves by day and night—even on Sundays.
   In their hands, all things become saleable. Electric light burns in their souls. They even measure what is incalculable. If it can't be counted, it doesn't exist!)

The poem concludes with the despair of an unfulfilled fantasy: these creatures ought to be shot—even their last gasp would be a *dernier cri*—but there are too many of them and they are too well connected, an ineradicable social phenomenon.

Benjamin is as explicit as Kästner himself in expressing his contempt for this 'yuppie culture' of his day. But he is no less fulsome in his repudiation of Kästner's poems, likening them to fish that have swum in the brackish waters of the daily press (where many of them were indeed first published) and grown fat on the detritus to be found there. The "melancholy" he discerns in these verses is that of the professional wit whose ironies have become routine. By holding up the mirror of poetic scorn to these ephemeral social types, he argues, Kästner is merely flattering them, affording them the illusion of their own complete humanity by forging a false identity between the world of work and the world of leisure. He derides Kästner's satire, along with that of Kurt Tucholsky and Walter Mehring, for ignoring profounder political conflicts and reducing the serious social issues of the day to a source of complacent amusement. Benjamin's contribution to the sharpening of political distinctions in the early 1930s is to stigmatize the popular publicists of the left as themselves merely fulfilling the function of "commercial agents" to marketable intellectual fashions, be they the revolutionary gestures of Expressionism or the documentary inventories of 'Sachlichkeit' (*GS* III, 279–83).

The note that Benjamin strikes in "Linke Melancholie" was to be echoed in other retrospective analyses of that brief period of economic stability in the mid-1920s. In Lukács's article of November 1932, 'Neue Sachlichkeit' is used to signify a phase in which the left-wing intelligentsia had, as he puts it, sought a rapprochement (*Wiederannäherung*) with the bourgeoisie (*L* 4, 11, 21). And among the subtle differentiations presented in Ernst Bloch's *Erbschaft dieser Zeit* (Heritage of Our Times) of 1935, it is essentially the same residual meaning of the term that dominates: 'Neue Sachlichkeit' is here synonymous with the subordination of imagination and idealism to "delight in the available earning opportunities and in the façade of stability" (*WA* 4, 256). In a general way since 1930, 'Neue Sachlichkeit' had become a slogan with which Marxists and liberals could taunt each other. In *Die literarische Welt* Willy Haas sought to play off the individualistic verve and exotic colour of Egon Erwin Kisch's prose against the "sociological" claims of Kisch's Marxist associates, thinking of 'Neue Sachlichkeit' as a "mechanistic" literary ideal specific to Communism (*LW* 6, 1, 6). Hans

Günther in *Die Linkskurve* (writing in 1932, but apparently without a knowledge of the arguments that Lukács was about to publish) speaks of that programmatic "Sachlichkeit" which excludes all theoretical foundation from its presentation of observed reality as something firmly linked with the policy of the liberal *Frankfurter Zeitung*, and thus implicitly with Ernst Glaeser and his associates (*L* 4, 6, 34 f.). Where the term 'Sachlichkeit' continued to be deployed with any sense of approval, it took on the sense of a consolidatory or even regressive cultural outlook. Heinz Kindermann distinguishes in 1930 between a "radical" Sachlichkeit, which is the product of the metropolis and aims at the mercilessly rationalistic "profanation" (*Entgötterung*) of the world, and an "idealistic" kind, which retains a sense of eternal values and of an inherently sacral quality in the physical world. Under "radikale Sachlichkeit", Kindermann lumps together all that appears to him overtly tendentious, laconically sceptical, or implicitly pacifistic ('Wesen', 365–69; *Antlitz*, 59–65). The "idealistische Sachlichkeit" he looks for is to be found in bucolic lyric poetry and in novels which celebrate the political values of expansionist nationalism (*Lebensraum*) and the "organic" community ('Wesen', 370–8; *Antlitz*, 66–82). The only exponent of reportage whom Kindermann can accommodate on the "idealistic" side of his scheme is Heinrich Hauser, whose politically quietistic presentation of the benefits of mechanization we shall consider in the course of Chapter 8 (*Antlitz*, 53).

Kindermann is able to invoke two precursors in his discussion of the cultural "physiognomy" of his times. One is the academic philosopher Emil Utitz, who had published a broad diagnosis of contemporary culture in 1927 under the title *Die Überwindung des Expressionismus* (The Overcoming of Expressionism). Utitz positively affirms the concept of 'Neue Sachlichkeit' as the appropriate means to arrest a process of cultural decline (*Kulturdämmerung*), and the meaning of the term that he has in mind is one that is firmly opposed to the analytical rationality of "civilization" (or of "Naturalism"), but is also opposed to the individualistic assertion of the will, which Utitz sees as the hallmark of Expressionism (*Überwindung*, 3–9). The "overcoming of Expressionism" which he proclaims in his title is to be accomplished by the integration of the human individual into a presupposed system of universal values (*Einreihung des Menschen in die seiende Wertewelt*): in aesthetic terms he was calling for a new classicism that harked back to Kant and Schiller, and in broader cultural terms he was seeking to restore a sense of the "sanctity" of physical existence which a one-sided rationalism had persistently eroded (*Überwindung*, 39 f., 96 ff., 183 ff.). Utitz's argument, in a word, was a combination of philosophical high-mindedness and political naivety, which Kindermann simplifies and vulgarizes. Kindermann's other precursor is less of a political innocent: he is Eugen Diesel, the son of the inventor of the Diesel engine, whose 1926 publication *Der Weg durch den Wirrsal* (The Way through the Chaos) had expressly embraced a racialist doctrine as the most promising antidote to the scepticism, relativism and general confusion of modern society. That aspect of Diesel's text represents for Kindermann an exemplary form of "resolute objectivity" (*Antlitz*, 48). In 1932 we find Diesel coining the expression "nationale Sachlichkeit" to denote a will to national unity that would transcend all party-political divisions (*LW* 8, 23, 5). Heinz Kindermann, after 1933, was to become a prolific author of works representing German literature in terms compatible with the spirit of National Socialism.[20]

It was a remarkable career that the term 'Sachlichkeit' had pursued during the years of the Weimar Republic. Around 1920, in all innocence, it had evoked the sober objectivity of outlook that was needed to confront the given realities of the post-war world. By 1924 it had struck up an association with the breezy vitalism and deliberate unsentimentality which dominated the public mood, especially in Berlin. During the 'stabilization phase' that followed it became securely attached to the hard-nosed matter-of-factness attendant upon industrial rationalization and technological innovation. The more firmly it became identified in public awareness with the enjoyment of material wealth and the culture of commercial interest, the more it was stigmatized by the intelligentsia as signifying a lifestyle and outlook bereft of personal identity and critical consciousness.

[20] See Josef Wulf, *Literatur und Dichtung im Dritten Reich: Eine Dokumentation* (Gütersloh, 1963), 234; also Alexander Bormann, "Vom Traum zur Tat: Über völkische Literatur", in Rothe (ed.) 1974, 304–33.

Its very adaptability, the sheer range of its connotations, allowed it to function as a freely available formula, the precise meaning of which would vary according to the personal taste and ideological orientation of the user. For a period from 1920 until about 1927 it could serve as an honourable watchword for self-consciously progressive writers; but as the political crisis of the early 1930s gathered, it was equally capable of lending a spurious air of 'objectivity' and factual 'necessity' to the dogmas of reactionary irrationalism.

These fluctuations and vacillations are mirrored in the works and public statements of literary writers of the period. Some of these we have noted already, others will be examined more closely in the chapters that follow. Heinrich Mann, Alfred Döblin, and Ernst Toller, each in his separate way, uphold a literary idealism which is pitted against what 'Neue Sachlichkeit' had come to signify. Feuchtwanger parodies the contemporary fascination with statistics, and satirizes the processes of popular acclamation as well as reactionary politics in his novel *Erfolg* (Success). Brecht pokes fun at the cult of technology, and in his *Mahagonny* opera he derides the ethos of consumerism. Horváth subjects the principle of commercial self-interest to more sardonic irony, and in his plays of the early 1930s he exposes the psychological mechanisms of "hypochondriac egoism", as he calls it (*GW* III, 147), in a variety of social contexts. The moral critique of the culture of 'Sachlichkeit' is pursued further in the novels of Joseph Roth, Hermann Kesten, Irmgard Keun, and—notwithstanding the strictures of Walter Benjamin—Erich Kästner. These are prominent examples of the critical realism in German literature between 1927 and 1933; they are linked in their very diversity by their critical detachment from the contemporary values their works reflect.

However 'new' the mood of 'Sachlichkeit' may have appeared to the German public of the 1920s, and however apt the term might seem in any description of social trends of the time, 'Neue Sachlichkeit' clearly cannot serve as an all-encompassing label for literary developments that follow Expressionism. What is revealed, in fact, in the variety of connotations which 'Sachlichkeit' takes on in the cultural discussions of the time, is a complex and involved system of perspectives and incipient ideological positions which it was open to writers to adopt, however experimentally, in the period between the collapse of the old Empire and the advent of Hitler. The question of what 'Neue Sachlichkeit' *was*, of what it *signified* in social, cultural, or moral terms, itself constituted one field of tensions among others in which German authors sought to orientate themselves and define their sense of purpose in the years that followed a lost war and a failed revolution. That is why, in our understanding of the literature of the Weimar Republic, any investigation of the meaning of 'Neue Sachlichkeit' should take its place—as it does in this book—*alongside* other lines of inquiry, not at the foundation of all inquiry.

2

Poetry for Everyday Use?

Nobody these days wants poetry, much less the lyric
variety.

Fritz von Unruh, *Phaea*, 1930[1]

Lyric poetry is surely something we ought to be able to
examine for its use value.

Brecht, 1927 (*LW* 3, 5,1)

On the face of it, the years of the Weimar Republic might appear
an unpoetic period. In the late 1920s it was the anthologies of
reportage-style prose—Glaeser's *Fazit* and Kesten's *24 neue
deutsche Erzähler*—that were being hailed as representative of
their time. Writing in 1927, Stefan Zweig bemoaned the passing
of public interest in lyric poetry, and of the journals that had
helped to sustain it through the previous decade.[2] And as early as
1922, when preparing a fresh printrun of his famous collection
of Expressionist poetry, *Menschheitsdämmerung* (Twilight of
Mankind), Kurt Pinthus noted that the volume he had originally
assembled in 1919 really marked the end of an era: he could see
no poetic writing of comparable significance that had appeared
in the meantime (*Menschheitsdämmerung*, 33 f.).

Such lamentations need to be put in perspective. A wealth of
poetic voices from the pre-war years remained active and influential during the 1920s. Rilke, whose earlier works were certainly being widely read at the time, reached the pinnacle of his
poetic achievement with the *Duino Elegies* and the *Sonnets to
Orpheus*, both published in 1923. Stefan George reissued a
number of his pre-war collections around 1920, and reaffirmed
his aesthetic creed of hieratic authoritarianism in 1928 with a

---

[1] Quoted by Reinhold Grimm in Grimm and Hermand, 21.
[2] See Stefan Zweig's preface to the *Anthologie jüngster Lyrik* published by Klaus
Mann and Willi R. Fehse in 1927, 1 f.

new cycle of poems entitled *Das neue Reich* (The New Empire).[3] The heritage of pre-war neo-Romanticism, too, was carried forward into the 1920s—for example, in the poetry of Hermann Hesse. And the complex legacy of the *Menschheitsdämmerung* collection itself, ranging as it does from vehement expressions of revolt and agitation (Becher, Werfel) to the contemplatively vitalistic (Däubler) and the mystically ecstatic (Stadler, Trakl), can also be found among the writings of the young generation of the late 1920s. As Hans-Peter Bayerdörfer (p. 444) has pointed out, in the very act of collecting the poetry of Expressionism into a consolidatory volume, Kurt Pinthus was aiding the dissemination of it on a wider scale than ever before.[4] When Stefan Zweig made his comment of 1927 about the loss of public interest in poetry he was writing the preface to a substantial anthology of work by young poets which reflected each of these influences in one way or another.

If this rich heritage of poetic styles is merely noted here without being discussed in detail, then that is not because I wish to downplay its importance. It is because I want to focus on some developments in poetic writing which are specific to the 1920s, and were received at the time as new and even scandalous, but which have had a long-term influence on critical perceptions of poetry. It took a long time for literary scholars to accept the anti-literary gestures of the 1920s as themselves contributing to the legitimate aesthetic effects of poetry; and it is only comparatively recently that general interest in linguistic theory has provided a ready vocabulary with which to describe those effects. What I particularly want to examine in this chapter is the sense in which functionalist approaches to the use of language during the Weimar period affected the practice of poetic writing in the short term, and the way we are able to construe that poetry in the longer term.

The sense of an ending that Pinthus was experiencing in 1922 was partly occasioned by sheer human loss: of the twenty-three

---

[3] Hans Norbert Fügen (Rothe (ed.) 1974, 334–58) shows how the poetic values associated with George and his circle were sustained well into the 1930s.

[4] Bayerdörfer (pp. 465 f.) specifically identifies the tones of Expressionist pathos in contributions to the *Anthologie jüngster Lyrik* of 1927 by Hanns Vogts and Hermann August Weber.

poets represented in his collection, seven were dead by the end of the First World War. But he was also acknowledging that the extraordinary ferment of Expressionist poetry, with its bold pursuit of visionary imagery and its radical experimentation with the means of linguistic expression, had been dependent upon a particular set of historical circumstances. What had appeared so new and creative at the time, he now recognizes, was largely attributable to the dismantling of established poetic conventions (*Menschheitsdämmerung*, 33). In his preface of 1922, Pinthus explicitly relates what he sees as the stagnation of the arts in Germany at the end of the First World War to the bewilderment arising from social and political dissolution. He also notices the inauguration of a cultural trend which was to be confirmed by the subsequent biographies of those Expressionist poets who had survived the War. Generally speaking, they were applying their energies to other pursuits than lyric poetry. Some—most notably Franz Werfel—were to achieve success in the 1920s as novelists, while others sought to establish themselves as dramatists, essayists, translators or—to borrow Pinthus's terminology—in more 'bourgeois' pursuits.[5] It was already apparent to Pinthus in 1922 that the peculiar vigour and adventurousness which had characterized German poetry between 1910 and 1919 could be neither reawakened nor developed further. What he saw happening to German poetry in the wake of that upheaval was a reversion to classical and Romantic models (ibid. 34).

In a longer historical perspective, too, the First World War clearly marked a watershed for poetry. Michael Hamburger, in his book *The Truth of Poetry*, speaks of a general "tendency towards retrenchment" in European poetry of the 1920s and 1930s (Hamburger, 181). In the works of W. H. Auden and T. S. Eliot, as well as in those of French and German poets, he recognizes a widespread recourse to national poetic traditions and the espousal of collective values—whether political or

---

[5] Among the poets featured in *Menschheitsdämmerung*, Yvan Goll (who incidentally moved to Paris and continued to write poetry in French in collaboration with his wife Claire), Edlef Koeppen, Karl Otten, and René Schickele turned predominantly to narrative prose; Walter Hasenclever and Alfred Wolfenstein tried to make their way as dramatists; Rudolf Leonhard became a regular essayist for *Die Weltbühne*; and Albert Ehrenstein and Paul Zech worked as translators. Else Lasker-Schüler also published very little new poetry between 1923 and 1932.

religious—following the experimental modernism, internationalism, and individualism which had been dominant before 1914. But Hamburger's view of these developments is more positive than might be suggested by such terms as reversion and retrenchment. His overall purpose in surveying poetic writing from Baudelaire to the 1960s is to give a more differentiated picture of developments than tends to be conveyed by studies which narrowly concern themselves with the emergence (and subsequent decline) of a modern poetry that is difficult, abstract, and hermetic. He shows that Baudelaire himself, who is often thought of as the progenitor of a conception of poetry that 'has no object but itself', was in practice very much concerned with the public functions of the arts. And he argues that poets since the mid-nineteenth century have worked in a complex field of tensions that stretches between a studious detachment from social reality as (in Mallarmé's phrase) a "brutal mirage" on the one hand, and a recognition of art as an instrument of social intervention and revolt on the other; between a self-absorbed fascination with language and its effects at one extreme, and an active engagement with the public functions of language at the other. When Hamburger uses the term 'classical' he is thinking either of the formal training in rhetoric which Baudelaire and other modern poets would have received at school, or else of certain historical periods in which the dominant attitude towards rhetorical usage was firmly wedded to the demands of public discourse and public institutions. What he sees happening to poetic writing after 1918 is, broadly speaking, a reassertion of the public dimension over the private; and in the German context it is Brecht above all whom he sees as establishing a new poetic idiom which is public in orientation, and which contrives to be "popular without condescension" (Hamburger, 193).

The period of the Weimar Republic was certainly one in which verse came to play a prominent part in public life. The precise nature of the role it played depended largely on the particular cultural milieu within which a poet was working. Functional lyrics were a natural medium for the nurturing of political sentiment, both on the Communist left and the Nationalist right; but at the same time a politicized middle-class intelligentsia provided the public for the satirical verses in which detached intellectuals gave vent, in cabarets and journals, to their disappointment over the political compromises of the post-war years.[6] A utilitarian approach to poetry was actively promoted as a modernizing tendency, by Brecht and others, and by the end of the 1920s the notion of functionality in poetry (*Gebrauchslyrik*) had become one of the shibboleths of cultural debate.[7] But at the same time, traditional poetic values were being cultivated even within the political movements which actively sought social change.[8] Traditional forms and idioms of poetic expression were indeed being revived across the whole spectrum of ideological positions. But traditionalism in formal terms did not preclude radicalism in content and expression, any more than an ostensible emphasis on functionality excluded the nurture of poetry as an autonomous medium of criticism. Even as they adopted modes of diction close to those of everyday usage, the more skilled poets did not fail to sustain a critical self-awareness about the elusiveness of truth, the difficulty of formulation, and the inherent opacity of language.

If we follow up Pinthus's observations by asking what motivated individual poets to adopt classical or otherwise traditional forms after 1919, some stark contrasts emerge, as we can immediately see if we compare the careers of two poets who featured in his *Menschheitsdämmerung* collection: Johannes R. Becher and Gottfried Benn. Becher's personal development, which is directly reflected in his early published verses, leads from anti-paternal revolt in the pre-war years, through excursions into drug-taking, sexual violence, and self-loathing, and

---

[6] Alexander von Bormann (1978) discusses the particular features of poems by the Communist Erich Weinert and the Nationalist Ernst Lissauer, and relates the various strands of politicized literary writing in the Weimar period to specific conditions of the organization of party politics at the time. On political songs of the Communist movement, see also Fritz J. Raddatz, "Lied und Gedicht der proletarisch-revolutionären Literatur" (Rothe (ed.) 1974, 396–410).

[7] The term 'Gebrauchslyrik' appears to have been coined by Kurt Tucholsky in a book review of 1928: see J. J. White, "The cult of 'Functional Poetry' during the Weimar Period" (Bance (ed.), 95). On the relation of the term to the vogue for 'Gebrauchsmusik', 'Gebrauchstanz', and 'Gebrauchsgraphik', see Willett 1978*a*, 162, 197.

[8] Christoph Rülcker, "Proletarische Dichtung ohne Klassenbewußtsein: Zu Anspruch und Struktur sozialdemokratischer Arbeiterliteratur 1918–1933" (Rothe (ed.) 1974, 411–33), discusses the strong sense of traditionalism which characterized the cult of the 'worker poets' of the 1920s, especially Max Barthel, Karl Bröger, Gerrit Engelke, and Heinrich Lersch.

on to an extravagant utopianism which manifests itself from
1916 onwards in impassioned appeals to religious redemption
as well as to insurrectionary politics. When Becher hails the
achievements of the Bolshevik Revolution in his poetry of
1918–19, he does so in terms of a stern punitive force capable
of purging the world of corruption and bringing about the transition to a new "holy empire" (*GW* 2, 18 f.: "Gruß des
deutschen Dichters an die Russische Föderative Sowjet-Repub-
lik"). Becher's commitment to Communism is transparently that
of a bohemian intellectual seeking a means to expunge all that
he has come to recognize as rotten in his personal background;
he openly says as much in a sonnet of the 1930s which begins:

> Was wär ich, ohne daß mich die Partei
> In ihre Zucht genommen, ihre strenge?!
> Ein wilder Spießer, der mit Wutgeschrei
> Sich selbst zerfetzt, und dabei eine Menge
> Von Alkohol vertilgt.

(*GW* 3, 715: What would I be, had not the Party taken me in hand
with its strict discipline?! A wild bourgeois, lacerating himself with
cries of anguish, and consuming quantities of alcohol.)

   The political conditions under which Becher was obliged to
operate after 1933, in exile in Moscow, put him under additional pressure to abandon his earlier avant-garde manner and
to cultivate an artificial traditionalism (Schäfer 1981, 96–106).
His later prominence within the regime of the German Democratic Republic—as Minister of Culture and author of the state's
official anthem—also made him an obvious target for the kind
of critique which sets out to expose the psychological roots of
political dogmatism on the left, as on the right (Rohrwasser).
But his identification with that now defunct regime has made it
perhaps a little too easy to dismiss the bulk of Becher's poetry
since the 1920s as the doggerel of a discredited political culture.
When he made the decision, in late 1919 and early 1920, to
work with traditional poetic forms, it was in a conscious effort
to move beyond the abstract expostulation that had characterized his Expressionist phase, and towards a more intensive representation of life's potential and society's turpitudes (*GW* 2,
601). Already at that time he was adapting his style to the
diction of popular verse forms, writing inspirational hymns and

balladesque accounts of individual experiences bound in consistent rhythms and regular rhymes or half-rhymes. Where he permitted himself the flexibility of free verse in order to evoke the strength and potential of the proletariat, he now did so in a vocabulary drawn from the everyday world of the workplace. But within the constraints he had imposed upon himself, he continued to write with the vigour and urgency of an undiminished moral imperative. Particularly in the collection *Die hungrige Stadt* (The Hungry City, 1927), Becher found simple but vivid language in which to express the social discrepancies that were opening up in a revived economy: luxury hotels and jazz bands for the wealthy, opulent displays of fresh foodstuffs in shop windows, and a growing army of the excluded who watch on with suppressed fury, an incarnation of social catastrophes yet to come.

> Das Heer der Arbeitslosen wacht im schalen Dämmer.
> Es wacht bei Tag. Wacht in der Nacht.
> Sein Wachsein ist ein Fluch dem Satten und dem Schlemmer.
> Das Heer der Arbeitslosen wacht...
>
> Es wacht heran die Zeit...Ein Fieber fegt
> Durchs Land. Wie Essen glühn, so brennen Menchenmassen.
> Ein lauter Wind in alle Fenster schlägt.
> Sie knallen auf. Die Flamme prasselt.

(*GW* 3, 18: The army of the unemployed watches in the twilight. It watches by day, it watches by night. Its watchfulness is a curse upon those who eat their fill. The army of the unemployed is watching... It watches that the time might come...A fever sweeps through the land. Crowds of people glow like furnaces. A bellowing wind beats in upon all windows. They burst open. The flame roars.)

The passionate commitment of Becher's exhortatory Expressionist poetry remains, but it is now contained within the framework of a conventional diction and versification.

No comparable moral passion had ever been apparent in the writings of Gottfried Benn. He had made a sensational entry onto the Berlin literary scene in 1912 with a cycle of poems which drew its subject-matter from his experiences as a medical student in the anatomy theatre and among the terminally ill. It was simply and brutally entitled *Morgue*. We would be wrong to suppose, however, that Benn's initial notoriety was simply based on the shock impact of his themes or of his ostensibly emotionless treatment of them. In his recent book on Benn, Hugh Ridley (pp. 36 ff.) points out that contemporary reviewers of *Morgue* responded to Benn's confrontation of the medium of lyric poetry with such subject-matter by interpreting it as a timely statement about the exhaustion of lyricism as a medium of emotional expression. Benn's subsequent development confirms that beneath his insistent depiction of the dismal materiality of the human condition there lay a deeper intellectual cynicism. He saw himself as the heir to a European culture in which all systems of belief had lost their credibility and the methods of scientific inquiry which had supplanted them afforded no hope of anything more than partial insights into the nature of existence. Benn's responses to this experience of nihilism were modelled on Nietzsche in two simple and obvious ways: from *The Birth of Tragedy* he adopted the watchword that existence could only be justified in aesthetic terms, and more generally he assumed the posture of Nietzsche's aggressive individualism, linked as it frequently is with disdain for any benefits that might accrue from the collective endeavours of a scientifically and technologically orientated civilization.[9] During the late 1920s Benn established a high public profile for himself—in essays, speeches, and a radio discussion with Becher—as a vehement opponent, not only of a specifically Marxist interpretation of history, but of any rationalist faith in historical progress towards a better society.[10] Benn's efforts to discredit any quest for an underlying meaning to history did not, however, prevent him from interpreting one contemporary development as an epochal advance: in 1933 he welcomed

[9] The dismissiveness towards nineteenth-century processes of 'socialization' is explicit in Benn's "Das moderne Ich" of 1920 (*GW* 1, 16 f.)—although it should be noted that the specifically anti-historicist thrust in the line "Fades Dakapo. Ach, die Idee in der Geschichte" (ibid., 10) was only added in 1928. Benn's self-image as an artist articulating a deeper 'totality' of knowledge than science can achieve is particularly apparent in "Zur Problematik des Dichterischen" of 1930 (*GW* 1, 77 f.).

[10] The text of the radio dialogue with Becher, in which Benn elaborates on his anti-historicist theme, is reprinted in Klein (ed.), 148–52. In "Kunst und Staat" (1927), Benn pours scorn on the notion of any state involvement in the promotion of the arts (*GW* 1, 41–51); and the opening thrust of "Zur Problematik des Dichterischen" (1930) is directed against all "optimistische, technisch-melioristische Weltanschauung" (*GW* 1, 67).

National Socialism as the harbinger of a new, higher biological type (*GW* 1, 440–9).[11]

Benn became the focus of intense scholarly interest in the 1950s and early 1960s as an author who had embraced in his poetry all the negative consequences of modernity. In a lecture on "The Problems of Poetry" which he gave at Marburg University in 1951 (*GW* 1, 494–532), Benn himself provided the arguments which made it possible to interpret his brand of poetry as invested with metaphysical significance, as the sole remaining means by which European culture might hope to transcend empiricism (see especially Lohner, 168–82). Analysing a typical example of Benn's later poetry, Reinhold Grimm (1961) showed with exemplary clarity how the constituent phrases of the work conveyed very little in themselves, but that a peculiar fascination arose from the interplay of the allusions—some intertextual, some mythical, some personal—suggested by those phrases: this was "absolute poetry", in which 'meaning' was created by the poetic arrangement or montage of phrases.[12] These were indeed the features that characterized Benn's poetry from the early 1920s onwards, and the formal framework he favoured for his purposes was an eight-line stanza with alternating rhymes—an elegant and pointedly artificial edifice within which to construct aesthetic order out of a reality that he perceived as inherently meaningless. His programmatic intention is already clear in early examples with such titles as "Schutt" (Rubble) and "Chaos". But what is particularly revealing in these poems of the early 1920s is the fact that they show Benn in the act of moving away from the realism that had characterized his earliest published work and towards the 'magical' arrangement of motifs that Grimm describes. In what appears to be his earliest composition in the new discipline of the eight-line stanza, a poem of 1922, the subject-matter is instantly recognizable as referring to the post-war Berlin scene. His rhyme

[11] The inconsistencies in Benn's attitudes to history are patiently analysed in Beda Allemann, *Gottfried Benn: Das Problem der Geschichte* (Pfüllingen: Neske, 1963).

[12] In 1967 Grimm showed with equal clarity how eclectic the arguments of Benn's "Probleme der Lyrik" were, and how misguided the premisses were upon which the cult of Benn as the representative German poet of modernism was based: R. Grimm, "Die problematischen 'Probleme der Lyrik'", in B. Hillebrand (ed.), *Gottfried Benn*, Wege der Forschung, vol. cccxvi (Darmstadt: Wissenschaftliche Buchgesellschaft, 1979), 206–39.

scheme, which in this instance precisely imitates the ottava rima form of the Italian chivalrous tradition, confers a haughty distancing effect upon his evocation of a world inhabited by blackmarketeers from the southern suburbs, pot-bellied burghers from the villas of the West, holidaying proles, and triumphant stockbrokers—a whirling mass of humanity driven by a libidinal energy that has no purpose beyond itself:

> Avant! Die Hosen runter, smarte Geister,
> An Spree und Jordan großer Samenfang!
> Und dann das Onanat mit Demos-Kleister
> Versalbt zu flottem Nebbich mit Gesang.
> Hoch der Familientisch! Und mixt auch dreister
> Den ganzen süßen Westen mitten mang—
> Und aller Fluch der ganzen Kreatur
> Gequälten Seins in Eure Appretur.

(*Gedichte*, 137: Onwards! Trousers down, smart spirits. Huge semen catch on the Spree and Jordan! And then, with a song, mix the ejaculate with demos-paste to a brisk nobody. Long live the family table! Keep stirring, mix the whole sweet West in too—and may all the curses of troubled earthly kind go into your ointment.)

Benn's intellectual point about the illusory nature of beliefs and the ultimate futility of social existence might remain explicit in one form or another in the poems he writes over the next few years, but it swiftly comes to be represented merely by isolated motifs or ciphers. Already in the "Schutt" poems of 1922, the reader is confronted with the task of establishing the implied connections between a fragment of popular song evoking a tropical sunset, the sexual connotations of 'drinking from cups', and a literary reminiscence of the death of Faust (*Gedichte*, 142 f.); or between intimations of subjugation in antiquity, the concept of heredity, and the "grimacing" of faith and fortune, as in the following incantatory stanza:

> Punisch in Jochen
> Heredität,
> Kranke Knochen
> Von Philoktet,
> Fratze der Glaube
> Fratze das Glück,
> Leer kommt die Taube
> Noahs zurück.

(*Gedichte*, 144: Punic in yokes | heredity, | sick bones | of Philoctetes, | faith is a grimace | fortune a grimace, | Noah's dove returns | with nothing.)

There is no simple correlation between Benn's poetry and the political stance he chose to adopt in 1933—and that fact in itself has helped to ensure that he remained a frequent object of intellectual controversy down the years.[13] Benn's insistent (and witty) deployment of the jargon of modern civilization in general, and of the medical profession in particular, acted as a barrier to the assimilation of his verses to the simple-minded dogmas of *völkisch* politics (cf. Bayerdörfer, 459). But in the arena of Weimar culture, Benn presented himself as the foremost representative of a poetic philosophy which took the aestheticism of the turn of the century to new radical extremes (Lamping 1989, 209). He assumed a public role—but on behalf of a poetry which was the opposite of a publicly orientated one, a poetry from which the very "gesture of communication" had been progressively withdrawn (Ridley, 78).

When Brecht too, in a diary note of June 1921, speaks of "feeling like a classic", then the reasons for this lie in his early attempts to define his own sense of purpose as a writer in opposition to the dominant trends he finds around him. The immediate context for his comment is an expression of revulsion towards the emotional excesses of Expressionist drama in performance;[14] but as Franz Norbert Mennemeier (pp. 9–24) has argued, the reflections with which Brecht responds to that experience contain insights which are relevant to the poetic practice he develops in the 1920s as well as to his work for the theatre. In the diary note Brecht firmly rejects an artistic practice which amounts to the impulsive articulation of an idea that is "not yet ready"; but as he discusses the merits of classical form he makes it plain that he is not interested in pursuing bland perfection (*Glätte*). What does interest him is the "service" that form provides, both in shaping an idea, and in contributing to

---

[13] It was a controversy about Benn's status as a representative modernist poet that sparked the famous "Expressionism debate" of the late 1930s: see H.-J. Schmitt (ed.), *Die Expressionismusdebatte: Materialien zu einer marxistischen Realismuskonzeption* (Frankfurt: Suhrkamp, 1973).

[14] It is in response to Alexander Granach's hectic performance in the role of the cashier in Kaiser's *Von Morgens bis Mitternachts* that Brecht notes, "Ich beobachte, daß ich anfange, ein Klassiker zu werden": Bertolt Brecht, *Tagebücher 1920–1922: Autobiographische Aufzeichnungen 1920–1954* (Frankfurt: Suhrkamp, 1975), 138.

a dynamic conception of the work of art. The work, as Brecht conceives it, should be "more than ready"; it should point beyond its own confines; it should convey a sense of its own provisional status, and indeed of the effort that was necessary to arrive at such a provisional statement.[15] One of the reasons why Brecht has come to be seen as the most important German poet to emerge after the First World War is the extraordinary versatility he shows in developing the potential for critical reflection out of an interaction between poetic form and content, between form and diction.

The poetry that is familiar to us from Brecht's *Hauspostille* (Household Devotions) of 1927, or from the songs of *The Threepenny Opera*, arose out of a ferment of quite diverse elements. In common with many older poets of the early twentieth century—including Benn and Becher—Brecht had absorbed the heritage of Rimbaud and had written poems in the mode of a hermetic 'absolute symbolism', in which the poem gives no explicit indication of what its imagery might be referring to (Steffensen, 24–8; Mennemeier, 25–38). Motifs which he knew from German translations of Rimbaud—from the Ophelia poem and "Le Bateau ivre" especially—appear in various poems Brecht wrote around 1920, where they are used to give sensuous expression to the fluidity of human existence and its physical oneness with the natural world.[16] In the course of the First World War Brecht had passed through his own experience of nihilism. In his case it was directly associated with the collapse of both clerical and imperial authority, to which he had evidently been bound by a strong sense of allegiance in early adolescence. In consequence, the idioms of ecclesiastical tradition and the icons of modern classical literature became for him a reservoir of disposable lin-

---

[15] Brecht, *Tagebücher 1920–1922*, "Man muß loskommen von der großen Geste des Hinschmeißens einer Idee, des 'Noch-nicht-Fertigen', und sollte hinkommen zu dem Hinschmeißen des Kunstwerks, der gestalteten Idee, der großen Geste des Mehr-als-Fertigen. Schon wieder abbröckelnd, schon wieder verblassend, hingehend, lieblich ausweichend, leicht gefügt, nicht sorgfältigst gesammelt, erschwitzt, versichert!"

[16] Steffensen (p. 23) speaks aptly of the "materialistic mysticism" that characterizes the poems "Vom ertrunkenen Mädchen", "Vom Klettern in Bäumen" and "Vom Schwimmen in Seen und Flüssen" especially. The special role of the verse translations of Karl Klammer in the development of German poetry in the early twentieth century is analysed by Reinhold Grimm, "Werk und Wirkung des Übersetzers Karl Klammer", *Neophilologus*, 44 (1960), 20–36.

guistic assets on which he was able to draw ironically throughout his subsequent writing career (see P. Schwarz, 62, 75–104). The poems of the *Hauspostille* challenge the ideological heritage of Christianity both in the overall conception of the collection as a personal "breviary" and through the use of poetic forms specifically derived from religious usage—the psalm, the chorale, the litany. The multiple resonances which Brecht is able to achieve through such ironic allusions to tradition are immediately apparent, for example, in the "Liturgy of Breath" (1924): the formal organization of the poem parodies the liturgical pattern of 'verse' and 'response', while the overt subject-matter is a discomforting narrative about the brutal imposition of 'law and order' on the margin of bourgeois society, and the recurrent wording of the 'response' travesties the evocation of natural harmony and tranquility in a poem by Goethe which would have been comfortingly familiar to middle-class readers. The intellectual challenge with which the poem confronts a reader is not that of seeking logical connections between the elements it contains, but rather that of reflecting upon the disruptive confrontation of one mode of diction with another. By keeping the reference to contemporary social violence vague, Brecht is able to focus attention all the more effectively on formal structures and turns of phrase which are traditionally associated with the mental habits of quietism.

Such subversion of inherited forms and material—Brecht himself spoke of the "Umfunktionierung" of poetry—is not something he contrived in isolation, however. Brecht was sustained in his ironic and multi-valent style by his participation in a new tradition of poetry for public performance, a tradition which had its roots in the cabaret culture that had developed since the turn of the century. Frank Wedekind had been a prime mover in that tradition, taking up the popular heritage of the "Moritat" or "Bänkelsang"—a ballad-style fairground entertainment which often took its themes from sensational criminal cases and characteristically presented them in ways which ostensibly demonstrated the interests of established communal morality. In his hands it became a vehicle for challenging the moral norms of the bourgeoisie. Wedekind had mastered the art of extracting innuendo and mock pathos from such subjects as the disgraced errand-girl ("Brigitte B.") and the unrepentant juvenile murderer ("Der Tantenmörder"). Other writers followed his example, developing the potential of the back-street ballad and the music-hall chanson for reflecting contemporary social tensions. This group of writers also cultivated the self-image of the poet as renegade and vagabond in a tradition which they knew to go back to the fifteenth-century French poet François Villon. The gentlest exponent of the new ballad tradition was undoubtedly Klabund (alias Alfred Henschke—the pseudonym was itself an allusion to the vagabond ethos), whose most vigorous collection, *Die Harfenjule* (Julie the Harpist), was published in 1927, only a year before his death. Others who helped to mould the character of the emergent cabaret culture were the Expressionist poet Alfred Lichtenstein (whose brand of irony has been fairly compared with Heine's,[17] but who was killed on the Western front in 1914), the anarchist Erich Mühsam, whose pre-war "Revoluzzerlied" (Revolutionary's Song) ironically enjoyed its greatest popularity within the working-class movement only in the wake of the failed revolution of 1918–19 (Bormann 1978, 261)—and also Joachim Ringelnatz, who regaled his audiences around 1920 with recitations about the bizarrely exotic exploits of the sailor Kuttel Daddeldu (Riha, 23–36, 102–6).

The "popular" style that Michael Hamburger identifies as characteristic of Brecht is part of the collective achievement of this developing tradition. The strong affinity that Brecht felt for Rudyard Kipling, another foreign poet whom he read initially in translation, is also related to his determination to speak in the language, and with the perspectives, of ordinary people (Willett 1984, 44–58). But what distinguishes Brecht's poetic effects from those of the cabaret culture generally is, again, the way he often works against the grain of received genres—popular or otherwise—rather than with it. A well-known example is the "Legend of the Dead Soldier" (1918), which brought him both critical acclaim and political acrimony in the course of the 1920s. Here Brecht has taken the rhythms and stock devices of the popular heroic ballads of the nineteenth and early twentieth centuries and redeployed them in a ringing satire of wartime propaganda (Riha, 72–81). His version depicts a

[17] See Patrick Bridgwater, *The Poet as Hero and Clown: A Study of Heym and Lichtenstein* (University of Durham, 1986).

soldier who has already opted for a "hero's death" in an act of desperation as the war drags into its fifth year, but who is pronounced fit for active service all the same, draped in the national flag, and marched out of town with all the panoply of a grotesquely inverted patriotic ceremony, including a priest swinging incense to mask the stench of decay:

> Mit Tschindrara und Wiedersehn!
> Und Weib und Hund und Pfaff!
> Und mitten drin der tote Soldat
> Wie ein besoffner Aff.

(*BFA* 11, 114: With an oompapah and a Bye for now! And wench and dog and priest! And in their midst the dead soldier, like a drunken ape.)

Elsewhere, in his ballad of the child-murderess Marie Farrar (1922), we find Brecht adopting the "Moritat" style as Wedekind had popularized it. But in his hands what might have been a straightforward vehicle of social indictment becomes ambiguous, and thus all the more disconcerting, in both its perspectives and its moral purport. The peculiarly insistent use of reported speech in this poem keeps the narrative hovering between the ostensibly dispassionate accumulation of evidence against the girl, based on her own testimony, and the expression of outrage at her social condition which becomes explicit in the final stanza. Another kind of tension is meanwhile generated by the recurrent refrain, which in this instance echoes the idiom of prayers of intercession: on the one hand it appeals for sympathy in a manner which presupposes an impulse to moral condemnation in the reader, and at the same time it questions the conventionality of the intercessionary idiom itself by confronting it with the stark physicality of Marie's experiences:

> Dann zwischen Kammer und Abort, vorher sagt sie
> Sei noch gar nichts gewesen, fing das Kind
> Zu schreien an, das hab sie so verdrossen, sagt sie
> Daß sie's mit beiden Fäusten ohne Aufhörn, blind
> So lang geschlagen habe, bis es still war, sagt sie.
> Hierauf hab sie das Tote noch gradaus
> Zu sich ins Bett genommen für den Rest der Nacht
> Und es versteckt am Morgen in dem Wäschehaus.
> *Doch ihr, ich bitte euch, wollt nicht in Zorn verfallen*
> *Denn alle Kreatur braucht Hilf vor allem.*

(*BFA* 11, 46: Then between her chamber and the toilet (before that, she says, nothing had happened) the child began to cry, and that upset her, she says, so that she pummelled it with both fists, without stopping, blindly, till it was silent, she says. And then she took the dead child straight back to bed with her for the rest of the night and hid it in the morning in the laundry. *But you, I pray you, do not fly into a rage, for all creatures need help above all.*)

By setting particular modes of diction off against each other, Brecht creates effects which are disruptive to the habits of mind associated with each one of them. Such techniques are not without historical precedent, and it may be that whenever Brecht confronts pious diction with life's cruelties in this way something of the heritage of Villon is in evidence. What is worth emphasizing here is the vigour and intensity with which Brecht applied those techniques to the public discourse of his own times. When he writes his own ballad about the life of Villon (*BFA* 11, 55 f.), it is in order to expound his characteristic themes of the immediate post-war period concerning the savouring of life, and of death, to the full. And in his famous self-portrait "Vom armen B.B." (Of Poor B.B., 1922), which directly imitates the manner of Villon, he is constructing a self-image which again says more about the shared cultural experience of nihilism, instability, and inhospitability in post-war Europe than it does about the personal biography of Bertolt Brecht (cf. P. Schwarz, 165 f.).[18]

Other new voices were helping to enrich the cabaret tradition in post-war Germany, foremost among them Walter Mehring and Kurt Tucholsky, who were instrumental in giving the topical chanson a keener political edge. Of the two, Tucholsky has probably enjoyed the more abiding popularity. It is in his songs that the disappointed revolutionary idealism of 1918–19 is most obviously translated into satire, throughout the Weimar period, and in his refrains the most innocent-seeming turn of phrase can acquire the force of a stinging moral rebuke as the full purport of his topical allusion unfolds (cf. Riha, 110–12). But it was Mehring who was the pioneer of political lyric in a more

[18] The aspect of role-play in Brecht's early poetry is stressed—not least as a counterweight to the emphasis on psychological interpretation in Pietzcker and to some extent also in Schwarz, P.—in the recent study by Philip Thomson (pp. 45–74, 89–95).

fundamental sense. He had a strong avant-garde pedigree: his earliest poetry had followed in the path of the radically analytical "Wortkunst" of August Stramm, and at the end of the First World War he was closely involved with George Grosz and John Heartfield in Berlin Dada and its ruthless dismantling of cultural assumptions. In December 1919, when the Dada movement was at its height, Mehring was invited to take a lead part in the opening show of "Schall und Rauch" (Sound and Smoke), the parodistic theatre that Max Reinhardt was then re-establishing, and he used the introductory *conférence* as an opportunity to sketch the role that cabaret might perform in the literary life of the young Republic.[19] What it could offer, he suggested, was a robust form of poetry for recitation (*Vortragslyrik*) conversant with the "political dialectics" of public life, and inoculated against the danger of "lyrical anaemia" by injections of everyday vernacular, from the argot of pimps and whores to the mumbo-jumbo of politicians and diplomats (Bayerdörfer, 439). The texts he published in 1921 under the title *Der Ketzerbrevier* (Heretic's Breviary) show how he put these precepts into practice. Despite that title, the parody of liturgical idiom does not have the pervasive implications in Mehring's work that it does in Brecht's, but it is through Mehring that the rhythms of jazz and the idioms of ragtime songs are introduced into German poetry. His liveliest numbers are a veritable festival of simultaneity and polyglotism, combining advertising slogans, and sensational news headlines into an acutely observed evocation of the pace and the commercial cynicism of post-war city life (*Chronik*, 117–34). In more sardonic vein, the same combinatory talent could assemble fragments of Berlin street wisdom into a cluster of ironic reflections on the urban lifecycle:

> Schließlich land't man treu und wacker
> Ausjebaggert
> Uff'm Acker,
> Sacht nich: meff!

[19] "Schall und Rauch" was the revival of a cabaret-style theatre that Reinhardt had originally established in 1902, and which he intended to serve once more as a parodistic counterpart to the high drama that he was offering in his Großes Schauspielhaus. The text of Mehring's "Conférence zur Eröffnung" is reprinted in Walter Mehring, *Großes Ketzerbrevier* (Munich: dtv 1975), 146–8.

Leichenschauhaus zahlt die Rente
Und verwendt dir
Zu Zemente,
Altes Reff!
Nächstes Jahr deckt's Jroß-Stadtpflaster
Deine Laster!
Denn wo Gottes Mühlen mahlen,
Wächst keen Jras mehr!

(*Chronik*, 142: In the end, you loyal trooper, you land clapped out in the cemetery, you've breathed your last! It's the mortuary'll pay your pension, and use you for cement, you old soak! Next year the city streets will cover up your vices! For where the mills of God grind, the grass never grows!)

What Mehring contributed to the development of poetry in the 1920s was above all a sharpening of critical awareness about the public resonances of turns of phrase.

In terms of literary history, Erich Kästner is bound to appear a late inheritor of the cabaret tradition. Between 1928 and the onset of National Socialism, Kästner published four substantial volumes in which he demonstrated a remarkable facility for turning the diurnal disappointments of contemporary life into eminently recitable verses. His rhythms and rhyme schemes are comfortingly familiar; his tone is one of cultivated undeludedness. Whether he is sketching the disillusioning experiences of his generation ("Jahrgang 1899"), or whether he is pointing up the socio-economic tensions of his time, he contrives a terseness of utterance which led not a few contemporary critics to see him—and to repudiate him—as the epitome of modish 'Sachlichkeit'.[20] It was an image that Kästner encouraged, evoking the end of a romance in the super-cooled terms of a "Sachliche Romanze", aligning himself squarely in a public statement of 1929 with the doctrine of 'usefulness' in poetry (*Gebrauchs-*

[20] The opening number of *Die Kolonne* in 1929 alluded specifically to the title of Kästner's first published collection, *Herz auf Taille* (Tailored Heart), as symptomatic of an alleged trivialization of the poetic craft in the name of 'Sachlichkeit'. Walter Benjamin, in his fulminatory essay "Linke Melancholie" (Left-Wing Melancholy) of 1931, described Kästner's poems as the progeny of the general culture of 'Neue Sachlichkeit', and accused him, together with Mehring and Tucholsky, of converting the revolutionary potential of contemporary social tensions into a lucrative source of amusement: *GS* 3, 281. For Heinz Kindermann in 1933 ("Vom Wesen der neuen Sachlichkeit"), Kästner had come to represent the paradigm case of an allegedly corrosive "radikale Sachlichkeit".

lyrik), and characterizing himself in a later poem as the 31-year-old owner of a little "verse factory" (*GS*, 1, 111, 135, 184). But the real significance of his poetry lies not in the flippancy, the matter-of-factness, the ready-made phrases he uses, but in the intellectual tensions he generates with them. Two examples from Kästner's first collection will serve to illustrate the point. At the level of universal accessibility, Kästner evokes the arrival of spring with all the knowingness of a seasoned city-dweller. It is the time of year when people take their coffee out onto the terrace or survey their flower boxes, and the freshness that they experience is as superficial as a new coat of paint: "Die Welt wird frisch gestrichen!" Even the poetic description of spring belongs to the well-worn routines of this human environment, and Kästner signals that fact in his title by combining an archaic term for spring, "Lenz", with one that is unmistakably derived from the language of lawyers and bureaucrats: "Besagter Lenz ist da" (Aforesaid Spring is Here). But then the flippant tone is itself set at a distance when the poem concludes with an admission that the emotional experience always feels new and authentic nevertheless (*GS*, 1, 60 f.).

For readers familiar with the German national heritage there is more to chew on in "Hymnus an die Zeit" (Hymn to the Times), where echoes of the patriotic verses of the early nineteenth century are intermingled with phrases which evoke a stolid bourgeois routine regulated by bureaucracy, doctor's orders, and pervasive servility. In one three-line sequence Kästner conjures up a whole culture of placid subordination by combining allusions to Goethe's grand description of a measured daily routine and to Max Schneckenburger's fervent battle-song of 1840 "The Watch on the Rhine" with an advertising slogan which appeals to an ethos of docility:

> Tagsüber pünktlich, abends manchmal Gäste.
> Es braust ein Ruf von Rüdesheim bis Oppeln:
> "Der Schlaf vor Mitternacht ist doch der beste!"

(*GS*, 1, 59 f.: Punctual by day, guests betimes of an evening. The cry goes up from Rüdesheim to Oppeln: "An hour of sleep at night is worth two in the morning!")

Sympathetic analysis of Kästner's poetic technique reveals the poignancy in what he is expressing: he reminds us how human experience is determined by historical circumstance, and he probes the senses in which the society of his day is impoverished of both emotion and idealism (cf. E. Schwarz; Last, 97–104). The cynical diction is a mask from behind which a still intact moral ideal peers through; the idyllic structures of the imagination which his poems invoke are mechanisms for exposing the brutal realities of life. Kästner speaks in the sound-bites of his time, but he does so in a manner which draws attention to the limitations they impose on human consciousness.

Alongside the manifestly public poetry of Mehring, Tucholsky, and Kästner on the one hand, and the demonstratively anti-public stance of Gottfried Benn on the other, there were poets who continued to cultivate the possibilities of lyrical utterance in a more measured and reflective fashion. Since critical interest has tended to focus either on the strikingly innovative or on the augustly traditional, there remain pockets of skilled poetic writing from the Weimar period to which literary history has arguably yet to accord due recognition. Walter Mehring may have had to wait until his death in 1981 before the implications of his poetic achievement received serious scholarly attention; but Max Herrmann-Neiße had to wait until his centenary in 1986 before the publication of his collected works made his full poetic stature visible. Herrmann-Neiße had been closely associated with Gottfried Benn since the heyday of *Der Sturm* and the literary salon of Else Lasker-Schüler, and it was an article of his on the merits of Benn's works, for example, which provided Becher and his Communist associates with a pretext for leaving the editorial board of the *Neue Bücherschau* and setting up a journal of their own, *Die Linkskurve*, in 1929 (Gallas, 36 f.). In a review of 1925, indeed, he held up Benn's café poems as a triumphant transcendence of the cabaret tradition.[21] He could make such claims with authority because he had himself been an active participant in Berlin cabaret around 1920, and the poems he published in *Die Aktion* and other outlets during the

---

[21] "Die Gattung Couplet ist gesteigert ins schonungslos Vernichtende, daß die Fronde der besten bisherigen Angriffschansons noch unter ihnen bleibt, weil jene Feindschaft innerhalb derselben Welt, diese aber brückenlosen Bruch bedeuten." Quoted in P. U. Hohendahl (ed.), *Benn—Wirkung wider Willen* (Frankfurt: Athenäum 1971), 108.

Weimar years show him to have been creatively involved in the cabaret style of poetry alongside Klabund and Mehring. In choosing the poems for the volumes he published during his lifetime he acted with evident discretion. But with his disciplined approach to versification, the purity of his diction and the judicious plasticity of his imagery, he maintained an eloquent style of ironic realism in his work, from his earliest descriptions of sexual experience and the public life of his Silesian home town around 1910, through to the suggestive metaphors of the laconic "Song of Chaos" from his 1927 collection:

Über das Land zieh'n Schwärme geflügelter Lügen aus Norden,
verdunkeln das Licht und trüben der Meere blauspiegelndes Blüh'n,
der weiße Strand ist von ihrem Unrat aussätzig geworden,
der Mond scheint nicht, es ergraut der Wälder sturmduftendes Grün.
. . . .
Wir ergeben uns, kauern uns verhüllten Hauptes an den Stein, den
    die Brandung
immer wieder mit schwarz anprallendem Haß überstürzt und endlich
    verschlingt.—
Vielleicht leben und trauern um uns morgen Sternenkinder, denen die
    Landung
in unser zerstörtes Weltall zu spät und sinnlos gelingt . . .

(*Gedichte* 3, 44: Over the land come swarms of winged lies from the north, darkening the light and dulling the blue-mirroring efflorescence of the seas, the white beach has grown leprous with their rubbish, the moon does not shine, and the storm-scented green of the woods turns grey. . . . We yield, cower with covered heads against the rock, which the breaking waves repeatedly devour with black crashing hatred, precipitately, definitively.—Perhaps we shall be mourned tomorrow by children of the stars, who manage to land in our devastated world too late and pointlessly . . .)

The German poet of the 1920s who is commonly represented as mediating between older poetic values and the intellectual demands of a technologized environment is Oskar Loerke. Without confining himself to a bland imitation of the eighteenth- and nineteenth-century German classics,[22] Loerke

---

[22] Lamping (1989, 227) draws a distinction between the conservatism of Loerke and the more truly reactionary traditionalism apparent in the poetry of such writers as Hans Carossa, Friedrich Georg Jünger, Rudolf Alexander Schröder, and Josef Weinheber.

worked predominantly with the formal models that they had established. From his earliest collection of 1911 onwards, he opened the subject-matter of his poems to the experiences of modern urban existence, but characteristically he related them to long-term historical developments and to the cultural heritage of antiquity. He maintained a sensitivity towards systems of belief that had held sway in the past, but he did so in the awareness that they had lost their ability to convince a sceptical and scientific modern consciousness. In both these senses, Loerke's poetry displays a curious bifocal quality. He himself speaks of a "dual consciousness of near and far", and of the need to maintain a balance—beyond all utilitarian claims on poetic expression—between the realistic and the romantic dimensions of modern cultural awareness (*Gedichte* I, 701–4); and that quest for balance is very much apparent in his collections of the 1920s. In *Die heimliche Stadt* (The Secret City) of 1921, when writing of the transience and undependability of that which is new, he invokes fidelity as a virtue capable of retrieving a sense of eternity that is otherwise scorned and denied (*Gedichte* I, 181 f.). And his 1926 collection, *Der längste Tag* (The Longest Day), contains a section called "The Magic Way", in which the human yearning to discern ultimate meaning in the objects of nature is offset by reminders of the inherent limits to human knowledge.[23] Loerke may speak of magical powers and ancient deities as if they were real, but he does so in order to grieve that they are no longer present possibilities for modern humanity. The gods are departing:

> Sie sammeln sich mit ihren Heeren
> Über den Städten Nineve
> Sie wollen diesen Abend noch in Ehren
> Und fahren aus der Welt dann hin auf je.
>
> Begehrst du ihren Ausblick zum Geschenk,
> So spüte dich hinan und hilf die Ösen

---

[23] In "Siderische Nächte" (*Gedichte* I, 265 f.), the intimation of cosmic awareness remains an earthbound emotional experience; and in "Die Vogelstraßen" (ibid., 255 f.) the hint that the flight of migrating birds might contain a "magical figure" susceptible of interpretation is linked to a reminder of the futility of trying to express such insight in words: "Und Bild um Bild erbangt nach einem Sinn | Ob Worten, die wir sonst im Sinne hatten." Bayerdörfer (pp. 461 f.) speaks of a "refraction" of the human yearning for communion with nature in Loerke's poetry, and finds a similar effect in the works of the religious poet Konrad Weiß.

Des stummen Trauerhornes am Gehenk
Dem letzten Knecht im Trosse droben lösen.

(*Gedichte* I, 273: They are gathering with their armies above the cities of Nineveh. They have come to celebrate this one more evening, then to depart this world for ever. If you wish to be graced by their sight, then hurry along and help the last vassal in the throng to release the fastening on his mute horn of mourning.)

As Dieter Lamping (1989, 227) puts it, among those German poets of the 1920s who remain in some sense modernists while also reacting against the experimentalism of 'first-phase' modernism, Loerke is a clear case of someone who is looking for a middle way.

Loerke's name is frequently linked in the secondary literature with that of Wilhelm Lehmann, and they were indeed personally associated during the 1930s. There is a distinction to be drawn between them nevertheless. The poems that Lehmann began to publish in 1929 are almost exclusively concerned with the description of natural objects and natural processes, and the effect of his rhymes and metres is often to suggest an intimacy with the rhythms of nature that was formerly the preserve of folk-song and fairy-tale. Loerke might articulate the human yearning to be as the souls of migratory birds (in his poem "Die Vogelstraßen": *Gedichte* I, 255 f.), but Lehmann, in a poem of January 1932, speaks directly of the mystical potency invested in the egg of the magpie:

Möchte das Nichts mich überfallen,
Suche ich nach dem Elsternei,
Trinke aus seiner Schale, damit ich
Der Sprache der Vögel kundig sei.

(*Werke*, I, 39: Should nothingness overpower me, I shall seek the magpie's egg and drink from it that I might understand the language of the birds.)

Loerke might allude to the 'magic' of naming things (*Gedichte* I, 369 f.);[24] but Lehmann really does strive for the magical evocation of nature's eternal round in his incantatory repetition of

---

[24] Lamping (1989, 225) cites Loerke's poem "Namen" from his 1930 collection *Atem der Erde* in illustration of the essential similarity between Loerke and Lehmann; but the complex framing motif of this poem, which amounts to a

botanical names—"Die Ulmennuß, der Ahornstich . . ." (*Werke*, I, 45: The elm-tree nut, the sycamore seed). Lehmann's poem "Abschied" (Farewell) of October 1934 still more explicitly evokes the human participation in nature's great round-song, and marks that sense of recurrence with the repeated line, "Weiß geäderte Stachelbeere" (White-veined gooseberries: *Werke*, I, 53). Marguerite Samuelson-Koenneker (p. 908 f.) sums up the distinction between the two poets aptly when she contrasts Loerke's acute sense of the interdependence of man and nature with Lehmann's quest for a poetic language which can appear to confer magical power over reality.

The strength of interest that German writers show in nature poetry in the early 1930s has been seen as a particular wave of retrenchment within the broader trend: in a phase when the public domain is riven by intractable political strife, many writers can be seen to be reverting to idyllic models for presenting reality (Schäfer, 1974). The cultivation of privacy constituted one variety of resistance to the collectivist tendencies which dominated the political world, and many of the writers who took this route were to become associated with the mode of literary activity under National Socialism that we know as "inner emigration".[25] It was a form of resistance which ran the risk of eluding public understanding. Already in 1931, when Lehmann sought to publish a poem about the moon which reflected self-consciously on the poetic act of evocation—"Ich spreche Mond"—and linked that reflection without explicit explanation to the myth of Diana and Endymion, then the poem was rejected by the *Vossische Zeitung* as "too complicated for our readers" (*Werke* I, 401). The hostility of leading newspapers to lyric poetry had been noted by Oskar Loerke in an address at Berlin University in 1928 (*Gedichte*, I, 696);[26] and

challenge to the air pilot to interpret the network of waterways below him as a chiromancer reads the future in the lines on a hand, is again an example of how Loerke confronts such human yearnings with the awareness of their inevitable frustration.

[25] For an introduction to the literature of the "inner emigration" see J. M. Ritchie, *German Literature under National Socialism* (Beckenham: Croom Helm, 1983), 111–32. Lehmann's first collection of poems, *Antwort des Schweigens*, was published in 1935 by Ernst Niekisch's Widerstands-Verlag.

[26] Loerke's text "Das Wagnis des Gedichts" was originally given as an address with the title "Formprobleme der Lyrik": see Schäfer 1974, 377.

the young poet Martin Raschke was aroused to a robust defence in 1930 by an article in the *Berliner Zeitung* proclaiming that "lyric poetry must die in order that progress may live" (Schäfer 1974, 377). Raschke was writing in *Die Kolonne* (The Column), a periodical which he had co-founded in 1929 precisely as a rallying point for those concerned to preserve poetry as a domain for the articulation of insights excluded from the fashionable demand for factual reportage. *Die Kolonne* provided an initial platform for a number of young poets who were to establish considerable reputations for themselves in later years—Günter Eich, Peter Huchel, and Gertrud Kolmar amongst them. But the programme that the journal was proclaiming at the end of the 1920s could not but appear to be an assertion of conservative values in both theme and outlook: the editorial statement which introduced its first number expressed a clear preference for rural subjects over urban ones, and for metaphysical schemes over empirical analysis.[27] The critic Bernhard Diebold was to challenge the young poets of *Die Kolonne* in 1932 with the view that they should come out of their contemplative shells and face up to the social crises of the day which were encroaching on the rural domain every bit as much as on the cities. The response that he got from Günter Eich was an emphatic denial that poetry should be expected to have any practical application whatsoever: "Gedichte haben keinen Nutzwert" (Schäfer 1974, 367).

In discussions of lyric poetry, as in the broader cultural debates of the Weimar Republic, the battle-lines were sharply drawn by 1930. Was poetry to be conceived in terms of social use-value or not? Was its subject to be the life of the industrial age or was it to be the realm of nature? Was it to restrict itself to recording observed phenomena or reach out for a sense of

---

[27] "Noch immer lebt ein großer Teil der Menschheit in ländlichen Verhältnissen, und es entspringt nicht müssiger Traditionsfreude, wenn ihm Regen und Kälte wichtiger sind als ein Dynamo, der nie das Korn reifte. [...] Wer nur einmal in der Zeitlupe sich entfaltende Blumen sehen durfte, wird hinfort unterlassen, Wunder und Sachlichkeit deutlich gegeneinander abzugrenzen. So kann auch im Bereiche der Dichtung ein Wille zur Sachlichkeit nur dann Berechtigung erlangen, wenn er nicht von Unvermögen, sondern durch die Furcht bedingt wurde, mit allzuviel Worten das Wunderbare zu verdecken. Denn zum Verzicht auf jegliche Metaphysik führt nun, daß die Ordnung des Sichtbaren Wunder genug erscheint."—*Die Kolonne*, 1/1 (Dec. 1929), 1.

the higher connectedness of things? If, in what follows, we focus particularly on the part that Brecht played in these controversies, then that is partly because it is his poetry above all that has come to be seen as pointing the way beyond such stark antitheses, and partly because his own intervention had served to sharpen the terms of debate in the first place.

In the autumn of 1926, *Die literarische Welt* announced a poetry competition for young writers, and invited Brecht to be the adjudicator. When his verdict was published in February 1927, he used the occasion to denounce the broad heritage of German poetry since the turn of the century because, with a few "lucky" exceptions, it strayed too far from what was for him the fundamental principle of "communicating an idea or a feeling that others might find it worth knowing about". What made great poetry valuable, he argued, was that it documented the manner of speaking of an important person; and for his own part he could see no such merit in the likes of Stefan George, or Rilke, or Werfel (*LW*, 3, 5, 1; *BFA* 21, 191–3). Brecht disclaimed for himself any special authority on, or indeed interest in, the subject of lyric poetry—not in any spirit of modesty, but as an expression of policy. Since poetry was made by human beings, he claimed, it ought to be possible for any human being to judge it. If anything needed to be assessed in terms of its use-value, then it was lyric poetry: "Gerade Lyrik muß zweifellos etwas sein, was man auf den Gebrauchswert untersuchen können muß."

Having read over 500 poems submitted by some 400 contestants, Brecht declared that he had found nothing amongst them to impress him. They had all revealed themselves as tender scions of a spent bourgeoisie; their poetry was all too innocuous, incurably sentimental, and innocent of the ways of the world (*weltfremd*). He decided to award the prize to none of them, and to recommend instead that *Die literarische Welt* publish a poem by Hannes Küpper about an Australian cycling champion, which runs as follows:

> Es kreist um ihn die Legende,
> daß seine Beine, Arme und Hände

wären aus Schmiedeeisen gemacht
zu Sidney in einer taghellen Nacht
He, he! the Iron Man!

Eine Spiralfeder aus Stahl sei sein Herz,
frei von Gefühlen und menschlichem Schmerz,
das Gehirn eine einzige Schalterwand
für des Dynamos Antrieb und Stillstand.
He, he! the Iron Man!

Dicke Kabelstränge seine Nerven wären
Hochgespannt mit Volt-Kraft und Ampèren
   Denn:
dieser künstliche Mensch sollte auf Erden
ursprünglich nicht Six-Days-Fahrer werden
Zu einem neuen Cäsar war er erdacht,
daher die ungeheure eiserne Macht.
He, he! the Iron Man!

   Und
bleibt auch alles nur Legende, so ist doch eines wahr:
Ein Menschenwunder ist es—Reggie MacNamara!
He, he! the Iron Man!

(Legend has it that his legs, arms and hands were forged out of wrought iron in Sydney one bright night. Hey, hey, the Iron Man!

That his heart is a steel spring, free from feelings and human pain, his brain a switchboard for the dynamo's energies. Hey, hey, the Iron Man!

That his nerves are thick cables charged with volts and amperes. For this synthetic man was not created to be a six-day cyclist, he was meant to be a new Caesar, that's why he was given his amazing iron power. Hey, hey, the Iron Man!

And even if all this is only legend, then one thing is still true: he's a human wonder—Reggie Macnamara! Hey, hey, the Iron Man!)

Brecht's action was generally received as a barbarous provocation. Disappointed contestants publicly complained that he had condemned them not for their poetry, but for their outlook (cf. BFA 21, 668); and Klaus Mann was prompted to organize a counter-attack, assembling an anthology of the rejected in collaboration with the poet Willi Fehse. The contents of that collection, which was published under the title *Anthologie jüngster Lyrik* in the autumn of 1927, serve if anything to prove Brecht's point: most of the contributions really do come

across as precious, sentimental, and pallid imitations of pre-war
poetic models.[28] But the publication gave Klaus Mann a platform from which to pour scorn on Brecht in turn for the coarse-
ness of his manners and the crassness of his taste for that jingle
about six-day cycle racing with a "profoundly unimaginative
American refrain" (*Anthologie jüngster Lyrik*, 161). Later
commentaries on Brecht's attitudes to poetry have similarly
tended to treat his verdict in *Die literarische Welt* as rather a
frivolous aberration, and even Jan Knopf in his extremely
thorough *Brecht-Handbuch* of 1984 (vol. ii, 487 f.) passes
over the matter as something of a burlesque escapade. The
points Brecht was making in that judgement do, nevertheless,
have a serious bearing on some of the things he was doing
in his own poetry of the mid-1920s, and the comments he
made about Küpper's poem provide useful pointers to the way
his thinking about the function of poetry was developing at this
time.

Brecht claimed to have come across the poem in a cycling
magazine, but this may well have been an embroidery of the
truth, as one of his better-informed critics—Gerhart Pohl in *Die
neue Bücherschau*—suspected at the time.[29] Küpper was not
such an entirely obscure figure as later accounts of the episode
tend to suggest, even if it has only recently become possible to
reconstruct his career in any detail (Cepl-Kaufmann). Having
trained as an actor after the war, Küpper worked as a sports
journalist in Berlin from 1923 to 1927 while trying, albeit
unsuccessfully, to establish himself as a poet and playwright.
From the autumn of 1927 he was to become the chief editor of
a not inestimable cultural journal, *Der Scheinwerfer* (The Spot-
light), associated with the civic theatre in Essen.

[28] Cf. Bayerdörfer, 469. Honourable exceptions are Erika Mitterer, who achieves
a certain dialectical intensity in her religious poetry, and Fred von Zollikofer, who
gives sustained expression to the tenacity of urban existence. A second anthology
by Fehse and Mann, published under the same title in 1929, contains work by a
number of poets whose reputations have proved more durable, among them Erich
Kästner, Paula Ludwig, and Marta Saalfeld.
[29] *NB* 4, 244: "Im Radsportblatt hätt' er's 'gefunden', neckt uns der Berühmte
'ziemlich leichtfertig'. Wir wissen, daß dieses 'Finden' von der Literaturgeschichte
höflich 'romantisches Beiwerk' genannt wird. Aber sei's. Küpper ist begabt, vielleicht nicht ernst und nicht bemüht genug, aber ein Kerl, der ohne Ullstein-Ruhm
etwas werden kann." *Die neue Bücherschau* published another of Küpper's poems,
"Nackte Seelen", in the October issue of 1927 (*NB* 5, 173).

Early in 1925, poems by Brecht and Küpper appeared together in an anthology published by the short-lived cultural journal *Das Dreieck* (The Triangle). Here we find Küpper writing in a spare and tightly argued free-verse style on the subject of religious awareness, on the demystification of the natural force of electricity, and—in what must nowadays appear distinctly self-regarding macho terms—on relations between the sexes (cf. Cepl-Kaufmann, 399–402).[30] It is unclear to what extent Brecht was aware of Küpper's previous publications when he decided to single him out for distinction in the poetry competition, and he had good reason to suppose that Küpper's name was not familiar to the general public (cf. BFA 21, 354). But the tone of the postcard Brecht sent him on 11 January 1927—asking him to send a handwritten copy of his "MacNamara Song", evidently so that Brecht could claim in *Die literarische Welt* that he possessed the original manuscript— suggests that they were already personally acquainted.[31] Between the publication of Brecht's verdict and Küpper's departure for Essen in the autumn of 1927, the two men were evidently in close contact: there are press photographs showing them together, both in Berlin and at the chamber music festival in Baden-Baden.[32] It is likely to have been during this period that Küpper sought Brecht's opinion on a play he had written, which he had unsuccessfully offered to professional theatre directors as early as 1925 (cf. Cepl-Kaufmann, 415). Whether or not Brecht was ever serious about promoting Küpper's career as a writer, he was certainly using Küpper's poem to promote a particular set of attitudes towards writing, without identifying himself irrevocably with those attitudes.

---

[30] Readers with a particular interest in gender issues will find a revealing representation of Küpper in the character of Wollank in Marieluise Fleißer's play "Der Tiefseefisch": *GW* I, 346–8.

[31] Brecht Archive reference: Z31/42–3. The handwritten postcard begins: "Lieber Küpper, bitte, schicken Sie mir, möglichst mit Rohrpost, Ihren McNamara Song, aber von Ihnen selbst geschrieben, bitte!"

[32] See Werner Hecht (ed.), *Brecht. Sein Leben in Bildern und Texten* (Frankfurt: Suhrkamp, 1988), 69; Ernst and Renate Schumacher, *Leben Brechts* (Berlin: Henschel, 1978), 88, 91. Following Küpper's move to Essen, contact was maintained for a few years through an extensive correspondence with Brecht's amanuensis and collaborator Elisabeth Hauptmann (now held in the Deutsches Literaturarchiv, Marbach). Brecht occasionally contributed items to *Der Scheinwerfer*, but without apparent enthusiasm.

The principle of 'usefulness' was to become an abiding theme of Brecht's work, and when he reflects in a poem of the mid-1930s on his own standing in the eyes of posterity, for example, the first of the reasons for which he hopes to be remembered is the fact that he wrote in praise of usefulness (*BFA* 14, 320f.).[33] When Brecht chose to commend Küpper's MacNamara poem for its work-a-day qualities he was patently mounting a challenge to that deep-seated assumption in German bourgeois culture that poetic writing belonged to a quite separate sphere of activity from everyday experience, that in the words of the nineteenth-century writer Karl Gutzkow it represented the "Sunday" of life (cf. Mandelkow, 391). But the issues associated with that challenge did not present themselves in unequivocal terms to Brecht in 1927. For one thing, the compliments he paid Küpper's poem are distinctly double-edged: it was an example of the best that Küpper was capable of, it could "conceivably" (*unter Umständen*) be sung, and its value lay in the fact that it documented public feeling on an interesting subject (*BFA* 21, 193). For another thing, Brecht was confronted with the limitations of the criterion of usefulness when finalizing the publication of his own early poems in the *Hauspostille* later the same year. In the introduction he wrote for the *Hauspostille* in 1927, Brecht ostensibly reaffirmed his commitment to the principle that a poem should make itself useful to the reader, but he simultaneously exposed that precept to ridicule by overstating the practical value of particular poems for specific purposes (the poems of the first section were intended to appeal to the emotions, and were therefore recommended only in small doses and only to those with a strong disposition; the "chronicles" were variously recommended for occasions of storm, snow, bankruptcy and persecution, and in one instance for singing on June nights—although parts of it might still be suitable into October; and so on). In other words, he was now distancing himself from the concept of 'use-value' in the crass form in which he had proclaimed it in *Die literarische Welt* by assimilating it to the parodistic use of 'instructive' forms which

---

[33] Other poems of the 1930s celebrate the use of artefacts and the "usefulness" of the classic texts of Marxism: *BFA* 14, 156f., 337f.

he had always intended to be reflected in the organization of the *Hauspostille*.[34]

There are some superficial similarities between Küpper's poem and Brecht's own work of the mid-1920s. This was the period when Brecht was working closely with the composer Kurt Weill on songs which reflect the fashionable themes and jazz idioms of the time. The style of the "MacNamara Song" is not far removed from that of Brecht's *Mahagonny* songs of 1926 (one of which Brecht had indeed quoted as a provocatively earthy motto to his judgement in *Die literarische Welt*), and the industrial imagery Küpper uses is close to that of the texts Brecht was to write in mid-1927 for a planned "epic" celebration of Germany's industrial community, the "Ruhrepos" (*BFA* 21, 205 f.).[35] But on closer inspection it becomes clear how different Brecht's poems are. The *Mahagonny* songs express basic human impulses in simple and direct terms, but by contrast with Küpper's unreserved celebration of human prowess they typically carry an ironic twist in their tail, an unmasking of the illusory nature of human yearnings. The "Ruhrepos" texts are strongly evocative of the power of industrial machinery; but whereas Küpper evokes mechanical force as if it were a desirable end in itself, and naively speaks of his champion cyclist as a potential "new Caesar", Brecht returns the machine to its human context, treating it as if it had a personality and social relationships of its own. The cranes of Brecht's poems are not only named (by the workforce), they are presented as workers who need to acquire the discipline that brings financial reward, as comrades with a stake in the socialization of the means of production (*BFA* 13, 374–8).

Having used Küpper's "MacNamara Song" as a gauntlet to fling in the faces of the traditionalists, the chief use that Brecht found for him subsequently was as a mental sparring-partner. The text in which he does so is the private note in which he is

---

[34] Among Brecht's posthumous papers there is a text which is assumed to be an unused draft of the cover blurb for the *Hauspostille*, and which expressly relativizes the notion of the use-value of the collection by stressing its private nature and the fact that its first "user" was the author himself: *BFA* 21, 202.

[35] Küpper represented the municipal authorities in Essen in negotiations with Brecht and Weill over the "Ruhrepos": see Eckhardt Köhn, "Das *Ruhrepos*. Dokumentation eines gescheiterten Projekts", *Brecht-Jahrbuch* (1977), 55 f.

most explicit about his opposition to 'Neue Sachlichkeit', and it casts Küpper in the role of the opponent who stands for 'Neue Sachlichkeit' (*BFA* 21, 354 f.). Brecht acknowledges that there is going to be a phase of intensive 'Sachlichkeit' in the theatre, as a necessary prelude to the development of anything more worthwhile. But he imagines a verbal duel taking place between himself and Küpper as members of the rising generation. For the nature of the difference between them, according to Brecht, is that he sees himself as someone who appreciates the value of new ideas *in the light of aesthetic considerations*, whereas Küpper does not. The conception of 'Sachlichkeit' that Küpper has come to epitomize in Brecht's eyes is one which is collectivistic in nature and orientated towards an external cause (*Sache*).[36] It is as if the cumulative effect of his dealings with Küpper and his writings had been to sharpen Brecht's awareness of the dangers of a 'Sachlichkeit' which allows the object under discussion to determine the terms in which it is discussed.

There is one further group of Brecht's poems from the mid-1920s which we have not yet considered, and which shows more clearly still how he was trying, in his poetic writing, to penetrate beyond that superficial and deterministic 'objectivity' which was associated with the fashionable conception of 'Sachlichkeit'. The sense of a coherent project behind this group of poems is most clearly apparent from the collection of ten poems which Brecht published in 1930 under the title *Aus einem Lesebuch für Städtebewohner* (From a Reader for City-Dwellers). Some examples from that collection had been published earlier, in the three-month period preceding the publication of Brecht's judgement in *Die literarische Welt*, between November 1926 and January 1927 (*BFA* 11, 349). Beyond the items included in the collection of 1930 there is also a sizeable body of other poems which are similar in character to the *Lesebuch*, regardless of whether Brecht himself ever expressly linked them to the collection.[37]

---

[36] *BFA* 21, 355: "Küpper nämlich geht es um die Sache, er ist kollektivistisch eingestellt; und was immer daraus für Unheil kommen mag, wer immer sich als Besitzer dieser Bezeichnung melden mag, ich behaupte jetzt einfach, um weiterzukommen, Küpper sei für neue Sachlichkeit. Ich aber bin gegen sie."

[37] The editors of volume 11 of *BFA* have adhered rigidly to the principle that only those poems which Brecht himself designated as "zum Lesebuch gehörig" should be published in the same volume as the collection of 1930. Poems which

What distinguishes this group of poems as a whole from Brecht's earlier work is the dry matter-of-factness with which they represent, and reflect upon, characteristic experiences of city-dwellers, without resort to colourful description or metaphor, and largely in the language in which ordinary city-dwellers would express themselves. Some of them focus on the anonymity and interchangeability of human predicaments in the city, on moments of estrangement and effacement, on the beginnings and endings of sexual liaisons (*BFA* 11, 170–2; 13, 367). Others evoke social transactions, acts of advice or exhortation, and in one case the brutal exercise of arbitrary authority (*BFA* 11, 162 f.; 13, 364 f., 371). As Brecht puts it in the closing poem of the 1930 selection, he has opted here to speak with the "cold and general" language of a reality which "you" (the imagined interlocutor) do not seem adequately to recognize (*BFA* 11, 165). A certain didactic thrust is implicit in the notion of a *Lesebuch*, and it is explicit in the poem just quoted. But the didacticism that we experience here is not yet one that is based on the conviction that a particular political conclusion should be drawn from the experiences that are being recorded. If there are hints of a potential for collective commitment in these poems, then it is shown to be a potential wrought out of the confrontation of individuals with the intractable and inhospitable realities of urban living.

This group of poems may fairly be said to represent a neglected portion of Brecht's writings. Marxist interpreters have tended to treat them merely as symptoms of a "behaviourist phase" that Brecht was passing through on his way to becoming a Marxist (cf. Knopf, vol. ii, 56 f.), while in the West these poems fell victim to a persistent prejudice against rigorous realism in poetry (cf. Lamping 1989, 210). Dieter Lamping, like Michael Hamburger before him, emphasizes the sense in which the realism of Brecht's poetry represents an expansion of the possibilities of poetic expression as well as a repudiation of traditional notions of poetry; but even he overlooks an important point when he speaks of the *Lesebuch* poems as exemplary "Gebrauchslyrik" in the "neusachlich" manner (Lamping 1989,

Elisabeth Hauptmann had identified, on the basis of her own judgement, as belonging to the same group, and which were so treated in the *Gesammelte Werke* of 1967, are consigned in the new edition to volume 13.

213). The *Lesebuch* poems do not simply document social reality. The closing poem of the 1930 collection claims only to be speaking "like reality" (making no apparent allowance for the individuality and "difficulty" of the addressee), it does not claim that the collection gives immediate and unproblematic expression to the reality of which it speaks. It would be linguistically naive to suppose that it were doing so, and what Brecht actually does in the *Lesebuch* collection suggests that he was well aware of this point.

The most obvious manifestation of self-consciousness in the presentation of the *Lesebuch* collection is the short statement in brackets which appears at the end of each of the first six poems. The opening poem bleakly enjoins the newcomer to the city to deny his friends, his origins, his thoughts, and ultimately his very identity, in order to avoid being called to account; but then we come to the end of the poem and read that this is "what I have been told". The third poem starkly expresses the desire to eliminate an individual, but then we are told at the end that this is "how we speak to our fathers". The effect is to force a reappraisal of the expectations which the reader—or listener[38]—has initially brought to the interpretation of what the body of the poem is saying.

Among the poems that Brecht selected for inclusion in the published collection of 1930, we may also be struck by rhetorical devices of a more specific nature. In the first two poems we find him applying elements of biblical or other stylized diction in ways which defamiliarize mundane experiences: "open, oh open the door . . ." and "we are with you in the hour . . . when hope departs from you" (*BFA* 11, 157–8). There is a conspicuous patterning of the argument, a symmetry or a rhythmic repetition, in individual poems. In poem number 2, which plays on the proverbial image of the superfluous individual as a "fifth wheel on the waggon", symmetrical presentation serves to highlight the psychological dynamics of the situation: the group does not initially recognize the signs that the luckless individual is acknowledging his superfluity, and by the time they do, he has lost sight of the

---

[38] Philip Brady (1972) points out that Brecht's thinking about the presentation of these poems may have been influenced by his interest in issuing them on gramophone records, and by his work with material for radio broadcasts in the late 1920s.

factors which had shown him to be redundant to the collective purpose. The strategies of self-discipline evoked in poems 4 and 5 are different in kind, but both are characterized by repetitive rhetorical structures. In the first instance the overall effect is to ironize the efforts of an individual to avoid effort. In the second, the repetition underscores the determination of a woman to overcome the hardships and humiliations that life has brought her, and thus reinforces the poignancy and tenacity of her commitment to the construction of a community for the future:

> Ich bin ein Dreck. Von mir
> Kann ich nichts verlangen als
> Schwäche, Verrat und Verkommenheit
> . . . . . .
> Ich bin ein Dreck; aber es müssen
> Alle Dinge mir zum besten dienen, ich
> Komme herauf, ich bin
> Unvermeidlich, das Geschlecht von morgen
> Bald schon kein Dreck mehr, sondern
> Der harte Mörtel, aus dem
> Die Städte gebaut sind.
> (Das habe ich eine Frau sagen hören.)

(BFA 11, 160–2: I'm just trash. I can expect nothing of myself but weakness, betrayal and depravity . . . I'm just trash; but I'll turn everything to my advantage, I'm on the way up, I won't be denied, I'm tomorrow's generation. Soon I won't be trash any more, but the tough mortar that cities are built of. (This is what I heard a woman say.))

Just as there are hints of the dialectics of struggle within individual poems such as this one, so too there are hints at dialectical connections between poems, between the self-discipline and the self-delusion (nos. 4 and 5), between the alienation and isolation (nos. 6 and 8) and the offers of advice and refuge (nos. 7 and 9). It was features such as these that led Philip Brady (1972) to look beyond the apparently documentary character of the *Lesebuch* poems, and to discuss the 1930 collection as an "essay in obliqueness".

A further point can be made about the scenic quality of these poems. The poems of the 1930 collection typically show individuals in alienating situations, whether we are dealing with sons in conflict with fathers or redundant individuals in conflict with the interests of a team. The ninth poem, indeed, presents us with a graduated sequence of scenes, it consists of four statements which document the varieties of nuance in which a man is offered a bed for the night in four different sets of circumstances (*BFA* 11, 164f.). And number 7—which, alone of the *Lesebuch* poems, alludes overtly to the likelihood that any serious attempt to change the conditions of urban life will be rewarded with victimization and criminalization[39]—takes the form of a monologue offering advice to a fugitive, and ends with the pithy (and untranslatable) phrase "Nichts zu danken". Without dispelling the mystery surrounding the relationship between speaker and addressee in the poem, that phrase on its own powerfully evokes an ethos in which mutual support may be taken for granted (there is no need to say thank you) and emotional bonding remains conventionally unexpressed (don't try to say it). In instances such as these we may detect that Brecht is beginning to articulate that sense of a social 'Gestus' which was to become an important, if elusive, concept for the organization of scenes in his later plays (cf. Brooker, 42ff.).[40] What is more germane to our present concern with the development of German poetry in the 1920s is the sensitivity that Brecht is displaying here towards the articulation of social relations in particular speech acts as well as in behavioural patterns. In the *Lesebuch* collection he has found techniques for drawing the reader into a critical evaluation of that process of articulation. Each poem is a reflection upon the reality of city living, but each reflection is presented in such a way as to invite critical reflection (cf. Bayerdörfer, 465; Mennemeier, 25).

In a private note of 1927, Brecht recorded his scepticism about the traditional notion of lyric poetry as a privileged medium of expression. When bankers and politicians express themselves, he noted, they are effecting a transaction; and as

[39] In his commentaries on Brecht's poems of 1938–9, Walter Benjamin noted that the *Lesebuch* poems had acquired a sense of eerie prophecy in the circumstances of exile, and went on to relate the surreptitiousness advocated in the opening poem, "Verwisch die Spuren", to the tactics demanded of an urban guerilla: *Versuche über Brecht* (Frankfurt: Suhrkamp, 1955), 80f. The frame of reference suggested by the poem itself, however, is not specifically political.

[40] In his 1939 essay "Über reimlose Lyrik mit unregelmäßigen Rhythmen", Brecht applies the notion of a "gestische Sprache", as developed in his theatrical work, to poetic writing, and describes its purpose as "die Vorgänge zwischen den Menschen als widerspruchsvolle, kampfdurchtobte, gewalttätige zu zeigen": *BFA* 22, 359.

patients we do something similar when we tell the doctor where it hurts. It seemed to him bizarre by comparison that we should expect lyric poetry to be a medium of "pure expression" (*BFA* 21, 201). The examples he was using point to the sense in which—without using the term, and possibly without having a technical term available to him—Brecht was alert to the pragmatic dimension of linguistic communication. As he had put it in his statement in *Die literarische Welt*, the fundamental gesture of communication is the expression of an idea or feeling that someone else may find it worth knowing about. It is his alertness to the inevitable social contextualization of what is "worth knowing" that manifests itself in the composition of *Aus einem Lesebuch für Städtebewohner*. This is also the sense in which Brecht's 1930 collection marks the culmination of a particular development in German poetic practice during the 1920s.

Hans-Peter Bayerdörfer draws attention to a general trend towards the foregrounding of the pragmatic functions of language in his article of 1983 on German poetry during the period of the Weimar Republic. We have noted in the course of this chapter some of the senses in which that trend manifests itself. We saw how the collapse of systems of authority in the course of the First World War had left Brecht in particular with a reservoir of idioms at his disposal, which retained their original ideological resonances, but could now be deployed at will for ironic purposes. We also noted how Wedekind, Brecht, and others adopted a particular voice or combination of voices in their ballads, for the purpose of disrupting conventional norms of response. The collage techniques of Mehring around 1920 (which are echoed by Kästner a decade later) bring about a still more drastic dislocation of the modes of public discourse, often coloured by the sardonic tone of Berlin street wisdom: "Where the mills of God grind | The grass never grows" (*Chronik*, 142). Arguably—and Bayerdörfer does so argue—the montage poetry of Gottfried Benn is a further radicalization of the possibilities of such allusive combination of phrases, but a radicalization which subverts the purposes of public allusiveness in their turn. In each instance, the act of quotation or allusion entails a process of intellectual construction, in which the formulation concerned is detached from its original functional context.

Brecht's *Lesebuch* poems step back from the intellectual assertiveness that characterizes both the social engagement of the cabaret culture and the anti-social aesthetic of Benn. They deal in the pragmatic currency of language in a more mundane sense, constructing social transactions in the vocabulary of everyday life, but also applying rhetorical devices which present those transactions for critical scrutiny. Brecht's 1930 collection challenges the naive notion of language as a transparent documentation of fact, just as his songs for the *Mahagonny* project and the "Ruhrepos" challenged the naive fascination with technological progress which he would have associated with the term 'Neue Sachlichkeit'.[41] In a general way, German poetry had opened itself up in the 1920s as a public medium for reflecting social reality, and the conception of what a poem was had shifted in the process away from "pure expression" and towards a self-awareness about expression as an act of intellectual construction. The conception of a poem implicit in Brecht's *Lesebuch* collection has moved one stage further: it has moved beyond the self-satisfaction of an intellectual construction of reality towards the self-critical display of the senses in which social reality is itself verbally constituted.

[41] In this sense, Michael Hamburger's assertion (p. 198) that Brecht treats statements as "solid reliable currency" also stands in need of qualification.

3

The Theatre as Political Community

> The stage took on a teaching function. Petroleum, infla-
> tion, war, social conflicts, the family, religion, grain, the
> meat trade became objects of theatrical representation.
>
> Bertolt Brecht (*BFA* 22, 110)

> The theatre fantasizes for the audience, and at the same
> time it lets the audience experience the products of that
> fantasy. [. . .] As collectivism grows, so does the power of
> fantasy.
>
> Ödön von Horváth (*GW* IV, 660 f.)

This chapter is about theatre rather than drama. In giving it that
emphasis, I am not overlooking the wealth and variety of
German dramatic writing in the Weimar period; indeed, I am
conscious that it would take a separate book to do justice to
that.[1] What I wish to concentrate on for present purposes,
however, within the span of a single chapter, is the role of the
theatre as the most public medium of literary communication
during the period of the Weimar Republic. To describe the
various conceptions of theatre which were prevalent at the time,
to set them in relation to each other and to the political climate
of the times, is a sufficient task for one chapter and a necessary
prerequisite for understanding the directions in which dramatic
writing was developing.

To approach those conceptions of theatre is immediately to

---

[1] H. F. Garten's *Modern German Drama* (London: Methuen, 1959) clearly stands
in need of updating; and while John Willett's *The Theatre of the Weimar Republic*
(1988) is up to date in its perspectives on the playwrights, it is not part of his purpose
there to analyse their approaches to writing drama. The subject is comprehensively
covered in German by F. N. Mennemeier, *Modernes deutsches Drama*, 2 vols.
(Munich: Wilhelm Fink Verlag, 1979).

confront some notorious ambiguities of German vocabulary. When we read discussions of the role of the theatre in the 'community' (*Gemeinschaft*), is that term being used in a sense which allows for the diversity of social relations and interests, or is it being used in implied opposition to a Western model of 'society' (*Gesellschaft*), and does it therefore carry the connotation of organic unity and a defining cultural identity?[2] When we come across the term *Geist* should we take it to imply a mental activity that is intellectual and analytical or one that is spiritual and integrative? The notion of community as something organic and spiritualized was certainly prevalent in discussions of the theatre at the start of the Weimar period, whether in the specific context of Expressionist drama or in relation to broader conceptions of the national culture. It is there that we may recognize aspects of that strong undertow of anti-modernity that characterized German cultural attitudes in the wake of industrialization. The new forms of theatre which became established in the course of the 1920s certainly conceived themselves as modernist in the sense that they were analytical and intellectualized, and that they engaged with the political tensions of an industrial society. But by virtue of that engagement, their intellectual analysis remained enmeshed in the historical realities of their time, and in the interests and perspectives of particular groups and institutions—which is to say that, whatever their aspiration to critical detachment, they were themselves specific manifestations of political community in a particular time and place.

The quotations from Brecht and Horváth at the head of this chapter are intended to provide an initial sense of the field of tensions in which the innovative developments in German theatre were taking place during the Weimar period. Brecht is looking back from the perspective of the 1930s at the attempt to expand the compass of theatrical representation, to break out of the limitations imposed by traditional drama, with its self-contained expression of interpersonal actions and relationships.[3] What he sees emerging in the peculiar conditions of

---

[2] On the importance of these categories in German social and political thinking around the time of the First World War, see Sontheimer 1962, 250–2; Pascal 1973, 22–32.

[3] On the broad historical relationship between the traditional conception of drama and the emerging practice of epic theatre, see Peter Szondi, *Theory of Modern Drama* (Cambridge: Polity, 1987), 7–10.

Berlin in the 1920s is a style of theatre which is inextricably linked with his name and with Piscator's, and which has become familiar to us as 'epic theatre'. By aspiration that new style of theatre is instructive, analytical, and receptive to the ramifications of modern social and economic organization which exceed the bounds of interpersonal relations. What is also familiar to us from Brecht's theoretical writings, however, is the continuous need he saw to develop presentational techniques for encouraging audiences to respond critically to what they were being shown. Horváth provides a perspective on that problem which complements Brecht's. His comment is made in the context of reflections upon the potency of communal bonding in an audience which shares a particular political outlook, and he is considering the potential of theatrical performance to make an audience critically aware of the subconscious impulses that determine its own social attitudes. In the course of this chapter I shall try to show how the various models of theatre developed during the Weimar period relate historically to each other, and to bring out the senses in which even a self-consciously critical style of theatre could run the risk of becoming aligned with the orthodoxies of a particular political subculture. Only in the light of such an inquiry do I think it is possible to assess the scope for a politically aware theatre to sustain and encourage critical openness in the circumstances of the Weimar Republic.

The notion of the theatre as a focus for a sense of community was particularly strong around 1918, and it was heavily laden with connotations of organic unity and ethical integration. In part this reflected the legacy of the theatre reform movement which had established itself in the first decade of the century. Reacting against Naturalist psychology in particular and Enlightenment rationalism in general, that movement had sought to cultivate an irrational mythical awareness as the basis for a cultural renewal inspired by the early writings of Nietzsche (Brauneck 1982, 63). Wagner had provided a model for a theatre of Germanic mythology at Bayreuth, and a number of similar projects for festival theatres were promoted during the Wilhelmine period. Something of that cultic nationalist ethos fed into the work of the leading theatrical impresario of the time, Max Reinhardt, who mounted large-scale productions of Greek classics and modern mystery plays in circus buildings and exhibition halls (including London's Olympia) in the immediate pre-war years; in 1913 he also produced Gerhart Hauptmann's contribution to the festival-play genre, the *Festspiel in deutschen Reimen*. A memorandum that Reinhardt drew up in 1917, describing the festival theatre he hoped to establish near Salzburg, is indicative of the way in which pre-war discussions of German cultural identity had invested the theatre with the status of a quasi-sacral institution aimed at transcending the divisions inherent in industrial society. His vision was of "a house for those high feasts which are to be celebrated once a year with full artistic solemnity, set apart from the everyday routine of the cities, in a place so distinguished by natural and artistic beauty that in the summer holidays, when people are freed from their cares and woes, it will become a popular place of pilgrimage" (Brauneck 1988, 122). Reinhardt's dream of summer festival plays at Salzburg was to become a reality in the course of the 1920s, and when he presided over the establishment of a grand-scale 'people's theatre' in Berlin in 1919—the Großes Schauspielhaus, funded by a "German National Theatre" consortium—it was presented to the public as a communal space in which the nation (the *Volksgemeinschaft*) could identify with its finest cultural products.[4]

A conception of the theatre as an instrument of moral renewal had also gathered strength as the social repercussions of the First World War made themselves felt. The revolutionary regime established in Bavaria in November 1918 under the local leader of the left-wing Independent Social Democratic Party (USPD), Kurt Eisner, envisaged, for example, that state-owned theatres would play a pre-eminent part in expunging commercial influences from cultural life and disseminating communitarian values (Rühle 1972, vol. i, 40). The man who, as Minister of Culture in that government, was to have carried out those parts of the revolutionary programme concerned with education and the arts was Gustav Landauer, a distinguished Shakespeare scholar

---

[4] Reinhardt's assistant Heinz Herald issued a statement on the occasion of the opening of the Großes Schauspielhaus which contained the following words: "Das neue Theater will eine Gemeinde um sich sammeln, die Gemeinde derer, die es erwartet haben, vielleicht ohne daß sie es wußten. Es will die Kunst der Volksgemeinschaft, aus der sie ihre besten Kräfte saugt, wieder näherbringen." (Quoted in Brauneck 1982, 379.)

and a philosophical anarchist, who had attracted a sizeable following among German intellectuals around the time of the First World War, including the dramatists Kaiser and Toller. The variety of socialism Landauer propounded was emphatically voluntaristic in nature and deliberately defined in opposition to the Marxism of the pre-war Social Democratic Party, which he interpreted as itself a product of the mechanistic and mercantile mentality of bourgeois society.[5]

The cultural policies of Eisner and Landauer were never put into practice because they were both assassinated in the first half of 1919, and their regime was first subverted by the Communist Party and then brutally suppressed. But their legacy lived on in the writings of Ernst Toller, who was also a leading member of Eisner's government.[6] Toller's first play, *Die Wandlung* (Transfiguration), tells the story of a young German-Jewish intellectual who welcomes the promise of national unity that the outbreak of war in 1914 had appeared to bring, is gravely disillusioned by what he actually witnesses in the course of the war, and emerges as a revolutionary agitator. The ending of that play, in which the young hero Friedrich persuades the masses not to march in response to hunger and material need, but to march instead in the spirit of a universal ideal of humanity, is a precise projection of Landauer's doctrine; and it is entirely fitting that, in a note on the play, Toller should have equated his conception of the political poet with a sense of religious mission.[7] In Karlheinz Martin, Toller also found a theatre director who fully sympathized with his ideal. The first production of *Die Wandlung* took place in September 1919 in the small Tribüne theatre which Martin had established in Berlin-Charlottenburg, and which he conceived as a shrine to "spiritual community" (*geistige Gemeinschaft*)—even if the price of

[5] See Gustav Landauer, *Aufruf zum Sozialismus* (Wetzlar: Büchseder Pandora, 1978[6]). Eugene Lunn, *Prophet of Community: The Romantic Socialism of Gustav Landauer* (Berkeley and Los Angeles: University of California Press, 1973), traces the influence of Nietzsche and of nineteenth-century *völkisch* thought, as well as philosophical anarchism, on Landauer's conception of voluntaristic socialism.

[6] For an extensive account of the Bavarian revolutionary government, and of Toller's role in it, see Dove, 60–87.

[7] See Toller, *GW* 2, 361: "Voraussetzung des politischen Dichters (der stets irgendwie religiöser Dichter ist): ein Mensch, der sich verantwortlich fühlt für sich und für jeden Bruder menschlicher Gemeinschaft."

seats made admission to that particular community somewhat exclusive (Patterson, 99).

The volume of essays on the contemporary theatre published by Max Krell in 1923 under the title *Das deutsche Theater der Gegenwart* provides intriguing corroborative evidence of the intellectual climate in which the role of the theatre in society was being discussed. It contains the reflections of Hans Poelzig, the architect associated with Reinhardt's festival theatre project, on the thinking behind that venture, as well as a variety of contributions on both the ideals and the practicalities of the theatre. It also contains, under the title "Epoche und Theater", an essay by Arnold Zweig (an author chiefly remembered for his later series of novels about the First World War), in which the theatre is described as the medium of a grandiose historical transformation for the German people. Zweig invests the theatre with the task of redeeming the true character of the German nation from the cynicism of its wartime regime and more generally from the "anarchy" of political and economic factionalism.[8] Zweig's vision of the theatre as a force for social cohesion is bound to strike us in retrospect as naive in its use of terms like 'national character' and 'community' which were subsequently to prove peculiarly susceptible to demagogic manipulation. His essay may nevertheless be seen as symptomatic of an intellectual revolt against the character of the times, particularly in the way that it appeals to the 'better nature' of the German nation by reaching back to a conception of the theatre as a 'moral institution' which Schiller had outlined in the eighteenth century. Schiller, too, had called upon the theatre to fulfil a role in the community formerly performed by religion, acting as a communal channel by which the precepts of the "better portion" of society could be disseminated among the populace. He, too, had hoped that the experience of a national

---

[8] Zweig's essay was originally published under the title "Das Theater im Volksstaate" in *Der Geist der neuen Volksgemeinschaft*, published by the Reichszentrale für Heimatdienst in 1919. On the general purport of Zweig's writings on the theatre, see H.-H. Müller, 153–7. For an account of Zweig's reputation as a dramatist around the time of the First World War, see Jost Hermand, "Das Licht in der Finsternis: Arnold Zweigs *Ritualmord in Ungarn* als prosemitisches Tendenzund Läuterungsdrama", in *Arnold Zweig: Psyche, Politik und Literatur (Jahrbuch für Internationale Germanistik*, Reihe A: Kongressberichte, vol. 32), ed. D. Midgley et al. (Berne: Peter Lang, 1993), 32–48.

theatre could help the Germans to realize their identity as a nation.[9] If we ask about the actual practical consequences for the theatre of the political transition from monarchy to republic, then two things stand out. For one thing censorship was abolished under the Weimar Constitution—although legal provisions still made it possible to prosecute literary authors for political reasons, and the licensing system still enabled the police to prohibit theatrical performances, as they did especially during the period of heightened political tension after 1929 (cf. Hannover and Hannover-Drück, 238–62). But no less important from the point of view of the functioning of the theatre as a public institution of the Republic was the fact that the court theatres of the various German principalities became converted into state theatres.

The abolition of censorship opened the way for unexpurgated performances of modern plays which had lain beyond the pale of Wilhelmine propriety. The official taboo was now lifted from the sexual themes explored in Wedekind's *Lulu* and Schnitzler's *Reigen* (La Ronde), for example—although in Schnitzler's case the scandal generated by the première of *Reigen* in December 1920 was sufficient for him to withdraw permission for any further public performances of the play. Obstacles were also removed from the performance of plays suggestive of radical cultural critique or touching on other issues sensitive during wartime—Sternheim's *1913*, for example, and the works of Kaiser and the younger Expressionists, which had begun to be staged sporadically since 1917, depending on local conditions (Willett 1988, 58 f.). The way also lay open for a fresh wave of plays which Günter Rühle (1972, vol. i, 56 f.) aptly calls "black Expressionism": Bertolt Brecht and Arnolt Bronnen, who were together thought of as the *enfants terribles* of German theatre when their works began to be staged in the early 1920s, were inverting the idealist visions of the Expressionists and

---

[9] "Die Schaubühne ist der gemeinschaftliche Kanal, in welchen von dem denkenden bessern Theile des Volks das Licht der Weißheit herunterströmt, und von da aus in milderen Stralen durch den ganzen Staat sich verbreitet. [. . .] wenn wir es erlebten eine Nationalbühne zu haben, so würden wir auch eine Nation." *Schillers Werke (Nationalausgabe)*, vol. xx (Weimar: Hermann Böhlaus Nachfolger, 1962), 97–9.

presenting an image of humanity which was firmly rooted in the physiological and the erotic.

The conversion of court theatres into state theatres was significant, not in the high-minded anti-commercial sense envisaged by the Bavarian revolutionaries, but because it brought a new pattern of political patronage to bear on the theatrical repertoire in general. A vivid illustration of the situation is provided by the career of Leopold Jessner, who was appointed in 1919 to what was at once the most prestigious and the most sensitive post under the new dispensation: Director of the Prussian State Theatre (Staatliches Schauspielhaus) in Berlin, the former court theatre of the Kaiser. In theatre history Jessner is remembered as an innovator in two specific senses. He experimented technically with the spatial dimensions of the acting area, stripping out all the clutter of naturalist representation and making ostentatious use of steps and podia, which became a celebrated idiosyncrasy of his productions. But his technical experimentation was put in the service of a more fundamental innovation in terms of theatrical interpretation: he harnessed all his stagecraft to the realization, not of dramatic psychology or the logic of the storyline, but of a central idea inherent in the play. In his 1926 production of *Hamlet*, the central idea he chose to highlight, in a palpably anti-monarchist spirit, was the notion of "something rotten in the state of Denmark". His choice of play for his opening production in 1919 was in itself a demonstrative political act; it was a text which had provided a veritable quarry of sententious phrases for statesmen and schoolmasters under the Empire, Schiller's *Wilhelm Tell*, and the central idea he emphasized was that of liberation from an oppressive tyranny. Lines of the original text which express patriotic fervour were cut from the performance, and if the memoirs of Fritz Kortner are to be believed, the tyrant Geßler (whom Kortner played) was kitted out in a costume which was distinctly redolent of the wartime German general staff—decorations and all (Brauneck 1988, 179–82). As Kortner reconstructs the incident, the politically self-conscious stylization of the production had already caused uproar in the auditorium by the time he himself arrived in the theatre, and the uproar was only dispelled by his intimidatory first entrance as Geßler towards the end of Act III (ibid. 180f.). Contemporary reviews indicate rather that serious disorder only broke out in Act IV (Fetting, vol. ii, 41–53). What is abundantly clear from the evidence, however, is that the radical abstraction of the production style (which is described in greater detail in Patterson, 88–90) was being used as a pretext for politically motivated disruption.

Jessner's conception of theatre was political in the broadest sense. His productions were responsive to contemporary political situations without sacrificing the principle of artistic integrity to a particular partisan line. It was a policy commensurate with the role of civic theatre in a republican state; but Jessner's subsequent career is also a poignant reminder of how susceptible state institutions can be to the dominant currents of political life.[10] When he directed *Wilhelm Tell* for a second time in 1923, French and Belgian troops had occupied the Ruhr, and it was an entirely different set of resonances that Jessner brought out in the text. The tyrant Geßler now became the wilful representative of an oppressive foreign power, and the Swiss peasants were presented as staunch patriots. The second performance of the new production was treated, moreover, as a state occasion, with the highest ministers of the government in attendance; and in the famous scene on the Rütli at the end of Act II the audience itself participated in the swearing of the oath of allegiance, and then sang the national anthem (Fetting, vol. ii, 44). Notwithstanding such displays of national solidarity, Jessner, as a Jew and a Social Democrat, was subjected to repeated agitation from the nationalist right during the 1920s, and eventually resigned from the post of Director in 1930 (Rühle 1967, 839, 1007). Like Max Reinhardt he was to die in exile in America in the 1940s.

Jessner's brand of theatre was also closely associated with a particular cultural tradition which had developed within the social democratic movement, the tradition of the Volksbühne (People's Theatre). Founded in Berlin in 1890, the Volksbühne movement had always been based on an uneasy alliance between avant-garde intellectuals and representatives of the organized working class. As Cecil Davies has shown in his

[10] The fate of the "Ruhrepos" planned by Brecht and Weill for the town theatre of Essen, as described in chapter 8, is a further example of the susceptibility of artistic projects to the pressures of civic politics under the Weimar Republic.

study of the movement, the pact that was struck between the two camps was one which satisfied working-class aspirations to self-improvement while also conforming, again, to the Schillerian notion of the theatre as a channel for disseminating ideas and sensibilites downwards through society. The founding principles of the movement were that it should provide ordinary workers with access to theatrical performances which were "morally uplifting" and of high artistic standard, as well as reflecting contemporary social issues (Davies, 21). As a historical phenomenon, the Volksbühne movement testifies both to the dominance of the theatre in German cultural life generally and to the significance of popular support in the development of the theatre as a cultural institution in the early twentieth century.

Starting on a small scale with special performances of new plays and with block bookings in the commercial theatre, the movement received a particular boost in 1905 when Max Reinhardt offered the Neue Freie Volksbühne (as the dominant faction of the movement was then called) special arrangements for Sunday performances at the prestigious Deutsches Theater. By the eve of the First World War, the movement was able to build its own theatre on the Bülowplatz (renamed Rosa-Luxemburg-Platz after 1945), and when economic circumstances became difficult during the war, Reinhardt again helped out by managing the theatre on a temporary basis, biding his time until he could realize his own project for a "theatre of the five thousand" (Davies, 71–86). While it had been part of the hope of the founders of the movement that the Volksbühne would provide a bulwark against commercialization in the theatre, as the movement had grown, political and commercial considerations had inevitably become intermeshed. In the years of the Weimar Republic, the way in which the management of the Volksbühne sought to cater to the tastes of its broad mass of subscribers led to its being frequently disparaged by left-wingers, Brecht included, as a mere ticket-selling organization. But its theatre stood nevertheless as an important institution in the cultural landscape of Berlin, an unmistakable monument to social democratic values (which the Nazis honoured by closing it down in the 1930s), and as a major house participating in the general circulation of the best theatrical talent of the day.

But the theatrical event to which the greatest, not to say the most inflated, expectations were attached in the immediate post-war years was the conversion of the capacious Circus Schumann building near the Friedrichstraße, under the auspices of Max Reinhardt, into the Großes Schauspielhaus. While the new theatre did not quite match up to the dream of a "theatre of the five thousand" as Reinhardt had described it in 1911, it was certainly imposing for its day, with a seating capacity of over three thousand, compared with one thousand at the Deutsches Theater and some two thousand at the Volksbühne. It incorporated the most advanced theatrical technology of the time, in the hope that it would be able to compete satisfactorily with the burgeoning cinema industry; it dispensed with the traditional hierarchical design of the auditorium, which was recognized to be part of the heritage of the cultural dominance of the aristocracy; and the acting area was no longer separated off from the auditorium by a front curtain, but on the contrary brought emphatically forward into the general arena by means of a large 'thrust stage' (cf. Styan, 111 f.). In the idealistic perspectives of the time, the circular arrangement of the internal space was seen to symbolize the integrative social function of the arts, the realization of an ideal 'theatre for the people' (Brauneck 1982, 379 f.)—even if, as one critic noted on opening night in November 1919, the manifest disunity of the German nation at the time was also apparent in the audience (Rühle 1967, 177). At the same time, the story of the Großes Schauspielhaus is a clear illustration of the problems that the theatre tends to encounter whenever it tries to operate as big business. After only one season Reinhardt became disillusioned with the practical implications of running the new house and left Berlin for a period in order to pursue his schemes for grandiose productions elsewhere. When he did return he was to confine his own productions in Berlin to smaller-scale traditional theatres. Meanwhile he entrusted his Berlin operations to his assistant Felix Hollaender, who persisted for a few years with a programme combining classics with major new plays; but by 1925 the Großes Schauspielhaus had passed into new hands and became a highly popular and lucrative venue for revues and operettas during the years that followed.

Herbert Ihering, the theatre critic who promoted new

approaches to theatre more vigorously than most under the
Weimar Republic, was to suggest in 1929 that Reinhardt had
left Berlin out of wounded pride over the criticisms levelled at
his early productions at the Großes Schauspielhaus (*Kampf*,
361). It was an interpretation with some superficial plausibility.
Reinhardt had been the darling of middle-class theatre audiences in Berlin ever since taking over the Deutsches Theater in
1905. He had demonstrated an extraordinary versatility, initially as an actor under Otto Brahm, the doyen of Naturalist
theatre, and subsequently as a director with an exceptional gift
for bringing out the skills of individual actors and blending them
into ensemble productions. As J. L. Styan puts it in his 1982
study of Reinhardt, he found "a style for every play", whether
it was classical or naturalist, exotic or expressionist; and it was
his theatres that had pioneered successive waves of new dramas
in Germany since the turn of the century. But vanity apart, the
responses of critics in 1919–20 were such as to direct Reinhardt's attention to perfectly objective reasons for the failure of
his grand pre-war project of an integrative theatre. Julius Hart,
a veteran campaigner from the times of the early Naturalist
movement, found the *Oresteia* an inappropriate choice of material with which to inaugurate the Großes Schauspielhaus
because he did not think it was a play that could move modern
audiences; and Emil Faktor, writing in the *Berliner Börsen-
Courier* found that the sheer scale of the arena exposed weaknesses in both individual performances and the overall
conception of the production (Fetting, vol. ii, 26, 29–33). Fritz
Engel in the *Berliner Tageblatt* was more enthusiastic, but wondered how the arena would sustain a play with a more complex
line of action—and Reinhardt's second production, *Hamlet*,
seems to have flopped for precisely that reason (Rühle 1967,
176, 204). The third production, in February 1920, was in one
respect more successful: Romain Rolland's *Danton* had been
written around 1900 with an anticipated 'theatre of the people'
in mind, and the tribunal sequence in Act III provided opportunities for sensational crowd effects, and for generating a sense
of popular involvement in the political action by stationing
actors among the audience to do their heckling. But the text was
compared unfavourably with Büchner's famous treatment of the
same material; Herbert Ihering questioned the psychologically

orientated interpretation of a text which cried out for an emphasis on its rhetorical qualities; and Paul Fechter, who had enjoyed
the *Oresteia*, found that the most effective moments of *Danton*
could have been achieved equally well by good acting on a traditional proscenium stage (Rühle 1967, 204–9). Beyond mere
divergences of taste, what was already making itself felt in the
critics' judgements was something of that diversity of aesthetic
orientation which was to lead German theatre in radically new
directions during the decade to come.

The conception of mass theatre which superseded Reinhardt's
in the mid-1920s was unreservedly populist, and its populism was in turn firmly wedded to a belief in the historical
mission of the proletariat. It found its own impresario in Erwin
Piscator.

   Like other members of the Dada movement who were to col-
laborate with him in some of his most important productions
of the 1920s—George Grosz, John Heartfield, Walter Mehring,
and Franz Jung—Piscator had come to see the experiences of
the First World War as the ultimate catastrophe of bourgeois
society. Like them he identified strongly with the cause of proletarian revolution at the time of the Spartakus uprising of
January 1919, and for the next two decades his intellectual
outlook was inseparably linked to the Communist Party. After
a brief spell in Königsberg (now Kaliningrad), where he experimented with a small theatre on the lines of Karlheinz Martin's
Tribüne, Piscator returned to Berlin in 1920 to organize a
mobile agitprop group. At a time when leading intellectuals in
the German Communist Party (KPD) still viewed art in general
and the theatre in particular as "too sacred" to be used as a
vehicle for a political message (Gallas, 27; Willett 1978*b*, 47 f.),
Piscator had committed himself to the most radical form of
politically engaged performance art. As Christopher Innes notes
in his account of Piscator's early career, agitprop—short for
'agitation and propaganda'—had developed in the early Soviet
Union as a branch of journalism, as an improvised means of
conveying information vividly and of confirming party policy
among newly activated workers and peasants. Not until 1923
did the Soviet Ministry of Culture attempt to standardize such
'living newspaper' performances; not until 1926 did the KPD

establish its own official agitprop troupe, the Rotes Sprachrohr (Red Megaphone), under Maxim Vallentin.[11] Working without a subsidy, Piscator would have experienced all the limitations of primitive performance conditions and a style of amateur acting in which speeches necessarily became reduced to slogan-like statements and the presentation of issues became stereotyped (Innes, 17–33). His first opportunity to take his imaginative ideas and his political commitment into the world of the professional theatre came in 1922.

As Piscator describes the next phase of his career in his book *The Political Theatre*, first published in 1929, it was an attempt to establish a radical alternative to the Volksbühne. The episode illustrates, however, the kind of compromises that are demanded of any radical innovator who tries to enter into a deal with the paying public. Through a chance encounter, Piscator was able to go into business with Hans-José Rehfisch, a lawyer turned playwright, who was in the process of buying up what had been a popular venue for light entertainment in the centre of old Berlin, the Central-Theater. In order to build up a regular clientele, Piscator started by offering serious—predominantly naturalistic—drama at low prices. He mounted productions of a satirical play by Gorky, a play by Romain Rolland about the Boer War which contained some easily recognizable contemporary resonances, and Tolstoy's *Power of Darkness*. He had plans for introducing a more pointed political message at a later stage—but the venture ran out of money before he could realize that part of his programme. In the autumn of 1924 the Central-Theater was sold to the brothers Alfred and Fritz Rotter, who restored it to its former use as a place of light entertainment. (During the 'stabilization phase' of the Republic, 1924–9, the Rotter brothers built an empire of nine such theatres in Berlin, which collapsed in its turn in 1932 under the impact of the Great Depression.)

Two opportunities came Piscator's way in 1924, however, enabling him to establish his reputation as a man of the theatre, and to secure a platform for the technical experimentation for which he is primarily remembered. First he was invited by the

---

[11] For an account of agitprop activity in Germany in the later 1920s, see P. V. Brady, "Playing to the Audience—Agitprop Theatricals 1926–1933" in Bance, 110–20.

Volksbühne to direct a play for which no other director could be found; and secondly he was invited by the KPD leadership to mount a show in connection with the second general election of that year. The production at the Volksbühne is frequently thought of—in accord with Piscator's own version of theatre history—as the first instance of 'epic theatre' (although there is another side to that story, as we shall see shortly). The author, Alfons Paquet, whose literary strength lay rather in the area of lyrical prose- and travel-writing, had fashioned a playscript out of an episode in the struggle of the working-class movement of Chicago with the title *Fahnen* (Flags). It told the story behind the execution of four activists and the suicide of a fifth, following a bombing incident which had been perpetrated by the police and fomented by a capitalist boss. Paquet himself described the text as a "dramatic novel". Piscator turned it into effective theatre by playing up the tableau character of the scenes and using slide projections to give particular definition to each episode in the sequence. The production had been mounted in a hurry, and was saved from disintegration only by a last-minute round-the-clock rehearsal which called for exceptional dedication from the actors. But according to contemporary reviews, when the first performance concluded with huge red flags being slowly drawn across the backdrop to the set on which the coffins of the martyrs lay, the audience responded with tumultuous applause (Davies, 97–9; Rühle 1967, 540–6). Piscator had found a simple but potent visual image with which to focus the anger and determination of a working-class audience.

The "Red Revue" which Piscator prepared for the KPD election campaign in 1924 went by the full title of *Revue Roter Rummel*. It brought him together with Felix Gasbarra, who was to become his political adviser-cum-minder throughout his subsequent productions of the 1920s, and it provided opportunities to combine agitprop techniques with slicker cabaret-style material. More importantly, it also led to a further commission from the KPD to mount a historical revue of the period 1914—19 to accompany the Tenth Party Congress in Berlin in the summer of 1925. Its title was one of the ringing phrases from German radical tradition, which was associated in contemporary minds particularly with the memory of Karl

Liebknecht: *Trotz alledem* (Despite All). The Großes Schauspielhaus was hired for the two performances (which was all
that the Party was willing to sanction) and the show was compiled from authentic speeches, newspaper articles and slogans,
photographs, and film obtained from government archives
(Innes, 42–54; Willett 1978*b*, 53 f.). It was this occasion that
enabled Piscator to try out a combination of conventional
stage performance with the most advanced technical apparatus
then available, blending them into a unified documentary
presentation.

The following year, working with another script provided for
the Volksbühne by Paquet, Piscator developed subtler techniques for incorporating the use of moving film into the dramatic action. The text, *Sturmflut* (Tidal Wave), was conceived
as a paraphrase of the Russian Revolution in terms of the underlying "driving forces of our time". Film was used as an extension of what was being acted out on stage, or to illustrate the
consequences of decisions taken by the characters, and in the
absence of film soundtrack, at one point a speech was read out
in synchronization with documentary footage of Lloyd George
(Innes, 89 f.; Davies, 101 f.). Piscator was pushing back the fron-
tiers of what could be represented in the theatre. At the same
time he was sailing as close to the wind as he dared politically.
When invited to direct Schiller's *Die Räuber* (The Robbers) at
the Prussian State Theatre in 1926, he provoked predictable
controversy by recasting the emphasis of the text entirely,
presenting the ruthless Spiegelberg as a true revolutionary in
the bolshevik mould and making the idealistic hero look like a
romantic fool by comparison. In March 1927 he also brought
the tensions within the Volksbühne movement to a head in
an episode which is thoroughly documented in his book *The
Political Theatre*.

The management of the Volksbühne appears to have been
seeking to contrive a compromise between the radical and conservative factions within its membership by asking Piscator, the
known left-winger, to direct a medieval costume drama with a
merely implicit political content, *Gewitter über Gottland* (Storm
over Gottland). The play centred on the figure of a legendary
fourteenth-century Baltic freebooter, Klaus Störtebeker, and on
the conflict between the communistic league with which he was

associated and the civic authorities of the Hansa towns.[12] Piscator made the play's political resonances explicit for contemporary audiences by prefacing the action with a film sequence
in which the medieval figures were seen marching down the ages
as they approached the camera, their costumes becoming progressively more modern, until the figure of Asmus, the guardian
of their communistic ethos, appeared as the very image of Lenin.
The author, Ehm Welk, raised no objection to this extrapola-
tion from the content of his play, although he did object that in
the process of bringing the figure of Störtebeker up to date and
making him appear as a proto-fascist figure, snatches of vulgar
modern jargon had been substituted for the substantial speeches
he had written for the character. But the theatre management
insisted that the film sequence be cut, thus precipitating a highly
public severing of connections between Piscator and themselves,
in the course of which Piscator received declarations of strong
support against this curtailment of artistic freedom from such
conservative figures as Thomas Mann and Alfred Kerr as well
as from his natural allies on the left. The episode has every
appearance of having been a calculated gamble on Piscator's
part: at the time of the production he had already secured substantial advance funding for an independent theatre of his own,
and he was able to split the membership of the Volksbühne,
taking a large number of ardent supporters with him. (A compromise arrangement was subsequently made, whereby the
young radicals could subscribe to Piscator's organization while
still remaining within "special sections" of the Volksbühne—
although these special sections were to be among the first
victims of the political retrenchment which began to affect cultural life in 1930.) Since the businessman who put up the cash
for Piscator's new venture did so on condition that the words
"proletarian" and "revolutionary" should not appear in the
theatre's name, it was launched as the Piscatorbühne (Davies,
104–11; Willett 1978*b*, 65–71 and 83).

In practical terms Piscator's triumph was short-lived. The
well-appointed theatre he rented on the Nollendorfplatz in western Berlin came close to enabling him to realize his technical

[12] An admirably clear account of the historical background to the plot of *Gewitter über Gottland* is given in Hugh Rorrison's English-language edition of Piscator's *The Political Theatre*, 135–7.

ambitions, but as a result of hiring a second theatre in order to run two productions in parallel his company became financially over-extended and was forced into liquidation by June 1928. A second Piscatorbühne equipped with still more ambitious technical facilities was established in 1929 under an independent licensee, but failed even more rapidly because of the politically insensitive nature of the opening production.[13] With the collapse of this second venture, a theatre collective was formed under Piscator's name, but the circumstances in which it operated suggest that the effective control of it lay with the Communist Party apparatus. After serving a short term in jail in 1931 for failing to pay the entertainment tax due on the first Piscator-bühne, Piscator escaped further professional embarrassment by taking up an opportunity to move to Moscow and work in the film industry there (Willett 1978*b*, 74–83, 98–100). None of this can detract, however, from the significance that was attached to the founding of the first Piscatorbühne as an epochal moment in German theatrical history.

Beyond all questions of political allegiance, Piscator's work was exercising an extraordinary fascination on a wide spectrum of German society. It was one of the country's best-known actresses, Tilla Durieux, who had persuaded the director of a major brewery that Piscator was worth backing; and the opening of the Piscatorbühne in September 1927 attracted the patronage of the rich and fashion-conscious of Berlin just as much as the radical working class (Rühle 1967, 791). The professional reputation that Piscator had established since 1924 also enabled him to command the loyalty of an extremely powerful team of associates. In addition to Felix Gasbarra and Leo Lania, who had become his closest dramaturgical assistants, he now had a group of authors, including Brecht, Mehring, and Mühsam, who were prepared to help adapt the texts for his

---

[13] *Der Kaufmann von Berlin* was based on a script by Walter Mehring and was conceived as a vehicle for displaying a social panorama of the period of hyper-inflation in the early 1920s. This conception was brilliantly realized with the help of ingenious film effects created by Laszlo Moholy-Nagy, who had been instrumental in pioneering the fusion of art and technology at the Bauhaus. But the opening performance ended—apparently against Piscator's wishes—with the body of a dead German soldier being swept away with the worthless money, the licensee became nervous, and Piscator found himself excluded from the theatre that had borne his name (Willett 1978*b*, 98–100).

productions. He could call on George Grosz and John Heartfield for designs and illustrations, and Hanns Eisler for musical settings. He had the film expertise of Curt Oertel, and the sadly short-lived Edmund Meisel as a specialist in the musical accompaniment of film. He had an ingenious set designer in Traugott Müller, and a dedicated stage manager in Otto Richter (whose sober accounts of the logistical difficulties encountered in the process of assembling, manœuvring, and operating the complex stage sets without adequate mechanical devices are quoted at length in chapter 16 of *The Political Theatre*). The theatrical experience that the Piscatorbühne promised was generating a sense of excited anticipation in the liberal as well as the left-wing press, and the reason for that was summed up by Axel Eggebrecht in *Die literarische Welt*: Piscator was offering a theatre that felt right for the times because it placed the representation of the nature of those times above any considerations of interpretative finesse, star performance, or ensemble work.[14]

It was the brilliance of the technical conception (if not always of the execution) at the Piscatorbühne that attracted the greatest critical acclaim. The opening production, *Hoppla, wir leben!* (Hoppla, Such is Life!) based on a script by Ernst Toller, presented a cross-section through contemporary society and its political factions. For it, Traugott Müller devised a multi-storey scaffolding set which made it possible to keep the various strands of the action simultaneously before the audience's eye, as well as providing for the fluid interaction of film sequences with individual scenes (cf. Patterson, 134—46). For *Rasputin*, which was adapted from a play by Alexei Tolstoy, Müller created a segmented globe, facets of which would open to reveal one or another dimension of the political intrigue which centred on the Russian imperial court; and as the curtain rose, the globe could be seen spinning on the revolve and appearing to catch fire, an intimation of the cataclysmic significance of the events that were about to unfold. It was *The Adventures of the Good Soldier Schwejk*, an appropriately rambling adaptation of Jaroslav Hašek's whimsically picaresque novel, that brought

---

[14] *LW* 3, 38, 1: "Dies ist *unser* Theater, endlich einmal eines, das den Zusammenhang mit der Zeit über den Erfolg einer einzelnen Inszenierung, eines Stars, eines gelungenen Ensemblespiels stellt."

the Piscatorbühne its greatest box-office success. With its low-comic perspective on the Hapsburg Empire at war, it provided a perfect vehicle for the popular Viennese comedian Max Pallenberg; but the production is also especially remembered for the sense of mobility and expansiveness that was created by the use of moving bands on stage and the projection of characteristically venomous cartoon films by George Grosz. Inventive use of the stage area also characterized the set that Müller designed for Leo Lania's *Konjunktur* (Boom)—a dramatically weak play by all accounts, but a pioneering attempt to bring the subject of international competition for oilfields into the theatre. Müller began with a bare stage and progressively constructed upon it an ever more elaborate assemblage of rigs and platforms in the course of the performance, a perfect symbol of the cumulative exploitation of natural resources (cf. Willett 1978*b*, 84–98).

What was achieved in the technical domain often seemed to be accomplished at the cost of the spoken word, at the cost of drama in its broad sense. The first production at the Piscatorbühne provides a poignant illustration of this point. *Hoppla, wir leben!* was not the work with which Piscator would have liked to open, but since none of the projects that his dramaturgical team had in mind was going to be ready in time, he fell back on the script that Toller was preparing. Toller's reputation as a dramatist was firmly associated with that revolutionary idealism of the 1918—19 period which, as Günther Rühle puts it (1972, vol. i, 47), was "conserved" by the theatrical production of Expressionist plays throughout the first half of the 1920s. The fact that Toller was serving a jail sentence between 1919 and 1924, without remission or parole, for his part in the Bavarian revolution meant that his status as a political martyr was highlighted whenever major productions of his plays took place. In *Masse Mensch* (Masses and Man), which Jürgen Fehling produced for the Volksbühne in 1921, and in *Die Maschinenstürmer* (The Machine Wreckers), which Karlheinz Martin staged in the Großes Schauspielhaus in 1922, Toller had presented the tragedy of the humanitarian idealist pitted against the forces of populist passion and material calculation. In *Hoppla* he was working with a similar line of dramatic confrontation. The plot centres on a fervent revolutionary idealist, Karl Thomas, who succumbs to a bout of insanity in 1919 and emerges from his asylum in 1927 into a society dominated by cynicism, nostalgia, and reaction. A central scene of the play alludes to the election of Field Marshal Hindenburg as President of the Republic in 1925, and Karl Thomas's chief antagonist is a fellow insurrectionary of 1919 who has in the meantime made an opportunistic political career with the Social Democrats. But the text as we know it is the result of compromises between Toller's dramatic conception and the demands of Piscator as producer.

It has recently been argued (Dove, 161–9) that when Toller started work on *Hoppla* in 1927 he conceived it as a comedy and as a kind of laconic leave-taking from the uncompromising idealism of his youth: according to this reconstruction of Toller's intentions, the relapse of Karl Thomas into insanity at the end of the play was a way of ironizing his single-mindedness, and the play as a whole was part of Toller's quest for a realistic basis for political action after 1924.[15] If this reading of the situation is correct, then it was Piscator's interventions that served to drive the scenario back into the Expressionist mould from which Toller was trying to escape, for it was Piscator who insisted that the play should end in Karl Thomas's suicide, and his comments on the matter in chapter 17 of *The Political Theatre* indicate that he was inclined to dismiss the character as a sentimentalist who is bound to come to grief in his conflict with reality (even if he also directed the actor Alexander Granach to play the character as a proletarian rather than the bourgeois figure called for in Toller's script). Contemporary reviewers generally deduced from what they saw that it was Toller's purpose to use the figure of Karl Thomas as a device for exposing the failure of Republican society to measure up to the ideals of 1919. Those who were in sympathy with Piscator's aims blamed any shortcomings of the script on Toller for failing to come up with the

[15] Dove's view has now been challenged by evidence drawn from two versions of the script for *Hoppla, wir leben!* which predate Piscator's interventions and reveal the inherent ambiguities in Toller's own conception of the characters. See Karl Leydecker, "The Laughter of Karl Thomas: Madness and Politics in the First Version of Ernst Toller's *Hoppla, wir leben!*", *Modern Language Review* 93/1 (Jan. 1998), 121–32.

right sort of play; Toller himself was left feeling that Piscator had ridden roughshod over the delicate composition he had devised.[16]

Beyond any narrow issue of the respective authority of author and producer, the controversy over *Hoppla* points to a fundamental limitation in Piscator's conception of theatre. What Piscator has to say about his productions in *The Political Theatre* is informative on their technical aspects, and on the shortcomings of the technical facilities with which he sought to create his effects. But it is indicative of his underlying approach to theatre that the most explicit statements he has to make on aesthetic issues come in chapter 8, which is entitled "The documentary play", and which is primarily concerned with *Trotz alledem*, the historical revue he compiled for the Communist Party Congress in 1925. Here he states plainly that factual substance (*Stoff*) was his chief concern (*Schriften* I, 65). He uses the term "art" only once, in connection with the emotional impact (*Erschütterung*) he assumes to have been achieved by showing film footage of the first infantry attacks and casualties of the First World War immediately after a stage scene in which Social Democrat politicians deliberate on whether to vote for war credits—and he can make that assumption because, as is clear from the context, he knows the perspectives that politically active members of the working class will bring to that subject (*Schriften* I, 70). What Piscator has to say on the matter of acting technique, in chapter 11, is similarly limited to a brief description of the "neo-realist" style of acting he sought to encourage. The criterion of documentary authentification is clearly at work again here in his demand that the actor's manner be "unfalsified, hard, unambiguous and open": when he asks his actors to adopt a "naturalness of movement and gesture", then it is in the interests of a performance which (in Hugh Rorrison's translation: p. 121)

---

[16] Conservative theatre critics tended to champion the author against the producer, notably Monty Jacobs (Rühle 1967, 792–4) and Alfred Kerr (Fetting, vol. ii, 361–6). Herbert Ihering acknowledged that *Hoppla* showed a sharper picture of social reality than Toller's earlier work, but felt that his dialogue was still characterized by a romantic fuzziness that Piscator was trying to leave behind (Rühle 1967, 797–9). The production was the subject of extensive debate in *Die rote Fahne*, where Piscator's depiction of the political struggles of the times tended to be played off against Toller's apparent defeatism and concern with dramatizing his personal experience (Brauneck 1973, 275–91).

should be "so scientific and so clearly analysed by the intellect that it reproduces naturalness on a higher level". The policy Piscator is outlining here is in part no doubt a response to critics who had lamented the subordination of the spoken word to the technological imagination in his productions.[17] It also takes us to the heart of the distinction that needs to be drawn between Piscator's approach to theatre and Brecht's (cf. Voigts, 108 f.).

The concept of 'epic theatre' as it developed in Germany during the 1920s has a dual lineage. If we follow Piscator's account of the matter (or Leo Lania's, to be more precise, since it was he who provided the original text for chapter 6 of *The Political Theatre*, to which Piscator added his own gloss in the version of 1963), the origin of 'epic theatre' lies in his production of Paquet's *Fahnen* at the Volksbühne in 1924. As far as Piscator is concerned, it was the extension of the stage action beyond its dramatic framework by means of film and documentary material that first created 'epic theatre': this was how the "spectacle play" (*Schaustück*) was converted into a didactic play (*Lehrstück*).[18] Herbert Ihering tells a different story when he reviews the development of directing technique in the German theatre from the perspective of 1929. He points to the emergence of an "objective, 'epic' style" in Brecht's production of *The Life of Edward II* (which Brecht had adapted from Marlowe's play in collaboration with Lion Feuchtwanger) in Munich, also in 1924. The essence of Brecht's directing style, as Ihering describes it, was distance: instead of building the historical figures up into "great" characters with a powerful emotional appeal (such as Fritz Kortner's portrayal of Geßler or Richard III must have had), Brecht had deliberately confined his actors to working with simple gestures and "cool, clear" diction, and had exposed the dramatic structure to scrutiny.[19]

[17] Such criticisms had also been levelled at his productions of *Sturmflut* for the Volksbühne (Arthur Eloesser) and *Die Räuber* at the Prussian State Theatre: see Rühle 1967, 695, 724.

[18] The implications of Piscator's position on the didactic force of theatre are well brought out in a recent essay by Graham Holderness, "Schaustück and Lehrstück: Erwin Piscator and the Politics of Theatre" (Holderness, 99 ff.).

[19] "Er forderte Rechenschaft über die Vorgänge. Er verlangte einfache Gesten. Er zwang zu klarem, kühlem Sprechen. Keine Gefühlsmogelei wurde geduldet. Das

Brecht himself, writing in 1927, emphasized above all the contribution to 'epic theatre' of another director whose influence on him went back still further: Erich Engel. It was Engel who directed the earliest productions of Brecht's *In the Jungle* (as it was then called) in Munich in 1923 and in Berlin in 1924, as well as the spectacularly successful *Threepenny Opera* of 1928; he had also engaged Brecht, together with Carl Zuckmayer, as dramaturgical assistants at the Deutsches Theater in 1924–5. His reputation was founded on the clear dramaturgical line of his productions of Shakespeare and of modern authors, and he stood out among the directors of his day as someone who encouraged his actors to take an intellectual approach to the dramatic argument they were enacting (Brauneck 1988, 317–27). In his note of 1927 Brecht mentions a particular feature of Engel's production of *Coriolanus* in 1925 which distinguished the style of "epic theatre" from that of conventional "dramatic theatre": Engel had isolated each scene of the play, presenting it as an entity in itself, rather than treating it as a contributory element in the linear development towards a dramatic climax (*BFA* 21, 197). It was Engel, in other words, who provided Brecht with at least one set of important insights which was to go into the famous tabulation of distinctions between "epic" and "dramatic" theatre which appears in his notes to the *Mahagonny* opera of 1930 (*BFA* 24, 85). Other qualities which Brecht admired in Engel's directing style were the judicious distribution of emphasis (*Gewichtsverteilung*), its clarity, sequentiality (*Abrollung*), and purity (*BFA* 21, 665).

In his public statements of the time Brecht was unstinting in his displays of solidarity with Piscator. At the time of Piscator's breach with the Volksbühne in March 1927, and subsequently, Brecht publicly defended his achievements in terms which are entirely consistent with Piscator's own conception of theatre, as the development of a "great epic and documentary theatre"

ergab den objektiven, den 'epischen' Stil." The context is Ihering's comparison of various approaches to producing classic dramas for modern-day audiences in his pamphlet *Reinhardt, Jessner, Piscator oder Klassikertod?* See Ihering, *Kampf*, 318. Brecht had described his own approach to theatrical performance in similar terms in the interview he gave to Bernard Guillemin in July 1926 (*LW* 2, 31, 1): "Ich bin für das epische Theater! Die Regie muß ganz nüchtern und sachlich die stofflichen Vorgänge herausarbeiten."

appropriate to the times (*BFA* 21, 196, 199 f.). Brecht had had to abandon one of his own projects in 1926 when he realized the limitations of drama for representing the processes of the international wheat trade,[20] and it was therefore without irony that, in a statement published in *Das Theater* in January 1928, he gave technologized theatre the credit for "pre-digesting" new subject matter which dramatists had not yet worked out how to handle, and for "training" audiences to receive that subject-matter (*BFA* 21, 220). It is also clear that he derived much practical benefit from his collaboration with Piscator during the 1927–8 season, particularly from his extensive work on *The Adventures of the Good Soldier Schwejk* (cf. Willett 1984, 87–106). Some of the differences between them are apparent, however, from the record of discussions they held in November 1928 about the possibility of adapting Brecht's *Drums in the Night* for the Piscatorbühne. Brecht's proposal that the central figure of the play, the anti-idealist Kragler, could be used as a basis for criticizing the failings of the revolution of 1918–19 is greeted by Piscator with the prompt suspicion that this would confine the conception of the piece to "individual drama"; Piscator's enthusiasm for the opportunity to show documentary material about the revolution which would bring out its positive appeal for audiences of 1928–9 is countered by Brecht's insistence that he can only write about social elements which were in decline in 1918 (*die Untergehenden*).[21] The private notes Brecht made during his period of collaboration with Piscator show quite precisely where the theoretical differences lay.

Brecht was particularly concerned about the sense in which Piscator's theatrical practice was technology-led, and about the way in which this was being perceived and presented in public. He records his strong disagreement with the theatre critic of the *Frankfurter Zeitung*, Bernhard Diebold, who had hailed the technological apparatus of the Piscatorbühne as a practical basis which would enable German writers to advance to a new form of drama. (In an earlier publication Diebold had spoken of

---

[20] See Elisabeth Hauptmann, "Notizen über Brechts Arbeit 1926", *Sinn und Form: Bertolt Brecht Sonderheft* (1957), 243.

[21] "Protokolle von Gesprächen über *Trommeln in der Nacht*" in Bertolt Brecht, *Schriften zum Theater* (Frankfurt: Suhrkamp, 1963), vol. ii, 272–93.

"anarchy in the drama" as characteristic of the Expressionist phase; the expectation that the theatre might provide a vehicle for overcoming that "anarchy" and restoring an integral German culture was evidently still alive in his mind in 1927.[22]) Brecht sees this as one example amongst others of the confusion about aesthetic issues which prevailed among bourgeois critics and theorists of his day. He acknowledges the advantages Piscator's technology has brought to the sphere of theatrical presentation—film enhances the realism of what can be seen in the theatre, moving bands lend a production mobility—but he denies that such modernization of theatrical equipment is *in itself* going to make a new type of drama possible (*BFA* 21, 225–7). Brecht's reasons for taking this line become clearer in a separate set of notes where he establishes a critical perspective on the very principle of a political theatre. The three arguments he develops here can each be seen to contain a critical thrust against Piscator's approach to theatre. First, Brecht defends the practice of treating old plays unsentimentally as "material" for modern productions, but rejects the practice of presenting them tendentiously.[23] Secondly, he objects more generally to "the requisitioning of the theatre for the purposes of the class struggle" because he sees that as a constraint on the development of new approaches to writing plays. Thirdly, and more revealingly still, he deplores the use of theatrical effects for generating a mere atmosphere of revolutionary fervour ("die pathetische Atmosphäre, die reine Nervenwirkung revolutionärer Stimmung") because this means falling back into the old "bourgeois" habits of "passive, reproductive" and "naturalistic" theatre—-and in this context Brecht pointedly places the word "naturalness" (the quality that Piscator demanded of his actors) in inverted commas. This text remains fragmentary, but the point at which it breaks off provides a clear enough indication of Brecht's chief reservation about the kind of theatre that

---

[22] Diebold's article "Die Piscator-Bühne", which had appeared in the *Frankfurter Zeitung* on 20 Nov. 1927, was also issued as a special brochure; a copy is held in the British Library, London.

[23] By implication Brecht is here expressing a reservation which applies to Piscator's 1926 production of *Die Räuber*, for example, although in public, again, in the Kölner Rundfunk discussion on "classics" that he conducted with Ihering in April 1929, Brecht praises that production for revitalizing Schiller's text: *BFA* 21, 312.

Piscator was offering: the true revolutionary transformation of theatre was not going to come about through technological means alone, however new and exciting they may be, but by using the art of theatrical performance (*Theaterkunst*) to "revolutionize people" (*BFA* 21, 233 f.; cf. 197 f.).

In private, Brecht was developing his own thoughts on how the technical apparatus of the Piscatorbühne *ought* to be deployed. He makes an extensive note on the function of film, treating it as a subdepartment of graphics. (Here he may have been influenced by the celebrated use of George Grosz's cartoon films in *Schwejk*; he was certainly still thinking in terms of the effect of *silent* film.) When he describes film as being essentially "static" in nature he is evidently thinking that, from the point of view of theatrical performance, the series of images that film reproduces is fixed and immutable:[24] what he senses to be missing in film as he knows it is that quality of judicious "Gewichtsverteilung" (distribution of emphasis) that he admired in Erich Engel's stage directing. He envisages a use for film as a kind of "optical chorus" within a production, and he is particularly interested in the effects created when film interrupts the stage action. What he had experienced in Piscator's productions had evidently alerted him to the possibilities for "dialectical" interaction between the various components of theatrical presentation (*BFA* 21, 210–12); and he put these new insights into practice in the *Mahagonny* opera which he was working on in 1928–9 with Kurt Weill and his old friend and collaborator Caspar Neher. The text of that work asks for back projection of film showing the restless masses of Europe streaming to the fantasy boom-town of Mahagonny, and Brecht's notes also mention the use of drawings by Neher in conjunction with specific scenes. With regard to the interaction of both music and design with the text, however, the principle that Brecht is keen to stress above all at this stage is the "separation of the elements": the various components should not be thought of as combining into an organically integrated *Gesamtkunstwerk*, but as providing contrasting and mutually critical perspectives on

---

[24] Brecht was to argue along exactly similar lines in discussions with Adorno in 1942: see *Arbeitsjournal* (Frankfurt: Suhrkamp, 1973), vol. i, 279 f. (quoted by Maarten van Dijk, "Blocking Brecht", in P. Kleber and C. Visser (eds.), *Re-Interpreting Brecht* (Cambridge: Cambridge University Press, 1990), 126).

each other (*BFA* 24, 79). In similar vein, Brecht was also able to argue that introducing film into the theatre need not lead to any diminution of the importance of the spoken word (as conservative critics of Piscator's productions had feared). On the contrary, the use of film to expound aspects of the stage action and its implications could help to take the strain off the dialogue; the actors no longer needed to expend words on conveying information to the audience, and when they did speak, their lines would therefore stand out all the more boldly as "free utterances" of the characters. In this way film had the potential to *enhance* the power of the spoken word (*BFA* 21, 196 f.).

Two general features characterize Brecht's theorizing about theatre at the end of the 1920s. One is his emphasis on the significance of form, which he saw as complementary to Piscator's emphasis on content (*BFA* 21, 278). The other, which is intimately connected with the issue of form, is his emphasis on "sociological" perspectives. For Brecht, as for his contemporaries generally, 'sociology' meant establishing the distinctive character of the present age through comparative study of forms of human society which had existed in the past. Since 1926 Brecht had been in close touch with the Marxist-orientated sociologist Fritz Sternberg, who was arguing strongly that the collectivist tendencies at work in the society of "late capitalism" had undermined the basis for individualistic drama as it had existed since Shakespeare's day. Brecht evidently found this emphasis on the historically changing nature of cultural needs a useful antidote to traditional aesthetic evaluations of drama (*BFA* 21, 202 f., 271, 674 f.). But such long-term perspectives could also provide an effective antidote to any mere enthusiasms of the moment. When Brecht met Piscator in November 1928 to discuss a possible production of *Drums in the Night*, he took Sternberg with him, and together they tried to prevail on Piscator to educate audiences about the underlying historical reasons for the failure of the German Revolution, rather than just trying to enthuse them for the revolutionary cause.[25] In a similar way, Brecht began to see the kind of theatre he was looking for as the outcome of a cultural development which

[25] "Protokolle von Gesprächen über *Trommeln in der Nacht*", loc. cit., 284.

stretched back over the previous fifty years. It had begun with the Naturalism of around 1890 and the first attempts to bring social themes into the theatre which were otherwise primarily being treated in the novel. It had reached a provisional culmination in the dramas of Georg Kaiser which, for all that they were individualistic in conception, presented their themes in a highly structured way which appealed to the intellect rather than the emotions. As Brecht claimed in a radio discussion of January 1929, it was Kaiser who had brought into the theatre that "cool, inquiring, interested attitude" that befitted audiences "in a scientific age" (*BFA* 21, 274 f.).[26]

At the same time it was apparent to Brecht that the audiences of the "scientific age" needed to be trained in the habits of observation appropriate to the world in which they were living. In February 1929 he published two articles in the *Berliner Börsen-Courier* (the paper for which Ihering wrote his theatre reviews), summarizing the position he had reached. The new subjects, such as the wheat trade, which were proving so difficult to present in dramatic form, nevertheless needed to be grasped in terms of human relations. In order to represent these, the theatre needed to abandon the premiss that acting necessarily involves inviting audience empathy for a character: the subject-matter exceeded the bounds of such empathy, it could only be understood intellectually, or as he puts it (appealing to the self-respect of the German intellectual tradition), "philosophically". The theatre had to adopt an approach which was "epic" in the sense of *telling* audiences about the world in which they were living, it needed a style of acting which was consciously demonstrative ("Bewußt darbietend. Schildernd"). Audiences for their part were inhabitants of a scientific world, but they had to be helped to abandon their preconceptions of what the (dramatic) theatre was offering them, they needed encouragement to develop the intellectual approach appropriate to that world. Brecht gives two examples of how acting technique might assist this process. Strikingly they are not taken

[26] In this context Brecht is evidently thinking in terms of continuity between Kaiser's dramatic technique and his own, whereas Sternberg invokes the Hegelian principle of a dialectical reversal (*Umschlag*) between the two authors. While Brecht had earlier been critical of the abstract way in which Kaiser presented human problems in his plays (as we noted in Chapter 1), he seems consistently to have admired the clarity of line in Kaiser's dramatic structures: see Schürer, 31–58.

from productions which do attempt to present "new subjects", but from old familiar dramatic situations; whether explicitly or implicitly, they relate to two productions running in Berlin in the 1928–9 season, namely *The Threepenny Opera* (which is formally the least innovative of all Brecht's plays of the Weimar period) and the version of Sophocles' *Oedipus* which was being performed at the Prussian State Theatre. They are examples, in other words, of how it may be possible within the framework of the existing theatre to encourage both audiences and actors to develop new habits of mind (*BFA* 21, 278–82).

The first example is an imaginary leave-taking scene. It need not be Macheath's farewell to Polly Peachum in Act II of *The Threepenny Opera*, but it easily could be: the gramophone recording of this scene, which was made shortly after the stage production, conveys a clear enough sense of how an impression of deliberate stylization was achieved by the actors, and of how Kurt Weill's music provided a detached, ironic commentary on what was being enacted (quoting mockingly, for example, from Macheath's earlier love song). Brecht envisages such a leave-taking as an almost ritual enactment of the process of establishing distance—between the characters, between spectator and character, between actor and character—in order to encourage "recognition" of what is taking place. The second example is based on the performance of Helene Weigel (the actress with whom Brecht had been living since 1924, and whom he was to marry in April 1929) as Jocasta's maid in *Oedipus*, and one reason why it is chosen is clearly because this is a role which is required to report what has occurred offstage. The maid reports the madness and suicide of Jocasta. As contemporary reviews of that production confirm, Weigel had spoken her lines penetratingly, but without emotion (*BFA* 21, 712). Brecht adds that she had sought to convey surprise (as opposed to evoking empathy) over Jocasta's frenzy, and by her diction and actions had focused the audience's attention on the "naked fact" of Jocasta's death, and on the need to grieve (*BFA* 21, 282).

In singling out *The Threepenny Opera* and *Oedipus* as "exceptions" to the general run of theatre productions in Berlin at the time, Brecht also expressly distanced himself, now, from the influence of Piscator (*BFA* 21, 278). The influence that Brecht was seeing had manifested itself in two very direct ways during the 1928–9 season. For one thing the Deutsches Theater sought to emulate the style of Piscator's productions, matching the theme of *Konjunktur* with a (rather superficial) play by Lion Feuchtwanger called *Die Petroleuminseln* (The Oil Islands), and also staging Ferdinand Bruckner's *Die Verbrecher* (The Criminals), which exploited the possibilities of the kind of set devised for *Hoppla* in order to present a multi-faceted picture of city-dwellers living in an atmosphere of financial hardship and emotional pressure. Secondly, a company of actors who had lost their jobs when the first Piscatorbühne folded came together as the Gruppe Junger Schauspieler and dedicated themselves to the performance of plays which addressed specific social issues of the day. It was this company that produced Peter Martin Lampel's *Revolte im Erziehungshaus* (Revolt in the Reformatory) in December 1928, a play which exposed the dehumanizing circumstances in which adolescent boys were being detained 'in care' (*Fürsorgeerziehung*), and which did indeed trigger institutional reform in this area (Rühle 1967, 903 f.). The same company also took up the issue of abortion legislation, which was the subject of a broad-based campaign for liberalization at the time, and in September 1929 they performed Friedrich Wolf's *Cyankali* (Potassium Cyanide), which documented the social pressures on young women who were resorting in their thousands to inexpert means of inducing abortions, often with fatal consequences (Rühle 1967, 956).[27] By the end of the year, Piscator had seized the initiative in this area in its turn. When the second Piscatorbühne collapsed in the autumn of 1929 and was converted into a theatrical collective, their first venture was a touring production of a play which took its title from the statute of German criminal law governing abortion, Carl Credé's *Paragraph 218*. Here Piscator took the principle of the theatre as a forum for public debate to its logical conclusion, placing actors in the audience who would rise and speak from the point of view of lawyer, magistrate, clergyman, or doctor;

---

[27] Contemporary discussions in the Reichstag, among the medical profession, and among the general public, are documented in Emmi Wolf and Klaus Hammer (eds.), *Cyankali §218* (Berlin: Aufbau Verlag, 1978).

and the theatrical action became formally dissolved into a public discussion with the magistrate's announcement that "the audience must decide" (Willett 1978*b*, 101).

In 1930, as Germany's political crisis deepened, producers and playwrights turned increasingly to material which reflected the origins of the Republic and the wartime circumstances which had led to the collapse of the imperial order. The new theatre season began in August with two productions which recalled the sailors' mutiny at Kiel in the closing days of the war. Theodor Plievier, who was to become famous after the Second World War for his novel about the Battle of Stalingrad, provided Piscator's theatrical collective with a dramatized version of his experiences in the German navy under the title *The Kaiser's Coolies*; and in *Feuer aus den Kesseln* (Draw the Fires), which went on at the Theater am Schiffbauerdamm, Toller gave a documentary (and rather sketchy) account of the Kiel mutiny of July 1917 as a pre-echo of revolution, and of the official responses to it. In November at the Volksbühne, one of the few theatres which possessed the technical means to mount productions in the manner that Piscator had established, the semblance of an entire battleship was constructed on the revolve for Friedrich Wolf's play *Die Matrosen von Cattaro* (The Sailors of Cattaro). It was this production that established Wolf's credentials as a skilful dramatist; it was also a theatrical event which emphasized the irreconcilable differences between the SPD and the KPD. A Communist Party member himself, Wolf had chosen to dramatize a revolt that occurred in the Austrian navy in February 1918, and he presented it as a moment laden with potent political symbolism. The Cattaro revolt had occurred at a time when it could draw on the inspiration of the Bolshevik Revolution in Russia, but when the prospects for insurrection on a comparable scale in the Hapsburg Empire proved in the event to be futile. Wolf conveyed a strong sense of the human realities of the situation by concentrating the action among the sailors of a particular ship as they struggled to establish new ways of dealing with the situation they had created for themselves, and he used the very isolation of the group as a means of investing the characters with a dignified self-consciousness about the exemplary nature of their actions. The final scene required the sailors to "vote" individually either

for commitment to the principle of revolution even unto death
or for capitulation and survival. It was a moment of theatrical enactment which prompted open altercations in the
auditorium when the capitulators were treated to taunts that
identified them with the Social Democrats (Rühle 1967,
1040–7).

In January 1931 Wolf came together with Erwin Piscator
and John Heartfield to produce *Tai Yang erwacht* (Tai Yang
Awakes), which took its theme from the attempted Chinese
revolution of 1927, an event which had excited much interest
in Communist circles in the meantime. This was to be Piscator's
last production before his departure for the Soviet Union, and
in a superficial way it marked a degree of convergence between
Piscator and Brecht—although (*pace* Patterson, 129) the sense
in which it adopted an "'epic' style of acting" as Brecht would
have recognized it appears to have been limited. In the context
of the more conventional theatrical architecture within which
Piscator was now having to operate, the traditional separation
of the audience from the action was overcome by extending the
Chinese-style wall posters of Heartfield's set design into the
auditorium, and also by showing the actors making up and
preparing themselves on stage before the performance started.
The dialogue was given an expository function, and potted
lectures on economic conditions and the parallels between
China and Germany were incorporated into the performance
(Willett 1978*b*, 104–6). In these senses the production was
overtly didactic, and it was recognizably in tribute to Brecht
(who had first used the term the previous year) that the show
was designated a "Lehrstück". But reviews of the production
indicate that, far from adopting the style of acting Brecht was
trying to promote, it had lapsed into the very naturalism of
which he had been so critical: not only the stage props, but also
the characterization, it was averred, could have come straight
out of Hauptmann's *The Weavers* of 1892 (Rühle 1967,
1062–8). The *Lehrstücke* on which Brecht had in fact been
working in the course of 1929 and 1930, with various groups
of associates, show once again how his thinking was running
ahead of any immediate concern with political agitation,
and indeed ahead of 'theatre' in its conventional modern sense
altogether.

The principle that underlies Brecht's conception of the *Lehrstück* is easily stated: it should be a learning experience for collective participation (cf. *BFA* 22, 351 f.). But in view of the prominence that has been given to the *Lehrstück* as a distinctive model of theatre in publications on Brecht in English[28] it needs to be stressed that this principle should be thought of as a leading idea behind the *Lehrstücke* that we find published under Brecht's name, rather than as the foundation of a theory that he was systematically putting into practice. The attempt has been made to construct a 'theory of the *Lehrstück*' out of the many notes of Brecht's which have a bearing on the subject (Steinweg), but that attempt is open to the objection that in order to construct a coherent theory it has to extract Brecht's statements from their precise historical context (cf. Knopf, vol. i, 422 f.).[29] Brecht was experimenting in 1929 and 1930 with forms of enactment which broke with the assumption that theatrical performance is one-way communication with an audience, and the title of the series in which he published the resulting texts from 1930 onwards was such as to emphasize their tentative nature: it was "Experiments" (*Versuche*). As experiments, the form that individual *Lehrstücke* took was dependent on practical circumstances—which is to say the circumstances of their realization in performance. Just three examples of such experimental performance were in fact realized in 1929 and 1930.[30]

The first occasion on which Brecht used the term *Lehrstück* appears to have been in the description of a text he had prepared for the Baden-Baden Chamber Music Festival of July 1929, and which for that reason has been published ever since as the *Badener Lehrstück vom Einverständnis*. "Einverständnis" here, as Jan Knopf argues (vol. i, 76 f.), is to be understood

---

[28] See Wright, 11–18; Rainer Nägele, *Reading after Freud: Essays on Goethe, Hölderlin, Habermas, Nietzsche, Brecht, Celan, and Freud* (New York: Columbia University Press, 1987), 113–34.

[29] In order to avoid an unnecessary proliferation of references in what follows, I refer readers to Jan Knopf's *Brecht-Handbuch*, which gives a very full account of the state of research on the concept of the *Lehrstück* and on individual *Lehrstücke*. For an extended critical assessment of Steinweg's findings, see also Ruping, 32–55.

[30] A fourth *Lehrstück*, *Die Ausnahme und die Regel*, was apparently prepared in 1930 or 1931, and first performed on a kibbutz in Palestine in 1938: see Knopf, vol. i, 114–19. In a note of 1937, Brecht also cites his 1934 play *Die Horatier und die Kuratier* as an example of the *Lehrstück*: *BFA* 22, 351 f.

not only in the sense of giving assent, but of adjusting human understanding so that it is in accord with reality. The *Badener Lehrstück* was closely associated with another short text by Brecht, a dialogue account of Charles Lindbergh's solo flight across the Atlantic, which was also presented at the Baden-Baden Festival,[31] and we shall have cause to consider the themes of both plays in the context of literary treatments of technology in Chapter 8. It was performed to a musical setting by Paul Hindemith, who was well-known at the time as a musical renegade and an experimenter with various practical applications for music (*Gebrauchsmusik*), and with accompanying visual displays by Caspar Neher. The *Badener Lehrstück* was described in a programme note as an "unfinished" attempt by its creators to clarify their thinking in the spirit of certain "musical, dramatic and political theories which point towards collective artistic activity" (*BFA* 3, 411). It took the situation of stranded airmen as a premiss on which to explore the issue of the human willingness to provide mutual help and its apparent absence from contemporary society, but it did so in ways which were partly abstruse and partly provocative. These included the notorious clowns scene in which, as it was performed in 1929, two upper middle-class figures "help" a lower middle-class figure by sawing his arms and legs off; and when Neher's selection of pictures of dead bodies caused unrest among the audience, Brecht promptly called for the sequence to be repeated—and subsequently wrote the repeat showing into the script (Knopf, vol. i, 80f.). In the context of a conventional theatrical performance, the audience evidently found itself excluded from the deliberative processes in which the producing collective had involved themselves.

The various versions of the texts that we know under the titles of *Der Jasager* (He Who Said Yes) and *Der Neinsager* (He Who Said No) have their origins in a text provided by Elisabeth Hauptmann for Kurt Weill when he wanted to prepare a school opera for a festival in Berlin in 1930 (Knopf, vol. i, 88). Brecht was asked to assist with the adaptation, and the variant texts record the stages of modification which he and Weill arrived at as they tried the play out with children at a Berlin school that

---

[31] *Der Flug der Lindberghs* was published as a play for radio in *Versuche* I, and is described there as a "Radiolehrstück" (*BFA* 3, 401).

summer. Both Weill's original project and the subsequent experimentation can be seen to relate to an established tradition of modern pedagogic practice in Germany, in which the enactment and improvisation of situations was used as a learning experience for the pupils rather than as a production to be performed for an audience (Voigts, 131–7). The central issue under examination in this instance was the circumstances in which a community was or was not obliged to provide help to an individual in need.

Die Maßnahme (The Measures Taken)—which has generally been regarded as the most controversial of Brecht's plays since the late 1940s, when attempts were made to link it with the regime of terror that had developed under Stalin (Ruping, 9 f.)— evidently developed out of work on *Der Jasager*, and in part as a critical reflection on it, in the course of 1930 (Knopf, vol. i, 92). It was concerned with the retrospective assessment of a situation in which a group acting in the interests of a collective purpose (the Communist revolution) had taken a decision to kill one of their number who was endangering that purpose; the text essentially consists of a dialogue between a chorus representing the collective interests of the Party and the four actors who represent the group of agitators and who reconstruct the circumstances surrounding their decision. The choice of subject here reflects the firm commitment to the Communist cause which Brecht had shown since late 1929, and which he shared with the composer who collaborated with him on this occasion, Hanns Eisler. The modifications that Brecht made to his text in the case of *Die Maßnahme* also show the degree to which he was prepared to accept instruction in political matters at this time: the changes were in response to criticism from within the KPD that the treatment of the subject was too abstract, and that Brecht's presentation of the teachings of the Marxist classics had not adequately reflected the way that political doctrine must evolve dialectically in relation to the practicalities of political struggle (Knopf, vol. i, 93–5, 101). The notion of *Die Maß-nahme* as a play for learning by participation is somewhat challenged by the fact that it was first performed by massed workers' choirs in the Berlin Philharmonie in December 1930—even if views expressed by the participants had been taken into account in the finalization of the text.[32] (It was repeated under similar conditions a number of times in the course of 1931 and 1932.) In circumstances such as these, it is difficult to imagine that the critical examination of behaviour which is embodied in the text was not subordinated to a collective celebration of the dogma by which that behaviour was motivated.[33] The occasion on which Brecht stressed most emphatically that the play was not intended for performance before an audience was twenty-five years later, when a Swedish right-winger wanted to perform it as an *anti*-Communist text (Knopf, vol. i, 104 f.).

In her presentation of the underlying principles of the Lehrstück, Elizabeth Wright (pp. 12 f.) is right to stress the importance of a distinction Brecht drew in a note of around 1930 between the pedagogic function that play-acting might fulfil in a future society and its scope within the society of the present; but her account of that note is distorted by the over-strong distinction she wishes to make between *Lehrstück* and 'epic theatre'. (We are closer to the truth with Walter Benjamin's description of the *Lehrstück* as a "special case" of epic theatre aiming at the erosion of the distinction between actor and spectator: *GS* II.2, 536.) The future situation that Brecht was envisaging, on the basis of his reading in classical Marxist theory, was one in which the interests of the individual had become identical with those of the state; in such a post-revolutionary society (if it can any longer be plausibly imagined) the distinction between actor and spectator would fall away, as would the distinction between economic base and cultural superstructure (*BFA* 21, 396; cf. 359). The practical possibilities Brecht envisaged for himself in what he saw as a "transitional period" towards the revolutionary transformation of society, however,

[32] An anonymous eye-witness account of a discussion which took place one week after the first performance records that the passage in which the Junger Genosse asks whether there is not an alternative to his death had been introduced in response to objections from participants. The same text records, however, that the notion of *Die Maßnahme* as a work intended more for the edification of the participants than of an audience met with incomprehension: Bertolt Brecht, *Die Maßnahme: Kritische Ausgabe mit einer Spielanleitung von Reiner Steinweg* (Frankfurt: Suhrkamp, 1972), 238, 277.

[33] A recent study which emphasizes the origins of the *Lehrstück* in innovative musical (as opposed to theatrical) practice aptly describes *Die Maßnahme* as a "political oratorio" (Krabiel, 4, 160–85).

were limited to either subverting or circumventing the apparatus of the theatre as it existed in the capitalist society of his day
(ibid. 396). What he describes in this connection as the "acti-
vation" of the public by theatrical performance is entirely consistent with the conception of an 'epic' style of acting as we have
seen him developing it in the late 1920s. The circumvention of
the established theatre by the use of lay actors, which he adum-
brates here as an alternative strategy for the short term, points
down the route he took with his play *Die Mutter* (The Mother)
in 1932—and it was in the notes to *Die Mutter* that he was to
give the most thorough illustration he ever gave of how his 'epic'
style differed from traditional approaches to dramatic presentation (see *BFA* 24, 150–90).

Die Mutter, which Brecht describes as related in style to the
Lehrstücke, was based on Maxim Gorky's novel *The Mother* of
1906. Brecht became involved in the preparation of an adaptation for the Volksbühne in the summer of 1931, brought in his
own dramaturgical collective (Elisabeth Hauptmann, Emil
Burri, Slatan Dudow, and Hanns Eisler), and together they produced a version which the Volksbühne management would
never have accepted. They converted a naturalistic account of
the circumstances surrounding the failed Russian revolution
of 1905 into a didactic presentation of developments which cul-
minated in the Bolshevik Revolution of 1917. The play was
performed by a combination of amateur and professional actors
(the professionals being drawn from the Gruppe Junger Schauspieler), with Helene Weigel in the lead role. Under close sur-
veillance from the police they gave a number of small-scale
performances in early 1932, some in public, and some in private
for representatives of working-class organizations (Knopf, vol.
i, 119–27).

To summarize the strategy Brecht had adopted in 1930–2, it
was one which led away from the mainstream conventional
theatre (as an institution of bourgeois society) and into close
association with the political movement which aimed at the
transcendence of bourgeois society by revolutionary means.
This had two implications for his theatrical practice. In the case
of *Die Mutter* he was working on a small scale, with lay participation, in order to promote the cause of the Communist
Party among the working class. In the case of *Die Maßnahme*,

he and Hanns Eisler could address themselves to mass audiences (again with lay participation), but in circumstances which largely presupposed an ideological commitment to Communism on the part of audience and participants alike. In certain respects, the views that Brecht was developing about the pedagogic value of play-acting can be seen to have positive potential for the educating of critically aware citizens within any model of democratic society:[34] it could help young people to reflect on their actions in ways which would make them useful to the state to which they belonged (here we could legitimately substitute the words "political community" for Brecht's "state"), and it could encourage an awareness of the relationship between "attitudes and gestures" on the one hand and "moods and trains of thought" on the other (*BFA* 21, 397 f.). But whatever pedagogic potential we might see in the *Lehrstück* model of theatre, what Brecht was doing in practice during the political crisis of the Weimar Republic involved a narrowing of the concerns of theatrical performance and an exclusion of perspectives that were critical of the cause he had adopted. His response to criticism of the partisan theme of *Die Mutter* was to conclude that it was in the nature of epic theatre to divide its public—by implication, along class lines (*BFA* 24, 183).

The course that Brecht took does not, however, constitute the only new development in German conceptions of theatrical activity during the period 1930–2. An alternative strategy was evolving at the same time within the conventional theatre, partly in critical response to the politicization with which Brecht and Piscator were associated, and partly in elaboration of the 'epic' style of acting that Brecht was promoting. Its chief exponent was the Hungarian-born Ödön von Horváth, and in so far as his conception of theatre has a label, it tends to be referred to as the 'critical *Volksstück*'.

Volksstück is an elastic term, generally used to distinguish a popular tradition of drama from the high literary canon. It is associated with a rich heritage of nineteenth-century popular

---

[34] Rainer Nägele (op. cit. n. 28 above, 115) points to an affinity between the Brechtian *Lehrstück* and Jürgen Habermas's conception of an ideal speech community. It is not possible to pursue that connection here, but it is one which may well repay close analysis.

comedy, especially as it was developed by Raimund and Nestroy in Vienna. The *Volksstück* tradition developed its own distinctive genres—the 'magic' play and the 'local' play—but it was a general feature of such plays that they portrayed characters who were not abstracted types, but recognizably based on living examples taken from the society for which they were performed.[35] The play which did most to secure Horváth's reputation, *Geschichten aus dem Wiener Wald* (Tales from the Vienna Woods), certainly carried distant echoes of that Viennese tradition, but the heritage with which he and his contemporaries were interacting probably lay closer to their own time, in the early Naturalist plays of Anzensgruber, in the regional comedies of the Bavarian Ludwig Thoma, and in the work of the popular comedians and ballad-mongers who had influenced Brecht in his early days (Balme, 81–92). It was a heritage of down-to-earth social drama which experienced an explosive renewal of interest in the Berlin of the mid-1920s.

The event which is often taken to mark the final eclipse of Expressionist drama on the German stage is the première of Carl Zuckmayer's *Der fröhliche Weinberg* (The Jolly Vineyard) in December 1925. It was by no means the first attempt at comedy in the 1920s; Kaiser, Toller, Unruh, Hasenclever, Hofmannsthal—all had turned to comedy at some stage in the post-war years, quite apart from Sternheim, who had never left it (cf. Knobloch). What made Zuckmayer's play different was the way it caught a particular public mood. And the way it did so was with earthy dialogue, strongly drawn characters representative of a rustic Rhineland situation, and a stock comic structure which endorsed the values of a rising social class. The action centred on the competition between a Rhine bargeman and a snooty student (the only character in the play who is given to open expressions of national pride) for the hand of the peasant-vintner's daughter: the bargee wins, and the student suffers various forms of derision before he too is paired off with a bride. With the political and economic crises of 1923 now seemingly well behind them, audiences evidently felt free to laugh at such matters once more (Rühle 1972, vol. iii, 9–11). Zuckmayer followed up his success with other plays in a popular sentimental

---

[35] See W. E. Yates, *Nestroy: Satire and Parody in Viennese Popular Comedy* (Cambridge: Cambridge University Press, 1972), 15–54.

vein, one about the legendary outlaw Schinderhannes and another about a famous circus family entitled *Katharina Knie*; and in 1931 he had another major success with *Der Hauptmann von Köpenick* (The Captain of Köpenick). Based on a legendary incident in 1906, when an ex-convict almost succeeded in deceiving the local authorities of the small town of Köpenick into providing him with money and identity papers by impersonating an army officer, it was another piece of astute comic writing which played on the deep-seated respect with which uniforms were regarded in German society. In the Germany of 1931 it was still possible to laugh at such things—just.

Another writer who later came to be recognized as an important contributor to the renewal of the *Volksstück* tradition in the 1920s is Marieluise Fleißer. It has been claimed on her behalf that her literary career was stifled after 1929, partly as a result of attitudes to women in the provincial society from which she came, and partly as a result of the personal intervention in her work of Bertolt Brecht. Brecht's early plays seem to have been an important stimulus to the writing of her own first play, *Fegefeuer in Ingolstadt* (Purgatory in Ingolstadt), in which she dramatized the experiences and social pressures of her strict Catholic upbringing in the Bavarian garrison town; and Brecht was evidently instrumental in securing a stage performance of the play in Berlin in 1926, but he insisted on making peremptory changes to the script. He went further in imposing his stamp on Fleißer's next play, *Pioniere in Ingolstadt* (Sappers in Ingolstadt), dictating aspects of the composition, giving the portrayal of the military a sharper satirical edge, and introducing material of a sexually explicit nature. The changes Brecht introduced provoked a scandal when this second play was performed in Berlin in 1929, the scandal isolated Fleißer from the society of Ingolstadt which was her major source of material, and Brecht's subsequent indifference to her situation left her adrift and unsupported (McGowan, 23–64).[36] Her skills in depicting the psychological dynamics of groups in a small-town situation make her plays, together with those of Zuckmayer and Horváth, a valuable source of instructive glimpses into the social psychology of the Weimar period; but of the three, it was Horváth

---

[36] Fleißer drew a satirical portrait of her experiences with Brecht and his circle in her play *Der Tiefseefisch*, but Brecht prevented it from being performed.

who went furthest in devising theatrical techniques for exposing the psychological determinants of social behaviour to scrutiny.[37]

As I have argued more fully elsewhere (Midgley 1983), the strategy that Horváth developed, both in theory and in practice, was to encourage an audience to identify with a situation in order to confront them all the more effectively with the disturbing truths that lay beneath the surface of that situation. *Geschichten aus dem Wiener Wald* begins a little like Zuckmayer's *Der fröhliche Weinberg*, with intimations of innocent delight in the joys of nature—except that the "romantic" status of the ruined tower which forms part of the set is quickly shown to be a social construct (and a business ploy), and the human relationships depicted soon turn out to be determined by malice and guile. Like Zuckmayer, Horváth uses drinking songs (as well as Strauß waltzes) to evoke companionable atmospheres, but only in order to reveal their hollow and deceptive nature. An aria from Puccini's *La Bohème*, played at a picnic on the banks of the "blue" Danube, might awaken pleasure or suspicion in a member of the audience; but it is also an ironic adumbration of the poverty and squalor to which the shopkeeper's daughter Marianne will be subjected when she follows her romantic impulse to abscond with a feckless lover. Horváth makes similarly diverse use of popular songs in *Kasimir und Karoline* (1932), which exploits all the "fun" of the Munich Oktoberfest as the background to a storyline which reveals the demoralizing effects of the Great Depression. The conventional structure of comedy or Volksstück, too, becomes an instrument of Horváth's strategy of audience enticement: his denouements play on our expectation of some kind of restoration of the status quo, but in *Kasimir und Karoline* this amounts to no more than a dispirited realignment of sexual relationships, and in *Geschichten aus dem Wiener Wald* it is a reunion bereft of joy in which Marianne submits to marriage to the brutal and self-righteous butcher next door.

---

[37] The sense of theatrical purpose that Marieluise Fleißer was to make explicit in later years shows a close affinity with the techniques developed by Horváth. As she noted of the characters in *Fegefeuer in Ingolstadt* in 1971, "daß die Figuren etwas Monströses haben, Konstruktionen sind, darin liegt die theatralische Poesie" (quoted in McGowan, 30).

As Horváth acknowledged when interviewed for Bavarian radio in 1932, he viewed the capacity of humans to behave as social beings with profound scepticism. When his works were 'rediscovered' in Germany around 1970, the manifest pessimism of his plot structures and his focus on the irrational aspects of life led some to see in him the very antithesis of the studied rationalism of Brecht. Others were quick to recognize that Horváth's conception of theatrical performance showed strong affinities with Brecht's, regardless of the differences in their philosophical outlook.[38] It was Brecht's terminology that Horváth echoed in the radio interview of 1932, describing his *Volksstücke* as "epic" in the sense that they offered a demonstrative representation of life: they were more "schildernd" than dramatic (*GW* I, 12). In the one substantial theoretical statement that Horváth left behind, the *Gebrauchsanweisung* (Instructions for Use), he emphasizes the need for non-naturalistic presentation in his plays: he asks for simple and colourful sets which sound rather like the illustrations in children's storybooks, and despite the regional colouring of the dialogue he writes, he insists that it should be spoken as stage German, not as if it were authentic dialect (*GW* IV, 663 f.). The *Gebrauchsanweisung* is a sketchy statement (though no more so than many of Brecht's notes of the 1920s), and it is occasionally flippant in its allusions to traditional theories of drama and to contemporary developments; but it says enough for us to be able to construct a clear sense of Horváth's purpose, and it is in that spirit that I paraphrase it here. He is aiming at a theatre that is rooted in the social reality of its time, but capable of enlightening audiences about themselves as individuals and as components of that social reality. He invokes the supposed civilizing effect on audiences of experiencing the enactment of their own anti-social impulses in the course of a play. (The example he gives is that of an audience of Communists seeing one of their kind brutally murdered on stage: on the one hand they are aroused to hatred for their enemies, but on the other hand their

---

[38] Franz Xaver Kroetz argues in *Weitere Aussichten* (Cologne: Kiepenheuer & Witsch, 1973), 522, that for the time being Horváth is a more useful model for political theatre than Brecht. Peter Handke's notorious proclamation that "Horváth is better than Brecht" is reprinted in Traugott Krischke (ed.), *Materialien zu Ödön von Horváth* (Frankfurt: Suhrkamp, 1970), 179 f.

own latent murderous impulses are stimulated by the action they are watching.) Like Brecht, he asks himself what the "pedagogic task" of the theatre might be in the future "proletarian" society that appears to be on its way, and his answer is that it should attempt to work with the emotional fascination that theatrical enactment exerts on an audience in order not just to "unmask" the figures on the stage (which would be "a cheap trick"), but to stimulate critical awareness of the structures of consciousness apparent in the community (the "collective") of which the audience is a part (*GW* IV, 660–2).

The principal means by which Horváth sought to achieve this "unmasking of consciousness" in practice was the careful structuring of his dialogues. Often he isolates a particular line with pauses, holding the audience's attention on the logical implication, or the inherent contradiction, in what a character is saying. The most telling effects are to be found in dialogues between the sexes, for it is there that the listener is most likely to be drawn into the simultaneous reconstruction of two contrasting trains of thought. A typical example occurs early in *Geschichten aus dem Wiener Wald*, where the butcher's one-word question "Böse?" is isolated from the flow of the dialogue and used as a pivotal point in the exposition of his relationship with Marianne. In the context of his train of thought it is a means of appearing placatory while continuing to assert a position of dominance: "Are you cross with me?" Her interpretation of it— as an indication of his desire to think of her as an evil person, "ein böser Mensch"—opens the way for the exposure of the authoritarian basis of his outlook through his very denial of it (*GW* I, 171 f.). In *Kasimir und Karoline* the dialogues between the two title figures typically hinge on Kasimir's desperate cleaving to 'a man's role' in the face of having lost his job, and Karoline's uncomprehending helplessness before the circumstances which prevent her from fulfilling the functions of 'a dutiful woman'. The dual experience into which the audience's emotional sympathies are drawn here is one in which mutual suspicion reinforces the very estrangement that either character fears, as is already apparent in the early exchange between Kasimir and Karoline in scene 5 (*GW* I, 259 f.). Even when a character has become identified with a position of superior insight in one respect (political analysis) he may reveal the irrationality of his mental impulses in another (sexual jealousy), like Martin in *Italienische Nacht* (Italian Night), the comedy in which Horváth satirized the complacency of Republican politicians in the face of the impending threat of fascism in 1930 (*GW* I, 142 f.). It is moments such as these that bear out Horváth's claim in the *Gebrauchsanweisung* to be surprising his audience with insights into human nature which they might otherwise be inclined to overlook.

In giving Horváth a position of prominence at the end of this chapter, I am not making any claim for the superiority of his model of theatre over others I have discussed. In certain respects, Horváth's theatrical strategies are just as clearly embedded in the circumstances of their time as anyone else's. It has been pointed out, for example, that his stylization of women as victims may have as much to do with the demands of theatrical impact as with the analysis of contemporary social reality;[39] and it can certainly be shown that he selects a particular section of society, the lower middle classes, in which to situate his plots because their characteristic attitudes and aspirations provide him with the impulses that feed his dramatic effects (Midgley 1983, 135 f.). What can be claimed on his behalf, however, is that, in the context of German theatre history under the Weimar Republic, his conception of the 'critical *Volksstück*' maintains the potential of the theatre as a place where an audience can be disabused of its comfortable assumptions about the factors which determine the social reality that is familiar to it. This is the sense in which Horváth's model of theatre challenges and complements those of Piscator and Brecht.

The status of the theatre as the primary medium for reaching large audiences during the Weimar period—when film and radio were still in the process of technical development—made for a particularly strong connection between theatrical activity and the political trends of the time. That is apparent in the early 1920s as much in the evidence of republican state patronage as it is in the idealistic attempts of Reinhardt or the Expressionists to achieve a sense of spiritual community in the theatre. The theatrical ventures of Piscator, which command strong public

---

[39] Cf. Ingrid Haag, "Das 'traurige Happy-End': Zur Struktur der 'Fräuleinstücke' Ödön von Horváths", *Austriaca*, 6 (1978), 169–86.

interest through the second half of the 1920s, bring a radical-
ization both of the technical approach to representing the
'reality of our times' and of the sense of political community,
wedded as they are to a Marxist-Leninist conception of the
dynamics of history. It was not least through a process of critical reflection on the practical implications of Piscator's approach to theatrical representation that Brecht developed his
thinking about how the theatre might nurture critical awareness
of how human experience is socially constituted; but the theatrical practice in which we find Brecht engaged in the early
1930s involves working within the confines of the Communist
movement and its specific sense of political purpose. Horváth's
conception of theatre cannot be said to transcend the circumstances of his time any more than that of Piscator or Brecht,
but it does provide an alternative perspective on the theatre as
a political community, and a model for theatrical enactment
which aims to nurture an audience's critical awareness of how
the social reality as Piscator and Brecht conceived it was in its
turn humanly constituted.

4

The Novel I: Representing the Times

The novel is not after the excerpt or the episode, it wants the whole thing.

Thomas Mann (*GW* X, 352)

I consider our age to be one of transition, but the distinction between an age of transition and one of fulfilment vanishes if the former recognizes its condition and acts accordingly.

Robert Musil (*GW* II, 1353)

The sense that an age had come to an end with the First World War and that a new one was struggling to emerge was not unique to the revolutionary left. It was shared by Thomas Mann, for example, who stated in his commemorative speech for the assassinated Foreign Minister Walter Rathenau in 1923 that the "bourgeois epoch", which had begun with the Renaissance, had reached its conclusion with the war and its aftermath (*GW* XI, 859). Indeed, the notion that European culture in its entirety was in a condition of terminal decay was given credence by Oswald Spengler's *Der Untergang des Abendlandes* (The Decline of the West), which began to sell well as soon as the first volume appeared in 1918. Spengler's arguments, based on the suggestive evidence of grandiose historical analogies, were such as to encourage the view that twentieth-century Europe faced an inevitable descent into barbarism, even if his methods were immediately criticized by professional historians and leading intellectuals (including Thomas Mann and Robert Musil).[1] At the same time, however, a countervailing attitude to

[1] For English readers there is an instructive early critique of Spengler by the historian R. G. Collingwood in the journal *Antiquity*, 1 (1927), 311–25.

history was being given currency by Theodor Lessing in *Geschichte als Sinngebung des Sinnlosen*, which appeared in four editions between 1919 and 1927, even if its furiously polemical style made it a less accessible text than Spengler's. Lessing's suggestive title was promoting the Nietzschean insight that the course of history is in itself meaningless, and that such meaning as we read into it is constructed in the act of interpretation.[2]

Against that intellectual background, it is unsurprising that literary writers should have sought to use the versatile potential of the novel in order to express something of the nature of the contemporary historical situation. But what kind of constructions were they to place on that situation, and how were they to reflect the problems inherent in its interpretation and representation? What were the implications of trying to relate the depiction of individual characters and events to a sense of the overall significance of historical experience in a period which was characterized by confusion and uncertainty? These are the main questions I wish to address in the present chapter, with reference to five works—by Thomas and Heinrich Mann, Döblin, Musil, and Broch—which may be seen as the most ambitious attempts between 1918 and 1933 to give encompassing literary expression to the distinctive character of the contemporary age. They are a heterogeneous group of texts, but it is precisely the differences between them that highlight the issues I have in mind. Taken together, they illustrate two kinds of development in narrative writing. One leads from the attempt to depict the individual case as representative of a more general experience (the brothers Mann) to a self-conscious construction of historical situations (Musil and Broch); the other leads from a reliance on the traditional authority of authorial narration (the Manns and Broch) to its problematization and ironization (Musil and Döblin).

The general idea that the novel was the most appropriate means for representing the nature of the modern age received a special

---

[2] Lessing's polemics against the "ideals and idols" of professional historians bear more than a passing similarity to the critical views developed by Musil in his essays of the early 1920s, although there is no obvious evidence of a direct connection between them. Cf. Rainer Marwedel, *Theodor Lessing 1872–1933* (Darmstadt: Luchterhand, 1987), 149.

boost in 1920 with the publication of Lukács's *Theory of the Novel*. This was a pioneering work in the sense that it treated the novel as an object worthy of the sort of serious intellectual attention which had previously been reserved in the German-speaking world for the more obviously self-contained form of the drama.[3] But the kind of sense that Lukács was making of the novel as a literary form had its roots in a particular brand of historicism characteristic of the German intellectual tradition. Lukács described *The Theory of the Novel* in his subtitle as "an essay in the philosophy of history"; he was out to show that the novel, with all its flexibility and diversity of composition, reflected the characteristics of the modern world in its form rather than its content.

Lukács constructed his image of the modern world in contradistinction to an idealized notion of antiquity, and in this he was following Hegel in particular, and a broad heritage of German cultural thinking generally which went back to Winckelmann in the eighteenth century. He pictured ancient Greece as a self-contained culture which could be readily grasped intuitively through the epics of Homer, for example; he saw Greece as an epitome of 'original' humanity which was 'at home' in its world and able to give that world direct, spontaneous, sensuous expression in its poetry. The form of the novel, by contrast, expressed for Lukács the estranged cultural condition of modern humanity, its "transcendental homelessness" (*Theory of the Novel*, 32). The reality that the novel had to depict was inherently "incomplete" and "fragmented", it was the reality of a world conscious of its transience, of its place in a historical sequence. The novel could not hope to embody a sense of cultural awareness in its entirety, as the ancient Greek epics supposedly did, but Lukács does present it as the attempt of modern humanity to *reconstruct* a sense of a total world-view. One of the semantic distinctions in Lukács's text which tends to be lost in English translations of it is that between the epic poem (*Epos*) as a variety of narrative text and "epopoeia" (*Epopöe*) as the active making of an epic account of the world. Lukács himself is admittedly less systematic than Hegel in his acknowledgement of this distinction, but it is a point which is nevertheless

[3] Hartmut Steinecke gives a concise account of the low esteem in which the novel was held in Germany around 1900 in his contribution to Bludau et al., 250–68; cf. also Scheunemann, 66–79.

fundamental to his argument. As he understands it, the novel is the *epopoeia* of an age for which the immanent meaning of life has become problematic, but which retains "die Gesinnung zur Totalität" (*Theory of the Novel*, 47), a phrase which is perhaps best translated as "the resolve to strive for totality".

It is totality of understanding with which we are concerned here, not any aspiration to an all-encompassing depiction of reality. As Lukács was to clarify the point in his later *Aesthetics*, 'totality' was intended to refer to the completeness of the literary work as an artefact on the one hand and the sense in which it contrives a unification of human awareness on the other (cf. Pascal 1970*b*). In trying to summarize Lukács's account of the way in which the novel may be said to achieve such 'totality' we inevitably lose sight of the intricacy of his allusion, but at the heart of his interest in the "inner form" of the novel is a particular conception of philosophical understanding. Unified human awareness, he argues, is no longer attainable in the modern world as an immediate sensuous experience, but only in abstract terms, as a system of derived concepts. Similarly, it is as a system of abstract principles that Lukács describes the "constitutive elements" which enable the novel to fulfil its distinctive role as the representative literary form of the modern age; they include the utopian yearnings of human individuals, the "formations" of the external social world, and the compositional organization (*gestaltende Gesinnung*) of a work capable of doing justice to those two independent dimensions of modern reality simultaneously. It is the relationship of balance between these "elements" that preserves the identity of the novel as something distinct from (subjective) lyricism and (objectivized) drama, and which prevents it from narrowing its focus to the merely idyllic or descending to the level of mere entertainment (*Theory of the Novel*, 60f.). When it comes to describing the sense of balance he has in mind, Lukács draws on a particular conception of irony developed by the early Romantics. That conception of irony amounts to a recognition of the provisionality of each act of self-recognition which the human subject executes in its pursuit of the absolute truth.[4] As Lukács applies the concept to the novel, it betokens a manifest recognition on

[4] Cf. Manfred Frank, *Einführung in die frühromantische Ästhetik* (Frankfurt: Suhrkamp, 1989), 301f.

the part of the narrating subject that it is itself caught up in a world which is "incomplete", "fragmented", and capable of systematic understanding only in abstract terms. It is by such "self-surmounting of subjectivity" that Lukács sees the novel achieving a "formal unity" which transcends mere abstract understanding and reflects the objective character of the modern world (*Theory of the Novel*, 64 f.). More than that, such "self-surmounting of subjectivity" is, as Lukács puts it, the highest freedom that can be attained "in a world without God" (ibid. 82).

Evidence that *The Theory of the Novel* directly influenced the nature of novel-writing during the Weimar period is slight. (It is strong only in the case of Hermann Broch: see Lützeler 1980.) What Lukács's book provided was a powerfully argued intellectual foundation for a conservative conception of the novel's purpose. As Lukács argues his case, the pursuit of unified understanding by means of the "self-surmounting of subjectivity" is firmly linked to the notion of a normative narrating subject mediating between the reader and the ostensible reality the text is depicting; and the kind of plot structure he envisages in his discussion of particular novels is one in which a "problematic individual" progresses to self-knowledge in relation to a pre-existing "system of ideas" (*Theory of the Novel*, 67–72). As he was to acknowledge in his foreword of 1962, his thinking had been strongly coloured by works of the type of Flaubert's *Education sentimentale*, with their German equivalent in the *Bildungsroman*. It is true that Lukács, like the Romantics before him, envisaged considerable potential for the novel to incorporate non-narrative elements, notably passages of lyrical expression or discursive reflection. But to use this sort of point as a basis for arguing, as Manfred Durzak (1970*a*, 37) once did, that *The Theory of the Novel* is compatible with an open-ended conception of the novel as an "experimental terrain for the permanent pursuit of meaning", is to elevate particular observations contained in Lukács's book above the overall structure of the theory in which he deploys them. Lukács's conception of the novel was to be challenged between 1925 and 1930 by the publication of works which did not share his philosophical premises concerning the nature of understanding and the function of the human subject. Durzak names the authors in question—Kafka, Döblin, and Musil—whom Lukács for his part could integrate into his account of twentieth-century literature at a later date only by representing them as symptomatic of a process of cultural disintegration.[5] The profound sense in which Kafka, whose fragmentary attempts at writing novels were published posthumously in the 1920s, expresses the characteristic uncertainties and anxieties of the modern age is well known; the introverted nature of his texts makes it inappropriate to include them in the present discussion. It is Döblin and Musil who will be discussed below as innovative novelists who give extensive expression to the social reality of their time, but in ways which transcend the boundaries of Lukács's argument.

Within the canon of authors whom Lukács consistently regarded as fulfilling his expectations of the novel, the brothers Thomas and Heinrich Mann were to enjoy a special prominence in subsequent years. By and large their works conformed to the model of an identifiable narrating subject acknowledging the provisionality of its own comprehension of the world; by and large their narratives made apparent that sense of a problematic relationship between the depiction of specific human experiences and the conceptual understanding of the world in which they take place, which is what makes the novel the representative form of the modern age in Lukács's sense. In their works of the early 1920s, however, both brothers were pursuing goals of a more specific nature. Both were working at a valedictory presentation of the pre-war world. Thomas Mann, in *Der Zauberberg*, was seeking to express the cultural and intellectual tensions of the time indirectly through the remote, but cosmopolitan world of a Swiss sanatorium; and Heinrich Mann was completing a trilogy intended to show the social and cultural factors which had brought Germany to war and defeat. In either case their works exhibit particular kinds of difficulty which faced an author who tried to present the story of 'problematic' individuals as representative of the nature of the times.

[5] See Georg Lukács, *The Meaning of Contemporary Realism* (London: Merlin Press, 1963), 17–46, 77 f. I have given a general account of Lukács's critical position in the 1920s and 1930s in my essay "Communism and the Avant-Garde: The Case of Georg Lukács", in E. Timms and P. Collier (eds.), *Visions and Blueprints* (Manchester University Press, 1988), 52–65.

The publication of Heinrich Mann's *Der Untertan* in 1918 was an emphatic gesture of separation from the old regime. It was also an immediate success, rapidly selling 150,000 copies (Winter, 47). The work had been written before the outbreak of war in 1914, and much of it had appeared in serialized form in a Munich-based magazine at the time, but the editor deemed it inappropriate to continue publication once the war had started (Weisstein, 115 f.). For *Der Untertan* is a trenchant satire of the attitudes and mentalities which had characterized the reign of Wilhelm II. The "loyal subject" (*Untertan*) at the centre of the action is Diederich Heßling, the heir to a provincial paper factory. He is depicted as an opportunistic small-scale industrialist who rises to power and influence on a tide of nationalistic fervour. He is also characterized as an epitome of servility—which is why the English translation of the work came to acquire the title *Man of Straw.*[6] He is more than that: he is the very model of an authoritarian personality, contemptuous towards those whom he can recognize as weak or inferior to himself, neurotically anxious about losing kudos, and unremittingly ferocious towards any force or sentiment which he senses to be threatening to the pyramidal system of power in which he is permitted to participate.

The depth of characterization and the wealth of historical resonance that Heinrich Mann built into *Der Untertan* prevent it from subsiding into mere caricature. He shows the processes of education and socialization by which the young Heßling absorbs the authoritarian impulses inherent in a patriarchal family, in school, church, and state. He shows him absorbing the ready-made attitudes of an assertive nationalism as a university student in Berlin, until he becomes a perfect mimic of the phrases and attitudinizing of the Kaiser himself. By making frequent allusion to the theatricality and the cult of self-congratulation which had characterized Wilhelm II's style of rule, the novel creates a sense of how the regime and its loyal supporters are deluding themselves.[7] It also shows the

---

[6] London: Hutchinson, 1947. Earlier versions of the translation had appeared in New York under the titles *The Patrioteer* (1921) and *Little Superman* (1945): Weisstein, 135.

[7] The quality of "masquerade" which characterized the life of Wilhelm II and his court is described by I. V. Hull, *The Entourage of Kaiser Wilhelm II, 1888–1918* (Cambridge: Cambridge University Press, 1982), 15–44.

mechanisms of political opportunism working to prevent effective opposition from other social types which exist alongside the "Untertan", notably the upholders of the democratic tradition of 1848 and the rising force of the organized working class. The rise to social prominence of a Diederich Heßling is the product of a multiplicity of social factors, in addition to his own instinct for coming out on the winning side.

The clearest illustration of this point is to be found in the trial episode in chapter 4, where another factory-owner is arraigned on a charge of insulting the Emperor. The offending remark had been made when, in the course of criticizing the arrogance of the aristocracy generally and the oppressive behaviour of the military on their behalf, the defendant had reached for the argument that Germany's royal houses were all "verjudet"— that they have been, so to speak, "infiltrated" by Jews—as a way of suggesting that they are no better than the rest of society. The state prosecutor is himself Jewish; in deciding to press the case he is motivated by careerist ambitions within the social climate as he finds it, and he plainly expects to find similar motives at work in Heßling. Heinrich Mann has constructed a situation, in other words, which is calculated to reveal the potency of anti-Semitism as a political force, not in the sense that it is overtly apparent in political or judicial decisions, but in the sense that it pervades the climate of assumptions about German identity in which such decisions are fashioned. The decisive moment in the trial, indeed, is the one where the defence lawyer—Wolfgang Buck, a liberal-minded young intellectual torn between a career in law and a career in the theatre—misplays his hand by boasting that the defence will, if necessary, demonstrate that the defendant's disparaging remark about German royalty has a basis in fact. It is this thought—unpalatable for those imbued with the patriotic ethos of the time—that generates an atmosphere of outrage in the courtroom which the prosecution is able to exploit and which provides Heßling with a platform from which to proclaim his loyalty to the Kaiser and all that he stands for. The speech in which Buck sums up for the defence is an oratorical tour de force in which he gives a damningly precise assessment of Heßling's character; but he loses the case by letting his anti-monarchist sentiments show through again.

What makes *Der Untertan* effective social satire is the balance that Heinrich Mann contrives between ridicule on the one hand and the serious depiction of sinister developments on the other. The hollowness of Heßling's pomposity is apparent to members of his society as well as to the reader. But he is able to rise to prominence within that society because of the combination of factors working in his favour; these include the ambition of the career lawyer and the vanity of the would-be democrat, as well as the background climate of racial prejudice and the entrenched interests of the aristocracy. It is the bandwagon effect of patriotic fervour that the novel exposes, the sort of political atmosphere which makes it possible to swing popular support behind a brazen monument to the Kaiser rather than a home for orphans. Once Heßling has become fired with a sense of the popular appeal of his cause he becomes adept at riding that bandwagon, and when elections are held for the Reichstag he is able to play his part in determining the political agenda, not in the sense that his monarchist faction attracts a great deal of electoral support, but in the sense that it compels the liberal and social democratic candidates to compete on its terms for the patriotic vote.

The richly ironic texture of *Der Untertan*, together with the essays and speeches that Heinrich Mann was publishing in 1918–19, established his reputation as one of the major figureheads of republicanism in Germany. (In the closing stages of the Weimar Republic his name was even advanced as a possible candidate for the presidency.) But the two volumes with which he continued his depiction of the Wilhelmine era reveal the peculiarities of his intellectual position and its weaknesses in relation to actual political developments.

Both volumes have generally disappointed the critics because they appear abstract in conception and uneven in composition by comparison with *Der Untertan* (cf. Weisstein, 128–31; Schröter, 169–81).[8] *Die Armen* (The Poor), which was actually published first, in 1917, extends the examination of pre-war

---

[8] Gnettner (pp. 64 f.) argues against this broad trend, but the prominence she gives in her discussion of *Der Kopf* to the notion of "ideal types" serves rather to emphasize the schematic quality of that work. König (pp. 135–299) defends the artistic integrity of *Der Untertan* by relating the labyrinthine complexities of its plot to the themes of Heinrich Mann's earlier works.

society into the world of the proletariat, but in its depiction of that world it fails to match the vibrant intimacy with which *Der Untertan* portrays the middle classes. The central figure of *Die Armen* is Karl Balrich, one of Heßling's shop-floor workers, who strives to educate himself, but dissipates his learning in a personal battle with his boss, rather than using it to the general advantage of his class. The theme that Heinrich Mann is developing here, in other words, is that of the failure of the enlightened mind to fulfil its social responsibilities, and it is that theme that links this slender second volume to the final volume of the trilogy. In *Der Kopf* (The Head, 1925), Heinrich Mann attempts—at great length—to depict the failings of Germany's pre-war social and intellectual élite.

The shortcomings of *Der Kopf* as a novel have been perceptively analysed by David Roberts (pp. 149–56). At the heart of the difficulties that Heinrich Mann created for himself with this work was the attempt to combine a critical account of Germany's political and diplomatic history in the run-up to the First World War with a more personal depiction of the fate of a generation of intellectuals under the reign of Wilhelm II. In certain respects the novel operates as a *roman à clef*, containing portraits of historical figures who actually determined the course of German foreign policy between 1900 and 1914 (these include Prince Bülow, who was Chancellor until 1909; Admiral Tirpitz, the chief architect of German naval expansion; and Theobald von Bethmann-Hollweg, who was Chancellor at the time of the July crisis of 1914). The central characters of the work, however, are two childhood friends and ideological rivals, Wolf Mangolf and Claudius Terra, who embark on their adult lives in the 1890s. Both become integrated into the power structure of the Wilhelmine Empire—Mangolf as a career politician and Terra as a minor director in an industrial empire modelled on Krupps—but the manner in which that integration is accomplished in the novel highlights the unresolved tensions in the artistic conception of the work. For one thing, our two intellectuals do not owe their rise to any factors which might appear representative of the political world the novel is reconstructing, but to an elaborate network of personal relations, the exposition of which occupies the first third of the text. For another, their close association with the destiny of their nation leads to a blatant departure from historical fact: the novel has Mangolf become Chancellor in July 1914, whereas in reality Bethmann-Hollweg remained Chancellor (even if he increasingly ceded effective power to the military) until July 1917. Stylistic features show how Heinrich Mann has tried to fuse the disparate elements of his novel together. Alongside the expansive psychological realism that characterizes much of the work there are moments of stark symbolism: Mangolf becomes Chancellor as the result of an assassination arranged by Terra in response to the news that Germany is mobilizing its troops for war, and on the closing pages the two intellectuals acknowledge the collapse of their respective hopes by shooting themselves (in a heavy-handed echo of the novel's title) "in the head".[9] The novel fails to achieve artistic unity, not so much because it combines a private plot with a public one, but because it combines a critical representation of the forces which actually determined the direction of Wilhelmine politics with a tragi-comic (as well as a psychologically self-absorbed) depiction of the intelligentsia which failed effectively to oppose those forces.

The question of the precise sense in which the characters of Terra and Mangolf are themselves based on real-life figures has proved contentious (see Koopmann and Schneider, 91 f., 121, 175–80). Those who approach *Der Kopf* with a strong awareness of the hostility which developed between the brothers Mann in the course of the war are bound to sense the resonances of that personal antagonism in the relationship depicted in the novel, especially in its intimate moments. Heinrich Mann himself, in the 1930s, pointed to other models among Germany's pre-war intelligentsia (Werner, 168). He linked the figure of Mangolf to the journalist Maximilian Harden, who had turned into an ardent proponent of German territorial expansion once the war began, although he had been a persistent critic of the Kaiser's policies beforehand. This suggestion is of limited interest, because Mangolf is consistently associated with the ethos of power throughout the novel, but it is a useful

---

[9] Roberts (pp. 155 f.) also draws attention to the "expressionistic" quality of certain early chapters in *Der Kopf*: their Novelle-like structure suggests that Heinrich Mann is attempting to express the 'essence' of a situation through the explosive evocation of an incident rather than through the suggested causality of extended depiction.

reminder of the senses in which the intellectual feuding between Heinrich and Thomas Mann always was related to broader public issues, even if in their case the arguments became coloured with personal innuendo.[10] As a model for Terra he pointed to the dramatist Wedekind. This seems a little more plausible, because some of the elements in Terra's early career—fairground, theatre, advertising agency—could have been taken direct from Wedekind's biography, and some of his later antics as an intellectual clown in high society carry something of the style of dialogue in Wedekind's plays. But to say this is to confirm that Heinrich Mann was publishing in 1925 a novel which contains a burlesque reflection of the role of the intellectual in society as he had himself previously proclaimed it.

Since 1910 Heinrich Mann had prominently identified himself with a particular conception of intellectual leadership, and his essay "Geist und Tat" (Mind and Action) is often seen as having inaugurated a brand of intellectual activism which was to become an increasingly important element in literary Expressionism during the decade that followed (cf. Anz and Stark, 263–8). In it he drew a sharp contrast between the political cultures of France and Germany, and held up the traditionally strong alliance between French intellectuals and the broad populace as a model for German writers to emulate. But in doing so he betrayed an inflated expectation of the influence that men of letters can hope to have on the course of history. The example he takes is that of the French Revolution of 1789, and he speaks of it as if it was the thinkers of the French Enlightenment alone who provided the people with an awareness of the values they needed to fight for. He sees "the rule of the people" as the means by which intellectual values might be asserted in Germany, too; but his conception of 'the people' is left as vague as Rousseau's notion of 'the general will' (*Essays*, 13 f.). The type of political commitment that Heinrich Mann was articulating in 1910 was one which opposed the interests of the intellect (*Geist*) irresolvably against the force and authority of entrenched power (*Macht*); it did not at that stage antici-

---

[10] Reed (pp. 190–5) shows how Heinrich Mann's Zola essay of 1915, which precipitated the severing of relations between the brothers, was polemicizing against a whole tribe of apologists for the war, even if specific phrases also carried a particular thrust against his brother Thomas.

pate the practicalities involved in the direct involvement of intellectuals in the exercise of power. When the Wilhelmine regime collapsed in 1918, Heinrich Mann's contribution to the revolutionary transformation of Germany was to call upon his fellow intellectuals to assist in educating the general populace in the kind of thinking that would be needed to sustain a Republic. He identified closely with the moral purism of Kurt Eisner's revolutionary government in Bavaria because it was attempting to provide precisely the kind of "school for democracy" with which he could sympathize (Berle, 84–92). He also sensed very keenly that the Republic as it came about in 1918 was not something which the broad population of Germany had struggled to achieve, but was largely the result of external pressures associated with the outcome of the war. Addressing the Political Council of Intellectual Workers convened in Munich at the end of November 1918, he called upon them to introduce into German politics "the moral laws of a liberated world" and to play their part in ensuring that a Republic which had arrived "as a gift of history" should now be provided with republicans (Kaes et al., 40).

In the novel *Der Kopf*, Heinrich Mann is using Terra as the mouthpiece for some political insights he had previously publicized in his essays and speeches. It is Terra, for example, who warns the old Chancellor Lannas (Bülow) that he will need to curb the economic power of the big industrialists if he is to preserve the authority of government, and who pleads for revolution from above in the interests of social justice and in order to arrest the drift towards war. But it is equally through Terra that the novel focuses very strongly on the psychology of the intellectual who is reduced to dismissive cynicism when confronted with a power structure that is not amenable to rational persuasion. The melancholy conclusion to which Terra appears compelled by wartime experience is that the involvement of intellectual talents in politics is ultimately futile because "society" has no use for it (*GW* 8, 647). David Roberts (pp. 153 f.) is perhaps overzealous in his pursuit of connections between this note of extreme disillusionment and the political situation in Germany in the early 1920s: when Heinrich Mann gave public support to the centrist government of Stresemann in its efforts to resolve the political conflicts of 1923, invoking the principle of a "dictatorship of reason" as he did so, then this probably reflects the patrician perspective which was an abiding feature of his political outlook (cf. Berle). The double suicide with which the novel ends is, of course, a gesture of profound resignation.[11] But it also reinforces the sense that Mangolf and Terra are dependent on each other, in death as in antagonism. As such it is a gesture of valediction from a world in which the intellectual principles of 'Geist' and 'Macht' were conceived in terms of mutually defining opposition. This is not to say that Heinrich Mann found it easy to adjust to the post-imperial world in which that clear sense of intellectual opposition to the structures of power had become a positive liability (he manifestly did not). But the major project to which he was to direct his attentions after 1925 was one which portrayed the humane intellectual in the role of political ruler, albeit in a French setting and a sixteenth-century one: it was his depiction of the life of Henri IV, which he completed only in 1938 (Roberts, 190–242).

In that wartime entrenchment of intellectual positions, Thomas Mann had played a role which could not easily have been predicted from his pre-war writings—even if Heinrich could claim in 1917 that he had seen it coming.[12] Thomas Mann's works, from *Buddenbrooks* in 1901 to *Der Tod in Venedig* (Death in Venice) in 1913, had been part and parcel of that critical, oppositional intellectual culture which had dominated German literary writing in the Wilhelmine period. But when the First World War broke out he was stung by the vehemence with which Western politicians and newspaper columnists were expressing anti-German sentiments, stylizing the war against Germany as a war to save civilization; and he responded, not by defending Germany's claim to be regarded as a civilized nation, but by attempting to define the values that Germany for its part was defending *against* civilization, and labelling

[11] Heinrich Mann's profound disillusionment in the last year of the war is documented in a draft letter to his brother Thomas of January 1918 (*Briefwechsel*, 118): "Ich bin nicht der Mann, Elend u. Tod der Völker auf die Liebhabereien meines Geistes zuzuschneiden, ich nicht. Ich glaube nicht, daß der Sieg irgend einer Sache noch der Rede werth ist, wo wir Menschen untergehen."

[12] Ibid. 111: "Die Gegnerschaft Deines Geistes kannte ich von jeher, u. wenn Deine extreme Stellungnahme im Krieg Dich selbst verwundert hat, für mich war sie vorauszusehen."

them "Kultur". In his essay "Gedanken im Krieg" (Wartime Thoughts), which appeared in *Die neue Rundschau* in November 1914, he spelt out the sense of rigorous distinction he had in mind. By 'culture' he meant a form of communal organization defined by its own sense of organic cohesion (*Geschlossenheit*) and characterized by distinctive styles and attitudes which could manifest themselves in some instances in ways inimical to 'civilization'; and opposition to 'civilization', as he expounded it here, entailed opposition to reason, to enlightenment, to the domestication of vital impulses, to *Geist*—which he described as anti-demonic, anti-heroic, "civilian" (*GW* XIII, 527f.). It was his first attempt to outline a political stance which he was himself to characterize as self-consciously "unpolitical".

The terms in which Thomas Mann was expressing his patriotism in 1914 were not in themselves extraordinary, related as they were to that heritage of late nineteenth-century cultural thinking which we saw to be at work in pre-war conceptions of theatre. Many writers and intellectuals were drawn into the patriotic fervour of the moment, and some, including Döblin, remained apologists for an aggressive military stance until quite a late stage of the war (Sebald, 19f.). What was extraordinary about Thomas Mann's wartime activity was the effort he put into elaborating his personal view of what it meant to be German. Fired by the criticisms he drew from prominent intellectuals in France and Germany (they included Romain Rolland and the pacifist writer Wilhelm Herzog, as well as his brother Heinrich), he spent much of the wartime period absorbing texts which could be seen as constituting a distinctive German intellectual tradition, from Fichte and the early Romantics to Nietzsche and that maverick conservative of late nineteenth-century politics Paul de Lagarde,[13] in order to reinforce his arguments for a conception of German national identity which was inherently anti-democratic, incompatible with the procedures of parliamentary government, and in a rather special sense, even anti-literary. It was these arguments that he published in 1918 as the *Betrachtungen eines Unpolitischen* (Reflections of an Unpolitical Man).

[13] For the implications of the thought of Paul de Lagarde, see Fritz Stern, *The Politics of Cultural Despair* (Berkeley and Los Angeles: University of California Press, 1961).

The profound sense of unreality that pervades the *Betrachtungen* is amply brought out in T. J. Reed's study of Thomas Mann (Reed, 201–22).[14] The text ignores inconvenient facts (which were known to Thomas Mann at the time of publication) about the actions of the German government in precipitating the First World War, to say nothing of those factors in Germany's political history which had given rise to a strong intellectual tradition of non-involvement in politics. It is also clear that Thomas Mann is constructing a picture of what it means to be German which is defined in opposition to the intellectual activism that his brother Heinrich had been calling for. When he uses the term 'Literatur' in the *Betrachtungen*, he means a type of literary writing which is analytical and partisan, by contrast with 'Dichtung', which implies an aspiration to all-encompassing poetic expression. And when he describes the type of writer—the "Zivilisationsliterat"—who has emerged in Germany itself as an exponent of the values of 'civilization' and 'democracy', then he describes his activities in terms of intimate familiarity: the "Zivilisationsliterat" is a figure known personally to the author as someone who desires and works for the downfall of the Kaiser (*GW* XII, 53–68). The ideal of Germanness that Thomas Mann constructs here does not, however, seek to *exclude* such oppositional tendencies. It is, on the contrary, an ideal which seeks to include and incorporate, reinterpreting such terms as 'democracy', of course, in ways which are compatible with the political heritage of hierarchical authoritarianism (the *Obrigkeitsstaat*) and the cultural heritage of introversion (*Innerlichkeit*). It is the capacity of German culture to absorb and sublimate conflicting tendencies that is offered as the justification for Germany's sense of historical mission on the world stage, and it is with a self-conscious sense of enfolding ambiguity that Thomas Mann expresses that sense of justification. As he puts it, it is Germany's destiny to serve as the arena, both geographical and intellectual, in which the "fraternal strife" of the nations of Europe (*GW* XII, 47) is at once fought out and brought to fruition (*GW* XII, 54: Mann himself makes this double sense of the verb "austragen" explicit).

Notwithstanding his wartime position, Thomas Mann was to become a passionate and eloquent defender of the Republic in

[14] For a full critical examination of the *Betrachtungen*, see Ernst Keller, *Der unpolitische Deutsche* (Berne: Francke, 1965).

the years to come. He responded to the violence of the nationalist right in the early 1920s by seeking to interpret the Republic as the true inheritor of traditional German values as he understood them.[15] He also responded promptly to the Nazi electoral successes of 1930 with a "call to reason", in which he gave a quite specific analysis of prevailing political and economic circumstances with a view to showing why it was in the national interest for middle-class voters to enter into an alliance with the Social Democrats.[16] In 1933 he even repudiated "the national idea", along with traditional middle-class prejudices against political and philosophical "materialism", as inappropriate to the needs of the moment.[17] The question of whether Thomas Mann became a truly convinced republican in the 1920s, or whether he was a mere 'Vernunftrepublikaner' supporting the Republic as the appropriate political expediency of the times, has generated controversy among English as well as German scholars.[18] What is clear beyond reasonable doubt, however, is that Thomas Mann did play a prominent part in trying to win the hearts and minds of the middle classes for centrist politics under the Republic, and that he was able to do so with an authority that was derived from his previous identification with nationalism and a distinctive sense of German cultural identity. But it was his self-questioning as a cultural nationalist, rather than his positive advocacy on behalf of the Republic, that went to determine the character of *Der Zauberberg* as he published it in 1924.

It is well known that the work had begun life before the war as a lightweight counterfoil to *Der Tod in Venedig*. In either case a character was removed from the 'normal' social world of his familiar German environment and experienced the manifestation of his own erotic impulses in response to an exotic figure in disorientating circumstances. For the famous writer Gustav

[15] "Von deutscher Republik": *GW* XI, 809–52.

[16] "Deutsche Ansprache": *GW* XI, 870–90.

[17] "Bekenntnis zum Sozialismus": *GW* XII, 678–84.

[18] Keith Bullivant argues that Mann was merely a bourgeois conservative reacting against manifestations of violence and obscurantism (Bullivant (ed.), 24–38); Martin Swales presents him as a sincere liberal humanist striving to give the Republic intellectual validation in the vocabulary of the times (Bance (ed.), 1–13). Discussions of Thomas Mann's political writings in Germany itself have been complicated further by the fact that, even after 1945, the tendency of the German intellectual tradition to separate the role of the poetic writer (*Dichter*) off from any concern with politics remained strong (see Sontheimer 1961).

von Aschenbach—who treats himself to a holiday in Venice, only to meet his death there—this involved a tragic confrontation with processes of internal dissolution which he was unable consciously to acknowledge. For the young trainee engineer Hans Castorp, whose experiences provide the narrative backbone for *Der Zauberberg*, a brief visit to his cousin in a Swiss sanatorium turns into a long stay during which the unanticipated responses of his own mind and body come as a comic revelation. He stays for reasons which make no clear distinction between the physical symptoms of tuberculosis and his sexual attraction to one of the patients, the Russian woman Clawdia Chauchat, which turns out to reflect a moment of adolescent homosexuality in his past. Indeed, the notion of sickness as a material manifestation of psychic forces is developed into an ironic commentary on Castorp's experiences, particularly through the series of lectures on "love as a factor in illness" given by one of the doctors at the sanatorium. What gives the work its problematic character, as well as its peculiar grandeur, is the process by which it grew between 1914 and 1924 from a story of comic 'deformation' (*Entbildung*) into a serious attempt to depict the growth to self-awareness (*Bildung*) of a representative young German (cf. Reed, 228–36).

The Swiss mountain provided a perfect terrain for imagined encounters. On it Hans Castorp meets figures who challenge and refine his sense of the person he is and of the national culture to which he belongs. The chief instrument of his developing self-awareness is the Italian writer Settembrini, a champion of Enlightenment rationalism, a natural pedagogue, a political activist and a sharp critic of the quietist self-absorption that he thinks of (echoing Nietzsche) as quintessentially German.[19] In short, Settembrini is a spokesman for the values of 'civilization' as Thomas Mann had sought to define them during the war years. It is Settembrini who warns Castorp of the dangers inherent in his abiding fascination with sickness, death, and the lure of the erotic, reinforcing those fixations by

[19] The use that Thomas Mann makes of "beer, tobacco and music" as emblems of Germanness in *Der Zauberberg*, together with his characterization of the world of German social convention as the "Flachland", carries strong echoes of the section in Nietzsche's *Götzendämmerung* entitled "Was den Deutschen abgeht": Friedrich Nietzsche, *Kritische Studienausgabe*, ed. G. Colli and M. Montinari (Munich: dtv, 1988), vol. vi, 103–10.

his very opposition up to a point, but also stimulating a spirit of critical inquiry and discovery (epitomized in his own watchword, "placet experiri"). In the second half of the novel, Settembrini is also provided with a worthy opponent, a man of comparable intellectual stature, through whom the more extreme implications of Thomas Mann's own wartime position are articulated; but it is perhaps through this figure, Naphta, that the reader is most likely to sense the effort and artifice by which Thomas Mann is trying to introduce a broad sense of European cultural crisis into his sanatorium storyline. Naphta is an extraordinary composite character, an East European Jew who has espoused Marxism and Catholicism in turn. His Jewish temperament is invoked as an ostensible explanation for the way he combines the impulses of a revolutionary intellect with the attitudes of a spiritual aristocrat, and his fervent commitment to the values of the counter-reformation is used to imbue his hostility towards modern commercialism with a passion for holy terror. Naphta is the character through whom Thomas Mann can distance himself from the severe anti-civilization views he had expressed during the war; but as a character he is also made to serve as the mouthpiece for various forms of anti-republicanism as they have meanwhile manifested themselves in the post-war world, including both ultra-reaction and revolutionary communism.[20]

This difficulty with the characterization of Naphta—the fact that his personality is constructed as a vehicle for amalgamated ideological impulses—is an illustration of what makes *Der Zauberberg* problematic as a depiction of the historical reality of the times. The sanatorium setting could accommodate a duel of ideas perfectly well, together with the wealth of cultural and historical allusion which provides the ammunition for it. It could also accommodate the positive education of Hans Castorp, not least by showing him responding with independence, as well as

[20] Anthony Grenville relates Naphta's views to the post-war phenomenon of National Bolshevism, with which Thomas Mann himself briefly flirted in a diary entry for Nov. 1918: " 'Linke Leute von rechts': Thomas Mann's Naphta and the Ideological Confluence of Radical Right and Radical Left in the Early Years of the Weimar Republic", *Deutsche Vierteljahrsschrift* 59 (1985), 651–75. On the reasons why the presentation of such a political confluence through a single character nevertheless remains problematic, see Claude David, "Naphta, des Teufels Anwalt", in Bludau et al., 94–106.

exasperation, to the proliferation of erudite reference with which the ideologues seek to undermine each other's arguments. Indeed, Castorp is shown finding his own way of rising above the "great confusion" of the debates between Settembrini and Naphta and experiencing, in his famous vision in the snow, the integrating power of love (in terms which echo St Paul's epistle to the Romans, chapter 6) as a principle which transcends intellectual antithesis. In all these ways, the novel could express the deeper resonances of Thomas Mann's conception of what it meant to be German, without unduly straining the sense of ostensible reality in the depiction of Hans Castorp's experiences. But it could reflect the political and social realities of the age only at one remove, as it were in the form of shadow play; and it is this limitation that creates further difficulties in the portion of the novel (the last quarter of the text) which comes after Castorp's vision in the snow.

Castorp stays on the mountain initially to await the return of Clawdia Chauchat, whom he has come to think of as the 'spirit of the place' (and whom the reader has come to recognize as the person onto whom he is projecting his inner needs). He stays ultimately to complete the symbolic references to the number seven which are developed in the text: he is to become a "Siebenschläfer", a figure who "sleeps" through a seven-year absence from the world of mundane society. He will depart from the sanatorium only in response to the call to arms of 1914, and very likely in order to go to his death on the battlefields of Flanders. The long final chapter, which tells of his experiences in the meantime, incorporates a critical reflection of the trends of the times, and of the 'representative' German mentality that Hans Castorp has come to embody. It is in this final chapter that we meet Mynheer Peeperkorn, the Dutch colonialist with whom Clawdia Chauchat returns to the mountain. He is a majestic figure, whose presence mysteriously defuses the confrontations between Settembrini and Naphta, taking the "spark" out of their debates; but he is simultaneously a pathetic figure, inarticulate, and doomed by a progressively disabling tropical disease. He is there to exercise charisma, to bring an enactment of charity and chaste reconciliation between Hans and Clawdia, but as a human figure he is also, in his turn, a parodistic representation of combined ideological impulses, those of vitalism and pietism.[21] It is in this final chapter, too, that the society of the sanatorium experiences its period of "great stupor" followed by the manifestation of a "great irritation" in which latent conflicts are discharged. There are squabbles among the Slav factions, a militant anti-Semite appears on the scene, and eventually Naphta and Settembrini provoke each other to a duel which ends as symbolically as any other aspect of their relationship, with the humanist firing into the air and the collectivist shooting himself in the head. It is in elements such as these that readers of the 1920s would have recognized allusions to the atmosphere of the pre-war years—but only to their atmosphere.

In these closing stages of the novel we also find reflections of the process of self-correction which Thomas Mann had personally undergone since the end of the war. Through the figure of Hans Castorp he now offers his readers an opportunity to participate in that process, which is in essence one of detachment from the thrall of Germany's Romantic heritage.[22] He tells us of Castorp's passion for music, and of his special fascination with the "Lindenbaum" song from Schubert's *Winterreise* cycle. He tells us how Castorp has developed a conscious awareness of the aesthetic principles entailed in that fascination, how he has come to recognize it (a direct echo of Romantic aesthetics here) as the expression of "a whole world of feeling and thought". When he goes on to tell us that the "world" in question is that of death, then that, too, is a fair interpretation of what is being intimated in Schubert's song. But even in a novel which is overwhelmingly characterized by narrative circumspection and tactful indirectness, what follows that moment in

[21] In all these senses, Thomas Mann had found a precise model for Mynheer Peeperkorn in the person of Gerhart Hauptmann. It was Hauptmann's sixtieth birthday which provided the occasion for Mann's speech "Von deutscher Republik" in 1922, in which he apostrophizes Hauptmann as the "king" of the Republic, as someone who provides an appropriate focus for popular respect in the political circumstances of the time (GW XI, 812; cf. also Reed, pp. 258–61).

[22] Reed (pp. 294–6) demonstrates the particular importance for Thomas Mann's post-war development of Ernst Troeltsch's pamphlet *Naturrecht und Humanität in der Weltpolitik* of 1923. In a short review of that pamphlet which he wrote for the *Frankfurter Zeitung* (GW XII, 627–9) Mann explicitly acknowledges that German Romanticism is a historical departure from the long European tradition of rationalism, and that he has himself lingered too long on the "magic mountain" of Romantic aestheticism.

the text is exceptionally circumspect. The song that Thomas Mann has identified as Castorp's favourite is one which would have been familiar to German readers as a charming icon of their national culture. Mann presents the points he now wishes to make about it as Hans Castorp's conclusions, and he does so in a manner which anticipates incredulity in the reader—"This was madness . . ."; "What was he talking about?" He broaches the subject in this surreptitious fashion because he wishes to show *by implication*, through the musings of Hans Castorp, that Settembrini had been right all along in his condemnation of Romantic aestheticism as "morbid", and because the point he is building up to, in the final paragraph of the section, is that the world-political role that "we" Germans have carved out for ourselves in the name of Romantic thought and culture deserves the description "earthly, all-too-earthly" that Nietzsche had slapped upon it in the 1870s (*GW* III, 903–7; cf. Reed, 268–71).

It is in this way that the narrative casts a pallor of doubt over the nationalist appropriation of Romanticism in the late nineteenth and early twentieth centuries. It is these associations that Thomas Mann is still working with when he concludes the work by sending Hans Castorp into battle with the "Lindenbaum" song (the siren-song of death) once more on his lips. It is through his deployment of this material that we can participate in the difficult process of emotional detachment from nationalist commitment which Thomas Mann was seeking to encourage—if, that is, we are able to read the novel with the eyes and the sensibilities of a 'Bildungsbürger' of the 1920s.

It would be facile to use the circumscribed nature of its manifest imagery as a basis for denying what *Der Zauberberg* contributes to the expressive range of the German novel. The world of the sanatorium, as the novel depicts it, is both a symbolic representation of the state of European culture and a space for critical reflection upon it. The technique of ironic allusion and cross-referencing reflects the way in which knowledge of the world must, of necessity, be intellectually constructed in the modern age. Indeed, the manner of composition comes as close as it is possible to get to a realization of the original Romantic project of "universal poetry". All these points (which are closely related, incidentally, to the general claims that Lukács made for the form of the novel) are brought out in the "Conversation on the Magic Mountain" which Erich Heller originally published in 1958 (Heller, 169–214). T. J. Reed argues—against a powerful legacy of misconstruction—that the allegorical character of *Der Zauberberg* is an effective, albeit indirect, medium for ironic depiction of the trends of the time around the First World War. More specifically, he shows how the ironic deployment of motifs has the effect of loosening intellectual connections from the rigidly antithetical positions of wartime polemics, and generally placing the material of German culture "in the perspective of humane purposes" (Reed, 248, 256). It may even be claimed that, in its very abstinence from direct depiction of mundane social experience, *Der Zauberberg* makes a breakthrough to the representation of reality as a perceptual "structure" which is "always more than immediate fact".[23] There are, nonetheless, limitations placed on each of these claims by the precise fictional framework of the novel: any wider social or political reality can only be refracted through the prism of the sanatorium setting, and the intellectual positions that are dismantled by the narrative are dominated by the specific perspectives of the author's personal past.

In their respective ways, then, both Thomas Mann's *Zauberberg* and Heinrich Mann's *Kaiserreich* trilogy had demonstrated the limitations of a personal storyline for the purposes of depicting what had been collectively experienced as the historical reality of the times. The limitations in question were partly a reflection of the intensely personal conflict between them at the time of the war, but they were also a consequence of the need to resort to symbolism in order to suggest ways in which the circumstances of a particular character are representative of a more general historical situation. When Hermann Broch attempted his depiction of the Wilhelmine era from the more detached perspective of the late 1920s and early 1930s, he took some quite deliberate steps to avoid those limitations.[24] In his

[23] See Ulrich Karthaus, "Thomas Mann: *Der Zauberberg*", in Lützeler (ed.) 1983, 95–109 (99).

[24] P. M. Lützeler examines the similarities of characterization and overall conception between Broch's *Schlafwandler* and Heinrich Mann's *Kaiserreich* trilogy in Koopmann and Schneider, 183–210; Hartmut Reinhardt discusses the relationship between *Die Schlafwandler* and *Der Zauberberg* in Kessler and Lützeler,

Schlafwandler trilogy he carefully determined in advance the intellectual scheme by which he wished to organize each phase of the action, and for each volume he devised a central character and a narrative style appropriate to the programmatic idea in question. Broch appears to have looked to Lukács for guidance, not only in his general understanding of the status of the novel in historical terms, but in aspects of characterization: the central figures of his trilogy show strong affinities with the three types of hero discussed in the typological section of *The Theory of the Novel* (Lützeler 1980). He displays an acute self-awareness about the role of subjectivity in interpreting the nature of the age, and about the need to "surmount" it, interpolating a series of discursive reflections into volume three, together with a first-person narrator as their ostensible author.[25] In a quite distinctive way the work also manifests its own aspiration to "totality"—which brings its own set of intellectual limitations with it.

All this should not be taken to mean that *Die Schlafwandler* is an entirely bloodless construction. It is a rich mixture of self-conscious composition, mythopoeic evocation, and discerning social observation. The first volume, *Pasenow oder die Romantik*, invites comparison with the novels of Fontane in its depiction of the social ambience of late nineteenth-century Prussia. It is set in 1888, the year of Wilhelm II's accession to the throne, and its central figure is a young army officer. The "Romanticism" with which Pasenow's name is linked in the title expresses itself in his relations with women, and in the almost sacral significance he attaches to his uniform. As a young aristocrat, his sexual initiation is provided by a call-girl (here, as in Thomas Mann's novel, it is a woman of Slav origin who is made to embody the lure of the erotic) to whom he is introduced at the

239–52. The strength of the similarity between Thomas Mann's perception of the post-war world and what Broch is attempting in his trilogy is apparent in Mann's 1923 speech in memory of Walter Rathenau (*GW* XI, 859) where he speaks both of a need for a sense of the absolute to overcome the "vice" of relativism that had characterized the bourgeois era, and of the danger of obscurantism that the thirst for an absolute can bring with it.

[25] The precise function of the first-person narrator Bertrand Müller within the overall composition of the trilogy has teased the brains of many a commentator. I have given my own interpretation of his role in terms of narrative technique, without claiming that this is a definitive explanation for his presence in the work (Midgley 1981).

officers' casino; the relationship endures for a while, but in Pasenow's perception of the world it becomes categorized as a dark and sinister aspect of his life, which must ultimately be suppressed. The woman he is to marry, on the other hand, a woman of his own class, is by the same token stylized into an object of veneration, an untouchable Snow White figure indeed. Readers who sense that Broch is here expressing characteristic male attitudes of his time may rest assured that he is very consciously doing so: Otto Weininger, whose writings have come to be thought of as epitomizing male sexual prejudices at the turn of the century, has been identified as a formative influence on Broch's thinking, in a broad philosophical sense as well as a sexual one (Ritzer, 55–68). Broch's depiction of Pasenow reveals its underlying ironic purpose only on the closing pages of the volume. First he takes the young man's self-consciousness to extreme lengths by having him spend his wedding night mounting watch over his bride—stretched out on her bed, but safely encased in his dress uniform. Secondly he rounds off by telling us that the couple did eventually have children, but that we now know enough to imagine the rest of the story for ourselves.

Like the second volume of Heinrich Mann's trilogy, *Esch oder die Anarchie* (set in 1903) focuses on the world of work in an industrial society. But what Broch is depicting here is the disorientation and deracination of a mobile workforce, rather than any experiences of the workplace as such. The story begins with Esch losing his job as an accounts clerk. He receives no help from any official organization of society, particularly not from the trade unionist he turns to, who is having to give strategic considerations precedence over the interests of an isolated individual. The sense in which Broch is here alluding to the reformist turn in Social Democratic policy of the time has been noted by Lützeler (1986a, 99). The "anarchy" that Esch experiences is not that of any particular political or philosophical movement, but a general sense that the world no longer "adds up", that the accounts no longer "balance". As he moves among the itinerant workforce of the Rhineland (labourers and entertainers) Esch seeks with cumulative desperation for the means to achieve restitution for the wrong he believes has been done to him; and Broch develops a fluid narrative style, a

sophisticated form of 'free indirect style' through which the
reader experiences, in certain passages, the erasure of any clear
boundary in Esch's experience between external reality and
internal fantasy. Although Broch certainly took notice of psy-
choanalytic theory, the imagery of "dream experience" he develops in the trilogy has more to do with Ernst Bloch's conception
of historical impulses which remain concealed from the conscious awareness of mankind in a particular epoch (cf. Lützeler
1973, 94f., 98–106).

The final volume, *Huguenau oder die Sachlichkeit*, depicts
the world of 1918 as one in which not only inherited political
structures are collapsing, but entire value systems with them.
Huguenau is presented as a contemporary type who has dis-
sociated himself from any form of moral restraint: he deserts
from the army as the armistice approaches, he devises a fraudu-
lent business arrangement as a means of extorting money and
property rights from others, and in the chaos of November
1918 he murders Esch and rapes Esch's wife. In the final chapter
he is described as living a life of opulence and respectability as
a typical south-west German businessman, still capable of
calling in the fruits of his unscrupulous contractual arrangements, but fully convinced that in his own terms he has always
acted rationally. Broch was himself an industrialist's son who
had turned his back on the commercial world in the mid-1920s
in search of philosophical enlightenment, and in choosing to use
the term "Sachlichkeit" in the title of his third volume he clearly
intended to suggest something about the general character of
the post-war world. But through the figure of Huguenau he also
wanted to intimate more than that. In this final volume he is
expressing a pessimistic view of the general development of
European culture since the Renaissance and the Reformation
(the two phenomena are fused, for the purposes of Broch's argument, into a single epochal moment). Broch's historical outlook
shows some superficial similarity with Spengler's account of the
"Decline of the West", sharing Spengler's interest, for example,
in the manifestation of the character of an age in features as disparate as its architecture, its philosophy, and its mathematics.
But Broch's chief interest is in the structures of knowledge which
have prevailed in the past, but have lost their authority or "plausibility" in the present; and he seeks to understand the histori-

cal development of the modern age as a process of "disintegration of values".

In *Die Schlafwandler*, in other words, Broch is depicting what have become the commonplaces of discussions about the nature of modernity—his theoretical excursions bear the traces of the thought of Max Weber and turn-of-the-century sociology, as well as neo-Kantian philosophy and the complex heritage of German Idealism (Vollhardt; Ritzer)—and he is interpreting them in wholly negative terms. His third volume speaks of the progressive rationalization of human activities; of the separation out of legal, commercial, and scientific thought from any integrating ethical system; of the privatization of religious belief; of the loss of an absolute reference point for moral judgement. Broch makes the "disintegration of values" palpable in the very composition of his third volume, breaking the narrative up into disparate strands, and he incorporates his theoretical analysis of historical processes as a series of essays, which culminates in an evocation of the possibility that human history might yet progress towards a recovery of integral meaning.

In terms of narrative composition, Broch was a highly self-conscious innovator. He wrote excitedly to his publisher in August 1931, as the final conception of his trilogy was coming clear in his mind, pointing to the works of James Joyce, André Gide, Robert Musil, Thomas Mann, and even Aldous Huxley, as indications that a new age had dawned, the age of the "polymathic" (*polyhistorisch*) novel (*KWA* 13/1, 151). If his own practice in *Die Schlafwandler* can be called avant-garde, however, it is only in the sense that he is trying to write prophetically, in anticipation of a future synthesis of philosophical awareness, conscious that he is living in an intellectual climate where the approach to knowledge has become predominantly analytical (cf. Lützeler 1983, 202 f.).[26] The nature of his prophecy becomes explicit in the final chapter of *Huguenau*, the "Epilogue", which provides both a conclusion to the essay series on the "disintegration of values" and an integration of

[26] Broch's letter to Daniel Brody of 5 Aug. 1931 states, "Sie kennen meine Theorie, daß der Roman und die neue Romanform die Aufgabe übernommen haben, jene Teile der Philosophie zu schlucken, die zwar metaphysischen Bedürfnissen entsprechen, dem derzeitigen Stande der Forschung aber gemäß, heute als 'unwissenschaftlich' oder, wie Wittgenstein sagt, als 'mystisch' zu gelten haben. Die Zeit des polyhistorischen Romans ist angebrochen." (*KWA* 13/1, 151)

the narrative material into the argument of those essays. The "Epilogue" is an elaborated profession of faith in the eventual reinstatement of an absolute system of values. It also encapsulates perfectly the circular nature of Broch's historical construction: the characters and events in the trilogy can serve as illustrations of underlying historical processes because it is presupposed that they are acting in obedience to those processes. Even when Huguenau gives his child a clip round the ear it is interpreted as an expression of his metaphysical, rather than his psychological condition (*KWA* 1, 709). The brutality and moral indifference that the trilogy depicts in the period around the First World War is explained as the behaviour of individuals who have become historically "value-free", and any "revolutionary" act is represented as the rationality of an oppositional "partial system" striving for totality in its own terms, in order that the contemporary world can be presented as the nadir of historical development which has to be passed through on the way to a "rebirth of values". The modern world as Broch understands it is not just a "world without God" (in Lukács's phrase), but a world in which abstract rationality is establishing itself as a hollowed-out negative image of God (*KWA* 1, 705 f.). This quasi-theological vision of history may have been productive in the sense that it created the framework within which a rich depiction of the modern world could be organized; but as an intellectual construction it can be defended only in the self-referential terms of its own deductive logic (Obermeier).[27] Broch's trilogy is perhaps the nearest literary equivalent to that determined pursuit of intellectual synthesis which Fritz Ringer (1969) describes as characteristic of the academic profession during the Weimar period.

In *Die Schlafwandler*, then, Broch was making an ambitious attempt to express an all-encompassing metaphysical expectation. It was an expectation which he was to abandon in the 1940s in favour of no less ambitious, but more down-to-earth efforts to influence the course of international politics (cf.

---

[27] For a full critique of Broch's philosophical arguments, see Menges. Vollhardt places Broch's arguments in the context of the philosophical trends of his time, without losing the sense of critical distance towards what those arguments are attempting.

Lützeler 1980, 57).[28] But by 1930, other developments in the German novel were making the metaphysical aspiration of *Die Schlafwandler* appear anachronistic. In their different ways, Döblin and Musil had set about depicting the characteristic conditions of the modern world, and the attempts of human individuals to live righteously within them, without resorting to the notion of a historical progression which might ultimately redeem that world from its uncertainties.[29]

By the time he came to publish *Berlin Alexanderplatz* in 1929, Alfred Döblin had long established himself as a prominent representative of the literary avant-garde, taking upon himself all the perils of ambiguity which bedevil the intellectual who campaigns for modernization before it is at all clear what the character of the new age is to be. The tensions in his outlook are plain to see, for example, in the essay "Der Geist des naturalistischen Zeitalters" (The spirit of the naturalistic age), which he published in 1924 (*Ästhetik*, 168–90). There Döblin is welcoming in a new age of materialism, but the language in which he describes it still carries the vestiges of an old spirituality. He argues that the theology of past ages is superseded, but he interprets the present in terms borrowed from the past, with trade and industry as the "*ecclesia militans*" of the new "naturalistic spirit" (and Soviet Russia, indeed, as its "messiah"). He asserts the priorities of a new culture of technology and physicality against the cerebral values of "humanist scholasticism", but he can define the cultural identity of the new age only in terms of the anthropocentricity it has lost (the Renaissance precept that man is the measure of all things is no longer applicable). He condemns the attitudes of cultural pessimism associated with

[28] Between 1936 and 1950 Broch was engaged in various efforts to secure international agreements on the need to guarantee human rights and human dignity: *KWA* 11, 195–396. For a critical assessment of Broch's political writings, see Hartmut Jäckel, "Hermann Broch and Politics", in S. D. Dowden (ed.), *Hermann Broch: Literature, Philosophy, Politics: The Yale Broch Symposium 1986* (Columbia, SC: Camden House, 1988), 93–106.

[29] Dagmar Barnouw, in her study of *Weimar Intellectuals and the Threat of Modernity* (1988), aptly distinguishes between the "homemade neo-idealism" of Broch (p. 245) and the "intelligent skepticism and muddled hope" of Döblin (p. 266), while Musil's "man without qualities" emerges from her analysis as a man "without redeeming ideas" (p. 120).

Spengler and Klages (that human cultures "degenerate" into civilizations, that the processes of modernization are depriving mankind of its "soul"); but when it comes to evoking the attitudes that are needed in their place he can offer only the vaguest of terminology, "social drive" and "collective being". In this essay Döblin was championing scientific and technological progress against the conservative instincts of German academic humanism, but in doing so he was also reaching out for a new totalizing sense of the position of the human spirit in the world (cf. Müller-Salget, 12–15).[30]

Even amid the turbulence of Weimar culture and politics, Döblin appears as an exceptionally restless and combative figure, eager for change and renewal, and provocatively resistant towards processes of consolidation. Part of the explanation for his actions has been sought in his personality and social origins (Kreutzer). He was a trained medical doctor and psychiatrist from an impoverished middle-class background, who had developed strong sympathies for the socially disadvantaged while also recognizing that his own position lay between the classes. Politically he was manifestly disappointed by the half-heartedness of the revolution of 1918, criticized the accommodation of the Social Democrats to inherited power structures in some acerbic essays of the early 1920s, and remained ferociously wary of party bureaucracies and the constraints of entrenched ideologies. His attitudes left him ultimately without any firm political allegiance (Alter; Müller-Salget, 249–59), but his cumulated experiences made him an acute observer of social and political behaviour. As a member of the Prussian Academy of the Arts (from 1928) he campaigned hard for literary writers to perform an active educational role in the interests of the political health of the Republic (Jens, 153–6). And in *Wissen und Verändern!* (Knowing and Transforming, 1931) he wrote a robust defence of the liberties of the individual citizen, which incorporated a historical account of factors that had militated against the develop-

---

[30] In some respects, Döblin may have been reflecting the thinking of the original Naturalist movement of the 1880s: it was the "spirit" of reality that Wilhelm Bölsche, for example, wanted to see captured in poetic writing in his early programmatic essay *Die naturwissenschaftlichen Grundlagen der Poesie* (Leipzig, 1887).

ment of a strong sense of individual political responsibility in Germany.

In general intellectual terms, too, Döblin is someone who refuses to be pinned down. He was the conscious heir both to the heritage of scientific specialization that had developed in the nineteenth century, and to a philosophical tradition which sought to transcend such compartmentalization of knowledge. Romantic 'nature philosophy', which aimed to overcome the opposition between spirit and matter and articulate a sense of the ultimate oneness of being, was an important influence on Döblin's literary writings, together with impulses from oriental religions (Mayer 1972, 32–50). The personal, the political, and the philosophical ambivalences all play their part in determining the character of Döblin's works. The result may be frustrating for any reader who approaches them in the expectation of being able to identify a clear authorial 'position'. But that is precisely the point: to read Döblin's novels is to encounter in-built resistances to the very pretension of the human intellect to interpret the world in terms of its own rational schemes.

Such resistance is already explicit in the programmatic statements Döblin was making before the First World War. As someone closely associated with the avant-garde periodical *Der Sturm* in Berlin, Döblin was among the first German writers to respond to the works of the Italian Futurists. He admired the vibrant dynamism and the representation of simultaneity in their paintings, but professed himself disappointed by Marinetti's novel *Mafarka le futuriste* when he read it in 1913, finding it characterized by tired metaphors and an outmoded aestheticism (*Ästhetik*, 113–19). Döblin criticized the "monomania" of Marinetti's prophetic posturing, and in his own literary manifesto, his "Berlin Programme" which was published in *Der Sturm* the following year, he issued a general call for the breaking of the "hegemony of the author". He was campaigning against the prevalence of rationalizing psychology in the German literature of that time. In its place, he recommended that his fellow authors adopt the discipline of his own professional speciality, clinical psychiatry: the literary text, like a set of case notes, should attempt to set aside preconceptions and allow the empirical world to speak as directly as possible. "I am not I," he wrote, "but the street, the lamps, this or that event, nothing more" (*Ästhetik*, 122).

A very similar impetus is apparent in Döblin's controversy with a fellow novelist, Otto Flake, in 1919. Flake had published a novel—*Stadt des Hirns* (City of the Mind)—which was predominantly written in the mode of psychological disquisition, and had furnished it with a foreword in which he claimed to be redeeming the novel by "exploding" it, with the intention of putting the reader into a "philosophical state" (Kaes, 376 f.). Döblin, in response, quoted from Marinetti in order to show that Flake's avant-garde aspirations were by now old hat; argued (with reference to the novels of Goethe) that the novel had been such a disparate form for so long that there was precious little left to "explode"; and again challenged the principle of a sovereign authorial intellect which was implicit in Flake's "philosophical" purpose (cf. Scheunemann, 118–24). He did not exclude the possibility that a work of art might express philosophical ideas, but he was quite insistent that its primary purpose was to communicate in ways which were "immediate to the senses (*anschaulich*) and affective": epics were there to serve a quite different function from ethics (*Ästhetik*, 137–51).[31]

Long before Brecht or Piscator had adopted the notion of an 'epic theatre' as the means of transcending the limitations of conventional drama, Döblin was invoking the concept of epic as a radical alternative to the conventions of the modern novel. "Epic" was his watchword in a campaign against the dominance of subjectivism which can be traced throughout his writing career. Around 1912 he is to be found, alongside the Expressionist prose-writer Carl Einstein, working at the depersonalization of narrative (Scheunemann, 79–94); and in a letter of 1947 he is still repudiating a tradition of subjectivism in the

---

[31] Manfred Durzak explores the circumstances of the controversy between Döblin and Flake, and makes a case for treating Flake's *Stadt des Hirns* seriously as a precursor to the kind of synthesis of intellectuality and sensuous depiction that we find in Broch and Musil. In the context of that purpose he overstates Döblin's argument, however, claiming that he is seeking to exclude intellectual cognition from the novel (Durzak 1970*b*, 301), which is not the case. In a later conference paper (Kessler and Lützeler, 209–20) Durzak acknowledges that Döblin has turned out to be the more significant influence on German novelists since 1945, even if Broch has received more attention from academics.

novel that runs from Goethe to Thomas Mann because it is contrary to his own conception of epic writing (Keller, 233). Even where he does acknowledge the significance of the individuality of the author (in his Berlin University lecture of 1928), he describes it as one of the "facts" amongst others that the epic work is empowered to encompass. In the same context he once more endorses his commitment to letting that "great story-teller (*Epiker*) nature" speak through the work (*Ästhetik*, 224–8). In 1927 Döblin went so far as to try his hand at monumental verse epic in *Manas*, a work which he thought of as treating the same themes as *Berlin Alexanderplatz*, but which is of intrinsic interest only as an expression of elemental human situations in the imagery of Hindu myth—although it was greeted with excited interest by Robert Musil at the time as an example of how the ancient need to "convert life into song" might perhaps be satisfied even in the twentieth century.[32] The more characteristic means by which Döblin sought to achieve his aim of "epic" depiction is montage. He had developed it in relatively simple ways in his early writings, but it was in *Berlin Alexanderplatz* that he applied it to greatest effect.

Berlin Alexanderplatz undoubtedly owes a large part of its reputation as a major work of fiction to the vividness with which it expresses the experience of living in a modern city. On the opening pages the sights, the sounds, and the general feel of the Berlin streets are evoked as the direct sensory encounters of the central character, Franz Biberkopf, who has just emerged, numbed and bewildered, from the secure routine of a spell in prison. There it is the immediacy of Biberkopf's experiences that is conveyed through the abrupt juxtaposition of phrases— jostling crowds, the cries of newsvendors and tram conductors, reflections in shop windows. But elsewhere the technique of montage can create a sense of the ramifications as well as the intensity of urban living. At the start of Book 2, where Biberkopf begins to face up to life in the city, Döblin allows the institutions of modern society to present themselves in a form familiar from directories and roadside signs, as pictograms; he adds snippets from public notices, a tram route, and a weather

---

[32] The appeal of *Manas* to Musil lay in the potential of rhythm, assonance, and repetition to achieve an effect of "Rausch" and a sense of elemental experience even in an age of intellectuality: *GW* II, 1674–80.

forecast; and he builds a picture of the inner suburb around the Rosenthaler Platz as if it had an organic identity of its own, with the lives of human individuals passing ephemerally through it. In his bold application of the montage principle, Döblin was evidently stimulated by the appearance in German translation of James Joyce's *Ulysses* and John Dos Passos's *Manhattan Transfer* (Mitchell; Duytschaever), as well as by what he had seen Piscator doing in his theatrical productions and by the practice of collage and photomontage developed by Dada artists since 1918. But as I have argued elsewhere (Midgley 1993), Döblin was using the technique of montage to suit his own purposes, and the manner in which he applied it allowed him an extraordinary flexibility in his deployment of modes of discourse. Even those portions of the text which read like statements of authorial purpose have to be recognized as elements in the compositional montage. As Axel Eggebrecht put it when he reviewed *Berlin Alexanderplatz* in 1929, Döblin was using expressive styles in the same way that other people use tram routes: he was riding each one just as far as he needed to before switching to another (*LW* 5, 45, 6).

One obvious advantage of the flexibility that Döblin achieves in this way is that it provides a ready means of placing the individual human destiny in a broader perspective. References to unemployment statistics and cuts in pensions and benefits accompany Biberkopf's breach with his drinking companions, just as an advertisement for hormone therapy and a snatch of lyric from a trivial operetta provide an ironic commentary on his experience of sexual impotence. When Biberkopf retreats from society in the face of deceit and humiliation, the narrative describes the character of the general area in which he has gone to ground, rather than the particular house where he is lodging; and when his hapless involvement with a gang of criminals leads to him being pushed violently from the getaway car, the text omits any immediate discussion of his injuries and evokes instead a new dawn, a new beginning, and the arrival in Berlin of a show-biz celebrity. There is a deliberate policy of relativization at work in the text which extends far beyond the contemporary social context of the action. The self-confidence and assertiveness with which Biberkopf confronts the city find echoes in references at various points of the text to 'conquerors' down the ages, from Hannibal and Caesar to the modern fraudster and the boxing champion. And when he finally succumbs to the series of hard blows that life deals him and undergoes a process of moral renewal, then that process is depicted as a descent through the various realms of earthly life, followed by regeneration, as it were, from biological first principles.

The montage of texts, in other words, serves a very different function in *Berlin Alexanderplatz* than the piecemeal documentation of contemporary reality that we find in the fashionable reportage of the 1920s. Döblin places his account of the personal experiences of Franz Biberkopf in a relationship of tension with a variety of traditional perspectives on human existence, some historical, some scientific, some religious. The struggle for the 'new' Biberkopf is represented allegorically as a battle between Death as the bringer of renewal and the Whore of Babylon as the preserver of old iniquity. The blows which bring the 'old' Biberkopf down are foreshadowed in a long description of the slaughter of animals in Berlin's central abattoir, and the sense of an analogy to Biberkopf's fate is emphasized by giving that description a heading taken from Ecclesiastes 3: 19, "Denn es geht dem Menschen wie dem Vieh". The implication is clear from the full text of that verse in the King James Bible, even if the emphasis of the English rendering is superficially different: "For that which befalleth the sons of men befalleth beasts; even one thing befalleth them: as the one dieth, so dieth the other; yea, they have all one breath; so that a man hath no preeminence above a beast: for all is vanity." As academic critics have long recognized, Döblin was incorporating seemingly disparate material into the work in order to convey a sense of the "resonance" (his term) between our experiences as individual human beings and the natural processes of the world at large.

The most systematic study yet undertaken of the resonances in *Berlin Alexanderplatz* is that of Otto Keller. Keller shows how Döblin's textual montage relates human behaviour to a variety of sets of opposing principles. Interpolated within the abattoir section, for instance, we find an evocation of the sufferings of Job; but this is not the biblical Job who is ultimately blessed for his endurance and his undiminished faith, this is a Job who bitterly reproaches God for his afflictions and is healed only when he abandons the presumption of judging the ways of God before the tribune of human reason. Döblin's story of Job, in other words, is a parable of self-assertion and of the salvation that is held out for those who show themselves able to surrender their self-importance. Döblin also reinterprets the story of Isaac, presenting him as someone who knowingly embraces the principle of self-sacrifice and thus overcomes the fear of death (Keller, 155–7, 173). Similarly, what is fundamental to the changes of attitude exhibited by Biberkopf at the end of his story is a relinquishment of the urge to assert himself as an immutable personality and an acceptance, not of passivity, but of the need to "let things come on" (*Berlin Alexanderplatz*, 493). The text is showing earthly existence to be organized in relation to polar possibilities, of which the most obvious are conquest and sacrifice, chastisement and healing, death and birth, decay and regeneration. Even the one actual description of the Alexanderplatz in the work, at the start of Book 5, is as a site of demolition and redevelopment—which is precisely what the Alexanderplatz was in 1928–9.

Beyond all this, however, Keller also shows us how Döblin has created a sense of human life as a dynamic play of forces between those polarities. The significance of individual motifs in the work is not fixed, but develops as its sense of context unfolds. At the point in Book 5 where Biberkopf's insistence that he is "someone you can depend on" is going to involve him, disastrously, with the Pums gang, Döblin interpolates a passage from Jeremiah, chapter 17, which tells us how he that trusteth in man shall be cursed, whereas he that trusteth in the Lord shall be like a tree spreading its roots beside a river. The biblical text would appear merely as a moralizing comment if it were not followed in its turn by a description of eery black waters in the depths of a forest, where snails lurk and plants decompose (*Berlin Alexanderplatz*, 215 f.). That passage in its turn might simply seem to be evoking the sinister obverse of the biblical text if it did not also carry associations with the thematic complex of decay and renewal which is developed elsewhere in the work (cf. Keller, 160–2). Motifs which are more specifically associated with the psychology of Franz Biberkopf similarly change their complexion according to circumstances. That patriotic hymn of 1840, "Die Wacht am Rhein" (Watch on the Rhine), which Biberkopf is given to singing in moments of panic and anxiety, is also what he chooses to sing in celebration of the reassertion of his manhood, and on the closing pages of the novel the wording of the same song can easily be modified into an expression of his new-found vigilance as a citizen. Other echoes of the military songs of his wartime past are used as intimations of male companionship at some points and as signals of bristling male rivalry at others. The motif of "paradise", first introduced as an expression of Biberkopf's naive dream of harmony in sexual union, can turn out to carry overtones of politically repressive "order"; and the presence of a serpent in paradise can just as easily be linked to Biberkopf's self-image as a "cobra" as to his perception of evil in others (Keller, 149 f.; Midgley 1993, 103 f.). Human behaviour is being presented to us here, not as the unfolding of any innate purpose or scheme of identity, but as the expression of complex and interactive systems of relation.

Among contemporary reviewers of *Berlin Alexanderplatz*, Walter Benjamin (*GS* III, 230–6) showed a deeper appreciation of Döblin's purposes than most; but even his verdict on the work was constrained by the historical perspectives that were dominant at the time. Benjamin expressed the difference between Döblin's "epic" technique and the customary characteristics of the novel in an eloquent metaphor, comparing the writer of epic to someone who lies on the seashore and garners what the ocean yields up, whereas the novelist takes us on a journey across it. He compared Döblin's montage of textual fragments to the evocative function of formulaic verses in ancient epic. He also recognized that Döblin was depicting the characteristic vocal assertiveness (*Schnauze*) of Berlin in order to show how it needed to be "cured". But in his closing description of *Berlin Alexanderplatz* as the "last, vertiginous, extreme extension of the old bourgeois Bildungsroman" Benjamin reveals his own preconceptions: this is his way of saying that the self-awareness Biberkopf is said to attain at the end of the work is merely that of "bourgeois consciousness", and that the work as a whole therefore merely extends the representative form of an age that is about to be transcended by a new kind of popular consciousness. For a more recent generation, grown sceptical

towards the political route to cultural transformation and ha-
bituated in the notion that all sense of social reality is linguistically constructed, the true measure of Döblin's achievement is
not to be found in the way the Biberkopf story ends—which
Döblin himself acknowledged to be arbitrary[33]—but in the very
fabric of the text. It is in the interaction between types of
discourse, each of which is in some sense recognizably "pre-
fabricated", that Döblin creates a new means of representing
the sense of 'reality' as it needs to be understood in the age of
the modern city (Scherpe 1988*b*).

The potential for critical awareness that such textual interaction carries is apparent, for example, in the evocation of the act
of manslaughter which had put Biberkopf in prison in the first
place (*Berlin Alexanderplatz*, 103 ff.). That incident is recounted
in the sort of dispassionate language (though not entirely free
from sexual innuendo) that we might expect of a police officer
or pathologist. Juxtaposed upon it we find a disquisition on
Newton's laws of mechanics, complete with mathematical equa-
tions, which parodies the modern-day approach to understanding the cause of death. On the other hand, the section has begun
with a burlesque play on mythical systems of understanding in
which the case of the former cement worker Franz Biberkopf is
contrasted with that of the ancient matricide Orestes, with the
world of ancient Greece subjected to ironic interjections in the
Berlin vernacular: here is Orestes cowering at the altar [try
finding a church that's open at night], cursed by the gods [as if
we can know that], having avenged his father by murdering his
mother [the one with the unpronounceable name], and so on.
Taken as a whole, the passage contrives an elaborate repudiation of both the conventions of tragedy and the principles of
physics as self-sufficient systems for understanding the human
act in question (Midgley 1993, 104–6). Through its incorporation of contrasting signals, in other words, the montage technique provides stimuli to reflection, not only upon the substance
of what the text is depicting, but upon the way our perceptions
of that substance are conceptually organized. It is in this sense
that Döblin's *Berlin Alexanderplatz* and Musil's *Der Mann ohne*

[33] See Döblin's letter to Julius Petersen of 18 Sept. 1931, which is reprinted in
Matthias Prangel (ed.), *Materialien zu Alfred Döblin's 'Berlin Alexanderplatz'*
(Frankfurt: Suhrkamp, 1975), 41–2.

Eigenschaften (The Man without Qualities), despite all their manifest differences as texts, show a degree of common purpose.

Like Döblin, Musil had a professional scientific background: he trained as an engineer between 1898 and 1903, in Brno and Stuttgart, did original work in experimental psychology, and took a strong interest in the latest thinking about the interpretation of the physical world. He also took an early interest in Romantic thought as an attempt to transcend the constraints of narrowly rationalist conceptions of the mind and its relation to the world of experience. Musil's early literary writings can be seen as contributions to the radical questioning of traditional subjectivism during the decade before the First World War; but instead of Döblin's aggressive challenge to the "hegemony of the author", we find Musil continuing to treat narrative literature as the natural medium for expressing personal feeling and insight, concentrating intensively on developing its potential to convey the fine texture of mental activity. Both his *Törleß* novel of 1906 and the extraordinarily dense texts of the *Vereinigungen* (Unions) of 1911 exhibit a passion for precision in the understanding of the intimate functioning of thoughts and feelings, as well as an imaginative use of analogy in the expression of psychic processes.[34]

It is the particular nature of Musil's scientific training that is of interest for the purposes of our present discussion. For his doctoral dissertation (which he submitted in Berlin in 1908) he wrote a critique of the Viennese philosopher Ernst Mach, who had achieved notoriety in the 1880s by demonstrating the artificiality of conventional distinctions between the observing subject and the material world, and by arguing that the reality we know is constituted in our sensations. Mach's work was important in its day because it helped to forge connections between the disciplines of physics and psychology which had not previously existed. Musil for his part firmly endorsed Mach's aim of eliminating metaphysical assumptions from the

[34] Andrew Webber, *Sexuality and the Sense of Self in the Works of Georg Trakl and Robert Musil* (London: Institute of Germanic Studies, 1990) has interpreted these texts in relation to both psychological thinking in Musil's day and to the post-Lacanian deployment of psycho-analytical thinking in textual criticism. For a good general account of Musil's literary practice in these pre-war works, see Dorrit Cohn, *Transparent Minds* (Princeton: Princeton University Press, 1978).

language of scientific inquiry. But in his dissertation Musil took issue with Mach's more polemical argument that the regularities established by mathematical interpretations of the physical world existed only as constructions of the human mind, showing by quotations from various of Mach's publications that he was himself obliged to assume that such regularities did reside in the facts themselves. Musil presents himself here, in other words, as someone who is fully convinced of the legitimacy of scientific methods for interpreting the natural world, but who is also acutely aware of the nature of the assumptions upon which scientific investigation must rest, however hard scientists try to eliminate presuppositions from their arguments. David Luft gives a very clear account of the intellectual background to Musil's early development, and summarizes it by saying that the education Musil completed in 1908 was "a virtual reconstruction of the nineteenth-century evolution of positivism in philosophy, physics and psychology" (Luft, 79). That education left Musil with a strong sense of the methodology needed to interpret a world conceived in terms of the functional interdependence of variable factors (which included the attitudes and behaviour of the person doing the interpreting). It was this highly developed sense of methodology that Musil brought to the interpretation of social and historical reality in the 1920s.

In the circumstances of 1918–19, Musil was a passionate advocate of the incorporation of German-speaking Austria into the German Reich. That is not in itself remarkable; "Anschluß" was a declared aim of most Austrian political parties, other than those on the conservative right, until it was prohibited under the terms of the Treaty of Saint-Germain in June 1919.[35] What is worth noting about Musil's public statements on the subject are the grounds on which he argues his case. He dismisses the notion of a specific Austrian culture as a nostalgic illusion which the non-German inhabitants of the old Hapsburg Empire had never shared; he wants to see what is left of Austria participating in the development of scientific, intellectual, and cultural activity at the highest level; and he argues that it will not be able to do so unless it acquires the level of economic activity and

[35] See F. L. Carsten, *The First Austrian Republic 1918–1938* (Aldershot: Gower, 1986), 5–8, 58–63.

bureaucratic efficiency which only the "Anschluß" with Germany can provide (*GW* II, 1030–42). Both the outbreak of the war in 1914 and the manner in which peace terms were concluded in 1919 came as severe blows to Musil's hopes for scientific and intellectual progress, and in essays of the early 1920s he argued for the continuing need to work around, rather than within the apparatus of the nation-state in order to achieve historical advances for humanity at large (Midgley 1994). But equally, he recognized that the manifestation of fervent nationalism in 1914, as well as the supranational idealism of 1918, was a feature of historical reality which needed to be acknowledged as such (*GW* II, 1059–62). The precepts that he wished to see applied to the investigation of such human realities were those of the same rigorous empiricism which he had learned to apply to the interpretation of the natural world.

Discussions of Musil as a writer on political issues have tended to be overshadowed by the kind of Marxist-orientated criticism which was content to pigeon-hole him as a liberal and a positivist (Böhme 1974). This fails to do justice to the acuteness of the critical awareness he shows in his political essays of the early 1920s. It is true that he accepts capitalism as the strongest and most flexible form of social organization available, but he also describes it as nothing more than a variety of "ordered egoism" (*GW* II, 1387). He does speak of the businessman and the career politician as positive instances of people who base their judgements upon factual evidence, but he also notes that they tend to speculate upon humanity's worst characteristics because these are the most reliable (*GW* II, 1085 f.). He rejected the Communist movement as a new kind of exclusive "church" (*GW* II, 1355),[36] but he also drew some important critical impulses from Austro-Marxist writings of the time (Strutz 1980). Musil was a severe critic of contemporary political attitudes on both left and right wherever he found the tendency to make ill-founded totalizing assumptions (which he saw as related to the German tradition of philosophical idealism). When he attacked Lagarde's notion of an organic national

---

[36] At the Kriegspressequartier in Vienna, where Musil ended the war, two of his subordinate officers were Franz Werfel and Egon Erwin Kisch. He recorded their insurrectionary activities of Nov. 1918 in his diary with detached amusement (cf. Corino, 262 f.).

identity (*Volkheit*), it was in order to argue that expressions of popular will were both heterogeneous in nature and influenced by the nature of the political apparatus through which they were articulated; the latter, he noted, stood in need of proper investigation (*GW* II, 1062 f.). When he repudiated anti-Semitism, it was in order to insist that the character of racial groups was determined by the individuals of which they were composed, rather than the other way around (*GW* II, 1065). When he published his trenchant critique of Spengler in 1921, it was in order to distinguish between any positive potential there might be in a "biological" perspective on the development of historical cultures on the one hand, and the development of "methods of thinking" in response to diverse historical stimuli on the other. Against Spengler's integrative notion of the "soul" of a human culture, Musil was emphasizing the role of material and contingent factors in determining cultural development (*GW* II, 1042–59). The very notion of an 'epoch' with its own distinctive character was something he regarded with intense suspicion, because he wished to stress the sense in which our knowledge of any historical period, including our own, has to be pieced together from fragmentary evidence (*GW* II, 1079, 1366).

In brief, the Musil of the early 1920s was someone who was working hard at the dissolution of false dichotomies in the contemporary discussion of political life, at the conversion of dualistic thinking into notions of gradation and transition (*Übergänge*: *GW* II, 1088). Among German literary authors of his time he stands out as someone who is prepared to accept the conditions of modernity, its rationalization, abstraction, and specialization (cf. Barnouw 1988). He is able to do so, not least, because he has recognized that diversification (*Vielspältigkeit*: *GW* II, 1361) is essential to the future development of society and culture. His contributions to political debate in the aftermath of the First World War are distinguished both by his sensitivity towards the processual nature of political negotiation in a democratic society, and by his explicit recognition that such "truths" as are to be had in the domain of human affairs are inescapably partial and provisional in nature (Vogt 1986; Midgley 1994). And even if Musil held himself somewhat aloof from public discussions of politics after 1923, those insights remain apparent as guiding principles throughout the text of *Der Mann ohne Eigenschaften*, on which he worked from about 1920 until his death in 1942.

Musil hit upon two ingenious devices which provide the fictional framework for his novel. The first is not unrelated to a traditional feature of the picaresque novel: he imagines a young Viennese intellectual—who is known to the reader only as Ulrich, and who shares a number of characteristics with the author himself—deciding to take a one-year holiday from life during the twelve months preceding the outbreak of the First World War. Ulrich, and through him the text, is thus provided with the space in which to experiment with personal relationships and to speculate upon the appropriate conception of morality for a modern, secularized age. The second device provides the novel with its elements of social comedy. It is based on the observation that Wilhelm II was due to celebrate his thirtieth anniversary as German Emperor in 1918, but that the Austrian Emperor Franz Joseph, had he lived, would have completed seventy years on the throne in the same year. Musil imagines a commission drawn from among the illustrious of Austrian society for the purpose of deliberating on the appropriate manner in which to mark the imperial jubilee. In view of the fraternal rivalry with Prussia which has provided the enterprise with a special impetus, it is generally referred to as the "Parallelaktion". As a fictional device it enables Musil to give free expression to the yearnings and expectations of central European society in the early twentieth century, while allowing the ironies of historical hindsight to speak for themselves.

Musil's name for the Austro-Hungarian Empire, "Kakanien" (derived from the fact that under the dual monarchy all institutions of the state were characterized as either "kaiserlich-königlich" (k.-k.) or "kaiserlich und königlich" (k.u.k.)), has established itself as a stock item of German vocabulary. As "Kakanien" is described in the novel (*GW* I, 32–5), it is a lost land in which the scope for human diversity was maintained within a regime of tact and moderation; where ethnic conflicts were absorbed and personal antipathies regulated by ceremony; where government was clerical by name but liberal by nature, and where parliamentary rule alternated with imperial decrees. It was a structure of political authority which allowed considerable latitude for individual creativity, which—as the laconic last sentence of the chapter puts it—is probably why it did not survive. Both irony and affection make themselves felt in that description. Musil's account of the pre-war world has a sufficiently firm basis in social observation for it to register the impulses (especially the nationalism and the militarism) which are going to precipitate the catastrophe of 1914; but his fictional framework also gives him opportunities to cast ironic sidelights on the post-war world in which he is writing and publishing. He can provide an unorthodox perspective on the modern world of ideas by having an Austrian general conduct a survey of it, and he can provide an anticipatory characterization of the cultural changes of the 1920s by having a Prussian industrialist speculate about them (*GW* I, 371f., 407f.). And in the racial views expressed by a young pre-war nationalist it is possible to recognize echoes of the post-war writings of Spengler and Klages (G. Müller, 21–6).[37] The picture Musil was painting of old Austria was also a self-conscious model of the twentieth-century world at large (*GW* I, 1905), and the text he was constructing was a self-critical exercise in interpreting that world.

The play of ironies out of which *Der Mann ohne Eigenschaften* is composed was described very clearly by Wolfdietrich Rasch in 1963, and its constituent elements have been explored in a variety of specialist studies subsequently.[38] The figure of Ulrich is the vehicle for serious investigation of the potentialities of the modern world, but he is also shown to be participating in the dilemmas of the actual historical world as the novel depicts them. Rasch (1967, 84f.) recognizes in Ulrich something of the personality type of the "Nörgler", as it had existed in pre-war Austria. It is a type also immortalized in Karl Kraus's *Die letzten Tage der Menschheit* (The Last Days of Mankind), the socially detached intellectual who is unable to apply his highly developed critical faculties in a constructive manner because his

---

[37] When interviewed about his plans for the novel in 1926, Musil stated explicitly, "Ich mache mich darin über alle Abendlandsuntergänge und ihre Propheten lustig." (*LW* 2, 18, 1)

[38] Christian Rogowski, *Distinguished Outsider: Robert Musil and his Critics* (Columbia, SC: Camden House, 1994) provides a judicious selective review of the critical literature on Musil for the English-speaking reader.

responses to the world as he finds it are overwhelmingly negative. It is his sense of his own lack of a motivating purpose that prompts Ulrich to explore the possible forms of sustainable moral orientation (his "utopias") in the course of the work, a project which will allow him to experience the implications of the absence of any ultimate foundation for morality. Among the characters with whom he associates, meanwhile, we see the same quest, and the same sense of lack, generating a willingness to grasp at the most illusory of notions if they seem to provide a foundation for their existence. Ulrich's cousin, the society lady whom he nicknames Diotima after the wise woman in Plato's *Symposium*, considers herself to be on "firm ground" when conversation turns to the idea of "boundless feeling" (*GW* I, 575). It is in his portrayal of Diotima's liaison with the Prussian industrialist Arnheim that Musil finds his richest opportunities to satirize the "hunger for wholeness" (in Peter Gay's term) as a prevalent feature of the German culture of the time—Arnheim being based on Walter Rathenau, whose writings Musil had criticized for their conceptual vagueness before the First World War (Barnouw 1985). But the flight out of social constraint into erotic adventure, which is an anguished possibility for Diotima, will also form a part of the experiments in living which Ulrich pursues with his "forgotten" sister in the unfinished second half of the novel. And while Ulrich's experiments are aimed at achieving a heightened sensitivity towards the interplay of psychic and sensual impulses of which human experience is composed, those same impulses are shown to manifest themselves in distorted or ossified forms in the impulsive fixations of his childhood friend Clarisse, and in the abiding obsessions of the sex murderer Moosbrugger.[39]

Not only the themes of *Der Mann ohne Eigenschaften*, but its compositional techniques, too, are placed in a relationship of ironic tension. The text works with traditional narrative techniques, but it does so in the awareness that narration in itself has come to be recognized as an inadequate means of

---

[39] Cf. Hassler-Rütti (p. 101): "Die Wirklichkeit befindet sich in permanent lebendiger Produktion und Konstruktion und resultiert aus dem dialektischen Prozeß intrapersonaler Motivation und äußerer Zufälligkeit. Gemessen daran beruht das Falsche, Wahnhafte im Bestreben, sie dauerhaft fixieren zu wollen."

expressing reality (Rasch 1967, 78–80).[40] Early chapters of the work make much of the fact that human personality has become a function of diverse impersonal factors, and that the individual human being has ceased to be a plausible measure of significance in the world of the twentieth century (*GW* I, 34, 150); but the coherence afforded by narrative sequence nevertheless remains a means of organizing awareness which Ulrich can acknowledge to be a desirable possibility (*GW* I, 649 f.). By comparison with most novels, *Der Mann ohne Eigenschaften* appears overwhelmingly characterized by discursive reflection; but each reflexive sequence is embedded in the exposition of a particular human situation.[41] Musil's approach to the presentation of the general human situation of Central Europe on the eve of the First World War is "essayistic" in a sense that is made explicit within the novel (as one of Ulrich's "utopias"): the term expresses the sense that the most appropriate means of evaluating a world which consists of a potentially infinite system of connections is in the manner of an essay, by examining the object from a variety of sides without claiming to be able to grasp it in its entirety (*GW* I, 250 f.). In that connection, the only sense of a 'whole' that is expressly acknowledged in the text is that of the constellation of functional relations in which the value or appropriateness of a particular act or property is to be assessed.[42] The inherent indeterminacy of such an "essayistic" manner of writing runs counter to any notion of a work of literature as a 'complete' expression of a world-view; and yet the essayistic explorations are contained within a text which, by virtue of its fictional framework, carries the implication that it is aspiring to become a coherent representation of a historical

---

[40] In one of his most explicit discussions of his authorial intentions, an excerpt from a letter of 1931, Musil expresses his sense of having compromised between the impulse to organize the narrative around the way the problems arise in Ulrich's mind, independently of temporal sequence, and an underlying conservatism in questions of style: *Briefe*, 496–9.

[41] The intention of developing the depiction of "lebendige Szenen", as well as an "ironische Grundhaltung", as antidotes to the dominance of "das Essayistische" was also explicit in the interview Musil gave in 1926: *LW* 2, 18, 1.

[42] In the words of Ulrich's reflection, "Der Wert einer Handlung oder einer Eigenschaft, ja sogar deren Wesen und Natur erschienen ihm abhängig von den Umständen, die sie umgaben, von den Zielen, denen sie dienten, mit einem Wort, von dem bald so, bald anders beschaffenen Ganzen, dem sie angehörten." (*GW* I, 250 f.)

situation, even if in practice it was never to be finished. The principle of the 'essay' challenges the traditional notion of a 'work', but it does so in a manner which allows the two possible ways of organizing perception to coexist in a dynamic relationship within Musil's text (Moser).

Indeed, the term "essayism" conveys only a narrowly stereotypical impression of Musil's manner of composition in *Der Mann ohne Eigenschaften*. Musil himself described the technique he was striving for as "constructive irony"; and by this he meant more than merely the converse of 'destructive' irony, he meant a practice of allusive formulation which 'constructed' a sense of the affinities as well as the differences between human beings. As he illustrated his point, it might mean depicting a priest in terms which also applied in certain respects to a bolshevik, or describing a fool in a way which also reflected something of the author (*GW* I, 1939). The effects of that strategy can be traced throughout the text in the form of an elaborate network of "intratextual relativizations" (Honnef-Becker). Musil deploys the traditional techniques of novel-writing in flexible ways which allow the narrative to slip in and out of the perspective of a particular character, or indeed in and out of the various perspectives in which an issue might present itself to that character's mind. Arnheim, reflecting on the relationship between rationality and intuition, is confronted with his subconscious awareness of his own father's business acumen as a quasi-mythical force (*GW* I, 545 f.); Ulrich is made to notice on a number of occasions how his own ideas take on a different complexion when they reappear in the thought sequences of others. It is a narrative technique which makes delicate play of the fact that a character's 'point of view' is itself composed of variables, a method of representing social reality which draws attention to the very procedures of narrative representation (Honnef-Becker, 51).

Like Döblin, then, Musil creates a new kind of reading experience which emphasizes the dynamic and provisional way in which our understanding of the world is constituted. Both authors pay a price for the new sense of dynamism unleashed in their texts: Döblin openly accepts that his way of ending *Berlin Alexanderplatz* is arbitrary, and Musil seems to have become too absorbed with the ramifications of his themes to bring *Der Mann ohne Eigenschaften* to a state of completion. The sense of fulfilment they offer a reader is to be found, not in any notion of a conclusion, but in the reflection of the continuous texture of human existence in the very fabric of their texts. Indeed, it was in a spirit of opposition to the will to systematize that they developed their respective techniques, Döblin working with the dynamic interplay of motifs among his textual fragments, and Musil with the interconnectedness of partial truths evoked in his multi-perspectival allusions. Both provided a radical challenge to the pretension that authorial subjectivity could reliably conjure up the sense of a general human situation—let alone an underlying logic of history—through the depiction of a 'representative' case. In its place they offered modes of composition in which the text itself became representative of the nature of lived reality in their time.

5

The Novel II: Facing up to Disillusionment

> The author naturally dares not hope that these pages of his might influence the natural processes of world events—but nevertheless . . .
>
> Ödön von Horváth (*GW* III, 147)

In a much-quoted phrase from his autobiography, George Grosz sums up the mood of the post-1918 world with the words "fury at having been deceived". In its precise context, he is using that phrase to describe an attitude which he and his fellow activists were trying to pass beyond.[1] It is also clear from the context that the deceit he had in mind was that practised upon an unwary populace by an imperial regime which had gambled on the military route to self-aggrandizement in 1914, and had refused to countenance any other prospect but ultimate victory even in the face of the slaughter and devastation for which the First World War is chiefly remembered. The fury of which he speaks is everywhere apparent in those familiar vengeful images for which Grosz himself became famous during the Weimar years (cf. Fig. 5).

For the generation of German writers born around the turn of the century, the pervasive sense of "having been deceived" unmistakably coloured their awareness of the social world in which they grew to adulthood; and when they began to publish in the 1920s, the expectation of deceitfulness profoundly determined the way they expressed themselves. Erich Kästner's first verse collection, *Herz auf Taille* (Tailored Heart) of 1928, is

---

[1] George Grosz, *Ein kleines Ja und ein großes Nein* (Hamburg: Rowohlt, 1955), 115. Precise context is of little concern to Peter Sloterdijk (p. 741), who sees the phrase as epitomizing the general character of German cultural attitudes in the 1920s.

Fig. 5. George Grosz, *Pillars of Society*, 1926

characterized by an attitude of wide-eyed undeludedness which is explicitly linked to that experience of growing up during the war. He presents his generation as having experienced its (dis-illusioning) sexual encounters early, while the men were away in the army, and as having been conditioned to regard the world with contempt—if they survived the carnage themselves. The post-war world he describes is one in which money talks, and the idealistic *sententiae* of 1918 have come to sound like self-parodies. The war dead lie with "filth in their mouths", while the hallmark of officialdom, whether secular or religious, is its utter lack of critical understanding (*Verstand*). His contemporaries Ernst Glaeser and Siegfried Kracauer, who both cut their literary teeth as contributors to the feuilleton of the *Frankfurter Zeitung*, show us variations on the same themes in novels which were similarly published in 1928. Glaeser's *Jahrgang 1902* (Generation of 1902), though reticent in its critical treatment of German society and very conventionally empathetic in its narrative technique, depicts a world in which the humane ideals of youth are first harnessed to a militarist ethos and then crushed by the experience of war. And through the young title figure of his novel *Ginster*, Kracauer presents all the pathos and misguided enthusiasms of the world of 1914 as if through the sceptical gaze of a seasoned observer: whether he is registering the tense excitement of the crowds on the day war breaks out or responding to the farewell letter of a friend at the front, Ginster contemplates the human activity around him as an ineluctible saga of self-deluding folly. When Walter Benjamin came to review the work of another young novelist (Hermann Kesten) in 1929, he noted something which he felt was indicative of a disturbing trend in recent fiction: the capacity of the critical gaze to register surprise (which had always been a hallmark of great satire) was in imminent danger of turning into a glassy stare.[2]

The better-known article on "left-wing melancholy", in which Benjamin sought to diagnose the ideology behind that decline of satirical potency, belongs among his more jaundiced commentaries on contemporary culture, as we saw in Chapter 1. The condition Benjamin thought he was dealing with was that

---

[2] "Der Nahblick, das erstaunliche Organ der großen Satire, hat nicht nur hier, nicht nur bei diesem Autor, seit kurzem etwas Glotzendes bekommen." (*GS* III, 172)

of a bourgeois intelligentsia for which all ideals were spent, scepticism had become automatic, and all that was being articulated was the hollowed-out shape of what had once been genuine feelings. He was thinking in terms of a left-wing radicalism that had degenerated into sterile oppositionalism, a retreat of literary writing, not just from political activism, but from any expectation of social effectiveness. It was this perception of German culture around 1930 that became firmly associated with the term 'Neue Sachlichkeit' as it was used in retrospective accounts of the period by Marxist literary critics, and indeed by such erstwhile participants in the culture of the period as Siegfried Kracauer.[3] It will be readily apparent from the novels I wish to discuss in this chapter in what senses they represent a melancholy moment for critical realism. But that does not automatically condemn them to sterility. Indeed, it is possible to discern amongst them a number of ways in which detachment from an ideal could give rise, not to an emotional vacuum, but to a critical energy which is brought to bear upon the circumstances which were preventing the realization of the ideal.

Among the novelists of the Weimar period, the most instructive case of a disappointed activist is actually a member of the older generation: Heinrich Mann. The disillusionment he displayed in the 1920s was related to the radical hopes he carried with him from pre-war days, and by the same token, it was his pre-war expectations that prevented him from exerting a significant influence in the post-war period. At the time of the armistice of 1918, as we noted in Chapter 4, Heinrich Mann presented himself as a leading upholder of the republican ideal while simultaneously acknowledging that the Republic had arrived as a consequence of military defeat rather than as something which the German populace had struggled to achieve. It was now the responsibility of Germany's intellectuals, he argued, to educate the republicans needed to sustain the new ideal (Kaes, 3–6). By

---

[3] It is as a collective state of psychological paralysis and as "a mentality disinclined to commit itself in any direction" that Kracauer describes the culture of 'Neue Sachlichkeit' in his book *From Caligari to Hitler* (Princeton University Press 1947), 165. See also Georg Lukács, *Deutsche Literatur im Zeitalter des Imperialismus* (Berlin: Aufbau, 1947), 54; Hans Mayer, *Deutsche Literatur seit Thomas Mann* (Reinbek: Rowohlt, 1968), 88.

August 1923, at the height of the Ruhr crisis, he looked back on four years of political and economic turmoil and warned that the principles of social justice and equal opportunity embodied in the Weimar Constitution had become hostages to the entrenched interests of a few powerful industrialists (*Essays*, 485–95). And when Gustav Stresemann was appointed Chancellor very soon afterwards, Heinrich Mann issued a public appeal to him to give strong leadership from the bourgeois centre in order to defend the integrity of the state against the personal ambitions of the "bolshevists of capitalism", and thereby to secure the loyalty of the small businessman and the ordinary citizen to the Republic (*Essays*, 474–84). It is with Stresemann's name above all that the ensuing 'stabilization phase' of the Republic is associated; but it was precisely during that phase that Heinrich Mann found himself manifestly at odds with the way German society was developing. In his essays of the time he chronicled the drift away from the principles of social responsibility and personal fulfilment that he held dear, and in his novels he looked for ways to give more concrete expression to his critical insights.

The essays show him contemplating the trends of the times with a mixture of bewilderment and alarm. He sees a shallow functionalism entering all areas of social life, from the world of work to the world of leisure. Mechanization and standardization are making themselves felt in women's fashions and in the development of mass tourism; popular entertainment has become collectivized and commercialized; the pursuit of happiness has become a matter of following the crowd; and the demystification of sex has led to a loss of the will to inquire into the nuances of sensual experience. Writing on the tenth anniversary of the armistice (*LW* 4, 45, 1), Heinrich Mann expresses concern at the attitudes of a young generation which seems bereft of social memory: they read nothing that has not been published within the last six months, and they are content to take the future as they find it.[4] By 1930 he was

[4] "Vor sechs Monaten war, wenn man sie hört, noch keiner da, und wer sie in sechs Monaten sein werden, findet sich. Sie lesen nur Bücher, die dieses Alter nicht überschritten haben. Sie ziehen aus Erlebtem keine Schlüsse, Gewesenes ist nicht einmal als Mahnung und Schatten noch da." (Heinrich Mann, *Sieben Jahre*, 540; quoted in Berle, 254.)

seeing the failure of the young to develop a strong individual personality as an ominous political factor because it was leaving them susceptible to a resurgent authoritarianism, to having their sense of purpose determined for them by others (cf. Berle, 201 f.).

In his novels of the later 1920s, Heinrich Mann was looking for ways, not just to reflect the social trends he was observing, but to influence attitudes towards them. In a statement of 1930 he is explicit about the need to use the art of the novel as a means of transcending social reality and helping to mould moral consciousness (Berle, 250f.). But the way in which he set about that task initially showed him still to be addressing his moral lesson at the older generation of Germany's governing classes rather than the young (and rather than a broader readership). It is still the issue of the irresponsibility of the older generation on which he is dwelling (as he had in *Der Kopf*); and it is still the literary conventions associated with that generation that he is applying, demonstrating his moral point by depicting the passive psychological experience of exemplary individuals. *Mutter Marie* (Mother Mary, 1927) tells the story of a woman who has abandoned her son at birth, leaving him to be brought up in a military family, and who rediscovers him in the post-1918 world living the life of a gambler, gigolo, and drifter. It is her experience of guilt, jealousy, and craving for her son's affection that the novel develops into a representative expression of the need for the older generation to learn to exercise responsibility towards the young. Only by painfully acquiring the attitudes of humility and renunciation, only by learning that it is not possible to 'buy' love, does she achieve the moral stature that makes her worthy to be a mother. *Eugénie* (1928) is set in the early 1870s, the time of Heinrich Mann's own infancy, and both the plot and the tone of the narrative are strongly reminiscent of the world of Fontane (and of Thomas Mann's *Buddenbrooks*). Konsul West and his French wife Gabriele succumb—he financially, she erotically—to the wiles of a mysterious speculator, whose eventual bankruptcy ruins their business along with that of many others. Here the experience of failure and humiliation is depicted in such a way as to emphasize the need for solid endeavour and communal responsibility as the foundation for well-being, as well as the need for personal commitment between husband and wife.

The title *Eugénie* relates to the performance of a play in the West's home on a festive occasion, which marks the climax of the action. Gabriele acts the role of the Empress *Eugénie* visiting her husband Napoleon III, who is being held captive in Kassel following the defeat of France by Prussia. The Napoleon role had been intended for the speculator Pidohn—who is, however, exposed and arrested before he can perform it. The novel also carries an alternative title, *Die Bürgerzeit*, which both holds it at a historical distance—this is the heyday of the nineteenth-century bourgeoisie—and emphasizes the sense in which the fate of the individuals depicted is intimately tied up with the historical fate of the Bürger as citizen in a united Germany. Wolfdietrich Rasch (1974) has given an illuminating reading of *Eugénie* (a work which has otherwise received little serious critical attention), showing how Heinrich Mann works into the texture of the novel some suggestive parallels between the Germany of the 1870s and the Germany of the 1920s. In either case the ethos of solid civic values faces the threat of 'napoleonic' adventurism; what had destabilized the virtuous bourgeois world of the 1870s had been the recklessness, both political and economic, of the era Heinrich Mann had depicted in his Kaiserreich trilogy. But Rasch also recalls (p. 475) that such subtlety of historical allusion was lost on young readers of 1928, who saw in the moralizing ending of *Eugénie* only the sort of triteness they associated with the novels serialized in middle-class family magazines. It has to be said that this response was fairly typical of the critical disdain to which Heinrich Mann's new novels were subjected during the closing years of the Republic (cf. Berle, 258 f.). But in *Die große Sache* (Something Big, 1930) he was at least making adjustments to his technique which enabled him to engage more closely with the dominant mentalities of the time.

Here he had hit upon a fast-moving plot which was designed to illustrate the power of human invention in a double sense. The industrial engineer Reinhold Birk, who has fallen into obscurity in middle age after an illustrious early career, lets it be known that he has invented 'something big': a new high explosive. The news fires the imaginations of his offspring, who set about trying to secure their own interests against the proprietorial claims of the firm for which they all work, and the plot that unfolds shows Heinrich Mann attempting to harness the dramatic potential of the popular detective novel, as well as the expressive potential of film.[5] Birk's son-in-law, Emanuel Rapp, is presented as the representative figure of a young generation that has lacked a productive focus for its energies—until this moment. But the unscrupulousness with which he is prepared to pursue his goal brings him into conflict with an array of figures (from the world of finance as well as the underworld) who are considerably better adapted to a life of unscrupulousness than he is. Rapp is married to Birk's eldest daughter Margo, who becomes private secretary to the general director, Karl August Schattich, in order to play him at his own game; but she has to endure disappointment, frustration, and the possible loss of her husband's loyalty, before circumstances bring her eventual victory on all fronts. (The most filmic section of the novel is one in which Margo pictures to herself what is going on among the other characters while she is herself an effective prisoner in Schattich's office, hooked up to a life-size marionette which symbolizes his manipulative power.) Margo's rival for Rapp's affections is her younger sister Inge, who turns out to be capable of using her sexual attractiveness without the least restraint in pursuit of immediate goals—and who ends up shot through the arm by Rapp at a point where he believes her to have betrayed him.

The positive case that can be made for this work as a critical reflection on its time has to be carefully separated from the various kinds of reservation which may be legitimately expressed about it. In his pursuit of an up-to-date storyline, Heinrich Mann draws on stock devices of popular fiction and the new media, but without the self-assurance with which, say, Brecht was doing so at the same time. The expression of his mistrust for post-war attitudes veers towards nostalgia when he makes Birk yearn for a return to more 'civilized' times, or when he characterizes Schattich's aristocratic wife in terms of the restrained eroticism of a bygone age. There are signs of vicari-

---

[5] Heinrich Mann's reflections on the detective novel—originally published in *LW* 5, 34, 1–2—are reprinted in Kaes, 371–2.

ous vengeance in his presentation of Birk as a 'proletarianized' victim of the inflation, and of ex-Chancellor Schattich as the chief perpetrator of a merciless plan to 'rationalize' the German economy.[6] And the denouement involves both outrageous contrivance and the arbitrary intervention of higher authority in order to settle the scores: it is an adventurous solo encounter between Margo and the big boss of the firm that leads to the disgrace of Schattich and the restoration of Birk and his family to favour. There is thus ample ammunition in the text for those who have sought to discredit it for its wilfulness or to present its populism as a crass inversion of Heinrich Mann's former aestheticism.[7] But at a distance of years it is perhaps easier to recognize what the tendentious criticisms of Heinrich Mann around 1930 overlooked, namely the instructive irony with which he deploys the familiar motifs of contemporary popular culture in the work.

If we expect *Die große Sache* to give us a realist *depiction* of contemporary society, then it may well look abstract and schematic; and if we expect it to provide a *constructive characterization* of the times, then it might appear wilful and hackneyed. But if we approach it as a *comedy of manners* composed out of easily recognizable cultural motifs, then we may be better able to see the critical potential of a narrative which unmasks the characteristic attitudes of the times while simultaneously acknowledging (through the figure of Birk) the practical limitations of any educative intervention. The story of the non-existent invention creates a dynamic and unpredictable situation in which each of the main characters—Birk included—experiences moments of discovery, some of which come close to

[6] Schattich is recognizably modelled on Hans Luther, who oversaw the stabilization of the monetary system in Stresemann's cabinet of 1923-4, who himself presided over a right-leaning government in 1925-6 (when he tried to circumvent parliamentary accountability by resort to a cabinet of administrative experts), and who actually achieved the ambition that Schattich is denied by becoming President of the Reichsbank in 1930.

[7] It is with reference to Gottfried Benn's notorious characterization of Heinrich Mann in a speech of 1931 as an aestheticist at heart, and to Thomas Mann's disdainful description of *Die große Sache* as "zur Farce gesteigert durch einen Ästhetizismus, der der Gemeinheit nur vorzuwerfen hat, daß sie nicht gemeiner ist und sie ins Überwirkliche hebt," that Schütz (1986, 117-24) constructs his dismissive account of this novel. He is manifestly doing so with a view to undermining the partisan account of Heinrich Mann's political career that had been constructed in the GDR.

a glimpse of outright catastrophe. The moralizing impulse which had seemed to dominate Heinrich Mann's two previous novels is here subjected to ironic reflection in the light of the learning experiences depicted in the narrative. *Pace* Berle (pp. 273 f.), the way the novel ends does not straightforwardly confirm any simplistic notion of the need to rediscover the meaning of joy ("Lernt euch freuen"). It is rather the case that the very fortuitousness of the happy ending is used as a means to develop the insight that the joy it is possible to take in *accomplishment* is invariably dependent on large measures of skill, hard work, and good luck—as opposed to calculation.[8] The exercise of deception, in which they have all—Birk included—become implicated in pursuit of their particular designs, has brought a *productive* disillusionment in its train.

The seemingly sanguine conclusion of *Die große Sache* admittedly did not hold up in the context of the times, and in his next novel it was as if Heinrich Mann was following up his social comedy with a naturalistic tragedy. Based on the life-story of the woman who was to become Mann's second wife, Nelly Kroeger, *Ein ernstes Leben* (A Serious Life, 1932) tells how a young woman born into poverty in a Baltic-coast village is drawn into a cycle of deprivation, criminalization, and corruption under the influence of a pair of amoral youngsters from Berlin. While this novel can clearly be read as an appeal for emotional sympathy towards the victims of social oppression, the laconic attitude displayed by the figures of authority in the work—the doctor who tends women broken in body and spirit by a life of incessant physical work, the police inspector who observes that all his suspects would be innocent if their full story were known—colour it with a melancholy scepticism about any scope for pursuing human happiness in the social world as it really exists in the early 1930s. There is here something of that sceptical detachment which had already begun to characterize the novels of younger authors than Heinrich Mann at an earlier stage.

Erich Kästner's *Fabian* (1931) is perhaps the classic expression of the young intellectual's sense of impotence in the face of

---

[8] Birk is made to qualify the terms of his own argument when the element of good luck in the denouement is pointed out to him: "Wenn ich Arbeit sage, meine ich Arbeit, Geschicklichkeit und Zufall. Die drei führen weit." (*Große Sache*, 451)

social developments. From the very start of the novel, Fabian comes across as a figure who has made despair at the impotence of reason into a guiding precept: he exercises his choices in life on the basis of sheer chance, momentary impulse, or wilful contradiction. He remains enough of a rebel to resent having to connive with a world that is busily organizing itself on the principles of commercial calculation (the world as 'plc' is one of his own images), but along the way he has adapted to a situation in which the only apparent outlet for his inventive capacity is in the field of "propaganda", i.e. marketing and public relations. His scruples serve only to hamper him in 'swimming with the tide'—an image which is converted into literal terms at the end of the novel, when Fabian drowns in an apparent attempt to rescue a boy who turns out to be quite capable of reaching the river bank unaided. There was a time when it appeared possible for liberal-minded critics to take Kästner's protestation of moral purpose at face value and defend this work as an 'honest' reflection of an unreasoning world (see Egon Schwarz in Wagener (ed.)). The difficulty for that argument, however, is that the world as experienced through Fabian's chance encounters comes across as an unrelieved sequence of saturnalian inversions: what he sees in newspaper offices is only the meretriciousness of media presentation, what he hears of industrial processes is only the absurdity of over-production, what he witnesses of political conflict is only a farcical street fight between a Nazi and a Communist, and his closest friend—who has dedicated his life to the investigation of Enlightenment rationalism and the practical goal of social improvement—is driven to his death by a malicious joke. What the work expresses is above all the disappointment of any Enlightenment expectation that humanity might yet prove capable of collective self-improvement. Its melancholy moment is famously captured in Fabian's own recollection of an Honoré Daumier cartoon which depicts "Progress" as a procession of snails—which are not only moving at snail pace, they are also moving in a circle.

It is a world of unreason that Lion Feuchtwanger, too, is depicting in *Erfolg* (Success, 1930)—even if he also asserts against it the notion of a rational principle at work in history. His subject-matter is drawn from the world of Bavarian politics around the time of Hitler's Munich putsch, and it gives him much scope for lampooning the pretensions of the Führer, the often trivial motives which swell the ranks of his movement, and the prevailing atmosphere of prejudice and atavism which provides him with favourable conditions for agitation. Feuchtwanger takes the case of a relatively innocuous 'political' prisoner (Martin Krüger is an art gallery director who has ostensibly been jailed for perjury) as a basis for exploring the prejudices and right-wing bias at work in the political establishment and the judiciary: the 'success' to which his title alludes is the kudos that becomes attached to any act that can command public support, for however brief a time, and regardless of its ultimate moral purport. But this is not a work that can be held up as an effective critical representation of the power struggles of the Weimar period. For one thing it makes National Socialism into too easy a target, stylizing it as a purely local phenomenon and making light of the passions and pathologies which were eventually to carry Hitler into office. For another thing, the focus of his depiction is less on actual political acts and attitudes than on the personal experiences of those who are themselves trying to make sense of events—on the Social Democrat lawyer Geyer who is collecting evidence of legal abuses, on the figure of Johanna Krain who campaigns to keep alive the memory of injustice, and on the creative writer Jacques Tüverlin who is clearly recognizable in important senses as the author's *alter ego*. It is through the foregrounding of these figures that Feuchtwanger's ostensibly historicizing account of "three years of a province" draws attention to the underlying tension in its own conception.

Two aspects of this novel may be said to reflect general characteristics of Feuchtwanger's work. First his approach to political bigotry is to expose it to ridicule rather than critical scrutiny. Public derision was to be the instrument of the downfall of the upstart dictator in the novel with which Feuchtwanger later satirized the Nazis in power, *Der falsche Nero* (The False Nero, 1936); and that expectation is explicitly anticipated towards the end of *Erfolg* when the image of the (disgraced) Führer on a cinema screen serves to discharge serious political tensions in laughter. Secondly, his treatment of political aspirations in his literary works is typically subordinated to a demonstration of the vanity of human strivings in a world that is fraught with incalculable factors. Whether he is depicting the power struggles of the ancient world in his *Josephus* trilogy (1932–45), or those of eighteenth-century Germany in his best-selling *Jud Süß* (Power, 1925), a dominant feature of his plots is the way that a personal triumph for an individual in one sense can be attended by catastrophic consequences in another sense. It is a similar pattern of development that he depicts in *Erfolg*. The personal aspirations of the Führer and those who back him culminate in a political debacle, while the efforts of those who campaign on behalf of the prisoner Krüger are forestalled by prejudice and malice—until, that is, altered circumstances (coupled with the intervention of outside forces in the shape of a Californian millionaire) enable them to bring his case to public awareness retrospectively. There is, in other words, a melancholy moment built into Feuchtwanger's plot which is, so to speak, temperamentally determined.[9] That moment is itself symbolized in the novel at the point where the writer Jacques Tüverlin looks back on his Bavarian experiences as a "fairground of justice"—a perception which is concretized in terms of a visit to a Munich fair, where all the old vanity and meanness is still apparent, all the old cynical representatives of public life are still present, and all the old negative qualities of the adult world are being replicated in the young (Book 5, chapter 17). It is a perception which exactly parallels the image of the world progressing in a circle as we find it in Kästner's *Fabian*. In the case of *Erfolg*, however, it is the manner in which the melancholy moment is compensated for that reveals the abstract nature of the novel's guiding idea.

Tüverlin's intervention in the social process—in the form of a "Book of Bavaria" and collaboration on a film about the victimized Krüger—is depicted in terms of a Nietzschean psychology that is not without interest in its own right. He has to experience his own moment of revulsion at the "eternal recurrence of the same" in human affairs before he can achieve that distance from his subject-matter which enables him to conceive it as a "vision"; and his labour on the book has to pass through a moment of emotional crystallization (stimulated by Johanna

---

[9] For a fuller analysis of *Erfolg* along these lines, see Hans-Harald Müller (in Lützeler (ed.) 1983); also Ulrich Weisstein (in Spalek (ed.)).

Krain's personal commitment to the memory of Krüger) before it can come alive as an artistic project. As Tüverlin's conception of his own role as an artist is presented (in Book 5, chapter 22), he is contributing to the advancement of the human race as a species by conferring a meaning (*Sinn*) on the otherwise contingent destiny of the individual Krüger. Here we may sense that Nietzschean psychology has been made to enter into a half-hearted alliance with the Enlightenment faith in an underlying rational process realizing itself in the history of mankind.[10] Through the figure of Tüverlin, Feuchtwanger is advancing the comfortably familiar notion that the work of art can convey a superior sense of the coherence of human experience than either empirically gathered evidence (represented by the documentary approach of the lawyer Geyer) or abstract analysis (represented by Tüverlin's own essay on Krüger). But in doing so he introduces a yardstick to which his own novel does not measure up. The aspiration to superior coherence remains an abstract idea in the text of *Erfolg*, while the world depicted in practice is composed of the random effects of human foible, rather than the plausible consequences of human agency.

Ödön von Horváth, in a less ambitious prose text, supplies the immediacy of depiction that is missing from Feuchtwanger's expansive account of provincial life. *Der ewige Spießer* (The Wandering Philistine, 1930) again presents contemporary humanity in a deeply sceptical light; and again it refers allusively to systems of rational understanding which have held sway in the past, but seem no longer to command credence in the present. The line which I have used as a motto for this chapter actually speaks in the original German of a world process that is "gesetzmäßig", i.e. subject to some law or principle of regularity; and the implication in context is that any such law tends towards the undermining of human ideals rather than their furtherance. I have translated Horváth's title as "The Wandering *Philistine*" for want of a more appropriate term in English, but what his word "Spießer" is really indicating is an attitude of

---

[10] I am thinking here particularly of Kant's postulation, in his "Idee einer allgemeinen Geschichte in weltbürgerlicher Absicht", of a "plan of nature" as the idea which will guide humanity towards a progressively more rational way of ordering their affairs. For the inconsistency (and inconsequentiality) of Feuchtwanger's attitude to the question of historical progress, see Hans-Harald Müller (Lützeler (ed.) 1983, 178f.).

quietistic conformity which the text shows to be capable of asserting itself in a variety of contexts that are not specific to social class. As Horváth puts it in his preamble to the work, the "Spießer" is "a compulsive egoist who tries to assimilate himself wherever he goes, and to falsify every piece of original thinking simply by appropriating it" (*GW* III, 147).

On the face of it, *Der ewige Spießer* accepts the cynicism of the times as a given from the outset. The young post-war generation, as Horváth presents them, live in the expectation that their fellow humans will try to put one over on them, and that their first intent must therefore be to secure their own material advantage, by deceit if need be. By contrast with his plays, however, where the impulses of egoism and malice tend to be exposed by moments of dramatic juxtaposition, the narrative medium allows Horváth to develop the sense of a personal history behind emergent behaviour patterns. For instance he shows the gradual stages by which a young woman "gets practical" after losing her job, namely by accommodating to the demands of her social environment and making "more productive use of her sensuality" (i.e. selling her body). In the course of her story a residual trace of that Enlightenment hope for humanity's collective self-improvement (or in Horváth's more laconic formulation, "a sign that humanity is capable of culture and civilization") is again allowed to show through: someone puts a job opportunity her way. But in this instance even the kind benefactor characterizes his own act in disparaging terms as a *minimal* gesture of solidarity from one "louse" to another; indeed the text concludes with the same character reflecting on his apparent selflessness as an occasion for self-congratulation. I have argued elsewhere that the technique of ironic disclosure in this work involves a degree of complicity between the narrating voice and the cynical attitudes of the characters (Midgley 1988, 29 f.). There are occasional moments when the narrator does express overt protest (at social injustice or attitudes towards prostitution), but more typically the ironic presentation of the character's perspectives presupposes a kind of reader who will recognize the damning allusions behind self-serving arguments and ideologies (such as the misrepresentation of the virtues of the profit motive, or the subtext of class bias in a film scenario). Horváth's narrative technique is that of the comic raconteur: he mimics the preconceptions of banal minds in order to render them accessible to wry scrutiny.

His *pièce de résistance* in this respect is the strand of plot which takes a wide boy from Munich on a journey to the World Exhibition in Barcelona. The narrative traces Alfons Kobler's perceptions (with interruptions) from the moment he achieves his 'windfall' by selling an unroadworthy vehicle for a princely sum, through a variety of irritating encounters with fellow travellers, to the moment when he returns home none the wiser. En route he has espoused the grand notion of European integration—Pan-Europeanism in the parlance of the times—but he has done so by assimilating it to his own private delusions and resentments: along the way he has lost out to a rich American (or more strictly to economic circumstances) over what had looked like the opportunity to marry an industrial heiress. The complicity of narrative perspective of which I have spoken makes it possible for Kobler to serve not only as an object of ironization, but also as a vehicle for the ironic exposure of the figures he encounters on his journey; and those figures between them go some way towards illustrating the intrinsic hollowness of contemporary ideals, as well as the capacity of lazy minds to debase them. Kobler runs into instances of democratic sentiment masking vulgar prejudice, and gross examples of blinkered Bavarian particularism. He meets a cultivated man whose professed love of Renaissance values barely conceals his latent political authoritarianism; and in the figure of the Austrian journalist Schmitz he encounters someone of indubitably superior intellect, whose professional life appears dedicated to the principles of liberal democracy and internationalism, but who is revealed in his private moments to be motivated by at best a sublimated form of egoism and base desire. In all these instances, the seeming unpretentiousness of Horváth's anecdotal style can be seen as serving a serious intellectual purpose: its very instability of perspective allows it to illuminate, case by case, the ways in which noble ideas and humane precepts can *become* corrupted as they are assimilated to the mental habits and physiological impulses of individual lives.

One common feature emerges, then, among the novels that Kästner, Feuchtwanger, and Horváth publish around 1930: they are all portraying a contemporary world in which Enlightenment hopes for the rational ordering of human affairs are being severely undermined. Kästner does so by presenting characters and events as impinging arbitrarily on the life of his central character; and Feuchtwanger does so by separating off the abstract notion of ultimate historical progress from his psychological depiction of actual human behaviour. Horváth at least provides a concrete sense of the processes by which Enlightenment ideals are undermined, in that he focuses on specific connections between banal human motive and intellectual corruption: it is in that sense that he keeps alive the potential for productive disillusionment within a sardonic view of contemporary humanity. If we now look at Kästner's *Fabian* alongside another group of social novels—by Hermann Kesten and Martin Kessel—then we see a different kind of family likeness emerging, namely a tendency for the disillusioning presentation of a far-from-ideal world to become absorbed into the personal concerns of the discomfited individual subject.

It might be said in Kesten's defence that he is telling a story of adolescent discovery. Josef Bar, the central figure of *Josef sucht die Freiheit* (Josef's Quest for Freedom, 1927) and *Ein ausschweifender Mensch* (A Dissolute Person, 1929), is growing up in pre-war Berlin, in impoverished living conditions, but with a grammar-school education. His personal disillusionment arises from the confrontation of his naive moral assumptions with the brutal inconsistencies of adult behaviour; and he does emerge towards the end of the second volume, following the outbreak of the First World War, as a revolutionary idealist who has come to realize that you need to wield power if you want to benefit others. To that extent he may perhaps be growing towards a kind of maturity that will enable him to act as a responsible citizen in the post-war world[11]—although when he does reappear as an influential journalist in *Glückliche Menschen* (Happy People, 1931) and *Der Scharlatan* (The Charlatan, 1932), his personal attitudes play no significant part in the narrative. Hans Wagener (in Becker and Weiß, 52) emphasizes the aspect of Enlightenment optimism present in Kesten's writing, his commitment to literature as a medium of

---

[11] It was the glimmer of a hope that Josef might yet "become a man" by committing himself to a collective cause that Walter Benjamin highlighted at the end of his review of *Ein ausschweifender Mensch*: GW III, 174.

instruction, and his evident belief in an unconditional, non-rel-
ativistic conception of truth. But the truth revealed in Kesten's
early novels is invariably a bitter one (it is the truth to which
the adolescent Josef must be awakened), and the manner of its
presentation in turn reveals a curious disunity in Kesten's technique of narrative representation. On the one hand Kesten
seems intent on preserving the effect of traumatized innocence
in his young hero. He does so by making Josef the clandestine
witness to the manifestations of sexual dalliance, emotional
blackmail, and moral betrayal which unfold before his eyes in
the small family flat like scenes from a Naturalist drama. Those
scenes culminate in the suicide of his eldest sister, who has been
seduced by the maternal uncle. But Josef, who has hitherto
enjoyed an exceptionally close relationship with his mother,
appears more shocked by the very manifestation of adult sexuality than by the way it is callously manipulated by the male
protagonists. On the other hand events are mediated by a narrating voice which speaks from the vantage point of a superior
(i.e. undeluded) knowledge of human affairs, and is able to
share ironic allusions to the contemporary world with an ostensibly unshockable post-war readership.

It might be supposed that the way in which the account of
Josef's experience is frequently interrupted by extended passages
which tell us about elements in the family drama (the stories of
the parents, the uncle, the sister) or about the personal histories
of other characters (the mother's admirer, the figures with whom
Josef associates at one time or another) is the result of the failure
of an inexperienced author to integrate his material consistently.
But there is a deeper reason for this imbalance. The authoritative narration conveys an (ostensibly reliable) sense of the (unreliable) world to which Josef is being required to adapt, and
against which he revolts. The substance of the revolt that drives
Josef's personal development, however, is exclusively derived
from his experience of sexual revulsion at the age of 13: it is his
overwhelming desire to break free from the world encapsulated
in that experience that motivates his abrupt separation (in succession) from mother, maternal uncle, and father. There is considerable potential, in the course of this pair of novels, for ironic
disclosure of the practical connotations of that 'freedom' that
Josef seeks. There are moments when individual perceptions of

what that world means are shown to shade towards either personal or political freedom, towards individual or collective
emancipation, towards a condition of freedom under the law or
the experience of liberation. But what could have been a revealing exposition of an important socio-political theme tends
invariably to collapse into the depiction of Josef's personal disappointments. Even after his moment of political insight—when
he has become associated with a group of anarchists in Holland,
after the outbreak of the First World War—his impulse is to seek
his 'freedom' in the apparent security of a new female partner;
and the woman concerned disappoints him again in a manner
which epitomizes the kind of intellectual conundrum that
Kesten has built into his narrative. Having previously warned
Josef that free speaking could cost him his freedom, she now
comes to stand for those who speak of fighting for freedom, but
mean only their own.[12]

When we move on to *Fabian* (1931), we find ourselves in the
world of a university graduate who finds that society at large
sets little store by either his academic training or his sense of
scruple: in Berlin he makes his way by designing cigarette advertisements (until he is made redundant), and in his home town
he is received as qualified only to write occasional theatre
reviews. Here we are dealing with a central figure who has a
highly nurtured skill in elegant periphrasis and memorable
repartee, a man of the world who appears inured to the colourful (and the brutal) manifestations of adult sexuality, but who
is brought low by emotional exhaustion and the experience of
moral treachery. And by contrast with Kesten we are dealing
with an approach to narrative composition which creates a
strong sense of the resonances between this central character
and his world. Kästner's novel displays the artfulness of its construction in the subtle symmetries of its plot elements. Fabian's
self-abandonment at the end is anticipated (and in large part
precipitated) by the suicide of his friend Labude; Labude's discovery of his girlfriend's infidelity anticipates (and perhaps helps
to predetermine) Fabian's suspicions of what is entailed when

---

[12] If we were to look for a German novel which fulfils the expectation of a developed political dimension in the account of a pre-war Berlin childhood, we should
have to turn to Döblin's *Pardon wird nicht gegeben* which, however, was not published until after the Nazis came to power, in 1935.

his own girlfriend, Cornelia, starts a career in film; and the way Fabian gives vent to his sexual jealousy (through a perfunctory affair with an older woman) closely mirrors what he imagines Cornelia to be doing with her film director. These are all ways of suggesting that the specific experiences of Fabian, lurid as some of them are, have a representative significance in the life of his generation. But in the last case the mirroring effect is also indicative of something more: it confronts the would-be moralist, when he comes to think about it, with the inconsistency in his *own* behaviour, and it points to the origins of that inconsistency in his inherent potential for psychological regression.[13] For Fabian's short-lived liaison with the woman from North Berlin—who 'mothers' him, while he alternates between aggressive sexual activity and impassivity—also mirrors the relationship which comes to dominate the second half of the novel: Fabian's relationship with his mother.

We see Fabian trying to resist the emotional pull of that relationship when his mother comes to stay in his Berlin bedsitter. We see him maintaining a rigorous sense of independence on an intellectual plane when he pursues the malicious injustice done to Labude, and indeed when he returns to confront what have come to appear as the hollow sentiments of his school education and the blinkered patriotism of provincial dignitaries. But his collapse into melancholy following the revelation of the circumstances of Labude's suicide also makes Fabian's childhood home an immediate, *compulsive* destination for him—he does not even stop to pack his bags. What we witness of his ruminations on the closing pages of the novel is still a struggle between self-respect and self-contempt, between the impulse to become involved and the impulse to withdraw (to look for a "goal" in the mountains), between the ideal of emancipation (which has been shown to carry a high emotional price) and

---

[13] The aspect of regression in Kästner's presentation of the social world, in his poetry as well as his narrative prose, has been emphasized in recent research. See particularly Dirk Walter, *Zeitkritik und Idyllensehnsucht: Erich Kästner's Frühwerk (1928–1933) als Beispiel linksbürgerlicher Literatur in der Weimarer Republik* (Heidelberg: Carl Winter, 1977), which is Marxist in orientation, and Andreas Drouwe, *Erich Kästner—Moralist mit doppeltem Boden* (Marburg: Tectum, 1993) (which sharply brings out the latent illiberalism in Kästner's morality as well as his implicit withdrawal from social responsibility).

regression—and by dint of chance (the circumstances surrounding Labude's suicide, the child in the river) it is regression that wins out.

Moving on one further year to Martin Kessel's novel *Herrn Brechers Fiasko* (Mr Brecher's Fiasco, 1932), we may well be struck by the strong kinship between Kästner's Fabian and Kessel's title-figure. Brecher is another university-trained young man working in what he sees as the "propaganda" department of a large firm (in this case a portmanteau service agency which deals in all manner of things from properties and investments to catering). But the focus of Kessel's narrative is more squarely and relentlessly on the sense of futility that comes of living in a highly organized world; and the element of moral protest that Kästner had articulated in the form of witty allusion has here become reduced to unrelieved sarcasm. The strongest feature of Kessel's novel is undoubtedly its concentrated expression of the ambience of office life—from the ergonometric design of its furniture to the special argot of the employees. He creates a powerful sense of an environment in which self-irony has become a habitual form of self-defence. It is the conditioned reaction to any anticipation of personal criticism (you say the novel you are reading is trash before anyone else does), and it is the communally shared response to any impending threat (whether it be the possibility of dismissal or the news of an attempted suicide). That habit of irony among the workforce is capable of generating penetrating insight, as when Brecher himself is described as a "living paradox" who is able to "singe people with his icy distance". But Brecher's own famous wit collapses into sterile contempt when he is himself dismissed: he sinks into demoralization and isolation, prowls the streets of Berlin as a very lonely "ghost" (even though the section in which he does so carries a title which alludes to the collectivist ethos of the Communist Manifesto), and ends up writing a suicide note that is one huge paean to the *servility* of the office routine. What Kessel gives us, in other words, is a vivid characterization of the emotive responses of a proletarianized intelligentsia to the intensifying experience of bureaucratization (which are very aptly described by Bernhard Spies in Becker and Weiß, 235–54), but it is a characterization dominated by the self-absorbed and self-pitying attitudes of the individual figure. Just as Brecher's protests remain impotently vocal, so too does the depiction of economic insecurity in this novel remain singularly abstract.

Against this background of self-absorbed intellectuality, Hans Fallada's *Kleiner Mann—was nun?* (Little Man—what now?, 1932) perhaps deserves more sympathetic understanding than it has often received from literary scholars. The work was clearly written with an eye to popular taste (which is part of the reason why it has been viewed with suspicion by Marxists, and with disdain by traditionalists), but it also contains a finely observed characterization of the white-collar worker as an important sociological phenomenon of the times. Hans Fallada (real name Rudolf Ditzen) had several years of work as a journalist behind him, and had published a highly acclaimed novel about the agrarian politics of North Germany, when he turned his attention to the situation of the "Angestellte", that segment of the working population employed in banks, offices, and the retail trade, whose significance within the German economy had steadily grown since the turn of the century.[14] As the drive for economic rationalization intensified in the 1920s, the "Angestellte" attracted attention from serious economic analysts, not least because their image of themselves as superior in status to the working class was being challenged by the brutal reality that their conditions of employment were essentially no different from those of any shop-floor worker.[15] The characteristic attitudes of these white-collar workers to their destabilized social position were described by Siegfried Kracauer in a series of case studies, which was serialized in the *Frankfurter Zeitung* in 1929 and appeared in book form in 1930. What Fallada did, drawing partly on Kracauer's information and partly on personal experience, was to integrate the observation of specific situations and mental impulses into a continuous narrative which shows the progressive impact of

[14] Statistical information on the growth of office work in relation to manual labour is provided in F. Croner, *Die Angestellten in der modernen Gesellschaft* (Frankfurt: Humboldt, 1954), and reproduced in Reinisch (ed.), 85. This trend has been used by economic historians as an important indicator of social modernization in Germany between the wars, notably by Detlev Peukert (1987).

[15] In the introduction to his study, *Die Angestellten*, Siegfried Kracauer was able to quote a 1928 publication by the economist Emil Lederer on precisely this point.

the Great Depression on a particular individual—or rather, on a marriage.[16] It is essential to the narrative effect Fallada is creating that his young couple should appear as innocent and, as it were, detached from the social background he depicts in his novel. He begins his story with the episode in which Hans Pinneberg proposes marriage to Emma (Lämmchen) Mörschel following the unexpected discovery that she is pregnant. He presents them as guileless in their pursuit of an 'honest' wage and 'decent' living conditions: only under the pressure of circumstances (when Pinneberg finds himself out of work in their Mecklenburg home town, and they move to Berlin) do they become obliged to collude in the dishonesty of others (in order to secure a job and cheap accommodation). They are to come across as passive victims of increasing economic hardship—which is made manifest in their descent from a furnished flat, via temporary accommodation with Pinneberg's mother, to illegal quarters in the loft above a small cinema, and finally to a cabin on a remote allotment—and they continually look inwards, to each other, for reassurance. Theirs is an innocence which carries certain implicit assumptions about social status. In the opening episode we see Pinneberg paying for Lämmchen's medical examination, even while protesting about the limits of his earning power, rather than queue for attention with the patients on insurance schemes. What we learn of Pinneberg's manner of dressing, as well as the couple's obsessive interest in items of furniture of limited utility value (a dressing-table, a 'proper' cradle for the baby), suggests a devotion to 'lifestyle' that is out of proportion to their actual financial circumstances. The precise reckoning of their living costs is designed to come as an unpleasant surprise for the reader, as much as for them. There is a pointed significance in the fact that the last symbol of his standing that Pinneberg is prepared to abandon is that stiff

[16] The precise relation between Fallada's novel and Kracauer's case studies remains a matter for dispute. When Helmut Lethen (1970, 165–7) asserted a strong affinity between the two works, he did so in order to emphasize the apparent impotence of the "bourgeois" (as opposed to the proletarian) subject in both instances. When Karl Prümm (in Becker and Weiß, 259–70) speaks of Fallada's novel as a "Gegenbuch" to Kracauer's, then he is arguing from the premiss that the isolation of observed phenomena carries a critical potential which becomes diluted in the "behaglicher Erzählfluß" of Fallada's narrative.

collar which distinguishes him from the manual labourer and marks him out in the jargon of the times as a "Stehkragenproletarier". Fallada's text registers other lifestyles which contrast with that of his central couple, not least that of Lämmchen's working-class family, through which the ideological rifts of the time are clearly shown to run. But it is only towards the end that Pinneberg himself, dishevelled ultimately, and relegated to the gutter in a quite literal sense, comes to realize how little difference there really is between his fate and that of millions of others.

When *Kleiner Mann—was nun?* was published in 1932, it excited considerable public interest. In *Die literarische Welt* it was described as having provided a unifying symbol for a nation that had appeared ravaged and divided against itself.[17] But the unifying symbol in question, Pinneberg and his nuclear family, is recognizably characterized in class-specific terms. This was brought out by Arrigo Subiotto in an essay which instructively contrasts the abiding ethos of the self-sufficient family depicted by Fallada with the working-class culture of solidarity portrayed by Walter Greenwood's novel *Love on the Dole* (Bance (ed.), 77–90). Helmut Lethen (1970, 156–67) makes a psychologically plausible point when he notes the complementary relationship between the enclosing mutual compassion of this particular model of the family and the particular anxiety generated by the competitive retail trade in which Pinneberg is obliged to work. And both Lethen and Subiotto highlight the psychic mechanisms by which Pinneberg comes to internalize the demands of economic rationalization as the measure of his self-worth: the thought that consoles him when he loses his job at the Berlin department store is that he was the one who had come closest to fulfilling his (exorbitant) sales quota. Fallada's novel depicts such responses *as* class-specific, as the expression of a particular social mentality; but at the same time he allows his narrative concept to be constrained by that mentality. There are moments when the potential of particular episodes for isolating

---

[17] *LW* 8, 31, 5: "Einer sprach aus, was alle leiden. Einem wurde Gestalt, was alle ahnen. So geschah das Wunder, an das wir nicht mehr glaubten: einer zersplitterten Gesellschaft, einem 'Interessenhaufen', einer Nation, die nichts gemeinsam zu haben scheint als die Not und den von ihr erzeugten Haß eines jeden gegen jeden, diesem mißhandelten Volk entstand in Falladas Roman ein Volksbuch."

and analytically presenting the social dimension of Pinneberg's behaviour—in the doctor's surgery, in the act of making a sale, or when signing on for unemployment benefit—could have been more fully exploited. But by contrast with Horváth, who does lay bare such moments of social interaction in both his prose and his plays, Fallada allows them to become absorbed into the flow of a sentimental comedy designed to appeal to a readership which shares the values and expectations of the couple themselves. That is the sense in which Fallada can be said to have compromised the critical potential of his precise social observation with his appeal to a particular kind of popular taste (cf. Karl Prümm in Becker and Weiß, 255–72).

That it was possible to work with the material of popular expectations and yet develop a potential for productive disillusionment out of it is demonstrated by the novels of Irmgard Keun. The expectations in question are those associated with new career opportunities for women, which had become a fashionable subject for fiction by 1930;[18] and Keun's critical interest is concerned precisely with the prospects for emancipation from that confining role of caring, resourceful wife and mother that Fallada depicts (and indeed from those other forms of stereotyped femininity which we find reflected in other novels discussed in this chapter). The main plot elements of her first novel, *Gilgi—eine von uns* (Gilgi—One of Us, 1931), might at first sight appear to be drawn from the standard repertoire of popular magazine fiction. An attractive young secretary is determined to get on in life, learns on her 21st birthday that she was adopted at birth, seeks out her true mother, falls in love, finds her true identity . . . —except that in Keun's version these elements turn out to be stages in a deepening of Gilgi's awareness of herself as an emotional and social being riven by competing demands and impulses. The device of the adoption story serves to accelerate the process of her separation from the stultifyingly conventional home in which she has grown up, from the mother who balefully cares and the father who blandly presides. It also

[18] Doris Rosenstein (Becker and Weiß, 287) mentions a number of shorthand-typist novels published in 1930 which may have provided contributory stimuli for Keun's early works. Ursula Krechel gives a succinct account of the cultural background to women's writing in the 1920s in her essay "Linksseitig kunstseidig. Dame Girl und Frau" (Wichner and Wiesner, 96–117).

introduces her to other modes of living which might have been hers but for the intervention of some arbitrary decision: the loveless luxury of her natural mother, or the squalid penury of the serving-woman who was given out as the natural mother at the time. Keun works with stark contrasts in this novel, as illustrations of the stark divisions in society that are being re-emphasized under the conditions of economic depression, and of the life-choices that may present themselves to a woman in Gilgi's position. She has a durable friendship with the dependably morose young socialist Pit, but, son of a rich father that he is, he epitomizes a brand of social alienation which serves only to confirm Gilgi in her drive for self-reliance. Her love for the bohemian writer Martin, on the other hand, is passionately sincere, but it utterly undermines the disciplined approach she has been used to taking towards her life. In the end she leaves him, not only because his profligacy would make him an unsuitable father for the child she has conceived, and only superficially because of the suicide of a young family which he has (perhaps) prevented her from forestalling. She leaves him because she has to renounce that part of herself if she is to regain control of her life.

By the standards of the conventional politics of the time, the perspective of *Gilgi* is clearly individualistic. The reviewer in the Communist *Linkskurve* concluded, emphatically and understandably, that whatever Gilgi was she was "not one of us" (*L* 4, 10, 27 f.); and readers of the Social Democrat journal *Vorwärts*, in which the work was serialized, objected that it did not accurately reflect the experiences of their working lives (Becker and Weiß, 277). At a time when the dominant interests of a politicized readership were still focused on the documentation of workplace experience, and indeed on the pressing issue of job security, Keun was showing her young heroine to be contemplating the lives of her fellow commuters as a dreary banality she wished to rise above, and even welcoming redundancy as an opportunity to absorb herself exclusively in her romance. But when such moments as these are viewed in the context of the novel as a whole, they can be seen as elements in a complex learning process which is far from unpolitical. What Keun is constructing on her opening pages—and faithfully reflecting in her sometimes brusque narrative tone—is the self-assurance of a 20-

year-old who is thoroughly in tune with the ostensible public virtues of the time. Gilgi at the start of the story is business-like in every aspect of her life, with a rigorously organized routine of earning, learning, and physical exercise, and a fierce determination to betray no sentiment and be beholden to no one. Gilgi by the end of the story has experienced the power of her own sexuality, the strength of her revulsion for self-indulgent lifestyles, and the imperative for solidarity in a world that makes no concessions to the weak. The collapse of Gilgi's immediate hopes is marked, as it is for Kästner's Fabian, by an abrupt decision to leave town, but the significance of her decision is the reverse of Fabian's: the solitary, vulnerable, pregnant individual who waits for the night train to take her from Cologne to Berlin is not seeking seclusion, but reintegration. It is the joy of involvement in the world of work that wells up emotionally amid Gilgi's grief and renunciation (even if the image used to represent that world is one of cogs in machines, suggested by a passing locomotive). The poignant hope that remains at the end of this text is that Gilgi's experiences have educated her to carry responsibility without forfeiting her humanity.

In *Gilgi*, Keun had adopted a narrative tone which blended perfectly with the heroine's states of mind; it could mark Gilgi's disdain for sentiment with tersely dismissive phrases, it could capture the warmth and expansiveness of her erotic awakening, and it could deftly note her fleeting thoughts and impulses at moments of tension and confusion. Keun preserves that lightness of touch in her second novel, *Das kunstseidene Mädchen* (The Artificial-Silk Girl, 1932), but she opts here for total mimicry of the mentality of the central character, couching the text in the monologue style of a diary-like *récit*. Again, on the face of it, this is a fictional construct with in-built limitations, in that it confines the diction and the ostensible concerns of the narrative to those of Doris, the out-of-work typist who dreams of being a star; but again there is a surreptitious purpose prompted by the circumstances of the time. Such dreams of fame and affluence had been helping to sell popular magazines throughout the 1920s, and by 1927 the model of the flapper as gold-digger had been firmly anchored in the public mind by Anita Loos's *Gentlemen Prefer Blondes*, which was serialized in the Ullstein Verlag's magazine *Die Dame* (cf. Lethen 1970,

33–5; Rosenstein, 55 f.). Keun—in a manner resembling that of Horváth's plays—derives intelligent comedy from that material by taking the figure of the girl-on-the-make and setting her down a few rungs on the social ladder. Doris thus comes across as a shabby and self-deluding version of the woman who tries to beat the men at their own commercial game, achieving at best petty triumphs and at worst major humiliations as she moves from her Rhineland home town to the metropolis in search of openings. The choice of narrative medium, then, is not only an apt way of expressing the character's progressive disappointment and demoralization, nor just an appropriate vehicle for illuminating Doris's attitudes with ironic juxtapositions (and not without sympathetic humour); it is also a way of speaking to a young female readership in the very terms of the marketing strategies that were simultaneously being aimed at them. It is again a subtle technique for drawing the reader into an involvement in, and a critical understanding of, the mentality that is susceptible to facile dreams of opportunism.

It would be possible to extend this discussion to include a number of other novels of around 1930 which use disillusioning narrative structures in order to enlighten or persuade, with a variety of aims in mind. Such a discussion might, for example, include Franz Werfel's *Barbara* novel of 1929, which presents a studied repudiation of the revolutionary fervour of ten years earlier,[19] or Arnold Zweig's equally purposeful exposure of political passions in his Palestine novel of 1932, *De Vriendt kehrt heim* (De Vriendt Goes Home), as well as his disillusioning accounts of wartime experience (which are discussed in Chapter 7, below). It might also include Erik Reger's *Union der festen Hand* (The Union of the Firm Hand, 1931), with its sobering exposure of the concentration of political power in the hands of an industrial oligarchy, to which I shall refer in the course of Chapter 8. But for present purposes I should like to focus on the novels which Joseph Roth published during the Weimar period, partly because they bring together several of the dimensions of disillusionment that I have been discussing in this chapter, but also because they exhibit a sombre variety of disil-

---

[19] As I have shown elsewhere, the experience of disillusionment depicted in Werfel's *Barbara oder Die Frömmigkeit* takes the form of moments of acute revulsion rather than considered evaluation: Huber (ed.), 125–38.

lusionment which sets them apart from the novels I have so far considered.

Roth's early novels contain some stark representations of the forces that were threatening the pursuit of democracy and social justice in the early years of the Weimar Republic, but at the same time they convey a sense of desolation at the pervasive presence of those forces. *Das Spinnennetz* (The Spider's Web), which was serialized in a Viennese workers' newspaper in 1923 before appearing in book form in 1924, shows some clear affinities with Heinrich Mann's *Der Untertan*, and with the French tradition of socio-psychological narrative which had served Mann himself as a model. Like *Der Untertan*, *Das Spinnennetz* tells of a young man's rise to power and influence aided by the anti-democratic and anti-Semitic prejudices he shares with others, of the way his ruthlessness is fuelled by his own cowardice and fear of retribution, and of how his manipulation of others makes him dependent on a "web" of machination and double-dealing—except that in the conditions of post-war Berlin the story acquires a heightened sense of urgency and savagery. The career of Theodor Lohse is initially motivated by his acute desire to regain the kudos that had been his as an army officer in wartime, there is nothing to restrain him from pursuing that career with acts of cold-blooded and semi-legitimized murder, and any intimation of a sense of political authority or human values which might help to counter the cycle of brutality is conspicuously absent from the circumstances that Roth depicts. Another 1924 publication, *Die Rebellion* (The Rebellion), presents what might perhaps be seen as a tragi-comic counterpart to the ruthlessness of Lohse. Here the central character, Andreas Pum, cleaves to the values of heroic patriotism for which he has fought (and for which he has sacrificed a leg) until a chance occurrence leads to his being identified in public perception as a detractor and a "bolshevik", so that he finds himself consigned to the ranks of the very "heathens" against whom he had previously railed. Pum is unjustly imprisoned, and gives an impassioned account of himself as a victim of social injustice when defending himself in court. But the psychological experience on which this novel concentrates is that of a man who has seen the fundamental assumptions of his existence turned upside down, and who ends his days positively welcoming the prospect of "going to hell" because of his profound disillusionment with God and the whole of creation. Both novels can be seen, from one point of view, as containing an unflinching diagnosis of the social and political climate of the early 1920s, and as ironizing social forces which are threatening to democracy. But they are both also case studies in human responses—nihilistic aggression in the case of Lohse, nihilistic despair in the case of Pum—to a world from which any sense of fundamental value and legitimizing authority has been removed.

It is again the situation of those returning from the war that Roth depicts in *Hotel Savoy* (1924), but he does so in a manner which is in one sense more direct while at the same time raising the theme into a symbolic dimension. The novel's narrator, Gabriel Dan, is making his way back to Vienna from captivity in Russia, and stops off in a Polish town where he has family connections in the hope of obtaining money that will help him to complete his journey. The hotel he stays in is like a chunk of Western civilization set down in an Eastern European environment, with its seven storeys stratified according to the wealth and status of the clientele. It provides temporary accommodation for a variety of figures who are searching for vestiges of a past life, or for pointers towards a future one. They include an American millionaire, Bloomfield, who returns to visit his old father and is instantly besieged by those who hope to benefit from his charity; and they include Gabriel Dan's former comrade-at-arms, the Croat Zwonimir Pasin, who welcomes any intimation of revolution with excited anticipation, and whose universal term for any wondrous or propitious occurrence is "America". Roth, in other words, is depicting a part-real, part-fabulous space in which the characteristic human hopes and fancies of the post-war period can be played out and ultimately disappointed. At the end of the text, Bloomfield has departed as mysteriously as he arrived, having learned that his father is dead; the narrator travels on, having earned a few days' wages helping Bloomfield cope with his throng of petitioners; and Zwonimir disappears on a night of insurrectionary confusion, in which the hotel itself goes up in flames. The experience of returning from the Eastern front is presented here with that sharply etched attention to concrete detail that characterizes all of Roth's works. But the narrative structure converts that concrete detail into a symbolic evocation of a general historical situation in which there can be *no return* to previous ways of life.

These early novels of Roth's, then, are imbued with a sense of irredeemable loss and abandonment which runs deeper than any of the more specific expressions of disillusionment with German society that we have so far considered in this chapter. It is not just that Roth, with his Galician Jewish background, is writing with a keen awareness of the depredations that war and revolution have wrought among the peoples of Eastern Europe. Nor is it simply that he is drawing, as has been shown to be the case, on a tradition of Eastern European Jewish writing in which motifs of unfulfillable yearning have a special place.[20] Joseph Roth, as was to become increasingly apparent as time went on, also shared something of that dismal Spenglerian vision which saw dissolution and cultural disintegration as inescapable features of the current phase of European history (Henze). It is surely that spirit of cultural pessimism that lends his texts their chilling perspicacity. The sense of irony that we find in his novels is not one that aims to unmask the motives and mentalities of characters in a social context, but rather a kind of bifocal vision: it is as if the depiction of immediate experiences and perceptions is brought into sharp focus by an acute sense of the hollowness that lies behind them.

To speak of such narrative irony as an expression of *resignation* is in one sense correct, in that Roth's view of the human condition is generally characterized by a stoic sense of the inevitable curtailment of hope. But to speak of his novels as solely or predominantly expressions of resignation is to overlook the passion that drives his depiction of loss and disorientation as immediate human *experiences* in the contemporary world.[21] In two of the novels Roth published in the later 1920s,

---

[20] On the significance of Jewish traditions in Roth's works, see Claudio Magris's contribution to Bronsen (ed.) 1975, 181–216; also Robertson in Chambers (ed.), 155–200.

[21] When Gotthart Wunberg (Kessler and Hackert, 449–62) presents *Hotel Savoy* as a "representative text" of the Weimar period, he does so in order to suggest that resignation was the dominant characteristic of the literature of that period—but the works in which he finds a particular affinity with *Hotel Savoy* are the novels of Kästner and Feuchtwanger which, as I argued earlier in this chapter, express a particular brand of resignation in the face of the contemporary world. What is more

that underlying passion manifests itself in specific narrative devices. *Die Flucht ohne Ende* (Flight without End, 1927) is the work in which his programmatic insistence on "reporting" rather than "inventing" led his contemporaries to associate him firmly with the 'neusachlich' vogue for documentary writing; but there is a vigour in the authorial narration of this text which distinguishes it from any run-of-the-mill reportage. What Roth is presenting here as the 'authentic' experience of a personal friend is a *shared* sense of profound disaffection towards the world that has emerged from the war. The central character, Franz Tunda, is forcefully confronted with the contingent nature of his personal existence as he makes his way back from captivity in Siberia, his social identity being determined by chance encounters, now with a Polish backwoodsman (whose surname he adopts), now with a company of Bolsheviks. But Tunda's sense of dislocation becomes all the more intense when he reaches the West and finds himself living a limbo existence—"between resignation and expectation", as he puts it—alienated from a bourgeois society which seems to function in obedience to mechanical laws of its own, and paralysed by the sense of his own superfluity. (Even his own fiancée fails to acknowledge his presence.[22]) Arnold Zipper, in *Zipper und sein Vater* (Zipper and his Father, 1928), also leads an unsettled and aimless life after leaving the army, apparently unable to muster sufficient independence of will to do anything constructive with the talents that his father had always been keen to develop in a practical way. In this instance the fact that the story is told from the point of view of an intimate acquaintance enables Roth to convey sympathy and understanding for both father and son. The authorial narrator here is again a figure who seems powerfully motivated to inform the world of a sense of estrangement in which he himself participates. His is a voice which sternly resists any psychological stereotyping that would hold the parental

interesting in Wunberg's argument is the case he makes for seeing *Hotel Savoy* as a metaphorical representation of a world that is no longer amenable to metaphorical interpretation, in the sense that there can no longer be any confidence about what a particular character or event stands for; for that argument points to a dimension in Roth's work which can be related to the depiction of metaphysical disorientation as we find it in Kafka, or indeed (as Wunberg makes explicit) in Musil.

[22] Rainer Wild's analysis of this work brings out the sense in which Roth shows relationships in post-war society generally to have become functionalized: Becker and Weiß, 34–6.

generation accountable (in the manner of Ernst Glaeser's *Jahrgang 1902*) for Arnold Zipper's malaise. His preferred conclusion is that he and Arnold would have done better not to return from the war at all.

As time goes by, then, Roth's works present vivid accounts of a certain kind of problem for his generation, but he does so in a manner which is increasingly distanced from any constructive engagement with the issues of the present. By 1930 he was being perceived as a prominent defector from progressive causes. He had repudiated his earlier association with radical socialism in the reports he had sent back from a visit to the Soviet Union in 1926. He was adding his voice to those who were protesting against the cultural trends of the times, not least in his essay calling for an end to 'Neue Sachlichkeit'. He had contracted to write for a reactionary newspaper, the *Münchner Neueste Nachrichten*. And in his novel about the afflictions visited upon an Eastern European Jewish family, *Hiob* (Job, 1930), he was manifestly adopting a 'mythic' rather than a realist approach to fiction.[23] In a much-quoted letter to Stefan Zweig of October 1930, Roth expressed his profound disillusionment with the world around him. Europe was committing suicide, he wrote, and what made that suicide so slow and painful was the fact that Europe was already dead. What he means by this becomes clearer when he goes on to profess incomprehension towards the political extremism of the present, and to speak of himself as a contemporary of the Europe that had died in the First World War, and more specifically of the old Austrian Emperor Franz Joseph (*Briefe*, 186). An attitude of despair towards the post-war world was not a new element in Roth's writing: it is present in a restrained form in his portrayal of Franz Tunda and Arnold Zipper, and it had been intimated earlier still in *Das Spinnennetz*, where the figure of Theodor Lohse is perceived from the point of view of a Polish Jew as the embodiment of a Europe bent on self-destruction. It is in the novel that Roth went on to write next, however, that his withdrawal from the contemporary scene becomes manifest.

Radetzkymarsch (1932), the work for which Joseph Roth is most commonly remembered, is not straightforwardly a

---

[23] For succinct accounts of these developments in Roth's career, see the contributions by Scheible and Schweikert in Arnold (ed.) 1982.

nostalgic reconstruction of the pre-war Hapsburg Empire. It is true that the text lingers over those frequent descriptive and reflective passages which capture the flavour and the ambience of a more measured pre-war life, with its peculiar combination of precarious multi-ethnic equilibrium, bureaucratic correctness, and hedonistic sensuality—those qualities which Claudio Magris (1966) has identified as salient features of the "Hapsburg myth" perpetuated by literary writers after 1918. But in Roth's presentation of that historical world, both society and the state appear imbued with the consciousness of their own impending demise.

A moment of disillusionment is built into the very first chapter, which depicts the creation of a political myth out of the spirit of self-delusion. At the battle of Solferino in 1859—a battle which led to the effective loss of Austrian influence in Italy, and which is remembered later in the novel as the moment when the rot set in—a young lieutenant saves the life of the still younger Emperor by pulling him to the ground just in time to avoid an enemy bullet. He is subsequently dismayed to find that the incident has been stylized by patriotic wishful thinking into an act of extravagant military bravery. The descendants of this "hero of Solferino", the Trotta family, are destined to live with an ambiguous legacy: on the one hand they are the beneficiaries of recurrent imperial favours, but by the same token their lives become inextricably identified with a legendary imperial order which is becoming increasingly ossified. Not only does it appear to be an open secret among high-ranking army officers and civil servants that Austro-Hungary cannot long hold together against the strains of its internal ethnic and social tensions, and that it is bound to lose any war it is compelled to fight; there are also more palpable intimations of decay which accompany the lives of the Trottas themselves. Young Carl Joseph, the grandson of the "hero of Solferino", experiences his sexual initiation at the hands of a married woman, only to find that she dies soon afterwards in childbirth (a childbirth for which he is by implication responsible). During the early stages of his army service he develops a bond of fellowship with the Jewish regimental doctor, with whom he shares a sense of emptiness, a sense of not belonging, and an awareness of the 'call' of his ancestors; the doctor is soon killed in a duel provoked by a malicious insinuation about the nature of Carl Joseph's relationship with the doctor's estranged wife. In the figures of Carl Joseph and his father (a district governor of the Empire) Roth depicts a way of life which, from one generation to another, has had any sense of purpose or conviction drained from the preservation of inherited practices. Carl Joseph himself eventually finds the "meaningless" death he has anticipated through an act of quiet defiance in the opening phase of the First World War: he fetches water from a well that he knows to be under enemy fire.

This evocation of the Hapsburg past, then, is far removed from the humoristic construction of a ramshackle "Kakanien" as we find it in Musil's *Mann ohne Eigenschaften*. It is not so much an expression of affectionate leave-taking from the pre-war world as the evocation of a life that is entirely composed of valedictions. The traces of post-war disillusionment that we can follow through Roth's writing take us far beyond the critical representation of the social and cultural condition of life in Central Europe. In *Radetzkymarsch* those traces lead in the direction of a resigned withdrawal from life itself.

In this chapter I have concentrated on a selection of authors who use the subtle potential of the narrative medium in order to confront the experience of disillusionment, and in some ways to generate productive responses to it. In the case of Heinrich Mann it is possible to relate that sense of disillusionment directly to the experience of political disappointment. He had recognized the concentration of economic power in private hands as the most immediate threat to the republican values he had proclaimed in 1918, and in his fiction of the later 1920s he was looking for ways to keep alive a sense of historical perspective in German political life, and to impress upon contemporary readers the need for social responsibility. In a less specifically political sense, the disappointed expectations of a liberal humanitarianism are apparent in the novels of Kästner and Feuchtwanger: it is there that we find the Enlightenment hope for the progression of humanity as a whole to a higher sense of reasoned social organization confronted with contemporary manifestations of wilfulness, irrationality, and malice. And in a sense which remains more wryly elusive (and constrained within a private adolescent perspective), Hermann Kesten is teasing out the senses in which the liberal pursuit of freedom is beset by both personal and social disruptive factors. Joseph Roth provides a contrasting case to these expressions of liberal protest: his disillusionment emerges in the course of the Weimar years as the historical pessimism of someone who has come to perceive the experiences of the early twentieth century predominantly in terms of political and cultural disintegration.

As expressions of concern for the pursuit of a humane order of social relations, the novels I have considered are frequently explicit in their repudiation of the public values which had come to prominence in the 'stabilization phase' of the Weimar Republic (i.e. 1924–9). They are particularly critical of the way personal lives are tending to become rationalized in accordance with the principles of commercial calculation. Heinrich Mann subjects the characters of *Die große Sache* to the experience of a frenzied pursuit of material advantage in order that they may discover the limits and the destructive potential of the contemporary lifestyle into which they have been socialized. Irmgard Keun presents her young women as committed—in Gilgi's case in a self-assured way, in Doris's case in a self-deluding one—to the calculated pursuit of personal advantage, in order subsequently to expose the inherent weaknesses of such an outlook. More direct repudiations of a shallow, mercenary materialism can be found in Joseph Roth's *Die Flucht ohne Ende*, and throughout the pages of Kästner's *Fabian*. In the narratives of Horváth, Keun, and Kesten, as well as Kästner, that repudiation is extended into more specific expressions of the sense that the dominant expectation in contemporary society has become one of mutual exploitation: human relationships at all levels have become imbued with a spirit of power-brokerage, with the sense that any interpersonal activity is being weighed up in terms of whether it represents a good or a bad deal. Beyond this sense of a disintegrative social ethos that these authors are registering at a personal level, there is also a sense of horror at the organization of humanity at the institutional level into a system of mutual disregard. Kessel, Fallada, and Heinrich Mann all express that sense of alarm in ways which transcend the immediate circumstances of economic crisis around 1930, even if the

terms in which they express it are respectively limited to personal anguish (Kessel), the threatened private idyll (Fallada),
and the lost liberal ideal of individual self-fulfilment (Heinrich
Mann).

The limitations of each of these works as a representation of
German society at a time of cataclysmic crisis are not difficult
to identify. Each focuses on manifestations of individual behaviour which are in most cases only tangentially connected to the
large-scale issues of economic reorganization, social depredation, and political allegiance. Their strength as narrative depictions of social experience, however, lies precisely in their focus
on human relations at the level of interpersonal transaction and
private conversation. If I were to sum up the senses in which I
think these novels achieve a positive critical potential in relation
to the social world of their time, then I would want to emphasize three things. First they provide a critique of the public
values of 'Sachlichkeit' as they had become consolidated in the
late 1920s, taking their characters (and with them the reader)
through a process of self-discovery which exposes the shallowness of those values. I see this happening particularly in Mann's
Die große Sache and the novels of Irmgard Keun. Secondly they
focus attention on those social developments which constitute
a challenge to the stability of a liberal society. This is manifestly
true of Fallada as well as Mann and Keun, and in their more
strident, egocentric way it is also true of Kästner and Kessel.
Finally they present an exposure of mentalities which are threatening to any pursuit of intersubjective understanding and the
peaceful settling of conflicts of interest. This is only superficially
the case with Feuchtwanger (whose characterization of Bavarian attitudes tends to *presuppose* their bigotry) or with Kästner
(who shows us only Fabian's knee-jerk frustration in response
to authoritarianism and reaction). It is very starkly the case in
the early novels of Joseph Roth. But I would say that it is most
effectively dealt with precisely by those authors who adopt a
small-scale approach to the depiction of social interaction,
namely by Ödön von Horváth and Irmgard Keun.

6

Remembering the War

"The war, my dear doctor, has been forgotten." "Worse than that, Herr Pont, it has been repressed."

Arnold Zweig, "Pont und Anna", 1925[1]

The time is fast approaching when the war will become a myth.

Joseph Ponten, 1927 (*LW* 3, 4, 1)

The narrative accounts of the First World War warrant a chapter to themselves for two reasons. They testify to the ideological contest that took place in the 1920s over the way the war should be interpreted in retrospect, and in doing so they illustrate the senses in which the post-war mood in Germany should not be viewed simply in terms of disillusionment or a retreat from ideologies.

There is, of course, a sense in which the war literature of other combatant nations can also be interpreted as a reconstruction of the experience in the terms of particular ways of looking at the world. The publication of Paul Fussell's book *The Great War and Modern Memory* in 1975 made readers generally more keenly aware of the senses in which the well-known English war memoirs by Robert Graves, Edmund Blunden, and Siegfried Sassoon, for example, were moulded by literary preconceptions as well as by personal experience. Cruel ironies and stark contrasts may have been among the commonly shared experiences of the effects of protracted and static warfare, but the narrative structures in which such memories are recalled can also be seen to relate to one or another kind of fictional prefiguration. In Sassoon's case it is the highlighting of symbolic contrasts, in the case of Graves it is the structure of comic anecdote. Fussell

---

[1] Arnold Zweig, *Der Regenbogen* (Berlin: J. M. Spaeth, 1925), 307.

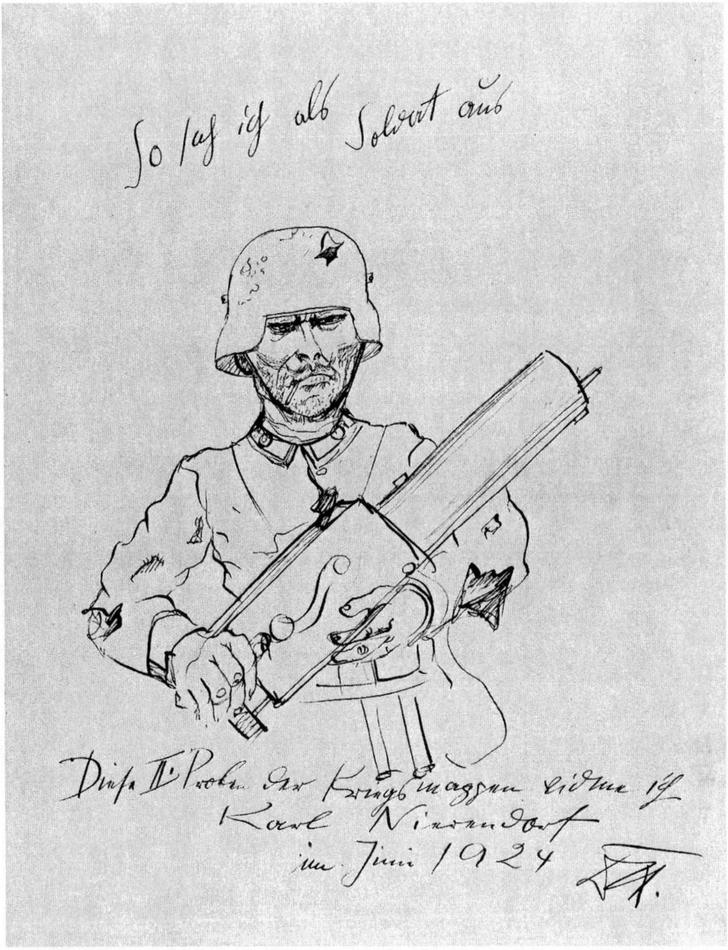

Fig. 6. Otto Dix, *This is how I looked as a soldier*, 1924

rather overstated his case when he tried to relate Erich Maria Remarque's *Im Westen nichts Neues* (All Quiet on the Western Front) to a German baroque tradition in imaginative writing, although he is certainly right in principle to contrast the contrived eeriness of some of Remarque's effects with the comic tradition he had recognized in the works of English writers.[2] But it is not my purpose here to take issue with the interpretation of details in depictions of the war by German authors. Rather I wish to emphasize the contrasts among those depictions, the implications of the narrative strategies adopted by particular authors, and the manner in which, in the context of Weimar Germany, the issue of how the war should be depicted became heavily politicized.

When reviewing some right-wing writings in 1930, Walter Benjamin commented that the Germans had lost the 1914–18 war in a double sense: first as a matter of historical fact, and secondly in that they had tried to forget it (*GS* III, 242). Benjamin's remark contained a polemical thrust, and a characteristically paradoxical point about the function of literature. He was blaming the forgetting of the war on the dull-mindedness of the bourgeoisie, while also implying that the fictionalization of the war in itself constituted a retreat from the reality of it. But he was also drawing attention to a pattern in German public responses to the war which might not be readily apparent from the standard historical accounts of the Weimar period.

There are obvious senses in which the war was never far from public consciousness. Commemoration of the war dead naturally became part of ceremonial state practice under the Weimar Republic; the cost of war pensions and the problem of caring for the war wounded remained abiding political issues throughout the period; and the perception of the Versailles Treaty as an unjustly imposed and punitive peace settlement provided right-wing politicians with a never-failing opportunity for agitation (cf. Whalen). At the same time, the awareness of the Great War as a major historical turning point and a source of opportunites for revolutionary change was nurtured on the radical left, and was kept before the public mind by Piscator's productions of the mid-1920s, for example. But there was something about the literary responses to the subject after 1920 which nevertheless made the war look like a forgotten experience. In the epochal novels of Thomas Mann and Robert Musil the war represents

---

[2] Paul Fussell, "Der Einfluß kultureller Paradigmen auf die literarische Wiedergabe traumatischer Erfahrung", in Vondung, 175–87. Fussell's allegations of Gothic fantasy in Remarque have been effectively refuted by Brian Murdoch (1993, 176f.).

a kind of vanishing point for the narrative, a threshold beyond which the text does not venture; and in Döblin's *Berlin Alexanderplatz* it represents a concealed memory which lies behind some aspects of the behaviour of the protagonist Franz Biberkopf, but without being explicitly evoked. There is even evidence that in the mid-1920s German publishers thought the subject had become unsaleable. Joseph Ponten, in the article of January 1927 that is quoted at the head of this chapter, was protesting at the exclusion of the subject of wartime experience from a literary competition announced by the S. Fischer publishing house.[3] Ponten, a nationalist and a deeply conservative writer, envisaged the war as the potential subject-matter for a great German epic in the manner of the *Iliad* or the *Nibelungenlied*, and within a very few years other nationalist authors were to attempt just such a treatment. But his comment about the war becoming the stuff of myth might also alert us to the senses in which the spectacular wave of war novels which did appear at the end of the 1920s represented a struggle for control of the memory of the war.

The phases in the literary treatment of the war to which Benjamin alludes have been reconstructed by Martin Travers in his 1982 book *German Novels on the First World War and their Ideological Implications, 1918–1933*. The immediate post-war years had seen the publication of many a volume of memoirs by high-ranking officers, largely concerned with the justification of their own strategic role, and insistent that, however things had turned out politically, Germany had not been defeated in the field. Particularly influential were the memoirs of the Grand Admiral of the Fleet, Alfred von Tirpitz, and those of the chief architect of Germany's campaign during its final year, Erich Ludendorff (soon to be associated with Hitler's attempted Munich putsch of 1923). Later historical analysis was to show how Ludendorff in particular had used his position in 1918 to ensure that responsibility for political decisions which looked like the actions of a defeated nation were safely entrusted to parliamentarians, as opposed to representatives of the imperial establishment. The effect of his actions at the time, however,

---

[3] Both Georg von der Vring and Ludwig Renn, who wrote their war novels in the early 1920s, had their works rejected by a succession of publishers before they finally appeared in 1927 and 1928 respectively: see H.-H. Müller, 95, 186.

was to create the potent political legend that the German army had been 'stabbed in the back'—a legend which the most painstaking investigations of a government commission in the early 1920s were unable effectively to dispel (cf. Travers, 30; Bessel 1988, 22).

Another popular form of publication between 1915 and 1919 was the diary-style account of front-line action. The perspective that dominates here is that of the more junior officer, the platoon or company commander, concerned with limited battlefield objectives and the personal qualities needed to accomplish them. Some of the most vivid accounts of the emotional experience of infantry action ever written are to be found in one of these works, Ernst Jünger's *In Stahlgewittern* (Storm of Steel, 1920). Such diary-style literature continued to be published in small editions well into the mid-1920s, and two examples written from more lofty perspectives were to be commended to English schoolboys for many a year to come as representing the humanity of the German officer and gentleman: Hans Carossa, *Rumänisches Tagebuch* (Rumanian Diary, 1924), and Rudolf Binding, *Aus dem Krieg* (From the War, 1925). Carossa writes as a medical officer, and shows sensitivity towards the human predicaments of war from within a staunchly unpolitical ethos which accepts the war as something inflicted as if by fate. Binding is eloquently critical of the devastation entailed by the High Command's strategy of attrition, and of the distortion of truth in official reports; but he writes as a staff officer for whom the rationale of the war and its sustaining ethos again remain beyond question (cf. Travers, 38–41).

Both the glory and the horror of war had found direct expression in the lyric poetry written between 1914 and 1918. But censorship, and probably also the sheer nearness of the experience, impeded the broader depiction of war as a social phenomenon. Even those Expressionist dramas which placed their treatment of the subject on the plane of existential spirituality and universalized grief could only be performed in private in 1918 (Patterson, 194). Reinhard Goering's *Seeschlacht* (Sea Battle) confines its action to the gun turret of a battleship, and its dramatic argument to the search for meaning in the face of death. Fritz von Unruh stylizes the experience of bereavement in *Ein Geschlecht* (A Noble Family). While the memory of gas warfare clearly influenced Georg Kaiser's choice of the title *Gas* for his dramatic trilogy of 1917–20, what that text provides is a highly intellectualized and notoriously abstract vision of humanity's inexorable progression through industrialization to eventual mutual annihilation. A clear sense of outrage at the relentless destruction of war is to be found in Toller's *Die Wandlung* (Transfiguration) of 1919, and equally clear echoes of it are to be found in some of his later plays. But while *Die Wandlung* makes use of both harrowing battlefield images and political satire, what it is primarily articulating is that volatile mood of social cataclysm and utopian counter-current which was all-pervasive in the literature of the immediate post-war phase.[4]

The one work of that time which stands out as an attempt to encompass the social behaviour of the German and Austrian nations at war—notwithstanding its openly apocalyptic title— is *Die letzten Tage der Menschheit* (The Last Days of Mankind) by the Viennese author Karl Kraus. Written by a process of slow accretion between 1917 and 1922, it suffers from compositional and ideological inconsistencies, but it captures aspects of the political responsibility for the war and the psychological collusion of society in it by presenting in dialogue form statements which had actually appeared in print during the course of the war (cf. Timms, 371–402). Running to over 600 pages, the work poses enormous problems for stage presentation (Kraus himself describes it in his preface, sardonically, as being conceived for a "Martian theatre"). But in its self-conscious use of montage and ironic juxtaposition it may be seen as pioneering a form of documentary technique which was to be used to some effect by later novelists and campaigners who sought to defend humanitarian values against the cynicism and the emotional appeal of the Nationalist right.

Those who attempted to promote views which were critical of Germany's wartime leadership faced repressive measures in the 1920s. The statistician and social democrat E. J. Gumbel published a pamphlet in 1919 entitled *Vier Jahre Lügen*

---

[4] The same may be said of many prose works which appeared around the end of the war, including Andreas Latzko, *Menschen im Krieg* (1917), Leonhard Frank, *Der Mensch ist gut* (1918), Bernhard Kellermann, *Der 9. November* (1919), and Hermann Hesse, *Demian* (1919).

(Four Years of Lies) which indicated, amongst other things, that the Kaiser's government had deliberately frustrated international peace initiatives since 1915. A leading member of the German League for Human Rights, Gumbel went on to chart the record of political violence in the early 1920s and to demonstrate the nationalist bias in the judiciary's response to it. But in common with other leading pacifists of the time, he faced a series of attempts to stifle him with law suits—all eventually dismissed—as well as a campaign to remove him from his university post at Heidelberg for his outspokenness. He was driven into exile by Nazi agitation in 1932 (Holl and Wette, 113–34). The revolutionary pacifist Ernst Friedrich mounted his campaign on an international level and with a multilingual text. In his book *Krieg dem Kriege!* (War against War, 1924) he combined two kinds of documentary evidence. He printed a unique collection of previously unpublished photographs exposing the horrors of the war, and interspersed them with complacent and bombastic utterances by military leaders and imperial politicians. Ernst Friedrich, too, suffered frequent litigation for alleged defamation, and a period of imprisonment in 1930–1 under a charge of high treason for the intended dissemination of anti-militarist literature among members of the army and the police.[5]

Judicial suppression faced others who—perhaps naively—sought to present their wartime experiences as symptomatic of the inhumanity of the old imperial regime. Heinrich Wandt assembled a veritable catalogue of corruption, iniquity, and brutality among German officers in occupied Belgium under the title *Etappe Gent* ("Etappe" implying the extended system of military administration behind the front lines). His book was initially banned in 1920, published in expanded form in 1924, and went on to sell over 200,000 copies in popular editions by 1929. Officers whom Wandt had portrayed in the book were unsuccessful in seeking a legal injunction prohibiting its sale, but Wandt was instead charged with military treason in 1924 and sentenced to six years in prison.[6] Bruno Vogel set about the

---

[5] See Douglas Kellner's introduction to Ernst Friedrich, *War against War!* (London: Journeyman, 1987).
[6] Cf. U. Baron and H.-H. Müller, "Weltkriege und Kriegsromane", *Zeitschrift für Literaturwissenschaft und Linguistik*, 19 (1989), Heft 75, 14–38 (18). Wandt published his own account of his imprisonment under the title *Der Gefangene von Potsdam* (The Prisoner of Potsdam) (Vienna: Agis, 1927).

systematic deflation of wartime clichés in a passionate tract, *Es lebe der Krieg!* (Long Live War!), but it was confiscated and banned on grounds of blasphemy, again in 1924 (Momber, 31-3). And the Communist J. R. Becher researched the effects of chemical warfare and its development during and since the war, working his findings into a novel in which he imagined its potential impact on civilian populations in a future war against the Soviet Union. His novel, which took its title from the formula for the poison gas Levisite, was also confiscated, and Becher was subjected to a protracted and inconclusive prosecution for high treason on the basis of this and other publications, which turned him into a literary cause célèbre between the years 1925 and 1928.[7] Coupled with the election of Field Marshal Hindenburg as President of the Republic in 1925, the judicial suppression of critical writings on the war has been seen as one of the clearest indicators that the economic stabilization in the years after 1923 was accompanied by a restoration of authoritarian power structures in German society (Bornebusch, 72 ff.; Bessel 1988, 33 f.).

Such was the background to the sudden resurgence of German public interest in the war at the end of the 1920s, and it helps to account for the palpable difference between the pattern of publications about the war in Germany on the one hand and that in Britain, France, and America on the other. While there had of course been painful and bitter memories to assimilate in the victorious western countries, too, there had at least been a certain continuity in the way that these had been articulated. Henri Barbusse's famous disillusioning novel *Le Feu* (Under Fire, 1916) had been published while the war was still in progress, and was promptly awarded the Prix Goncourt. (An English translation appeared in 1917; a German translation was published in neutral Switzerland in 1918, but military censorship prevented the immediate dissemination of it in Germany itself.) Roland Dorgelès was able to publish his novel *Les Croix de bois* (The Wooden Crosses) in 1919, but a German translation had to wait until 1930. The war novels of John Dos Passos and E. E. Cummings appeared in America in the early 1920s, and in England both R. H. Mottram and Ford Madox Ford

---

[7] Cf. Kaes, 145-7. A full documentation of the Becher case can be found in F. Albrecht et al., *Aktionen, Bekenntnisse, Perspektiven* (Berlin: Aufbau, 1966), 65-127.

were publishing trilogies about the war between 1924 and 1928.[8] Even Hollywood moved rapidly through a documentary phase in the immediate post-war years, and by 1925 King Vidor's *The Big Parade* was openly exploring the cruel ironies of war; it might not have been a runaway box-office success in America, but in Germany it was banned.[9] In so far as accounts of the war were available to the German reading and cinema-going public in the mid-1920s, by contrast, they constituted a mixture of military self-glorification and romantic nostalgia.[10]

The "return" of the war in German fiction which occurred at the end of the 1920s was thus in part a response to a genuine thirst for information which had been denied to the German public, but it was not without its aspect of cynical calculation. Remarque's *Im Westen nichts Neues* began to be serialized in the *Vossische Zeitung* precisely on 10 November 1928, the eve of the tenth anniversary of the armistice. It was not the first of the German war novels to appear. The liberal *Frankfurter Zeitung* had serialized Arnold Zweig's *Der Streit um den Sergeanten Grischa* (The Case of Sergeant Grischa) in the summer of 1927, and had followed this in the course of 1928 with Siegfried Kracauer's *Ginster* and Ludwig Renn's *Krieg* (War). Remarque was also acquainted with the novel *Soldat Suhren* (Soldier Suhren, 1927) by Georg von der Vring which he reviewed, together with some earlier works by Ernst Jünger, at the time he was preparing his own novel.[11] But publishers were evidently still cautious

---

[8] On the steady output of war novels in English during the 1920s, see Bruno Schultze, "Fiction and Truth: Politics and the War Novel", in Stanzel and Löschnigg, 297–311.

[9] See Kevin Brownlow, *The War, the West, and the Wilderness* (London: Secker & Warburg, 1979), 176–90; Hans Sochaczewer, "Der verbotene Film 'The Big Parade'", *LW* 3, 18, 7.

[10] See Rüter, 13–24; Bornebusch, 37–60; H.-H. Müller, 20–35. When the literary scholar Ernst Jirgal published a broad survey of war literature in 1931 under the suggestive title *Die Wiederkehr des Weltkrieges in der Literatur* (The Return of the World War in Literature), he listed well over 200 war books by German and Austrian authors which had appeared in the course of 1929 and 1930, whereas the titles which dated from before 1928 were predominantly by foreign authors.

[11] Erich Maria Remarque, "*Soldat Suhren—Ringen an der Somme—Das Wäldchen 125—In Stahlgewittern—Das Frontbuch*", *Sport im Bild* (Berlin) 1928, no. 12, 895–6. In addition to the evidence of textual borrowing from nationalist authors discovered by Rüter (pp. 47 ff.), it is conceivable that the section in Remarque's chapter 8 about Russian prisoners of war and the "Befehl" that makes them enemies of the German soldier was influenced by Zweig's *Grischa* novel, and that

about the prospects for war novels, and when Remarque approached them in 1928 he had difficulty persuading them to accept his manuscript. Even when he signed up with Ullstein in August 1928, the contract contained clauses which insured the publisher against the possibility of poor sales (Howind, 58). At the same time, however, this influential publishing house threw its efforts into promoting *Im Westen nichts Neues* as *the* novel which, ten years after the event, was finally going to tell the truth about the war. The book version was deliberately held back until 31 January 1929 in order to keep appetites keen and to avoid competition with the Christmas market; and on the day of the launch, three different Ullstein papers carried full-page articles about Remarque by well-known authors, using the novel's title as a banner headline. Finally, when sales took off, the book's commercial success was itself presented in the promotional literature as proof positive of the truthfulness of what it depicted—the hype was complete.[12]

As Angelika Howind notes, it was the advance publicity for the novel that was also responsible for creating a cynical legend. In an announcement of the serialization, published in the *Vossische Zeitung* of 8 November 1928, Remarque was stylized into a simple soldier with no literary background, who had just sat down one day to write down his wartime experiences: his novel was to be "the first true monument to the Unknown Soldier". Documentary authenticity was evidently considered a prime selling-point; and in the interests of this, the publisher also insisted on deleting a sentence from the prefatory note to the book. In the form in which readers are familiar with it, that note describes the book as neither an indictment nor a confession. As Remarque had originally typed it, it also denied—above all—that the novel represented an *experience*, "for death is not an experience for him who is confronted by it" (Howind, 59,

---

his description of injuries owes something to the publications of Ernst Friedrich or J. R. Becher.

[12] Further details of the publication history of *Im Westen nichts Neues* are given by Eksteins (pp. 276f.), but his account is marred by a curious animus against Remarque for aspects of the publicity for which he was clearly not responsible. The fullest study of the publication and subsequent reception of Remarque's novel is Johannes Brautzsch, "Untersuchungen über die Publikumswirksamkeit der Romane *Im Westen nichts Neues* und *Der Weg zurück* von Erich Maria Remarque vor 1933", Diss. Potsdam, 1969.

63). Even the small amount of laconic self-awareness that these words convey was incompatible with the image of the author as naive autobiographer which the marketing strategy required. The publisher's imposition of an inauthentic identity on the author (on the pretext of promoting the 'authenticity' of his book) is one reason, incidentally, why Remarque's subsequent statements about his intentions in writing the novel must be treated with particular caution. Another is his evident difficulty in coping with the political controversy that arose around his novel.

What we find if we strip away the misleading claims of Remarque's publisher is—in the words of Herbert Bornebusch (p. 118)—the artful reconstruction of an ostensibly personal experience from the stuff of collective memory. What prompted the controversy was the way the text persistently deheroicized the war.[13] Each chapter is carefully organized around its own particular constellation of themes which were to become commonplaces in the depiction of the experiences of the common soldier. The soldier's most fundamental concern, as evoked in the opening chapter, is not the fighting, but the fulfilment of bodily needs. The company is tucking into double rations; only as we read on is it gradually disclosed that the reason for this good fortune is that half their force was killed or wounded in the previous day's action. Apart from eating, their concerns are with catching up on sleep and providing as best they can for the rigours that lie ahead. The second half of the chapter takes us on a visit to a comrade whose leg has been amputated in the field hospital. Only here do we begin to get a sense of the background of the characters we have been reading about, in the shape of recollections of schooldays and the teachers who had dinned patriotic sentiment into them until they had joined up. Only gradually, again, does the unpleasant truth emerge that the survivors have an ulterior motive for their visit, namely to scavenge the dying man's boots. The picture of army life that Remarque is building up is one that is reduced to the horizons of basic material need: these young men are alienated from the standards of home and civil institutions, not so much in the sense that they have discovered the nationalist clichés to be a cruel delusion

---

[13] For a summary of the critical reception of Remarque's novel, see Gollbach, 293–305; H.-H. Müller, 66–93.

(they prefer not to think too deeply about what has got them into the situation they find themselves in), but by simple habits of mind.

The story that follows is similarly composed of ironic juxtapositions. The pathos of watching the amputee Kemmerich die is set against the impersonal routine of death in the military hospital. The first account of the experience of artillery bombardment and gas attack is followed by the carnivalesque episode in which the group celebrates the incarceration of one of their number for a deliberate act of insubordination by stealing and roasting a goose. The long, central sixth chapter, which evokes the experience of trench warfare—the remorseless logic of attack and counter-attack, the violent rage engendered by an atmosphere of kill-or-be-killed, and the nerve-racking cries of the wounded by night—is framed by examples of the macabre humour of men accustomed to the ever-presence of gruesome death. It is followed again by relaxation: a period at rest, an illicit night of love with some French women, and a spell of home leave which serves only to reinforce the sense of a gulf of misunderstanding between serving men and civilians. The closing stages of the narrative renew the depiction of the intensity of experience at the front, with the narrator telling of his first experience of hand-to-hand combat, and of the slow death, at his hand, of a Frenchman with whom he shares a shellhole. "What war really means", in this account, is the mutilation and debilitation he observes while hospitalized with a leg-wound; and back in the trenches, he finds his comrades eliminated one by one around him until we are informed, in the short final paragraph, that he too was killed, a month or so before the armistice, on a day when activity was so typical of the war routine that all was reported to be quiet on the Western Front. In a very deliberate way, the fiction constructs its account of a young generation cut off from their pre-war roots, isolated from the population at home, and relentlessly destroyed by a carnage that no one had anticipated and no one seems to understand.

The narrator has a name—Paul Bäumer—but his social identity is only vaguely defined. He is characterized as sensitive and artistic, and accustomed to a higher social perspective than "the poor" (although his own parents are described as worn down by labour and privation). But it is not his character that matters to the way the novel works so much as his constant presence as an accompanying voice, guiding us through events in the present tense. It talks us through the army routine, the sensations of exposure to attack, the fear and apprehension, the physical oppression, and the special sense of intimacy with the earth and of group solidarity associated with those experiences. At the same time it retains, in its moments of lyrical reflection, an awareness of the now distant promise of youth, innocence, and cultured civility. In short, it is a voice which guides the reader on an imaginary journey into a realm which is by definition remote from the shared reality of peacetime society. The contrived pathos of Remarque's final paragraph reinforces this impression by intimating that Bäumer's is a voice speaking to us from beyond the grave. In an important psychological study of the soldier's experience at war, Eric Leed has described the transition by which the infantryman in particular becomes separated from his former identity and from the community to which he used to belong, and initiated into a new one (Leed 1979). A crucial factor, surely, in the enduring popularity of Remarque's novel is the contrivance by which it gives an uninitiated readership the illusion of participating in the infantryman's experience of separation, alienation from his home background, and integration into a community defined by the distinctive varieties of suffering it had shared.

In the wake of Remarque's spectacular success, the German book market became swiftly flooded with narrative accounts of the war. The Viennese scholar Ernst Jirgal, who surveyed the literary treatment of the war in 1931, listed over 200 such publications in German between 1928 and 1930. It was characteristic of this wave of war literature that it placed a high priority on the claim to first-hand 'authentic' experience, and it became a commonplace to speak of these writings as the testimony of a 'war generation' that had finally found its voice. Reviewers were for the most part concerned to judge these works from the point of view of whether or not they created a sense of how the war had 'really' been (cf. Prangel, 61–4). The atmosphere of tense controversy in which these critical assessments took place is reflected in the terms of the questionnaire in which the Ullstein Verlag, at the end of 1929, invited readers to evaluate

Remarque's novel: did they or did they not find it truthful, pacifistic, offensive, a danger to youth, and a threat to religion
and morality (H.-H. Müller, 66)? The question of literary merit
was simply not a major concern at the time. But if we want to
develop an adequate sense of the terms in which wartime experience was being reconstructed, then we need to consider the
distinctive narrative approaches which authors adopted for
that purpose, as well as the manifest ideological content of
particular works.

To start at the most simple level of depiction, Ludwig Renn's
Krieg (War), which was written in the early 1920s and published
shortly before Remarque's novel in 1928, aspires to do nothing
more than give a mundane account of what the physical
experience of wartime service had been like for the ordinary
infantryman. But in the circumstances of the time, that alone
was sufficient for the work to be recognized as a self-conscious
break with the tradition of self-justifying officer memoirs. The
author was in fact himself an officer and aristocrat by the name
of Arnold Friedrich Vieth von Golssenau, who had served in the
war in the rank of Captain, and had subsequently joined the
Communist Party. It appears that the *Frankfurter Zeitung*, keen
to emphasize what was new and different about the work,
insisted that it be published under a pseudonym and that the
author's true identity be kept secret for six months after the start
of serialization (H.-H. Müller, 186f.). The pseudonym he chose
was the name of his protagonist. Nothing in the text itself
betrays any sign of political allegiance, and the work was initially reviewed in positive terms in the nationalist press as a
faithful depiction of the war.[14] The first-person narrator is a
common soldier who works his way up through the ranks
between the moment of mobilization in 1914 and the armistice
of 1918, and is decorated for bravery along the way. He takes
part in various battles on the western front, and describes the
distinctive experiences of the front-line fighter: advancing,
coming under fire, taking casualities, the euphoria of attack, the
recognition of one's own shock responses, and the apathy that

[14] It is only at the very end of Renn's sequel, *Nachkrieg* (1930), that he makes
his political allegiance explicit, but in the course of 1929 he had explained his sense
of ideological purpose in the Communist journal *Die Linkskurve* (1, 1, 11–14 *et
seq.*). Cf. Bornebusch, 91–7.

results from protracted exposure to danger. His emotional responses and the conclusions he draws from his experiences are reported only in lapidary fashion, and there is liberal use of onomatopoeia in the evocation of events on the battlefield. In so far as there is any sense of conscious literary orientation in the work, it comes with the brief allusion to Grimmelshausen's *Simplicissimus* novel, which Renn's protagonist is given as a birthday present. The implication, in context, is that the wartime experience of the persona Renn has created is that of a simple figure buffeted by the events of world history and the decisions of others, and for whom the ignorance and uncertainty surrounding those decisions is part of the characteristic experience. Renn's professed intention was to break with the insistence of the memoir tradition that there had been a higher purpose behind the carnage, and foremost among the conclusions he draws from the experience of battle is that sacrificing lives is in itself pointless. But the inescapable consequence of the narrative stance he maintains is that the reader is not provided with any explanation of what is happening and why.

Of all the German writers of the period, the one who is most commonly referred to nowadays in discussions of the immediate experience of battle is Ernst Jünger, and the substance of his writings undoubtedly provides justification for this situation. But although he worked doggedly throughout the early 1920s at his diary-style accounts of battlefield experience (and continued to revise them subsequently), his writings received relatively little attention until after Remarque's success. Even then it appears that they were more sympathetically received in England, where Remarque's novel had stimulated interest in the German side of the picture, than in Germany.[15] Jünger's narrative stance is that of the participant—he tells the story of his own wartime service as an infantry officer, in the course of which he was wounded several times and highly decorated—and of the unflinching observer. His texts bear vivid testimony to the heightening of sensory awareness that comes with living in the face of perpetual danger. As a contemporary reader commented, his descriptions are distinguished by a clinical quality,

---

[15] See Hans-Harald Müller, "'Herr Jünger thinks war a lovely business': On the Reception of Ernst Jünger's *In Stahlgewittern* in Germany and Britain before 1933", in Stanzel and Löschnigg, 327–39.

as if he has gone about the battlefield carrying a bag of quick lime, but then forgot at the decisive moment to scatter it.[16] A soldier's first encounter with a dead body, Jünger notes, leaves a precise image seered on the mind, and he specifies: the black crust of blood in the hair, the bluish lips set off against the whiteness of the teeth, the hand driven like a claw into moss and soil.[17] His narrative reconstructions are consistently frank and undeluded about what this war between industrialized nations entails. In the early stages, the adjustments that need to be made are to a life of dirt, physical labour, and vigilance. The fighting, when it comes, is the application of a learned craft, intensified in its effects by the release of pent-up vital energies. By the time we reach the campaigns of 1918, Jünger is describing sustained artillery bombardments as the unleashing of elemental destructive forces (the "storms of steel" evoked in the title of his first volume), but affirming all the more strongly in that connection his faith in military strategy and the ability of his own troops to prevail. Often he adopts the perspective of a superior vantage point from which to describe the activity of stormtroopers overwhelming a defensive position or the devastating impact of artillery fire, and the more practised his writing becomes, the more stylized his descriptions. By the time we reach *Feuer und Blut* (Fire and Blood, 1925), the reconstruction of momentary perceptions is palpably moulded by the technique of literary analogy. From the edge of a crater he observes the after-effects of a direct hit on his company. A pack of shadowy figures is clambering up the sides of the crater, and from the bottom a "magical light" shines forth, which his next sentence identifies as the combustion of machine-gun ammunition. He goes on to recognize a mass of bodies seriously wounded by the exploding shell. But in his evocation of them they are "squirming like amphibians in a boiling sea, like the damned in a Dantesque vision" (*Feuer*, 81).

It became fashionable in the 1980s to view Ernst Jünger as a major representative of literary modernism. The basis for that view was provided by Karl Heinz Bohrer, in his book *Die Ästhetik des Schreckens* (The Aesthetics of Terror, 1978), in which he constructed a cultural lineage for Jünger which ran

[16] Erik Reger, *Kleine Schriften*, vol. i, 80.
[17] *Der Kampf als inneres Erlebnis*, 12.

back to the aesthetic play on the imaginative power of terror in works by Oscar Wilde, Edgar Allan Poe, and E. T. A. Hoffmann. More specifically, Bohrer argued that the sense of reality as dissolved into isolated and terrifying images, which Jünger's writings undoubtedly convey, places him in a tradition which runs from the dandyism of Baudelaire to the literary shock techniques of French Surrealism (Bohrer, 140–3). What was misleading about Bohrer's argument was not so much the account it gave of Jünger's descriptive practice (which no doubt does evoke physical sensations with a directness that excludes the intervention of moral control, as Bohrer says), but the way it appeared to turn amoral sensationalism into *the* defining feature of the modernist heritage. It did so by excluding from that heritage the dimension of rational self-critique and self-irony which can be found in Baudelaire, in Wilde, in Nietzsche, and even in André Breton (to say nothing of Musil and Döblin), and by excluding from its own analysis the ideological perspective of Jünger's depiction of war.

Jünger presents the war of attrition as a process of quasi-Darwinian selection, from which the front-line fighter emerges, tempered and vulcanized, as a new breed. Intellectually he was seeking to uphold the ideal of heroic individualism with which he had entered the war in the face of the collective experience of indiscriminate destruction. The collection of essays in which he attempted to resolve this intellectual problem, *Der Kampf als inneres Erlebnis* (Battle as an Inner Experience, 1922), is highly eclectic. It contains passing allusions to the aesthetic theories of Kant and Schiller, as well as to the Nietzschean conception of intoxication (*Rausch*). The assertion early in the text that war is "the father of all things" is merely a simplistic version of what Nietzsche has to say in *The Gay Science* about cultural achievements as the outcome of ruthless struggle. Jünger also draws selectively on Spengler's *Der Untergang des Abendlandes* (The Decline of the West), insisting repeatedly that fighting is something fundamental to human affairs, an elemental expression of the life-force, and thus an essential means of cultural renewal. The political thrust of his argument is directed against the liberalism of the Republic, against the Enlightenment principle of tolerance, and against any belief in a rational path of historical progress. To experience war only in a spirit of suffering and negation, he concludes, is to experience it only contingently, "externally", and thus to endure it "as a slave". His construction of the memory of the war is thus fundamentally related to that current of existential 'decisionism' with which the radical nationalism of the 1920s sought to justify political action in terms of an unbridled assertion of the will.[18]

These intellectual attitudes are already manifest in the way he describes the infantry war in his first volume, *In Stahlgewittern*. He speaks of the modern battlefield as a machine that draws ever increasing numbers of men and supplies into a maelstrom of destruction, but he expressly denies that the infantry war has become degraded to a mass slaughter; on the contrary, the actions of the individual remain decisive and the hand-to-hand fighting has found its men of the hour, "princes of the trenches" in whose grim determination "the blood" speaks (pp. 107, 210 f.). Their heroism is a blend of the animal and the divine; the vital will of the nation expresses itself in the unleashed drive to kill (pp. 227, 134 f.). Danger is an occasion for experiencing the virtues Jünger associates with "enhanced manliness", and the hardened fighter is someone who has braved every terror and learned to regard it with contempt (pp. 24 f., 84). A page later he describes the "landscape of horror" created by an artillery bombardment, including the body of a small girl lying in a pool of blood. A toast to fallen companions at the end of a day is simply a part of the fighter's routine (p. 127). A man endures out of a sense of duty, but he does so because his individual will has become invested in the fate of nations that is being decided by the massive deployment of destructive forces in which his personal death has become an irrelevancy (pp. 162, 226 f.). The fighting has acquired its own rationale, independent of strategic or political, to say nothing of humane, considerations.[19] Those who are tempted to read Jünger's writings as if they yielded a more 'authentic' account of the war than the novels of the late 1920s ought to take note of the senses in which

[18] For a critical analysis of political decisionism, and of Jünger's contribution to it, see Christian Graf von Krockow, *Die Entscheidung: Eine Untersuchung über Ernst Jünger, Carl Schmitt, Martin Heidegger* (Stuttgart: Ferdinand Enke, 1958).

[19] This sense that the fighting has become its own rationale is indeed made explicit in Jünger's original foreword to *In Stahlgewittern*: "Das war der deutsche Infanterist im Kriege. Gleichviel wofür er kämpfte, sein Kampf war übermenschlich."

he, too, is subjecting the experience to a retrospective stylization. It was in a spirit of almost anarchic individualism and
vitalism that Jünger celebrated the war; that is what distinguished his attitude from that of more conservative nationalists.
Only gradually did he adjust his intellectual outlook to accommodate the aspect of political organization in the modern state,
and even then it was his experience of military organization at
the front that provided his model for a totalitarian state of the
future.[20]

Jünger did not contribute directly to the wave of war fiction
that appeared in 1929–30, but something of his ethos is apparent in the writings of other authors who responded to the challenge of Remarque's novel by constructing alternative myths of
the war from a nationalist perspective. Werner Beumelburg,
who had previously contributed a number of volumes to the
nationalist historiography of the war,[21] published *Die Gruppe
Bosemüller* (1930), which tells of the fate of a small group of
fighting men in the battle of Verdun. The circumstances in which
these men are placed yields an ideal setting for an imagined test
of survival instinct, discipline, and comradeship. They know
they are involved in a battle which takes an enormous toll of
lives, in which they are up against huge odds, in which platoons
are buried alive and men are driven mad. Against that background, the officers Beumelburg depicts come across as model
leaders: a major who can restore the confidence of others with
his tactical planning, a captain who exudes "icy" logic, and a
giant of a lieutenant, who has self-consciously made the battlefield his home and moves about it with the unfailing self-
assurance of a phantom. Beumelburg's one foil for the valour
of his protagonists is a martinet sergeant-major who becomes a
figure of fun in much the same way as the equivalent character
in Remarque's novel.[22] His common soldiers may experience

---

[20] Cf. Prümm 1974; H.-H. Müller, 283–95; Harro Segeberg, "Technikverwachsen: Zur Konstruktion des 'Arbeiter' bei Ernst Jünger", *Der Deutschunterricht*, 46
(1994), 3, 40–50. Jünger's political tract *Der Arbeiter* is discussed in Chapter 8,
below.

[21] Beumelburg's chronicle of the war, *Sperrfeuer um Deutschland*, which
appeared in October 1929, rapidly became a best-seller: see Vogt-Praclik, 60 f.

[22] The fact that this character goes by the name of Benzin, and that his bowel
control regularly fails him when danger approaches, suggests that he is also conceived as a scurrilous parody of Renn, who is similarly frank about his spontaneous
physiological responses to danger.

moments of doubt, confusion, or indolence, but only in order to overcome them. Once committed to the task of storming strongly defended positions, they are characterized exclusively in terms of single-mindedness, the euphoria of assault, and a capacity for exemplary loyalty and self-denial. The figure of Bosemüller himself is presented as a dreamer, a bit of a poet, and a proud father, but also as a fearless fighter who, having visited his wife and new-born son, returns to his platoon with a renewed sense of commitment to its group ethos and common destiny. In Beumelburg's representation of the comradeship of battle, it is precisely that experience of group loyalty that paves the way for a new sense of national identity.

Verdun had been the site of the first attempt of the war, initiated by the German High Command early in 1916, to conduct a campaign of attrition. By concentrating a massed artillery and infantry assault on Verdun, General Falkenhayn hoped to break French morale by drawing increasing numbers of their troops through the "mill" of his bombardment in defence of a stronghold heavily imbued with symbolic significance for either nation. The battle had remained in public memory for the deployment of previously untried technological weapons— poison gas and flame-throwers, as well as large calibre guns— and for the huge numbers of casualties on either side.[23] For the Catholic author Josef Magnus Wehner, as for Beumelburg, Verdun provided a legendary setting, and in *Sieben vor Verdun* (Seven before Verdun, 1930) Wehner set out to write precisely the sort of epic vision of the war that Josef Ponten had anticipated in 1927. He did so by combining a sense of prophetic foreboding—five of his seven warriors are destined to meet a gruesome death—with the heavy inference of an opportunity lost. Wehner prefaces his narrative with an explicit critique of the reticence of Falkenhayn, precisely because his strategy had not made it a supreme objective to capture the citadel of Verdun; and he illustrates the point in the course of his narrative by describing the frustration of stormtroops who are ordered to hold their position rather than press home their advantage, or who advance so quickly that they come under fire

---

[23] For a recent account in English of the thinking behind the battle of Verdun, and of its consequences, see Holger H. Herwig, *The First World War: Germany and Austria-Hungary 1914–1918* (London: Arnold, 1997), 179 ff.

from their own artillery. By way of contrast, Wehner stylizes the Crown Prince (who is otherwise remembered for having warily kept his distance from the front and for maintaining a lifestyle of leisured luxury during the war) into an embodiment of the will to achieve that objective by all-out assault, and presents the enormous sacrifice of lives at Verdun as an expression of the subliminal yearning of all Germans for unification into a greater German Reich. Wehner's characterization is still cruder than Beumelburg's. His infantrymen carry stereotyped traits of emotional and artistic sensibility, as well as valour, but they are above all presented as victims of a vicious and barbaric enemy (capable of bayoneting unarmed prisoners) as well as of the incompetence of an old-fashioned military leadership. Ennobled by its allusion to Aeschylus' *Seven against Thebes* and by religious intimations of life after death, Wehner's novel celebrates its dead heroes as lives sacrificed for the redemption of an ancient dream of pan-German unity (cf. Travers, 180–92).

Clearly, such novels as these are not simply commemorating the experiences of the past war. They belong to the retrospective cultivation of the legend of a 'front generation', and of the unified sense of purpose in what that generation had fought for, which came to play an important role in the defining of political allegiances in the early 1930s.[24] Another contributor to this vein of war writing was the National Socialist Hans Zöberlein, whose *Der Glaube an Deutschland* (Faith in Germany, 1931) appeared with a foreword by Hitler evoking the "heritage of the front". Zöberlein writes in the first person, and from the perspective of a simple soldier for whom allegiance to his group is never at issue. He describes the battles on the western front in which he participated between 1916 and 1918, and does so at great length, in order to emphasize the aspect of heroic endurance in that participation. His Nazi belief in German racial superiority is explicit in the text, his evocations of the enemy are frequently tinged with contempt, and he recalls the actions of revolutionaries and striking munitions workers as a direct betrayal of 'the front'. For Zöberlein, as for Beumelburg and Wehner, the front-line fighter is not simply sustained

---

[24] For a discussion of the role this notion played in the politics of the Weimar Republic, see the final chapter of Bessel 1993.

by his faith in the national cause, he is the true embodiment of that cause and the harbinger of a new spirit which will transcend decadent 'civilization'. But the most accomplished, as well as the most ambitious of these attempts to present the war as the source of a new nationalist mythology is Franz Schauwecker's *Aufbruch der Nation* (The Nation on the March, 1929).

Schauwecker, like Jünger, had emerged from the First World War with the conviction that the soldiers it had produced were a new breed characterized by the ultimate refinement of manly virtues.[25] What distinguishes his *Aufbruch der Nation* from the common run of nationalist war fiction of 1929–30 is the sense of historical context he gives to his narrative. In the process he also reveals more of the social pathology behind the nationalist mythology of the war than is immediately apparent from the other authors discussed so far. The persona through which Schauwecker reconstructs the learning experience of war is Albrecht Urach, a professional-class young man who breaks off his university studies in 1914, welcoming the outbreak of war as a liberation from the constraints of a peacetime society dominated by materialism, calculated careerism, and the intellectual discipline of academic specialization. At the front, Urach embraces the surrender of intellect in a double sense: he relishes the spontaneity of his own instinctual responses to danger, and he enjoys becoming blended into the collective, the mass of German fighting men. For Schauwecker, as for Jünger, the confrontation with horror is an important element in the forging of a new heroic identity, and he lingers over the description of the mass of pulped flesh left behind by an exploding shell. (Once more, the scene is Verdun.) But what matters above all for him is the stylization of front-line experience into a more authentic expression of 'life' than anything that can be found in the world of the civilian. The gulf of understanding between the front and home, which is described by many veterans of twentieth-century wars, is presented here as the difference between the fighters

---

[25] In his memoir *Im Todesrachen* (1919), Schauwecker writes of the war veteran as "eine neue Art von Mensch, ein Mann in höchster Steigerung aller männlichen Eigenschaften": quoted in U. Baron and H.-H. Müller, "Weltkriege und Kreigsromane", *Zeitschrift für Literaturwissenschaft und Linguistik*, 19 (1989), 75, 14–38 (17).

who have discovered their 'true nature' and the abstract patriotism of those who have no real appreciation of what the fighters are defending because they cannot share their experience.
The nationalism Schauwecker evokes for readers in 1930 is one
which is no longer defending the homeland of 1914, but projecting a new sense of collective identity for the future derived
from the surrender of individuality and critical rationality on
the battlefield. That is the sense that lies behind the paradoxical conclusion his protagonist reaches at the end of the novel,
namely that Germany had to lose the war in order to discover
itself as a nation. Through his sustained characterization of
Urach and the depiction of his concrete experiences, Schauwecker lends substance to the otherwise abstract impressions
conveyed by the anti-rational existentialism of radical right-
wing thought in the period.[26]

The radical nationalists did not have the field to themselves,
indeed their sales figures before 1933 failed to rival those of the
more successful of the anti-war novels.[27] We have already seen
the sense in which Ludwig Renn's *Krieg* (1928) was attempting
to counter the tendencies of a heroic recollection of war. In other
specific ways, too, works published before Remarque's novel
can be seen to be challenging the glorification of war. Siegfried
Kracauer's *Ginster* (1928) contrives a particularly marked
critical distance towards wartime events by adopting from
the outset the perspective of a self-conscious outsider. The title-
figure has acquired his nickname (the German word for gorse
or broom) as a schoolboy. Whether he is witnessing attitudes at
home or in the army, Ginster confronts wartime clichés with
that sharpness of gaze that is characteristic of so much of the
new writing of the later 1920s. He is a persistent sceptic towards
patriotic sentiment, is bemused by the way military saluting
becomes a conditioned reflex among his contemporaries, and

[26] The terms in which Schauwecker characterizes the pre-war civilian world
strongly suggest that he is participating in that current of post-war anti-modernism
which consciously repudiated Max Weber's characterization of modern society as
inescapably "disenchanted" (cf. Bolz).

[27] Kornelia Vogt-Praclik (p. 48) notes that the nationalist war novels generally
lagged far behind the anti-war novels in terms of sales, and only achieved best-seller
status in the course of the 1930s, with the aid of official promotion by the National
Socialists. For indications of sales figures in particular instances, see Gollbach;
H.-H. Müller.

notes with irony that Germany's internal political differences have been laid aside in favour of the ferocious denunciation of foreign nations. A prime example of the satirical edge to Kracauer's narrative is the section midway through the text in which Ginster responds to the news that his home town is planning to dedicate a cemetery to the honour of its fallen sons. As he notes, many of the dead would thus be better accommodated than when they were alive, but the bronze that might have gone into the creation of their monuments has gone into the manufacture of armaments, and in any case, "it was unfortunately not possible to return the soldiers in the desired state of completeness". Ernst Glaeser's *Jahrgang 1902* (Generation of 1902, 1928), which ranked among the best-sellers of 1928–9, presents the adult society of wartime through the eyes of an adolescent protagonist and exposes the operation of personal motives under the cloak of patriotic euphoria, although the focus of the narrative is on the emotional and psychological tensions at work in the youthful narrator himself. In *Soldat Suhren* (Soldier Suhren, 1927), Georg von der Vring also adopts something approaching a childlike perspective in his depiction of the process by which the war relentlessly destroys the personality and sensibility of his self-pitying poet-protagonist.[28] (Arnold Zweig's *Sergeant Grischa* novel, which also appeared a full year before *Im Westen nichts Neues*, will be discussed together with other works by Zweig at the end of this chapter.)

Remarque's example provided an impetus for more directed counter-attacks from the left. Theodor Plievier, who was to go on to write epic accounts of major battles of the Second World War as well as a documentary novel about Germany's political transition in 1918, was prompted to write *Des Kaisers Kulis* (The Kaiser's Coolies, 1929), which was hailed in the press as a "nautical Remarque". Based on a combination of research into the naval mutinies of 1917 and Plievier's own pre-war experience in the merchant navy, the work was too political for the Kiepenheuer Verlag, but not political enough for the

---

[28] Hans-Harald Müller (pp. 94–104) also discusses Alexander Moritz Frey's medical orderly novel *Die Pflasterkästen* and Karl Federn's *Hauptmann Latour*, as well as the works of Glaeser and von der Vring, as critical accounts of wartime service which were written before *Im Westen nichts Neues*, although they were not published until 1929.

Communist *Linkskurve*, whose reviewer would have liked to see the story extended to the insurrection of 1918–19 (cf. Travers, 111 f.). In so far as the work expresses a political orientation, it is that of the anarchist movement to which Plievier had remained close throughout the 1920s. This comes out particularly in his stylization of the stoker Albin Köbis, who was executed for an alleged infraction of military discipline in 1917, into an anarchist martyr committed to a negotiated peace without annexations.[29] *Des Kaisers Kulis* gives a graphic account of shipboard life, emphasizing the stark contrasts between the luxuries enjoyed by the officer class and the regime of repetitive drill and privation suffered by the ratings. Whatever the precise relationship between Plievier's plot and his historical sources, the work was received in the liberal and left-wing press as a welcome critique of militarism, and on the right as a defamation of the German fleet.

The most self-conscious reconstruction of wartime experience from a proletarian viewpoint is Adam Scharrer's *Vaterlandslose Gesellen* (1930), the title of which is a phrase coined by Wilhelm II in order to denounce the pre-war Social Democrats as an unpatriotic crew. Narrated in the first person, this heavily autobiographical novel tells the story of Hans Betzoldt, who is a factory worker in Hamburg at the start of the war, and someone accustomed to taking part in socialist anti-war demonstrations. As the newspapers begin to carry stories of Belgian and Cossack atrocities, Betzoldt is made increasingly aware of his political isolation in the circumstances of the moment, given that his own party has voted to support the war effort. His wartime experiences are divided between spells of work in munitions factories and service on both the western and the eastern front. In the army, as well as at home, he witnesses at first hand the perpetuation of social injustice behind the veneer of wartime solidarity. He particularly denounces the 'comradeship of the front' as a sham which is only maintained in the face of imminent death; the old class distinctions and privileges reassert themselves as

---

[29] Cf. Hans-Harald Müller's introduction to Theodor Plievier, *Der Kaiser ging, die Generäle blieben* (Hamburg: Konkret Literatur Verlag, 1979), 16. The background circumstances to the execution of Köbis are explained in F. L. Carsten, *War against War: British and German Radical Movements in the First World War* (London: Batsford, 1982), 118 f.

soon as his company withdraws from the front line. Elucidat-
ing the familiar tag that the war would soon be forgotten if the
combatants received equal pay and provisions, which is cited by
Remarque and others, Scharrer identifies a hierarchical social
structure as responsible for keeping men at their military tasks,
particularly behind the lines.[30] But his narrator also testifies to
the increasing depredation of skilled labour and the demoralization which sets in after the destructive campaigns of 1916.
The narrative ends with his participation in the munitions
strikes and revolutionary insurrection of 1918.

Edlef Koeppen's *Heeresbericht* (Higher Command) invited
comparison with the technique of Karl Kraus when it appeared
in 1930 because of the satirical use it makes of authentic
wartime documents. In addition to quoting from military and
governmental proclamations (the ruler of each combatant
nation claims, for example, that he has God on his side),
Koeppen opens up ironic perspectives on the perceptions of the
war being cultivated among the general populace by reproduc-
ing circus and music-hall programmes which include representations of the sinking of the Lusitania, or of "our heroes in
France" followed by a spectacular "final apotheosis". As the
text progresses he also blurs the boundaries between history and
fiction by including ostensibly documentary material relating to
the young soldier who provides the personal storyline in the
work, Adolf Reisiger. Reisiger shares certain biographical details
with Koeppen himself. He enthusiastically volunteers for service
in 1914 and advances to the rank of lieutenant, but is ultimately
confined to a mental asylum after openly condemning the senselessness of the slaughter. As the narrative is constructed, Reisiger
is the reader's naive witness to situations and military procedures, the purpose of which remains a mystery to him, but the
effects of which he can observe at first hand. Assigned to an

---

[30] "Es ist längst ausgemacht—auch für den stupidesten Sohn des Vaterlandes—,
daß gleicher Lohn und gleiches Essen die Disziplin derer, die den Krieg als eine
Badekur ansehen, so völlig zersetzen würde, daß der Krieg auch nicht einen
Tag länger dauern würde. So ist denn überall dafür gesorgt, den hohen und weniger
hohen Herren das Durchhalten zu ermöglichen." (*Gesellen*, 182.) For a full
account of the political background to Scharrer's novel, see Hans-Harald Müller,
"Kriegsroman und Republik: Historische Skizze mit einer Interpretation von
Adam Scharrers proletarischem Antikriegsroman *Vaterlandslose Gesellen*", in
M. Brauneck (ed.), *Der deutsche Roman im 20. Jahrhundert* (Bamberg: Buchner,
1976), 222–52.

artillery battery, he experiences the men's relief as the tension and uncertainty of the anticipation of an attack give way to mechanical activity when they are ordered to give rapid fire. Seriously wounded, he learns of the gruesome routines of a field hospital, but can find no other rationale in his life than to return to his unit. As an observer in the front trenches, he witnesses the combination of mechanized routine and desperation required to repel a frontal infantry attack under covering artillery fire. Assigned to desk duties behind the lines, he discovers to his horror that, here too, he is directly implicated in the preparation for murderous acts. He becomes gradually initiated into the material realities behind such abstract notions as 'the front', 'the enemy', and 'the chain of command'. But what he never loses—and it is this that lends the work its emotional poignancy—is his sense of the value of individual lives sacrificed, something which is obscured by the statistics published in the daily bulletins.

Koeppen prefaces his text with a statement by the military censors of 1915 proscribing the publication of extensive accounts of the war by persons who are not in a position to assess the significance of specific events in their broader context. By confronting the personal (and necessarily limited) experiences of Reisiger with fragments of documentation which point to the broader historical context of those experiences, he achieves two ends: he demonstrates the need for any assessment of overall significance to take the form of active interpretation of the connections between fragmentary items of information, and he keeps alive the sense of glaring disparity between the official manipulation of information and the devastating effects of wartime experience at a personal level.[31] That is the sense in which Koeppen's novel makes a positive and substantial contribution to the task of constructive disillusionment with regard to the memorialization of the war in the context of its time. But as Herbert Bornebusch (p. 152) has noted, it is a mode of composition which presupposes "a (bourgeois) public of criti-

---

[31] For detailed discussion of the effects created in Koeppen's novel, see Brian Murdoch, "Documentation and Narrative: Edlef Koeppen's *Heeresbericht* and the Anti-War Novels of the Weimar Republic", *New German Studies*, 15 (1988–9), 1, 23–47; Jutta Vinzent, *Edlef Koeppen—Schriftsteller zwischen den Fronten* (Munich: iudicium, 1997), 114–43.

cally reflecting individuals" capable of recognizing the irra-
tionalities that sustained the war and willing to respond to an
appeal to their consciences on behalf of its victims. The effects
of *Heeresbericht* depend chiefly on the pathos generated by the
discrepancy between the suffering of individuals and the relentless momentum of the military machine which exacts that
suffering.

Arnold Zweig, too, built on that sense of discrepancy between
the suffering individual and the machinery of power, but his
novels distinguish themselves from other German war fiction of
the time by their extensive exploration of the social and political dimensions of the war. The means by which he conducts that
exploration is the technique of omniscient narration cultivated
by the major nineteenth-century European novelists. The ele-
vated character of his literary style, particularly in the first of
his war novels, *Der Streit um den Sergeanten Grischa* (The Case
of Sergeant Grischa, 1927), did not endear him to critics of the
time whose expectations were attuned to the public demand for
'sachlich' reportage.[32] But that novel was among those which
enjoyed a printrun of over 100,000 within a very few years, and
both in that work and in the volumes he added in the early
1930s Zweig conferred social and psychological depth on the
depiction of situations which were part of the common experience of participants in the war.

Der Streit um den Sergeanten Grischa tells the story of a
Russian prisoner of war who tries to make his way home in the
spring of 1917, is captured using a false identity, and is ultimately shot as a spy even though his true identity (and implicit
innocence) has been established. Zweig presents that story as a
test of the moral probity of the German imperial regime. The
exercise of arbitrary authority by the overall commander in
occupied Eastern Europe, General Schieffenzahn (who is modelled on Ludendorff, and whose draconian approach to the issue

---

[32] Ernst Jirgal (p. 222) described *Der Streit um den Sergeanten Grischa* as "arg
literarisiert" by comparison with the other war novels he was reviewing; Kurt
Tucholsky (*GW* 5, 410) also objected to the contrived nobility of Zweig's style. On
the relationship between Zweig's self-conception as a writer and the background
culture of 'Neue Sachlichkeit', see David Midgley, "Schreiben um der Vergeistigung
des Lebens willen: Das Verhältnis Arnold Zweigs zur Neuen Sachlichkeit", in D.
Midgley et al., *Arnold Zweig–Poetik, Judentum und Politik* (Berne: Peter Lang,
1989), 97–110.

is fuelled by his fear of Bolshevik infiltration), is opposed by an array of figures whose sense of a moral imperative makes them determined to defend Grischa to the limits of their capabilities. The group includes a divisional commander, General von Lychow, whose strong sense of traditional Prussian values makes him insistent that the exercise of power should have a demonstrable moral foundation, but also means that he will ultimately confine his actions in the matter to 'official channels'. The divisional legal officer under Lychow's command is a Jew by the name of Posnanski, whose ethical commitment to the case is expressly related to the strength of his belief in Mosaic law. Posnanski in his turn is assisted by a young intellectual, Werner Bertin, who is moved by a sense of fellow-feeling as well as moral outrage and who, on the eve of Grischa's execution, conceives the idea for a drama based on the affair which will present it as a danger sign overlooked by the authorities of the time.[33] An impulse which these three figures share is to interpret the case of Sergeant Grischa as a manifestation of hubris on the part of the regime, as the "writing on the wall" for imperial Germany. And that interest in the individual case as a sign of the times is extended in the text into interpretations along both Marxist and Talmudic lines by members of the local population: the fact that the narrated events reach their conclusion in November 1917 enables the text to carry discrete allusions to the Balfour Declaration, which promised the establishment of a Jewish homeland in Palestine, as well as to the Bolshevik Revolution in Russia (cf. Midgley 1980, 48–52).

The fact that Zweig's novel (in accordance with his own experiences of military service) focuses on the operation of authority behind the lines brings certain advantages when it comes to an extended depiction of the nation at war. He treats each phase in Grischa's story as an opportunity to highlight the position of particular individuals within the overall structure of authority. The power of command which keeps men at their posts and impels them, under certain circumstances, to carry out inhumane acts is sharply evoked at various stages of the action. The

---

[33] Zweig himself originally used the case as the basis for a drama in the immediate post-war years, and something of the Expressionist spirit of protest on behalf of a universalized conception of suffering humanity remains apparent in the novel.

conflicting personal motives of the combatants as the third winter of the war comes to an end are initially intimated, not through the thoughts of Grischa himself, but through those of a German soldier on sentry duty. Fear of execution or transfer to the front weighs heavily in the minds of the ordinary soldiers who find themselves directly or indirectly implicated in Grischa's fate, particularly in the case of the man on guardhouse duty who forestalls a last-minute attempt to abduct the prisoner. The suppressed rage of those who have witnessed the horrendous sacrifice of lives in pursuit of national self-aggrandizement erupts, ironically, at an officers' party held to mark the third anniversary of the outbreak of war (more precisely, of the British declaration of war in response to the German violation of Belgian neutrality). But Zweig also investigates the mentality of those who exercise power and influence in the circumstances of the time. He explores the psychology of Schieffenzahn, a career soldier who, unusually in the German context, comes from a middle-class background, and who has cultivated the extraordinary intellectual skills required for the strategic conduct of the war as a way of compensating for his low social status and winning the favours of his aristocratic fellow-officers. He works into his text references to the socio-economic dimension of the war, particularly through the figure of Albin Schilles (based on the industrialist Hugo Stinnes), a guest at Schieffenzahn's table who has read the fortune of the German war effort in the falling value of the mark on international exchanges, and is taking care to transfer his personal assets into foreign currency. As a counterpart to the manipulations of the capitalist, Zweig ends the work with an intimation of the growing power of skilled labour under the conditions of war: it is not so much the fact that an engine-driver dares to halt his train in order to pick up a straggler bound for home leave as the nature of the comments his act attracts that leaves the reader with a pronounced sense of the significance of the closing date of the novel, late November 1917.

These are the ways in which *Der Streit um den Sergeanten Grischa* lays bare both the operation of power structures which contribute to the perpetuation of the war and the factors which make those power structures vulnerable in the longer term. But Zweig also has a distinctive way of dealing with the question of how to 'make sense' of the war. The anti-war novels of Remarque and Renn have no answer to that question: for their protagonists it can only represent a dangerous distraction from the immediate task of surviving under the conditions of front-line fighting. Koeppen's protagonist, devastated by the evident senselessness of the slaughter he has witnessed, turns his back on the world for as long as the war lasts. The radical nationalists filled that vacuum of 'meaning' by stylizing the fighting itself into an expression of the struggle for life and collective (racial) dominance. One way in which Zweig addresses the issue is by extricating it from the context of the battlefield and presenting it as a personal and psychological adjustment to the prospect of death. He shows Grischa 'making sense' of his impending execution by relating it to his own complicity in the slaughter, embracing the Talionic principle that whoever has spilt blood shall have his blood spilt in turn. It is a principle that has been articulated for him by the pious Jewish carpenter alongside whom he finds himself working, articulated moreover in a context which emphasizes once more the symbolic significance of Grischa's death for the regime which kills him rather than for himself. But in his acts and his private thoughts, Grischa becomes identified in the closing stages of the novel with the willed acceptance of atonement, the forgiveness of iniquity, and the dream of a more equitable future life which might transcend the terrible divisions of a world at war. The other way in which Zweig addresses the issue is by presenting the war as an educative experience.

The two further volumes which Zweig published respectively in 1931 and 1935 focus on the personal development of Bertin between the outbreak of war and his transfer to the position of legal clerk that he occupies in *Der Streit um den Sergeanten Grischa*. In the first of these novels, *Junge Frau von 1914* (Young Woman of 1914), Bertin participates in that seemingly liberating experience shared by many young intellectuals of the combatant nations in 1914. He is swept along by the patriotic fervour of the moment, and unashamedly seeks to justify the war as a "tragic" confrontation in the terms of the philosophical idealism with which his education has imbued him: he would happily give orders to fire on the Strasbourg Minster if called upon to do so because that is what the situation seems to demand. He welcomes the physicality of military service and the sense of being incorporated into a social collective, although the detached narrating voice also brings out the irony of the mindless conditioning to which Bertin is subjected in the course of his military training. The abandonment of civilized restraint which this process encourages becomes apparent when he dominates and violates the fiancée with whom he has enjoyed a rich and mutually fulfilling relationship in the months preceding the war. Although the novel ends with the endorsement of that relationship in a highly conventional wedding, this is not before the consequences of Bertin's act have been extensively depicted, namely the humiliation and suffering of the fiancée, who is left alone to face the rigours of terminating an unwanted pregnancy and the potential menaces of a censorious society. Bertin's own path to self-recognition and critical self-awareness leads through the active service he experiences, not in the front line, but as part of that supportive machinery sustaining the ferocity of the fighting, once more, at Verdun.

In an essay he published in 1929, Zweig was insistent that the only appropriate way to depict the social behaviour of a nation at war was as an extension and intensification of peacetime conflicts.[34] That principle is especially well observed in *Erziehung vor Verdun* (Education before Verdun), where Bertin is brought face to face with the administrative dimension of the war, and with the opportunities it provides for petty bureaucrats to exercise the power and authority that is denied them in civilian life. He experiences this aspect directly when his humanitarian behaviour towards French prisoners exposes him to ridicule and victimization at the hands of his immediate superiors; and he experiences it indirectly when he becomes a witness to the way the Captain of a supply unit contrives to bring about a man's death under enemy fire in order to conceal the truth about his own corrupt administrative practices. In the figure of the dead man's brother, Lieutenant Kroysing, Zweig creates a character who embodies precisely those 'manly' attributes which the radical nationalists had emphasized and heroized in their novels.[35] Kroysing is an imposing presence and the epitome of a technocratic warrior who survives in the devas-

---

[34] Arnold Zweig, "Kriegsromane", *Die Weltbühne*, 16 Apr. 1929, 597–99.
[35] For a detailed analysis of the characterization of Kroysing, see Hans-Harald Müller, "Militanter Pazifismus: Eine Interpretationsskizze zu Arnold Zweigs Roman *Erziehung vor Verdun*", *Weimarer Beiträge*, 36 (1990), 12, 1894–1914.

tated landscape and subterranean fortifications of Verdun by adopting an unashamedly amoral view of life, and who thinks nothing of drawing the entire supply company concerned into the 'mill' of the Verdun battlefield in order to exact vengeance on his brother's killer. It is through the agency of Kroysing above all that Bertin is enabled to recognize that the prosecution of this war depends on the unleashing of primitive instincts on the one hand, and on the systematic exercise of social subjugation on the other. It is in the company of Kroysing's sappers that Bertin visits the front-line trenches. He approaches the occasion as a sensational escapade, and it provides him with a moment of participation in the exhilaration of destruction as he peeps over the breastwork to observe the artillery barrage. But in the dugout where the troops await the call to attack, Bertin makes a discovery which undermines the heroic expectations he has brought with him. What he recognizes, as the earth groans above him and the wan-faced infantrymen smoke their cigarettes, is that these men, too, are just carrying out orders. They are the "proletarians" of war. But the truth that hurts is that what determines the actions of men going into battle is ultimately no different from the oppressive command structure he knows from his own company (*Erziehung*, 245).

The 'education' Bertin experiences in the novel is neither consistent nor conclusive. He learns of the contradictory impulses lurking within himself, and within human nature generally; and he learns of the unbridled ruthlessness at work in the world around him; but at the end of the text he is still digesting his wartime experiences and working at the interpretation of them under the fraught political circumstances of post-war Germany. In the course of showing what Bertin goes through during his months at Verdun, however, Zweig explores the appeal of precisely those opposing tendencies we have seen to be at work in the wave of war novels published in 1929–30. For as he struggles to make sense of his situation and the iniquities he witnesses, Bertin is wooed by competing ideological factions. To the right there is Kroysing, who remains doggedly committed to the national struggle for dominance, and to the pursuit of a personal position of dominance within that struggle. To the left there is a pair of class-conscious workers in Bertin's company, Pahl and Lebehde, who recognize in him a brand of intellectual who could with profit be recruited to the class struggle. What Zweig depicts in *Erziehung vor Verdun*, in other words, is more than the outcome of his own personal experiences as a soldier and a writer. From the vantage point of his all-seeing narrator, he gives a critical exposition of the various standpoints from which the contest for the meaning of the war had been fought during the crisis years of the Weimar Republic. Of all the anti-war novelists of the Weimar period, it is Arnold Zweig who provides the most effective conceivable refutation of the nationalist heroization of the war because he makes the psychological and social dimensions of the behaviour of men at war transparent to the reader, and thus contributes directly and self-critically to an understanding of the personal and ideological factors which made the interpretation of the war such a sensitive issue after the event.

7

The City and the Country

A "new cultural era" is beginning in which Germany becomes a slave to Berlin.

Wilhelm Stapel (1930)[1]

What we heard was the voice of provincialism, of local art, the art of the soil, of the utterly flat countryside.

Alfred Döblin (1931)[2]

A powerful tradition of anti-modernism, which accompanied the industrialization of Germany in the second half of the nineteenth century, saw the city as an emblem of all that was abominable in modern society, a place where human relations became fragmented, productive effort became harnessed to a mean commercialism, and political idealism was subordinated to base material interest. The utopian thrust of that tradition is most clearly apparent in the writings of Paul de Lagarde (1827–91), who nurtured the dream of undoing the processes of industrialization and restoring Germany to a harmonious patriarchal order based on an agrarian economy, an aim which was to be achieved by means of colonial expansion into Eastern Europe.[3] Lagarde's proposal, which ran counter to the dominant political trends of his lifetime, met with growing sympathy around the turn of the century, at a time when an earnest reform movement was looking for ways to alleviate what it saw as the unwholesome influence of urban life on the culture of the nation and the attitudes of the young (Bergmann, 85–112). Widely read

[1] Wilhelm Stapel, "Der Geistige und sein Volk", *Deutsches Volkstum*, 12 (1930), 1 (quoted in Kaes et al., 424).
[2] Alfred Döblin, "Bilanz der 'Dichterakademie'", *Vossische Zeitung*, 25 Jan. 1931 (quoted in Meyer, 70).
[3] See Fritz Stern, *The Politics of Cultural Despair* (Berkeley and Los Angeles: University of California Press, 1961), esp. chapter 4: "The German Nation".

publications of the 1890s—Julius Langbehn's *Rembrandt als Erzieher* (Rembrandt as Educator, 1890) and Max Nordau's *Entartung* (Degeneration, 1893)—also reinforced the perception of the city as harbouring all that was debilitating and decadent in modern society. Such intellectual anti-urbanism can be seen to feed into political plans for territorial expansion at the time of the First World War, and subsequently into Nazi ideology.[4] Following the Versailles Treaty of 1919, the emotional link between abhorrence towards urban culture and outrage at Germany's loss of overseas colonies found expansive literary expression in Hans Grimm's novel *Volk ohne Raum* (People without Space) of 1926 (cf. Zimmermann 1976).

This anti-urbanism is accompanied in German literature by an equally strong idealization of peasant life. This tradition, which begins as a conservative commemoration of traditional rural communities and distinctive regional cultures in the course of the nineteenth century, acquires a recognizable *völkisch* accent in the wake of the First World War (Rossbacher; Zimmermann 1975).[5] It is from the perspective of the provincial middle classes that the figure of the peasant farmer comes to be stylized as an embodiment of true nationhood which needs to be defended against alien (especially Jewish) influences and the supposedly corrosive effects of modern civilization; and it is out of the experience of the territorial defence of the nation in the First World War, and out of a yearning for the security of national community in the face of the divisions of the Weimar period, that the notorious evocations of a mystical connection between the blood and the soil—*Blut-und-Boden-Literatur*—emerge.[6] Norbert Mecklenburg (pp. 114ff.) uses Gustav Frenssen's autobiographical novel *Otto Babendieck* of 1926 as a basis for establishing a stereotypical model of the reactionary provincial novel. The setting for the work is Dithmarschen (on

[4] See Bergmann, 164ff., 354ff. The Nazi ideologue Alfred Rosenberg, for example, speaks of the cities as poisoning the life-blood of the nation, and calls for their reduction to small towns as part of a programme of "de-proletarianization": *Der Mythus des 20. Jahrhunderts* (Munich: Hoheneichen-Verlag, 1930), 550–5.

[5] For an account in English of the German regional novel as it developed around 1900, see also Jethro Bithell, *Modern German Literature 1880–1950* (London: Methuen, 1959), 346–58.

[6] For a summary of the features of *Blut-und-Boden-Literatur* and a selection of representative texts, see Ernst Loewy, *Literatur unterm Hakenkreuz* (Frankfurt: Fischer, 1969), 96–145.

the North Sea coast of Schleswig-Holstein), the world beyond the familiar domestic realm is presented as a source of threatening influences, characters are treated as having fixed personalities and fixed destinies, and the narrative structure slavishly follows the example of the nineteenth-century novel of personal development. Frenssen's writing aspires to be more than just 'Heimatkunst', and seeks to present the local community as a microcosm of worldly experience; but the manifest aesthetic criteria of the work rest on the assumption that all great art is rooted in a sense of regional, and indeed tribal, identity. It was Frenssen's works that provided the platform for the true exponent of *Blut-und-Boden-Literatur*, Hans Blunck, in the course of the 1920s and 1930s.[7] The traditionally strong sense of an association between the ideal of integral personality and the cultural traditions of rural communities also enabled more reputable authors who had begun as exponents of a conservative resistance to the depersonalizing effects of liberal capitalism—Emil Strauß, Hermann Stehr, and Erwin Guido Kolbenheyer—to accommodate to the Nazi ideal of national community (*Volksgemeinschaft*) after 1933 (Bormann 1974; Heimann).

Important as this sense of a dichotomy between city and country is to an understanding of the cultural traditions from which the Nazi movement drew sustenance, it provides only a limited, indeed a one-dimensional impression of the relationship between city and country which actually existed in the broader literary culture of Germany in the early twentieth century. Recent research has shown how complex the interaction between the respective perspectives and attitudes of urban and rural culture was, even within the reform organizations and youth movements which rebelled against the constraints of urban living in the decades before the First World War.[8] Mecklenburg's study of the regional novel in the twentieth century (which examines works by Hermann Broch and Uwe Johnson as well as Frenssen) also showed us that it is far too

---

[7] Cf. Bithell, 351–6. At a later date Emil Strauß also followed suit with a celebration of farming life in the service of the nation set in his native Swabia, *Das Riesenspielzeug* (1935).

[8] See Edeltraud Klueting (ed.), *Antimodernismus und Reform: Beiträge zur Geschichte der deutschen Heimatbewegung* (Darmstadt: Wissenschaftliche Buchgesellschaft, 1991).

simplistic to associate the city categorically with the forces of modernism and the provinces with those of reaction. And in the context of his sociological analysis of the representation of rural life by authors born between 1880 and 1914, Peter Zimmermann (1975, 127f.) was bound to acknowledge particular examples of critical and realistic depiction which stood out from the dominant *völkisch* trend that interested him. In the main sections of this chapter I have tried to look beyond the stereotypes associated with the dichotomy between city and country, and ask about the specific implications of literary responses to the city on the one hand and provincial life on the other. But first it is worth recalling precisely why this sense of a dichotomy acquired such a strong political significance in the intellectual debates of the Weimar period.

There were two obvious reasons why Berlin became the particular focus of acrimonious debates about the relationship between the city and the country in the course of the Weimar period, and together they show how closely intertwined the politics and the culture of the Republic were. First, it was the seat of central government. While Berlin had been the capital of Germany since 1871 by virtue of being the residential city of the king of Prussia, the powers of federal government were strengthened under the Weimar Constitution to the extent of allowing the central collection of taxes, but the individual states were left with considerable scope to defy that central power and to assert their own traditions.[9] The political resentments which lingered in the nationalist press of the provinces are exemplified by a leading article from a Swabian newspaper of 1919 reprinted in Anton Kaes's *Weimar Sourcebook* (1994, 414f.). There the "spirit of Berlin" is equated with the alleged defeatism of civilian politicians at the end of the war, and the city is viewed as too receptive to alien influences ever to command respect as the capital of a united Germany. The latter point links up with the second reason why Berlin became the target of ever more vehement attacks in the right-wing press as its reputation as a cultural metropolis took off in the course of the 1920s. It was vilified as the breeding-ground of *Asphaltkultur*, of all that was seen as inimical to traditional German values.

[9] See A. J. Nicholls, *Weimar and the Rise of Hitler* (London: Macmillan, 1968), 33–5.

Berlin was stigmatized as a city without character, as having no "society", as a place where mere technicians associated in a merely mechanical fashion (Meyer, 17 f.). As the impact of social modernization came to be felt in the wake of economic recovery in the mid-1920s, Berlin was accused in the pages of the radical conservative journal *Deutsches Volkstum* (German Nationhood) of active "provincialization", in the sense of subjugating other regions of Germany to its own cultural trends. By 1928 a contributor to the same journal was presenting the capital as a "monster of civilization" relentlessly devouring what was traditionally understood as "culture" (Meyer, 21). Insinuations against the prominence of Jewish influence in cultural institutions were a common feature of such attacks. The leading editor of *Deutsches Volkstum*, Wilhelm Stapel, was a self-conscious champion of "old Prussia" against "new Berlin", who had begun his journalistic career in the pre-war reform movement (writing for *Der Kunstwart*) and whose political attitudes were steeped in Johann Gottlieb Fichte's romantic ideal of organic nationhood. While he did not shy away from wishing "a few years of the most brutal fascism" on Germany in 1926 as a way of putting the ideological commitments of vacillating intellectuals to the test, he shared the fate of many right-wing radicals when the National Socialists consolidated their power after 1933: isolated, ignored, and appalled by the sheer vulgarity of Nazi propaganda. But in 1930, as the political struggles intensified in a climate of economic crisis, Stapel launched a consolidated journalistic campaign against Berlin. Writing under the title "Der Geistige und sein Volk"—the term "der Geistige" chosen to evoke a conservative conception of intellectual activity and its relation to the concerns of "the people" in contrast to the implied carping of mere "intellectuals"—Stapel denounced Berlin as an intellectual cesspit spreading its contagions across the provinces despite the best efforts of decent folk to combat them in local theatres and the regional press. He recalled the resistance of the pre-war reform movement to the dominance of urban culture, and called upon the countryside to rise up against Berlin (Meyer, 8–11; Kaes et al., 423–5).

Stapel's rallying-cry was promptly taken up in the *Süddeutsche Monatshefte*, which devoted a fifty-page supplement in

March 1930 to the denunciation of Berlin as a doomed city, mired in corruption and suffocating in its own nihilism, and intent on dragging the provinces down with it. These sentiments were echoed over the following year in the *Süddeutsche Monatshefte*, and also found support in other journals such as *Der Kunstwart* and *Die neue Literatur*. The influence of Stapel's campaign was spreading through a newly consolidated network of right-wing publishing outlets (Meyer, 32–7). By comparison, the response of Berlin intellectuals to the onslaught was sporadic and ultimately ineffectual, perhaps because the general terms of the argument were already familiar.[10] Kurt Tucholsky, in *Die Weltbühne*, drew attention to press hostility towards Berlin in 1927 and 1928, but as so often, his irony was double-edged. He invited readers to consider why the provinces, which were so quick to condemn Berlin, were also so keen to adopt its ways; but he conceded that it was precisely "out in the country" that the real Germany lay, and that the petty-mindedness which was commonly thought of as a provincial characteristic was equally at home in the power structures of the capital itself. The best hope he could hold out was for a steady extension of such democratic culture as existed in Berlin into regions where it was distinctly under-represented at present (*WB* 23, 499–501; 24, 405–8; cf. Kaes et al., 418–20). Far from lending him support, Willy Haas in *Die literarische Welt* took Tucholsky's 1927 article as an occasion to denounce the arrogance of Berlin's Marxisant radical intellectuals (*LW* 3, 17, 5 f.). In *Das Tage-Buch* in October 1931, Alfred Kantorowicz gave a robust defence of Berlin as the home of all that really mattered in German culture, but this was fully eighteen months after the right-wing onslaught (*TB* 12, 40, 1563–7). *Die literarische Welt* gave the issue judicious treatment in 1932—assessing Stapel's publications in the context of a general review of the literature of German nationalism, looking for ways to drive a wedge between his reactionary high-mindedness and more rabid anti-Semites, and subsequently attempting to depoliticize the controversy by devoting a number to the literary depiction of landscapes by authors of widely varying persuasions (Meyer, 39 f.)—but by this time it was most unlikely that such intellectual

---

[10] Already in 1920, Tucholsky refers to provincial antipathies towards Berlin in ways which suggest they are tediously familiar: GW 2, 439.

subtleties would have any effect on the tides of German politics.

Just how serious the campaign to "bring down Berlin" was emerges still more vividly from the machinations which took place during the same period within the literary section of the Prussian Academy of the Arts. The Academy had existed as an institution of the Prussian state for over 200 years, but only in 1926 was it decided to add a literary section to it; and given the representative nature of such a body under the circumstances of a united Germany, the question immediately arose of how, and indeed whether, the membership of that section should reflect the national character of German letters, as opposed to the cosmopolitan character of literary activity in the capital. Ideological conflicts were initially masked by formal and practical considerations: the Academy remained a Prussian, not a federal institution, and it was easier for members to attend meetings if they were resident in or near Berlin. But by 1928 the issue of the representative status of the countryside as opposed to the city became explicit, and explicitly directed against cosmopolitanism, when the nationalist Wilhelm Schäfer (who was about to move to Berlin) was nominated for president of the section (Jens, 96 f.). In the same year traditionalists among the membership pointedly opposed the election of Alfred Döblin to the Academy because of his reputation as a literary modernist, because he was publicly identified with the culture of Berlin, and because he had spoken out clearly in favour of the Academy committing itself openly to the Republic (Meyer, 53 f.). The protest of Erwin Guido Kolbenheyer against Döblin's views on the grounds that the Academy should remain aloof from politics soon proved to be disingenuous. In October 1930, at a plenary meeting of the section, Kolbenheyer gave a speech which emphasized the notion of an organic connection between the literary writer—*Dichter*, as opposed to *Schriftsteller*—and the nation; and under Schäfer's chairmanship the meeting was persuaded to vote in favour of new standing orders which reduced the effective power of the Berlin residents by specifying that resolutions could normally only be passed by the annual assembly (Jens, 101 f.; Meyer, 61–4). When Schäfer subsequently presented this coup as a triumph for the nationalist tendency, the Berlin group—in which both Döblin and Thomas

Mann played a leading part—managed to countermand the decision of the October meeting in a manner which compelled Kolbenheyer and Schäfer to resign, but which was bound to appear to the outside world as underhand. Under the presidency of Heinrich Mann the literary section of the Prussian Academy did, for the next two years, champion intellectual freedom and a conception of literary activity as founded in individual responsibility as opposed to "national community"; but in 1933 it was Kolbenheyer and Schäfer who effected the transition to a Nazi-controlled organization (Jens, 116–37, 181–218; Meyer, 64–86).

It was in the context of these events of 1930–1 that Döblin made his much-quoted remark about the spokesmen of the "utterly flat countryside". It was an expression of exasperation at the determination with which Schäfer's group had sought to capture the organization and harness it to the conceptions of a narrow and backward-looking nationalism. The terms of Döblin's polemic were an inversion of the invective which conservative nationalists had heaped on Berlin. As he explained in the *Vossische Zeitung* in January 1931, what the Berlin group had been confronted with was a delegation from "the country" which spoke with the voice of "provincialism, of local art (*Heimatkunst*), the art of the soil, of the utterly flat countryside, an old romantic ideal", a voice which spoke from "dark orphic depths" and stigmatized Berlin as a place where "business (*Betrieb*) was pursued for business's sake" (Meyer, 70). He was summarizing a situation in which "Berlin" and "the country" had become the respective rallying cries of two factions between whom there clearly lay an unbridgeable ideological divide.

Berlin was peculiarly suited to a role as emblem of the modernization process in both positive and negative senses. The rapidity of industrialization in the second half of the nineteenth century made a bigger impact there than in any other German city. The population of Berlin grew from 900,000 at the time of unification in 1871 to two million by the turn of the century, and with the extension of local government boundaries to create Groß-Berlin in 1920 it became a city of four million inhabitants, nearly four times the size of Hamburg, to say nothing of

Germany's other major towns. More significantly, that rapid growth affected the character of the population and its social life. Throughout the period between the 1860s and the First World War, a majority of the population had not been born in the city, but had moved there—from Slavic countries and from Western Europe as well as from elsewhere in Germany—in pursuit of employment. It became a commonplace by the turn of the century to describe Berlin as a colonial settlement on the plains of Eastern Europe, as a frontier town, indeed, in the American sense (Schäfer 1989, 110). But the dynamic nature of that process left the city with a marked lack of civic identity, something with which it has been reproached ever since (as preparations are made for Berlin to become the capital of Germany again, it is often the parochial character of Berlin's politics that attracts comment in newspapers published in other German cities). The settlers brought their small-town habits of mind with them, creating pockets of local custom and economic interaction which remained to a considerable degree 'foreign' to each other. The representational character of Berlin as a royal city was not developed to anything like the extent of Munich or Dresden or Vienna; intensive land speculation in the nineteenth century, coming on top of Berlin's earlier function as a garrison town, confirmed the dense and dismal character of much of its housing as "barracks to rent" (*Mietskasernen*),[11] while those who had profited from the rapid industrial expansion displayed their status with notorious eclecticism. This combination of factors conferred on Berlin a general reputation for provisionality, instability, and continual change. In a phrase coined by Karl Scheffler in 1910 (and much quoted ever since), it seemed that Berlin was destined "always to become and never to be".[12]

It may fairly be objected that this characterization of Berlin by Scheffler carries the traces of a prejudice which is rooted in old humanist assumptions about the nature of human commu-

[11] This aspect of Berlin's social development was sternly analysed by Werner Hegemann, *Das steinerne Berlin: Geschichte der größten Mietskasernenstadt der Welt* (Berlin: Kiepenheuer, 1930).

[12] This formulation appears on the final page of Karl Scheffler, *Berlin, ein Stadtschicksal* (Berlin: Erich Reiss, 1910), and is repeated at the end of the revised version of 1931, *Berlin: Wandlungen einer Stadt* (Berlin: Bruno Cassirer).

nities.[13] It is by comparison with an idealized view of Vienna, or Paris, or even London, that Scheffler assesses the apparent absence of "personality" in Berlin; and the processes of economic modernization, social differentiation, and organizational rationalization can no doubt be seen to erode the semblance of collective identity in many of the cities of Europe and elsewhere in the course of the twentieth century (cf. Scherpe 1988*a*). But there are nevertheless real senses in which Berlin was pioneering those experiences for the German-speaking world. When Scheffler revised his book for publication in 1931, he was anxious to convey a more positive image of Berlin as a cradle of the new era which had arisen in the wake of the First World War. He was able to point to new civic projects for developing the major public concourses, to the extension of the local railway network, opening up access to outlying areas for excursions and recreational purposes, and to the way that modern communications were encouraging a dispersion of the city's population, thereby carrying the effects of urbanization out into the countryside. But his endorsement of dynamic change is not unreserved: he is still troubled by the absence of coherent identity in Berlin, and he conveys a sense of eeriness when describing how the city centre has migrated—from the Alexanderplatz, to the shops and fun palaces of the Friedrichstraße, and further west to the Potsdamer Platz, and the Kurfürstendamm (p. 68).[14] Scheffler's fastidiousness shows in his evocation of the (shapeless) masses who have replaced the officers and the burghers as the dominant element on the streets, and in what he has to say about the seeming uniformity and the temporariness of the architecture that has arisen to house those masses (pp. 177 f. 233).[15] His enthusiasm for the outlook of Berlin as the way of the future seems to mask a certain apprehension: it is a

[13] Scheffler's criteria are apparent in the remark that Berlin is "keine der Hauptstädte, in denen sich die schöpferischen Kräfte einer ganzen Nation ein für allemal konzentriert haben": *Berlin: Wandlungen einer Stadt*, 17.

[14] It was partly in order to halt this westward drift that the director of city planning in Berlin, Martin Wagner, with strong commercial support, vigorously promoted the redevelopment of the Alexanderplatz in the second half of the 1920s (see Boberg et al., 126 ff.).

[15] The latter point appears to contain a thrust against the planning regime of Martin Wagner, who had accepted the principle that the city should renew itself in accordance with the needs of each successive generation (see Boberg et al., 127).

"cold-blooded utopianism" that he reads into the by now legendary resilience of the populace.[16]

Walter Mehring captured the bustle and dynamism of 1920s Berlin in his early cabaret lyrics; and George Grosz and Otto Dix reflected the social disparities and injustices in their acerbic caricatures. But in the course of the decade, the art world also discovered a new painter of everyday Berlin in Gustav Wunderwald. The city he depicted was not that of the new civic developments, but that of the older industrial ones: the looming blank walls of the tenements (sometimes covered with shrill advertisements), the factories, and the heavy iron railway bridges that crouch over the streets and waterways. He made the ostensibly drab and depersonalized Berlin his speciality (Fig. 7). There was no apparent evidence that Wunderwald had ever been schooled in a particular artistic tradition, although the critic Paul Westheim, who championed him, later claimed to recognize an affinity with Utrillo.[17] Westheim acclaimed him as a 'natural', who painted the environment he knew with the intimacy of someone who had grown up in it (in reality he had moved to Berlin in 1912 at the age of 30), revealing its melancholy charm to viewers who would otherwise overlook it; and he admired the technique with which Wunderwald could organize stark surfaces into a compositional whole with its own sense of rhythm. But Westheim's main reason for publicizing Wunderwald's work was that he felt here was an artist with the *potential* to become the representative painter of the new Berlin, of its peculiar "atmosphere of being devoid of atmosphere", in a word, of its "Sachlichkeit".[18]

The task of conveying to a broad public, both within the capital and beyond it, what life was actually like in this new Berlin fell to the feuilleton section of the major newspapers. Many feuilleton articles of the Weimar period provide vivid first-hand testimony to the trends and atmospheres of the times, although they have to be read, of course, as the attempts of indi-

---

[16] Scheffler speaks of Berliners as possessing a "Genialität, die kalten Blutes des Geistes der Utopie fähig ist und die bei dem Deutschen der Zukunft Pate steht": *Berlin: Wandlungen einer Stadt*, 190.

[17] See Hildegard Reinhardt (ed.), *Gustav Wunderwald: Gemälde—Handzeichnungen—Bühnenbilder* (Berlin: Nicolaische Verlagsbuchhandlung, 1982), 52.

[18] Paul Westheim, "Gustav Wunderwald", *Das Kunstblatt*, 11 (1927), 2–5; reprinted in Reinhardt (ed.), *Gustav Wunderwald*, 111 f.

Fig. 7. Gustav Wunderwald, *By the S-Bahn in Wedding*, 1927

vidual writers to construct an image of city life in the light of
their own expectations and those of their anticipated readers (cf.
Prümm 1988; Bienert, 5–20). Heinrich Mann in 1921, writing
in the conviction that Germany needed to develop democratic
habits of mind, lighted on a conversation between a policeman
and a strike picket as evidence of the erosion of previously

strong class distinctions, and viewed the emergence of ironic turns of speech as a "human" way of mastering unfamiliar impressions (Jäger and Schütz, 13–19).[19] Otto Flake, on the other hand, visiting Berlin from Munich in 1923, registered the stressed and unhealthy appearance of the populace by comparison with pre-war years (Jäger and Schütz, 20 f.). Joseph Roth, who wrote for two leading Berlin newspapers as well as placing his articles further afield in the early 1920s, took the reader on little excursions into unknown territory behind the surface appearances of the city, the world of black-marketeers and abortionists, the unemployed and the homeless. He stripped away the pretence that the new jazz cult was anything more than a way of playing at being uncultivated, and he described the coldness that had entered the souls of the poor and the down-and-out. The Berlin Roth discovered was an intrinsically unstable and unsafe environment. Indeed, when he became the first designated Berlin correspondent of the *Frankfurter Zeitung* in 1923, he dipped into the repertoire of apocalyptic Expressionism in order to evoke the chaos and violence of the city at a time of roaring inflation: "The dollar dances jazz numbers on Jacob's ladders, hands wave through the air and hinder the traffic. Beggars writhe at street corners, and the ailments they display to enforce their demands are their working capital. Prophets pass through the streets and preach war or peace to a desperate mob. Human beings are nailed to the swastika, and the bells proclaim: Judas is risen!" (*Werke* 1, 930 f.) The context is an article which contrasts the madness of the world at large with the comparative sanity of the inmates of a particular mental asylum.

Bernard von Brentano, who succeeded Roth as Berlin correspondent of the *Frankfurter Zeitung* in 1925, brought with him the clipped and matter-of-fact style of the rising generation. In his feuilletons, the monumentality and dynamism of Berlin are enthusiastically accepted as an inherent feature of the new age, and the representative 'reality' of that age is sought in the sensational technical and sporting events, at the film premiers, and among the crowds on the Kurfürstendamm—the Kurfürstendamm because that is where the scene is constantly changing,

---

[19] Heinrich Mann's article was reprinted, as a gesture of republican resolve, in the *Vossische Zeitung* of 21 July 1929: Jäger and Schütz, 350.

as seasonal fashions come and go, as new shops and cafés replace the old (Prümm 1988, 94–8). For Brentano, crowd scenes suggest the primacy of the collective experience over the individual life, with or without intimations of the power of a machine age (*Wo in Europa*, 57, 100). From 1925 to 1930 is the period in which such visitors as Harold Nicolson note the charm of fashionable Berlin (Kaes et al., 425 f.), others record the erotic fascination of its consumer districts and its night life (Jäger and Schütz, 24–33), and *flânerie* becomes established as a fashionable form of resistance to the pace of city life.[20] In the early 1930s, finally, Berlin becomes the terrain of the sociological investigator. In his famous study of white-collar workers, which appeared as a series of reports in the *Frankfurter Zeitung* before being published under the title *Die Angestellten*, Siegfried Kracauer aimed to build a picture of society in mosaic style, analysing the personal catastrophes and the obdurate mentalities of middle-class employees as the institutions for which they worked collapsed (Prümm 1988, 98–103; Bienert, 163–74). The Kurfürstendamm he describes in 1932 is a street where nothing is built to last, and the memories of yesterday are all too easily obliterated by the surface appearances of today (Jäger and Schütz, 112–16). As Ernst Glaeser put it in 1931, what could be observed in Berlin was merely the concentration of phenomena which were characteristic of the general cultural development of Germany during the Weimar period; in the dismal circumstances of economic crisis, he described Berlin as the "megaphone" for the hubris and the illusory boom of the mid-1920s (*LW* 7, 19, 1 f.).

It is in the early 1930s that we find Berlin most closely associated with the mood of disillusionment in the novels of the younger generation. The Jewish editor Miermann in Gabriele Tergit's novel *Käsebier erobert den Kurfürstendamm* (Käsebier conquers the Kurfürstendamm, 1931) wanders the streets after the funeral of an employee's little daughter, who has died of tuberculosis, apparently aggravated by hardship. The next day Miermann, too, will die after receiving his dismissal notice. It is a "dead city" that he experiences, a city of shuttered façades,

---

[20] As Walter Benjamin noted in his review of the work (*GS* III, 194–9), Franz Hessel cultivated the manner and the mystique of the nineteenth-century *flâneur* in *Spazieren in Berlin* (1929). Cf. Kaes et al., 420–2; Bienert, 78–83.

silhouettes, and delapidated houses awaiting demolition. Such life as he encounters on the Friedrichstraße is ephemeral and meretricious, a world of pimps, transvestites, and sham Chinese pubs (pp. 262–4). Erich Kästner's Fabian is making play of his general disaffection when he compares Berlin with a madhouse and adds, "The East is inhabited by criminals, the centre by fraudsters, the North by misery, the West by fornication, and doom dwells in all directions." (He is introducing the city to his new-found girlfriend from the provinces. She asks what comes after the doom, and when he answers, "Imbecility," she tells him that her home-town has already reached that stage: *GS* 2, 83 f.) It is the irony of impotence that pervades the street descriptions of Martin Kessel's *Herrn Brechers Fiasko* (1932), too. When Kessel sets his scene in the Friedrichsstadt office quarter, what he evokes is on the one hand a diffuse landscape of banal ugliness, and on the other hand the daily routine of a humanity whose working and leisure lives are institutionally organized for them. It is in an atmosphere of purposelessness and impending redundancy that the city streets provide Kessel's characters with a bleak backdrop for their ruminations on futility and loneliness, while "Berlin" appears as a shadowy opponent, the very abstractness of which makes it impossible to combat it effectively.[21]

But there is much in Glaeser's comments of 1931 that points beyond the mere mood of the moment. Here was someone who had identified himself firmly with the new 'sachlich' trend in writing—as a feuilleton writer and as the editor of the *Fazit* collection of contemporary prose in 1929—expressing fundamental unease with the nature of the society that had developed in Berlin. A migrant from small-town Germany himself, like most other writers of the time, Glaeser emphasizes from the outset that he is not about to deliver a defence of the provinces; but he speaks with repugnance of the "unbridled idolization of success" in Berlin. Arguing against Alfred Kantorowicz's view

[21] See especially Brecher's reflections on p. 323: "Berlin aber ist ein Fall, es wird stets ein schattenhafter Gegner bleiben, dem es gewachsen zu sein gilt. Man lebt nicht dahin, sondern trotzdem oder neben alledem. Märchen, Skepsis und Kritik, die Elastizität als Lyrismus, die Zersetzung als Trauer und Witz, das Projekt und die Theorie als radikaler Ernst, im Schatten als Schwindel und Großmannssucht, als Zauber oder als fauler Zauber—in solchen Kategorien bewegt sich diese Stadt, es ist ihr Lebenselement."

of the dynamic character of Berlin life as an expression of a will to learn and an absence of prejudice, he sees it as a symptom of how anarchic life has become. The pace and intensity of life, and the capacity for rational organization, leave him with a pronounced sense of the lack of any defined goal or meaning to all this activity. Glaeser, in short, articulates the melancholy moment that resides within the pursuit of modernization for modernization's sake, or for the sake of keeping up with the trend.

The standard clichés about Berlin—that it had no stable cultural identity; that its character was moulded by utilitarian rationality; that its physical development was determined by technical requirements rather than organic growth; that its pace of life had no other rationale than itself; and that its human transactions were exclusively driven by the circulation of goods and services—were echoed by those who worked there and wrote about the city, regardless of where they stood on the political spectrum. The image of life in Berlin as frantically going round in circles without a sense of ultimate purpose, which seems to have become a commonplace by 1929,[22] is already a part of Kurt Tucholsky's journalistic vocabulary in 1919; and in 1920 he evokes the mood of new political departures in terms of sitting in a tube train which is on the move, but without knowing what the destination is (*GW* 2, 130, 438 f.). The "rasender Reporter" Egon Erwin Kisch extracts an allegory of the emptiness of human endeavour from a six-day cycle race at the sports arena on the Potsdamer Straße, in which each participant peddles away like fury, but never significantly alters his position in relation to the pack. Crowd participation in such spectacles may be a form of protest against utilitarianism and mechanization, Kisch notes, but if so, it is characterized by the same fanatical pointlessness as the money-earning routine it is protesting against (*GW* V, 227–31). What Tucholsky and Kisch describe with satirical piquancy in the early 1920s is merely extrapolated into plangent denunciation in Hermann Kesser's account of life on the Potsdamer Platz in *Die neue Rundschau* in 1929. Here life has become reduced to a mechanical process, the truth is mass-produced, and the God that reigns is that of

[22] The examples cited by Bienert (pp. 226 f.) in support of the general point all date from 1929.

trade and business: "He is the tireless revolutionizing energiser—without aim. [. . .] He pulls down, rebuilds, converts, draws new lines, founds, bankrupts, liquidates, redevelops. His creation is called profit." (Jäger and Schütz, 131–7)

In both their positive and their negative aspect, the dynamic processes of the city were part of the lived experience of Weimar authors, but the longer-term perspectives in which they perceived them owed much to a pre-established discourse about the nature of historical development. On the positive side, Georg Simmel had given a balanced assessment of the implications of urbanization in his essay "Die Großstädte und das Geistesleben" (Big Cities and the Life of the Mind) of 1903. He acknowledged that the increased specialization of economic activity in the city, and the growing tendency for human needs to be met through impersonal institutions, brought with them the danger that individuals were required to serve those institutions in one-sided and purely functional ways. But at the same time he stressed the cosmopolitan character of the big city and the wealth of opportunities it offered for personal choice and initiative, which made the small town feel restrictive by comparison.[23] The underlying liberalism of Simmel's analysis of urban society provides an important strand of intellectual discourse on the city which carries through, for example, into the cheerful endorsement of modernity by Robert Musil.[24] The ironic manner in which Musil describes the city ambience in the opening chapter of *Der Mann ohne Eigenschaften* (Man without Qualities) is not merely a way of teasing the reader about the stock conventions of narrative fiction; it is also a jovial way of evoking the senses in which the substance of city life consists of a largely depersonalized system of functional relations.

But there was a darker side to Simmel's perception of the development of the modern world, and he expressed it in an

---

[23] See Georg Simmel, "Die Großstädte und das Geistesleben" (1903), in *Das Individuum und die Freiheit* (Frankfurt: Fischer, 1993), 192–204.

[24] More specific echoes of Simmel's arguments are to be found in Musil's essays of the early 1920s, where he stresses the social diversity generated by the energy and inventiveness of technological development, and accepts that, as a natural consequence of that development, older forms of social bonding are being replaced by relationships established in the workplace: GW II, 1087, 1362.

essay of 1910 on the "concept and tragedy of culture".[25] Here he constructed a dichotomy between human creativity and its own products, describing a world in which man is inevitably alienated from his social environment because the creative impulses of the individual are constrained by the ossified forms of human culture that already exist in the external world. This pessimistic dimension to the discussion of cultural development was taken to an even bleaker extreme by Oswald Spengler after the First World War. In *Der Untergang des Abendlandes* (The Decline of the West), Spengler described the development of human cultures generally in terms of biological life-cycles. As he saw it, all documented cultures begin as vital and creative organisms, but are doomed to end in intellectual abstraction and the exhaustion of vital potential, a condition which Spengler calls "civilization". That much is explicit in Part I of his disquisition, which he published in 1918. In a major section of Part II, which appeared in 1923, he presents the contrast in lifestyle and mentality between the metropolis and the provinces as both irreducible and an inevitable feature of the historical pattern he has in mind. He describes the metropolis (*Weltstadt*) as a stony colossus which marks the endpoint of the development of a culture; in explicit contrast to the vitality and organic character of a "young" culture, the metropolis is equated with notions of petrifaction and sterility (*Untergang*, 672–84). The implications of Spengler's historical vision were firmly repudiated at the time by major authors—Musil, Döblin, Thomas Mann[26]—but the suggestive power of his arguments manifestly pervaded the intellectual discourse of the time in both direct and indirect ways. What he had to say about cities and civilization found echoes in the works of Hermann Broch and Jakob Wassermann, for example, although it should be emphasized that both were

[25] Georg Simmel, "Der Begriff und die Tragödie der Kultur", in *Philosophische Kultur: Gesammelte Essais* (Leipzig: Verlag von Dr. Werner Klinkhardt, 1911), 245–77.

[26] Musil gave a critical analysis of Spengler's analogical method under the humorous title, "Geist und Erfahrung: Anmerkungen für Leser, welche dem Untergang des Abendlandes entronnen sind" (*GW* II, 1042–59); Döblin emphatically rejects the distinction between "Kultur" and "Zivilisation" in the opening sentence of his essay "Der Geist des naturalistischen Zeitalters" (*Ästhetik*, 168); and Thomas Mann, who had set great store by that distinction in his wartime writings, distanced himself publicly from Spengler in 1924 (*GW* X, 172–80).

looking for ways to transcend Spengler's pessimism through ethical insight.[27] And by the same token, authors who were eager to espouse the modernization process also seem to have found it difficult to address the subject without engaging in some way with Spengler's vocabulary.

In Brecht's writings of the mid-1920s, for example, the city provides a focus for a variety of mutually contradictory motifs. Cities are built to outlast us, and they are doomed to crumble in their turn; they call forth the wrath of God (like Sodom and Gomorrah), and they embody man's defiance of divine ordinance; they are the way of the future, and they are the scene of man's inhumanity towards man. Brecht's stylization of himself in the poem "Vom armen B.B." ("Of Poor B.B.", which dates from 1922) presents him as a *poète maudit* who is "at home" in the city, and whose every spiritual need is met by such emphatically mundane objects as newspapers, tobacco, and brandy. All that will remain of the great cities of modern times, this poem suggests, is the wind that passes through them—the wind which is a common symbol of transience in Brecht's early works. The logic behind this nihilistic gesture is made explicit in a poem of December 1925 entitled "Bidi's view of the great cities" (Bidi being the form of his given name, Berthold, which Brecht liked to retain with intimate acquaintances). Here the motif of transience appears as a consoling thought in the face of what everyone is saying about the coming dominance of the cities, it negates the prevailing opinion that "this petrifact" is here to stay. But the world of the city, the world of civilization, is also one from which the consoling metaphysical certainties of earlier times have disappeared. As this poem puts it, the stars still shine as they did for your daddy, but the Great Bear is no longer to be seen. And the closing lines suggest an appropriate response to these circumstances: "Du, der sie sah | Betrachte sie kälter." (You who saw them, regard them more coldly: *BFA* 13,

---

[27] David Horrocks draws attention to both the historical pessimism and the over-schematic contrasts drawn between the city and the country in Broch's *Schlafwandler* trilogy (Bance, 38–52). Wassermann frequently invokes the notion of petrification in his discussions of modern society during the Weimar period (see S. H. Harris, "The Tradition of Humanist Narrative in the Work of Jakob Wassermann", Diss. Cambridge, 1997, 13–32); and in his 1934 novel, *Joseph Kerkhovens dritte Existenz* (Munich: Albert Langen & Georg Müller, 1982, 67) he describes the city as a withered organism and as "organisierter Tod".

307.) Coldness, the emblem of lost comfort, which was presented in "Vom armen B.B." as something inherited that the poet has brought with him to the city, appears here as an attitude to be consciously adopted, as the attitude required by the modern, urbanized world.

After some early brushes with Berlin in the period 1920–2, Brecht settled there in 1924—although he usually retreated to the gentler landscape of his native Bavaria for the summer months. Over the next few years he accumulated a large number of poems which register in one fashion or another the coldness, the hardness, the brutality, of the city environment. Some of them evoke the trauma of self-alienation which can arise from living in a mass society where individuals become anonymous and interchangeable (the woman I slept with for seven years greets me politely in the hallway and passes me by, it feels as if I have moved out and someone else is living in my underwear: *BFA* 13, 368). Some of them imitate the matter-of-factness with which personal disputes are regulated (when he came home he found his suitcase by the door, that made him think: *BFA* 13, 367), or the ruthlessness with which authority could be exercised in the workplace (Fall in! Why are you so late? Now wait! No, not you, that one! *BFA* 13, 371). Others come close to a dramatization of irate or reflective responses to experiences of betrayal or rejection.[28] The selection from among these poems that Brecht published in 1930 under the title "From a Reader for City-Dwellers" is as if designed to display for scrutiny the mental and rhetorical attitudes associated with particular social situations, as we saw in Chapter 2. The collection contains indications of the survival strategies which city-dwellers may adopt, but it also has its puzzling aspects.

One of the ten poems imitates the mode of political instruction, but the lesson it ostensibly puts across is that "they will make mincemeat of you". Another offers advice on how to live on the run; but the opening poem, which ostensibly instructs the reader on how to avoid attention, carries the theme of self-effacement beyond anything that may be needed for political struggle. What the city has taught the speaker in this instance

---

[28] The poems in question are more conveniently gathered together in the old Suhrkamp *Werkausgabe* (Frankfurt 1967, 277–95), which was prepared by Elisabeth Hauptmann, than in the new Berlin and Frankfurt edition.

(as we seem bound to conclude from the final stanza, which concerns the preservation of anonymity in death) includes a panic response which leads to the total denial of personal involvement in any aspect of historical development.[29] The third poem, which was also published separately under the title "To Chronos", evokes the ambition of the young generation to supplant the old, and in doing so, brings out the ruthlessness of the modernization process. The young are keen to "talk with the stones", i.e. to adopt an attitude of mind appropriate to a new and inhospitable environment, but are also explicit about their intention to take possession of their father's house with all its furnishings and to make the old boy disappear like smoke up the chimney. The fifth poem presents a counter-image to this, but one which again establishes a relationship between commitment to the world of the future and the severity of struggle in the present. It tells of a woman who has repeatedly had to surmount degradation, drug-addiction, disease, and low self-esteem in order to reassert her vitality and establish a sense of purpose in her life. She has a vision of herself as no longer the "scum", but the "hard mortar" of which cities are built; she identifies, in other words, with a future urban world, but what is required of her in order to participate in that future is the effort of self-overcoming and a hardening of her attitudes towards herself and others. Brecht's city poems, then, explore a number of themes which together suggest the variety of personal and social factors which contribute to the making of the modern world. Among the human responses to that world displayed in the poems are the need for evasiveness and the impetus towards retreat and self-destruction, as well as the exercise of solidarity and organization. In so far as his "Reader for City-Dwellers" can be said to offer instruction on how to live in the city, its lessons are presented as fragmentary and hard-won, and they

---

[29] "Sorge, wenn du zu sterben gedenkst I Daß kein Grabmal steht und verrät, wo du liegst I Mit einer deutlichen Schrift, die dich anzeigt I Und dem Jahr deines Todes, das dich überführt!" (*BFA* 11, 157) It is necessary to stress this aspect because it poses a problem for any interpretation of the poem which seeks to invest it with political meaning, as Walter Benjamin does (*Versuche über Brecht*, Frankfurt: Suhrkamp, 1955, 80f.). It is also worth noting that, when revising the collection for publication in 1938, Brecht changed the final line of this poem from "Das wurde mir *gesagt*", which might seem to imply instruction by a third party, to "Das wurde mir *gelehrt*", which leaves open the possibility that the responses described have simply been instilled by the urban environment (cf. *BFA* 11, 350).

involve arguing with, as well as against, contemporary perspectives on civilization as a process which entails the "petrifaction" of human relations.

In *Rise and Fall of the City of Mahagonny* (first performed in 1930), Brecht examined a common response to those pessimistic perspectives in its turn. Mahagonny is a boom town created precisely by the urge of contemporary humanity to *escape* from civilization; it is the place where the gratification of all desires is permitted—provided that you can pay. The dramatic situation Brecht constructs here lends itself to the ironization of the conflicting impulses which make up a money-based urban society. The unrestrained pursuit of human appetites is shown to create a hell on earth, a society that need fear no natural disasters because it is equally capable of creating its own, and at the final curtain, street demonstrations are still campaigning for the free reign of precisely those tendencies which were recognizable at the time as contributors to economic catastrophe: inflation, urban chaos, and the ethos of every-man-for-himself. The *Mahagonny* opera was a provocative attempt to pose moral issues through the ironization of social trends (and, as the notes to the work make plain, an experiment in using the apparatus of commercial theatre to expose the ethos of commercialism). But beyond that, Brecht's attempts in the course of the Weimar period to dramatize the historical processes which made the modern city what it was came to nought. *In the Jungle of the Cities* (1924) shows only the self-absorbed battle of wills between two enigmatic individuals in the setting of a story-book Chicago, with the struggle itself apparently providing the only sustaining rationale in their lives.[30] During the mid-1920s Brecht worked with Elisabeth Hauptmann on other projects for depicting the drift of populations to the cities and the nature of economic competition in the cities, and it appears to have been the failure of these projects that led him towards the theorization of an 'epic' approach to theatrical presentation on the one hand and to the reading of Karl Marx on the other. The evidence of the manuscript fragments that remain—published under the title "Jae Fleischhacker

---

[30] When *Im Dickicht der Städte* was revived at the end of 1927, it was dismissed by the reviewer of *Die literarische Welt* as a faded relic of Expressionism (*LW* 4, 1, 7).

in Chikago"—suggests that what made it impossible for Brecht to convert his material into a coherent drama was the tension between the habit of looking to personal rivalry for plot motivation and the supra-personal nature of the economic forces involved, as well as the difficulty of making plausible connections between the acts of individual traders and the movement of prices. Looking back on the experience in 1935, Brecht said that what had made him abandon the work was the recognition that the behaviour of world commodity markets was inherently irrational (*BFA* 10, 271–314; 1073 f.).

It was almost a commonplace in the immediate post-war years that the city represented a challenge to the literary writer, a subject which had yet to be conquered. Brecht noted in his diary in 1921 that somebody ought to do for the city what Kipling had done for the subject-matter of British imperial conquest: in the urban "jungle" he saw another promising source of heroes, colonizers, and victims.[31] Heinrich Mann noted that Berlin, and the new age it was fostering, was an ideal theme for epic treatment, and Otto Flake echoed him in this—although Flake wondered why, in 1923, nobody yet appeared to be taking it on (Jäger and Schütz, 19–20). The two works of the 1920s which did make the attempt—Paul Gurk's novel, *Berlin* (which was written between 1923 and 1925, although it was not published until 1934) and Döblin's *Berlin Alexanderplatz* of 1929— provide good evidence, not only of the adjustments in cultural outlook which were necessary in order for the literary writer to come to terms with the city, but also of the extent to which the solutions found were themselves moulded by the intellectual controversies of the time.

Gurk's novel tells of the last year in the life of an elderly man who sells books from a barrow. Eckenpenn is a native of Silesia who retains a strong, indeed a romantic affinity with the natural world. Even his perception of the time of day is expressed in references to the changing colour of the daylight. He lives in the hope that the lyric poetry he wrote in his youth will find a sympathetic reader among the populace, but what he fears is confirmed by the up-and-coming young writer, Dr Seidenschwanz: such poems are now seen as sentimental and hopelessly out of

---

[31] Bertolt Brecht, *Tagebücher 1920–1922. Autobiographische Aufzeichnungen 1920–1954* (Frankfurt: Suhrkamp, 1975), 145.

date. It is from Eckenpenn's perspective as a street figure and a denizen of cheap bars and cafés that Gurk constructs his composite picture of what life is like in Berlin. Eckenpenn is the reader's witness to the outward manifestations of toil and bustle, to court cases, suicides, and fatal road accidents. He experiences the city traffic as an "explosion" of sound, in his eyes even the people in the cars seem as if they are made of iron. Before his stall, individuals come and go as if by chance, or at any rate, according to where their business takes them, and they refer to emotional experiences, if at all, with a callousness which emphasizes the gulf between Eckenpenn and the world around him. Eckenpenn's suicide at the end of the novel is ostensibly triggered by the fact that he is about to be evicted from his room for failing to pay the rent. But long before that point he has come to see himself as representing the "dying soul" of Berlin.

It has often been said that Gurk mythicizes the city,[32] but the precise senses in which that is so carry a number of specific implications. For one thing, the city he portrays is like a compilation of all the faults with which Berlin's enemies had ever reproached it: mindless bustle, depersonalization, and a social environment that compels individuals towards depravity and crime. In Eckenpenn's private thoughts it is also explicitly associated with pacifism and the encroachment of foreign influences (p. 164). The world of industrial production is seen only in Eckenpenn's imagination, as a cyclops' cave in which workers are continually devoured, or as a bleak subjugation of humanity to the demands of mechanization, culminating in the image of a ceaseless cycle in which animal carcasses are hoisted on a conveyor-belt in order to be stripped, portioned, consumed, and returned to the soil that fed them (pp. 95 f.). 'Life', by implication, is a dwindling potential that exists beyond that world of work. Secondly, Gurk dehistoricizes the society he depicts. The structure of his narrative is related to the seasons of the year,

[32] Gurk himself is quoted by Manfred Schlösser, in his afterword to the novel (p. 360), as saying that in his writing he repeatedly attempted to depict "den ewigen Mythos vom Sterben der Seele an der Zivilisation, an der Verruchtheit der Großstädte, an den eigenen Grenzen". Wolfgang Wendler emphasizes the aspect of the Expressionist heritage in Gurk's "mythicization" of the city (Rothe 1974, 171). Hermann Kähler, *Berlin—Asphalt und Licht* (Berlin: Dietz Verlag, 1986, 205–9) presents Gurk's novel in crude Marxist terms as a petty-bourgeois mystification.

rather than to any sense of progression in the life of a human community, beginning with the first intimation of spring and ending in the depths of a severe winter. Politics is merely a dimension of that world from which Eckenpenn knows himself to be alienated, and its violence erupts into his field of vision like an emanation from the sewers. Thirdly, the perspective from which this picture of society is constructed is that of a social group conscious of experiencing its own demise. Eckenpenn and his closest associates—a retired history professor who becomes one of Berlin's traffic victims, and a former circus artiste who goes by the name of Fox Randolfini and has a penchant for self-ironizing cultural allusions—belong to a world of bourgeois literacy and courtesy which is constantly reminded by the toughness of the Berlin environment that it has had its day. And finally, Gurk's mythical construct also represents the city as an entity which provides a kind of private religious test for the protagonist. Eckenpenn even stylizes Berlin from time to time, in the manner of a medieval epic, as a wicked princess. He makes one attempt, in midsummer, to escape the clutches of the city, only to find that they are extending—kraken-like, as he puts it— into the surrounding countryside. But two thoughts present themselves vividly to his mind subsequently. One is that the dominance of the city will prove inescapable in the context of his own life (p. 190), and the other is that, much as he might reproach the young with living only for the present, he is bound to recognize how devoid of substance his own life has become, with the result that it is incapable of realizing itself in the present (pp. 220 f.). The emotions associated with the moment of his death are defiance of the city on the one hand, and on the other hand a love that has endured against all the degradation he believes himself to have witnessed.

Döblin's depiction of Berlin does not shy away from acknowledging the city's chaotic uncertainties, its criminality, its brutality, and its power to corrupt; but it absorbs these aspects into a broader representation of human vitality and its place in the natural order of things. The city provides an opponent for Döblin's protagonist, as it does for Gurk's, but the opening pages of *Berlin Alexanderplatz* encourage the interpretation that it is the combative impulse with which the ex-convict Biberkopf responds to the experience of disorientation and insecurity that creates that sense of opposition. Biberkopf takes Berlin on, having resolved to lead a decent life, and it keeps knocking him down—until it becomes apparent that the fault lies in his own obstinate nature rather than in his environment. The traditional association of the big city with corruption is evoked with the figure of the Whore of Babylon, but the precise context is a strictly allegorical representation in which she fights to hold on to the old recalcitrant Biberkopf, and is defeated by Death, who enables the new one to emerge. Like Gurk, Döblin makes use of the slaughterhouse as a source of symbolism, treating it indeed to one of the most vivid and sustained descriptive passages in the work, but it is not the symbolism of a mechanized existence that Döblin extracts from it. The slaughter evoked in *Berlin Alexanderplatz* is the work of skilled men, and a necessary contribution to the feeding of the city. It is the particular actions of their trade that acquire symbolic resonance within the work: the swinging of an axe anticipates the way that Death will slice away at Biberkopf's unyielding identity in order to bring about his transformation, and the repeated blows which fell the animals anticipate the metaphorical blows of fate that will bring him low. The section-heading reminds us, in a line from Ecclesiastes, that the fate which awaits man is no different from that of beasts, and the explicit imagery of the passage makes suggestive connections to the themes of destruction and renewal, of recalcitrance and broken resistance, of death and regeneration, which are woven into the broader fabric of the narrative, as we noted in Chapter 4.

Whereas Gurk presents the life of the city in the form of external impressions reflected in a single central consciousness, Döblin dispenses with that central subjectivity and looks for ways to allow the various dimensions of city life to speak for themselves. The famous montage sequences of *Berlin Alexanderplatz* which incorporate snippets of hackneyed verbal exchanges as well as fragments of official documents, weather forecasts, and the details of tram routes, display the transactions of the city in the very language in which they take place. These are the features of Döblin's text which make it justifiable to claim that it succeeds in evoking those dimensions of city life which elude more conventional narrative approaches, including the seemingly abstract organization of urban society and the impersonal functionality of language in the city environment (cf. Scherpe 1988*b*). But if we take account of the full range of textual material that Döblin has built into the work, then I think we are bound to resist the implications of Klaus Scherpe's thesis that *Berlin Alexanderplatz* is above all a representation of the city as a "functional void" in which human communication acquires an "inorganic" character.[33] What Scherpe's argument overlooks are the subtle connections between organic and inorganic categories which are to be found in the play of motifs in Döblin's text. The slaughterhouse sequence is a case in point. As a pig is clubbed senseless and its throat is cut, we are told that it passes from the biological realm into that of metaphysics and theology, and finally into the inorganic domain of physics. The imagery of that sequence provides suggestive links to Döblin's reworking of the stories of Job and Isaac; and quotations from Jeremiah as well as Ecclesiastes evoke cycles of decay and regeneration which entail an intimate relation between the animate and the inanimate sphere (cf. Keller, 154 ff.). Döblin deploys his imagery, in other words, in ways which allow it both to convey vivid impressions of the ramifications of city life and to keep before the reader's eye the sense that the city is itself a manifestation of human energy which participates, like all earthly life, in the ultimate oneness of being.

In his essay of 1924 on the "spirit of the naturalistic age"— which begins with a firm repudiation of Spengler's dichotomy between 'culture' and 'civilization'—Döblin had spoken of the modern city as just one more manifestation of the evolutionary drive for biological diversity, expressed through the human impulse for collective activity. He explicitly rejected the prejudices of those who favoured the country over the city and spoke of a loss of 'soul' when they should be concerning themselves with the specific mutations of the 'soul' under the conditions of modern society. And he emphasized both the collective nature of urban culture and the biological character of the forces that create it by likening cities to colonies of bees, termites, and coral (*Ästhetik*, 171–81). Alongside the other themes it evokes (these include themes of a moral and existential nature), the imagery

---

[33] See pp. 168 and 170 of the English version of Scherpe's text. As the expression "functional void" indicates, Scherpe is trying to make Döblin's text conform to the description of Berlin to be found in Ernst Bloch's *Erbschaft dieser Zeit*.

Döblin develops in *Berlin Alexanderplatz* is also an elaboration of this line of thinking about the biological character of the city. Perhaps that accounts for the emphasis we find there on the assimilation of the individual into a collective body, an emphasis for which Döblin also attempts to compensate on the closing pages of the work with the intimation that Biberkopf has also learned to think for himself. Döblin, it seems, was countering the prejudices of those who would denounce the city as an embodiment of rational organization and a mechanical way of life, not by asserting the specific virtues of those qualities, but by hinting at connections which indicate that life in the city is every bit as much a product of natural organic processes as life anywhere else on earth.

The representations of provincial life to which I now wish to turn all contain indications of how the political and economic developments of the 1920s were making themselves felt throughout Germany, and among the novels which appeared in the early 1930s there are reflections of the responses to those developments in rural areas which created campaigning opportunities for the National Socialists. Each of these works raises questions of perspective, of the point of view from which a particular image of provincial life is being constructed. But together they also illustrate a more general phenomenon. A common reference point in discussions of the tensions between the city and the country in German literature is Friedrich Sengle's essay of 1963, "Wunschbild Land und Schreckbild Stadt". Sengle had suggested that there was something peculiarly German about the tradition of negative representations of city life, which seemed to go back beyond the impact of industrialization in the German-speaking world and to have emerged in the seventeenth and eighteenth centuries as a complement to the idyllic depiction of life on the land in the literature of the rising middle classes. But that was not the whole of Sengle's argument. Part of his purpose was to point out that, within the strongly regional literature of the nineteenth century with its often parochial content, there had developed what he called a "broader urbanity" of outlook which transcended the stark antithesis between urban and rural culture. He saw that urbanity exemplified in the balanced treatment of social diversity to be found in the

works of Fontane and Thomas Mann, and he also associated it
with the robust narrative traditions of Southern Germany,
where industrial conurbations had not developed so freely and
the sense of alarming contrasts between city and country was
therefore less marked. Sengle's "broader urbanity" is not to be
found in equal measure among the works I wish to discuss in
this section, but his concept provides a useful initial indicator
of what distinguishes these works as a group from the reactionary stylization of the German provinces as bastions against
the encroachment of modernity, and thus what makes it worth
considering them as critical appraisals of the provincial life of
their time.

Leonhard Frank's depiction of contemporary life in his home
town of Würzburg in *Das Ochsenfurter Männerquartett* (The
Ochsenfurt Male-Voice Quartet, 1927) is difficult to categorize
because of the ambivalence with which it treats the character of
provincial life on the one hand and the modernizing impulses
of the time on the other. The work makes no bones about the
constraints of small-town life, but at the same time it explores
the range of emotional experience and the potential for personal
fulfilment which is available within those constraints—which is
why critical judgements of the work have varied between reject-
ing it as the construction of a nostalgic idyll and lauding it as
a masterpiece of realist narrative.[34] Frank had earlier given a
sharply critical account of life in Würzburg in *Die Räuberbande*
(The Band of Robbers, 1914), a tale of youthful rebellion
against the authoritarianism embodied in the power of the education system and the Catholic Church. He now shows the adolescent rebels of that pre-war work grown into independent
tradesmen and craftsmen—true representatives of the 'Mittel-
stand'—whose livelihoods have been ruined by the devaluation
of the currency in the course of the war and its aftermath. Their
performance as a male-voice quartet (before an audience of

---

[34] Weissenberger (1975) sees the work as a lapse into idyllic representation,
whereas Schmeling (1989, 88) emphasizes its critical potential. Among the early
reviews of the novel, Richard Huelsenbeck acknowledged its depiction of what he
called "primitive" human emotions, but gave the somewhat misleading impression
that the evocation of small-town atmosphere ultimately dominated over the characterization of individuals (*WB* 23, 984–85), while Axel Eggebrecht hailed it as the
consummation of a ten-year struggle in Germany for forms of literary expression
adequate to the times (*LW* 3, 44, 5).

peasants) in the nearby village of Ochsenfurt, which gives the novel its title, is consciously presented as a mere episode in their lives, a semi-burlesque attempt to escape from hardship, which provides them with a momentary sense of purpose and rekindles something of their old camaraderie, but which is never really going to bring them fame and fortune, and cannot provide a substitute for real work. By the end of the narrative, the four have been restored to apparent well-being by a series of fortuitous events which include an advantageous marriage and the death of a well-off aunt. But the fragility of that well-being has been kept in view all along through the depiction of seemingly incidental circumstances. A pensioner commits suicide because his life has become meaningless; an infant dies, apparently from a combination of hardship and negligence; and one of the group is arrested on suspicion of having murdered the usurer whose actions had brought about his bancruptcy a few years earlier (although the usurer's death eventually turns out to have been accidental). Christian Schmeling (p. 90) is surely right to argue that the ostensibly happy ending to Frank's novel retains the sense of its own illusoriness. The gaiety and banter which characterize relations within the group of men are on the one hand a token of mutual loyalty based on shared experience, but at the same time they are shown to be a mask that is worn against the ever-present possibility of despair. And the sober evaluation of material advantage which surfaces intermittently in the depiction of interpersonal relations in the work shows how the distinction between good husbandry and mean-mindedness is largely a matter of perspective: the aunt over whose modest inheritance branches of a family quarrel has herself shown apparent indifference at the impending death of her first husband, calmly sewing the garments she needs for his funeral while he lies beside her paralysed by a stroke.

It is particularly through his depiction of the younger generation that Frank opens up perspectives on the relationship between this small-town world and developments further afield. The sons of the 'robbers' are shown to be growing up in the same mould and with the same (provincial) street-wisdom as their fathers. But as they grow up it becomes increasingly apparent that the only way out of the limitations of this background is through education and training. In the course of his characterization of Hanna Lux, the 16-year-old daughter of one of the group, Frank notes that there were at that time more would-be shorthand-typists in Würzburg than there were type-writers. And Thomas Kletterer, the 19-year-old son of another, has recognized that his best prospects lie in an economics degree and work in the real America (as opposed to the adventure-book America which had fascinated his father's generation). Into the convolutions of his plot, Frank works two strands of narrative which bring these two youngsters into contact with the currents of modernity which are running through Europe. One of these is the murder-mystery element, in the course of which Thomas confronts a Swiss anarchist whom he suspects of being the real murderer; here Frank implicitly repudiates the radicalism of his own earlier Expressionist phase, for which he is often better remembered, by presenting the 19-year-old Thomas as an expo-nent of 'Sachlichkeit' in a positive sense, namely as a clear-headed rational appraiser of objective circumstances, and the older militant activist as a 'Romantic'. The other strand involves the introduction to the town of a pair of exotic visitors, the young optician Dr Huf, whose profession brings him tem-porarily to the local clinic, and his actress sister. On the one hand the experience and sophistication of this couple bring out the backwardness and inarticulateness of the locals, but on the other hand they are pointedly presented as rootless figures who are clinging to metropolitan Europe in preference to the even more limited cattle-ranching society of South America, where they grew up. The presence of Dr Huf as a rival for Hanna's affections makes for a heightening of the erotic awakening Frank depicts through the figures of Hanna and Thomas, an experience in which both the need to exercise sexual restraint and the awareness of their inability to express their emotions verbally have a poignant part to play.[35] And the fact that the final page of the text shows us both the physical consummation of the teenagers' relationship and the melancholy departure of Huf and his sister lends weight to the sense that personal fulfil-ment is more likely to be found within the intimacy of small-town society than in a life of sophisticated itinerancy. But again,

[35] The delicacy with which Frank was able to evoke the physiological basis of desire in characters who could not verbalize their emotions for themselves, par-ticularly in *Karl und Anna* (1927), was much admired at the time.

this ending is double-edged. Thomas and Hanna have discovered the strength of their mutual attraction, but by yielding to it they also appear resigned to perpetuating the eternal round of provincial life in the annexe to the parental home which has been built with just such a marriage in mind.

The critique of a repressive Catholic culture which had strongly characterized Frank's pre-war novel, and which is touched on again in connection with his depiction of adolescent eroticism in *Das Ochsenfurter Männerquartett*, takes us directly to the heart of Marieluise Fleißer's treatment of provincial life in the 1920s. The two plays for which she became known at the time derive their dramatic strength from the power of social constraints in her home town of Ingolstadt. *Fegefeuer in Ingolstadt* (Purgatory in Ingolstadt), which was first staged in 1926, explores the destructive potential of sexual desire when it is associated with the experience of social exclusion. A young man who has been ostracized because of his physical unattractiveness tries to obtain love by means of psychological blackmail when he discovers that one of the local girls is pregnant and seeking an abortion. It has been plausibly argued that the language of the text shows the influence of Expressionist drama in general and Brecht's early plays in particular (McGowan, 35 f.). But what gives the dialogue its peculiar vigour and poignancy is the way that, in the effort to articulate the powerful emotions that govern their behaviour, the young protagonists resort to biblical idioms and the language of precisely the inherited moral system that constrains their self-awareness. The second of the two plays, *Pioniere in Ingolstadt* (Sappers in Ingolstadt), unmistakably bears the marks of Brecht's intervention, which triggered a major theatrical scandal when the play was staged in Berlin in 1929 (McGowan, 51–7). The structure of *Pioniere in Ingolstadt* is determined by the montage effect that Brecht was keen to pursue at the time: each scene is designed to bring an aspect of the social tension in the situation into stark relief. The situation in question is the relationship between the townsfolk and the soldiers stationed at the local garrison, and the tensions arise from the predatory sexual activities of the soldiers. Fleißer's characterization of the women in this instance concentrates more on bringing out the bruising effects of sexual suppression and social dependency. Her female protagonists exemplify the stark alternatives of a life of prostitution on the one hand and the vulnerability that comes with romantic delusion on the other.

A clash of wills between the sexes also provides the plot for the novel she went on to write, but the way she contextualizes that theme opens up particular issues about the nature of provincial society. The work exists in two versions, which do not differ radically, but which highlight the two sides of an ambivalent picture in their respective titles.[36] The original title of 1931, *Mehlreisende Frieda Geier*, refers to the female protagonist, who works as a travelling saleswoman dealing in flour not only to support herself, but also to ensure that her younger sister receives a good education, and who resists the advances of the young shopowner Gustl for the sake of economic independence. The collected works of 1972 contain a revised version, *Eine Zierde für den Verein* (A Credit to the Club), the title of which alludes to Gustl's prowess in the local sports club. It is Gustl's skills as a swimmer and a life-saver that have attracted Frieda to him. The narrative shows the relationship disintegrating under the impact of his insistence on being the dominant partner. What starts as a wryly observed courtship turns into a destructive trial of strength; what starts as possessive love turns to vengeful cruelty. The man who displays rational self-control in his area of expertise descends to acts of abject petulance and threats of calculated violence in the effort to bind Frieda to him. But what makes the novel more than simply another study in the psychology of aggression is the depiction of background circumstances which contribute to the stigmatization of Frieda as the guilty party rather than Gustl. He has two kinds of institutional momentum on his side. One is the tribal character of the club, in which he will remain a living legend provided that he maintains a degree of self-discipline. The other is the traditional conception of the family, represented by his own mother, who has laboured in pursuit of his success and will not hear a word said against him. In the face of these social pressures, it is the self-willed woman rather than the dom-

---

[36] The revised version smoothes out the narrative style in certain respects, and expands on some of the descriptions of historical circumstances, including a reference to the desecration of a Jewish cemetery (*GW* 2, 183 f.).

ineering man who is exposed to loss of standing, loss of business, and public menaces.

It is open to serious question whether Fleißer succeeds in developing the narrative potential of her themes satisfactorily in this novel. Early reviewers criticized the fragmentary character of the chapters, the melodramatic quality of the villainous figure (the only character in the work, incidentally, who is explicitly presented as an emanation of the city) whose dastardly dealings give Gustl the opportunity to recover his self-respect, and the resort to a stereotypical Bavarian brawl at the end.[37] What makes the work a revealing document of its time, nevertheless, is on the one hand the account it gives of female resistance to the dominant social traditions of provincial Germany, and on the other hand the way it puts the trend of 'sachlich' description to work in the narration of that account. When looking back at her first play, Marieluise Fleißer noted that it had arisen out of a collision between her small-town Catholic upbringing and the outlook of the big city (cf. McGowan, 23). That sense of collision is apparent in the very fabric of her novel. Her description of the town, which she situates halfway through the text, is terse, almost to the point of disdain. This former garrison town is small and self-contained, and because of the consequences of inflation and economic recession—exacerbated in this instance by the reduction of Germany's standing army under the Versailles Treaty—it is said to be poised between life and death. The desperation of the struggle for economic viability enters into the characterization of the relationship between Frieda and Gustl, as well as into what is shown of the relationship between them and their customers. But a certain brusqueness also characterizes the narrative tone from the outset. Whether she is describing the status-consciousness of the male or the tactical self-assurance of the female, Fleißer treats each moment of human behaviour with that same quizzical scrutiny that we have seen to be characteristic of the young writers coming to prominence in Berlin in the late 1920s. It is as if each 'take' on the psycho-dynamics of provincial life has

---

[37] See Günther Rühle (ed.), *Materialien zum Leben und Schreiben der Marieluise Fleißer* (Frankfurt: Suhrkamp, 1973), 146–51.

been prepared with the sceptical gaze of a city readership in mind.[38]

Lion Feuchtwanger, who appears to have been the most decisive literary influence upon Marieluise Fleißer alongside Brecht, gives an equally uncomplimentary picture of Bavarian society in his novel *Erfolg* (Success, 1930), but he does so from a rather different perspective. Writing with the suave assurance and the narrative flow of the practised historical novelist that he was, he contemplates the life of the province from a position of intellectual superiority. Feuchtwanger, who was himself a native of Munich, satirizes Bavaria as a backward rural society, where outsiders and nonconformers automatically attract prejudice, and where matters of great political consequence are ultimately determined by the popular currents of parochial self-regard. His satirical approach is epitomized by the way he describes the factors which keep the three Chairs of History at Munich University occupied by Catholics: one was endowed by the bishopric, the second is devoted to the history of the Bavarian state, and the third is occupied by a senile scholar who has dedicated his life to the intricacies of the "biological" history of the city of Munich, including the stuffed elephant which came into the possession of the Duke of Bavaria following the siege of Vienna in 1683, and who is left in the post simply because the politicians want to keep a Protestant out. Feuchtwanger's treatment of the National Socialist movement is similarly cavalier— although it should be borne in mind that his novel was conceived and largely written before the economic crisis of 1929–30 brought the Nazis serious electoral support. In effect, the movement is presented as the local variety of protest politics: it merely harnesses the predisposition of the populace to blame all manner of personal and economic setbacks on a conspiracy of freemasons, or Jesuits, or Jews, and is said to attract malcontents in Munich in the same way that the Communist Party does in Berlin. There are elements in the work which are clearly modelled on the real-life figures and events surrounding Hitler's attempted putsch of 1923. But as we noted in Chapter 5, Feuchtwanger's purpose in depicting contemporary events is to

---

[38] It is this quality in the text that makes *Mehlreisende Frieda Geier* less straightforward to read as a critique of contemporary society than Sabine Becker suggests in her analysis of it (Becker and Weiß, 212–34).

suggest an underlying momentum in historical development which ultimately carries the vanity of all such human endeavours before it. It is for this reason that scholarly interest in the work has moved away from interpreting it as a reflection of contemporary history, and towards seeing it as a Jewish intellectual's attempt to construct his sense of historical identity in relation to the manifest threats of the contemporary situation (Müller-Funk 1981; 1987, 61–74).

Where we do find a careful evaluation of the factors which assist, and limit, the appeal of National Socialism in rural areas is in Anna Seghers's novel *Der Kopflohn* (The Reward, 1933), which is set in 1932, but which was not published until the Nazis were in power and Seghers was already in exile. As in several of her later novels, she builds her plot around the situation of a fugitive: an unemployed worker from Leipzig, Johann Schulz, is on the run for the manslaughter of a policeman, and takes refuge on the farm of a relative in the region Seghers knew best, Rheinhessen. Since it is harvest time, Schulz's presence as a labourer is inconspicuous at first; the question is, how will the rest of the community respond as that excuse wears thin and they become aware that there is a price of 500 marks on Schulz's head? Particular characters have their own motives for not denouncing him. A rich farmer does not want to stir up trouble at a time when his children are getting ready to marry. A Jewish cattle-trader, who knows the experience of social marginalization although he has extensive business dealings in the area, keeps the secret out of a sense of fellow-feeling. Others simply decline to get involved, perhaps because they do not see it as any of their business, perhaps because they are habitually wary of doing anything that might be to someone else's advantage. It is only through the agency of a Nazi Party member that Schulz is eventually denounced.

Through the verbal exchanges between her characters as well as her exploration of their psychology, Seghers creates a strong sense of the atmosphere of rural life, in which a cautious pragmatism inhibits the actions of individuals, but also limits their horizons. She shows what it implies in practice that the traditional priority of the peasant is to protect the property and assets on which the family's livelihood depends, and to do so all the more jealously in times of hardship. But she also confronts

her peasants with a predicament in the form of aggressive elec-
tioneering by the Nazis, who have made their recruits in the
area, individuals who are fired by a sense of national humiliation in the wake of the First World War as well as seeing the
Nazi movement as a force which will help them keep the products of their labours. Part of the fascination of the work lies in
the way it presents individual responses to the Nazis' campaign
tactics, to the rallies, the tin-rattling, and the mystique of uniforms. The locals are shown to be cautious and uncertain, afraid
to give offence and slow to enter into any commitment—
although when election day comes, many of them vote Nazi
anyway.

Seghers, who had joined the Communist Party in 1928, was
evidently trying to provide an exposé of the factors at work in
rural areas which militated against the advancement of Marxist
politics. The election campaigning she describes in the novel is
effectively limited to a straight fight between Nazis and "reds",
with the "reds" coming off worse. But the overall effect of the
work is far from dogmatic. It depicts the German peasantry as
a social group with its own powerful humanitarian instincts, as
well as showing what was going to make it hard to win them
over to any kind of broader political solidarity.

Hans Fallada, in North Germany, took a gloomier view both
of the character of provincial life and of the prospects for
opening it up to literary portrayal. His pessimism is apparent
from an article he contributed to the opening number of *Die literarische Welt* in 1925, where he invited readers to consider
what sort of books people read in Outer Pomerania: "Was liest
man in Hinterpommern?" They might, he surmised, pass the
time of an evening reading kitsch romances (Hedwig Courths-
Mahler); and they might collect, alongside reference works on
animal husbandry, the memoirs of First World War generals or
such anti-Semitic fantasies as Arthur Dinter's *Die Sünde wider
das Blut* (The Sin against the Blood, 1917). Here was, he concluded, an unconquered territory as far as German art and literature were concerned—and one that was likely to remain so.[39]
It is in an imaginary Pomeranian town, Altholm, that Fallada's

---

[39] *LW* I, 1, 4 f. Fallada's concluding remark reads: "Künstler Deutschlands, hier
liegt eine große Provinz, die zu erobern euch vorbehalten ist! (Ihr werdet sie nicht
erobern.)"

first novel, *Bauern, Bonzen und Bomben* (Peasants, Bigwigs and Bombs, 1931), is set, and through the mouths of various characters the text betrays something of its author's frustrations with small-town life, as well as depicting some of the factors which contributed directly to the downfall of the Weimar Republic.

As a journalist on the regional newspaper for Schleswig-Holstein, Fallada had been a witness to the conflicts between the farming community and the local authorities which erupted into violent confrontation and a sensational trial in 1929. Günter Caspar, in his study of Fallada, provides extensive information on the self-defence organization (the *Landvolk*) which had spearheaded the farmers' actions, and on the circumstances which created fertile ground for Nazi agitation subsequently; but he also points out that the prominence given to the peasantry in the title *Bauern, Bonzen und Bomben* was a product of the aggressive marketing of the work under the political circumstances of 1931 rather than an accurate reflection of its content (Caspar, 17 f.). It was almost unwittingly that Fallada had opened up his text to issues of far-reaching political purport, and his decision to avoid a documentary approach in the novel, transferring the farming life of Schleswig-Holstein instead to a fantasy Pomerania, has the effect of blurring the sociological features of the rural life he depicts (cf. Caspar, 21 f.), even if it also enables him to emphasize the senses in which the provincial community of his novel is representative of Germany as a whole.[40] But what the critics generally admire in the work is the vivid evocation of the machinations of rural politics, based on the first-hand impressions Fallada had obtained from the court proceedings.

Altholm is a town of close-knit social connections where individuals live in a high degree of mutual dependency and a constant awareness that the misfortunes that have befallen them or their families are common knowledge in the community. In that atmosphere, the actions of both the local Bürgermeister (a Social

---

[40] In his short preface to the novel Fallada writes, "Die Gestalten des Romans sind keine Fotografien, sie sind Versuche, Menschengesichter unter Verzicht auf billige Ähnlichkeit sichtbar zu machen. Bei der Wiedergabe der Atmosphäre, des Parteihaders, des Kampfes aller gegen alle ist höchste Naturtreue erstrebt. Meine kleine Stadt steht für tausend andere und für jede große auch."

Democrat) and the newspaper editor who agitates against him take the form of petty intrigue among those local figures over whom they hold sway in one sense or another. The plot shows a progressive hardening of attitudes among the parties to the dispute: those in authority see their prestige being put to the test and decide to demonstrate their resolve, while the peasants grow suspicious and resort to violence, which calls forth a violent response from the police. But the focus of the narrative is on the behaviour of the individuals involved rather than the interests and motives which have brought the dispute about. An undertow of anti-Republican sentiment makes itself felt in many quarters and for a variety of reasons. The newspaper editor is a cynical conservative who holds the socialists responsible for the ills that have befallen the nation since 1918; minor officials are nostalgic for the insignia of the old Reich and the days of prosperity they associate with it; the peasants are generally resentful of what they see "the state" as having done to them. Against that background, the Bürgermeister is portrayed with a measure of sympathy for his situation. He has become adept at fighting local battles with local weapons, and has displayed both energy and skill in the promotion of local government projects. But he has lost sight of quite how dependent his activities are on the party bureaucracy (to which the term "Bonzen" in the title alludes), falls from favour, and is transferred to another rural outpost when he presses for a greater degree of autonomy. It is a self-renewing cycle of mistrust that Fallada depicts as characteristic of his model of provincial life.

Among the representations of the German provinces during the Weimar period, it is at the margins of the old Reich, rather than in its heartlands, that the potential for a supra-national, European perspective is explored, and the deleterious impact of modern nationalism most keenly felt. René Schickele's trilogy *Das Erbe am Rhein* (The Heritage on the Rhine, 1925–31) tells of a regional culture subjected first to Prussian regimentation after 1871, and then to the abrupt imposition of French standard expectations when Alsace was ceded to France after 1918. Schickele presents the population of Alsace as embodying a variant of German culture well suited to mediating between the nations, but as alienated by the policies of the two national governments concerned; and the third volume of the trilogy, *Der*

Wolf in der Hürde (The Wolf in the Fold), shows the erosion of old-style cultural particularism by the circumstances of the Weimar period, as the movement for local autonomy becomes a vehicle for political opportunism on the part of unscrupulous individuals. In his recent study of German novels of provincial life, the Polish scholar Miroslav Ossowski has also drawn attention to a Silesian author who provides a counterpart to Schickele's depiction of Alsace—and a counter-model, indeed, to Arnolt Bronnen's notorious *O.S.* of 1929 (the initials refer to the campaigning over whether Upper Silesia should remain part of Germany), which makes heroes of the nationalist agitators. August Scholti's novel *Ostwind* (East Wind, 1932) depicts a young man's complex path towards the acceptance of his German cultural identity in the circumstances of the time. The work is candid about the restrictions and economic disadvantages of provincial life, about the backwardness of the Polish peasants, and about the brutality of German measures to suppress Polish language and culture in the area. In its depiction of the Weimar period, it is critical both of Polish nationalist agitation and of the complacency of the German Republican government towards campaigning for the support of the Silesian populace (Ossowski, 202–12).

In one way or another, the novels of provincial life we have so far reviewed in this section show the fault-lines that were opening up in the German-speaking world in the course of the social and political developments of the early twentieth century. It is with ambivalence that Leonhard Frank explores the tension between new opportunities and old emotional securities in his Würzburg novel, whereas Marieluise Fleißer brings an unsentimental critical gaze to bear on the challenge to a traditional understanding of gender roles entailed in a new conception of economic independence for women. Seghers and Fallada describe the tension between peasant communities and modern political organization; Schickele and Scholti explore the impact of centralized national government on the delicate ethnic balance of cultural border areas. And we find the disdain of the metropolitan intellectual towards the provinces built into the narrative fabric of the works by Feuchtwanger (who deploys it with greater self-assurance) and Fallada (who deploys it more tentatively). But there was at least one other narrative tradition at work in Germany at the time which treated rural life neither as locked in to a confrontational relationship with urban culture, nor as a crudely idealized alternative to it; and it was undoubtedly one of the traditions Friedrich Sengle had in mind when he coined his phrase about the "broader urbanity" of German regional literature that belied its ostensibly parochial concerns.

Bavaria may have acquired a reputation as a provincial back-water following the installation of a reactionary political regime in 1919, but it nevertheless remained the home of a literature which combined regional subject-matter with a sense of universal humanity. Among the writers who represented this Bavarian tradition, Ludwig Thoma is often unfairly remembered for having thrown in his lot with the political reactionaries of the region shortly before his death in 1921—evidently out of a sense of repugnance for the centralizing tendencies of the Republic. But he was no idealizer of rural life, treating the Bavarian peasant rather as a butt of robust comedy in narrative works which are clearly aimed at a town-based or professionally educated readership. Closer to the actual experience of peasant life is Lena Christ, whose novel *Madam Bäurin* (Milady the Peasant's Wife), which appeared in the year of her death, 1920, focuses precisely on the tension between town and country and its eventual resolution. Her plot concerns a romance between a peasant's son and the daughter of a lawyer's family who come to stay for their summer holiday, which is sternly resisted by both mothers because they find it difficult to countenance making concessions to the other's way of life, and which gives the author ample opportunities to give voice to the attitudes and the implicit values of either side. In the Weimar period, the specific character of this Bavarian tradition was carried forward above all in the prolific writings of Oskar Maria Graf.

Graf's depiction of rural communities shows a clear affinity with the nineteenth-century village novel—Gotthelf and Tolstoy are among the few literary models he ever acknowledged—but he makes no concessions to the idealization of peasant life, and his jovial appreciation of human diversity shows in his treatment of the dynamics of social change in the wake of industrialization. His first novel, *Die Chronik von Flechting* (The

Chronicle of Flechting, 1925), is based on the history of his ancestors, who had migrated to the Starnberg area from the Tyrol in the early nineteenth century. The story he has to tell is one which involves adapting to a relatively closed peasant community by accepting a lowly position in its pre-established hierarchy: the first generation makes its way by fabricating hand-made farm implements and trying to sell bread to the peasants (who are used to baking their own). Prospects for the baking trade, as for other elements of the local economy, improve when the Bavarian royal family shows interest in a nearby residence, and the social character of the area changes. The extension of the railway brings the development of the tourist trade, but also factory-produced implements which supplant the old hand-made tools. The hazards of participating in the property boom associated with these changes is illustrated by the history of one member of the family who over-extends himself with ambitious building projects financed with borrowed money, and ends up committing suicide. The work ends with an evocation of the area in the 1920s, with speculators thriving on continuing economic opportunities related to the tenderly nurtured legend of Ludwig II.

An article by Kai-Uwe Ruf (1987) has set out very clearly the senses in which *Die Chronik von Flechting* resists the stereotyping tendencies of the sentimental 'Heimatroman'. There is no suggestion here that any one locality is preferable to another; on the contrary, characters are explicit about having occasion to be just as merry, or just as miserable, anywhere on God's earth. Graf's narrative implicitly accepts that the society of Flechting is susceptible to processes of social change which are determined by the political and economic developments of the wider world. Indeed, the character of wealth itself is shown to change in response to the industrialization of the mid-nineteenth century, as money takes over from fixed property in the hierarchy of values. As for the family Graf depicts, they experience disintegration and dispersal in the course of these changes, but the spirit in which the family's fate is presented is one in which the differences between individuals show in their particular ways of responding to the vicissitudes of life, and what they have in common is simply the attempt to make the most of the circumstances in which they find themselves.

Graf was given to distancing himself from the fashionable modernism of Weimar culture, self-consciously insisting on his image as an ingenuous provincial writer. But when he spoke, in the self-presentation he was asked to write for *Die literarische Welt* in 1931, of preferring the ambience of the provinces because it was easier there to see people for what they were and to recognize that they were the same the whole world over,[41] the remark is an accurate reflection of the catholicity of outlook which characterizes his work as a whole. The stories he published in the course of the Weimar period (and for which he made no more pretentious claim than that he had been the one who had written them down) bear witness to the attentive ear of a man who recognized the foibles of human nature equally at work among the inhabitants of both the city and the country. Among his *Kalender-Geschichten* (Stories from a Calendar, 1929) there is one which not only illustrates the continuity of human experience between city and country, but which might also stand as a brief parable of the relationship between provincial experience and the way it came to be presented in the literature of the time.

The title of that story, "Der Ruhm trügt" (Fame is Deceptive), points to the vanity of urban literary culture, which obeys a momentum quite distinct from the personal experiences that go to make literature in the first place. The opening statement explicitly repudiates the notion of a rural idyll: that, we are told, is something which you can only experience if you come from a well-off city background. The protagonist Jakob Torberger, by contrast, is the orphaned son of a bricklayer, who leads a tedious life as an assistant teacher in a village school, and only comes alive when he spends his holidays (and his savings) in the city. He otherwise spends his leisure hours writing. His acquaintances in the city assume that he is writing about the joys of nature, but in reality he is writing the novel of his own early life. The work becomes a best-seller, and an object of controversy, because it catches the mood of the times and the public interest in the harrowing effects of war, revolution, and inflation. When he can no longer enjoy the freedom of anonymity,

---

[41] "Daß ich aus der Provinz bin [. . .], das hat viel für sich. Schon deswegen nämlich, weil ich mit der Zeit herausgebracht habe, daß die Menschen überall gleich sind und weil man sie in der Provinz schneller und leichter sieht." (*LW* 7, 19, 8)

Torberger becomes filled with revulsion for the literary trade of the city, which continually feeds on notoriety, and longs for the obscurity of the coutryside. But far from retreating from the urban scene, he learns to live out the role that circumstances have fashioned for him, publishes a few more novels, and marries his aristocratic patroness. The man from the country, in other words, embraces a literary destiny which is inseparable from the urban culture that fostered it—and in due course his fame is superseded by that of a younger generation, by the next phase in the cultural life-cycle that humanity creates for itself in city and country alike.

8

Technology versus Humanity

Sieh, die Maschine:
wie sie sich wälzt und rächt
und uns entstellt und schwächt.

Hat sie aus uns auch Kraft,
sie, ohne Leidenschaft,
treibe und diene.

(See, the machine: | how it rolls and takes its revenge |
deforming us and weakening us. | Even if it takes its
strength from us, | let it impassively | drive and serve.)

Rilke, *Sonnets to Orpheus* (1922)

Rilke might seem an odd choice of author with whom to begin
a chapter on technology. In general he treats the impact of
modern technology with fastidiousness and manifest suspicion.
The architecture and the power sources of an industrial age
are evoked in the seventh of his *Duino Elegies* (1922) as
emblems of a depersonalized world bereft of religious sensibility, and when Rilke goes on, in the ninth elegy, to look for
human accomplishments worth praising, then it is from the
realm of old-fashioned craftsmanship that he draws his examples: the ropemaker, the potter. In the sonnet from which
the above quote is taken, it is with apparent reluctance that
Rilke acknowledges the claim of the machine to be commemorated as an undeniable feature of the contemporary world
(*SW* I, 742); and in the next sonnet in the sequence he evokes
the notion of a rapidly changing world only to counter it
with the consoling thought that all that is transient passes over
into the domain of mythical antiquity, where it may yet be celebrated and sanctified in song. Later in the same collection he
is still more explicit about the threat posed to cultural tradition
by the machine if it once takes hold of our minds, and he asserts

against that threat the celebration of everything in this world that remains nonetheless "enchanted" (*SW* I, 757). I would therefore not go so far as Karl Robert Mandelkow (1987, 403 f.), who places Rilke's acceptance of the presence of machinery in the modern world on a par with that positive affirmation of technological development which is commonly associated with the culture of 'Neue Sachlichkeit'. Rather, it is the ambivalence of Rilke's sentiments that leads me to think of them as representative of literary responses to technology in the 1920s. The din of the machine-room, his sonnet is saying, has taken its place in the world of human experience which poetic writing should strive to commemorate, but the heaving momentum of mechanical production must be subordinated to human needs if it is to be prevented from deforming and enfeebling human nature.

Technology became a major public issue in the 1920s, partly because of the process of technical modernization associated with Germany's national recovery after the First World War, and partly because that modernization process was confronted by an intellectual tradition which was deeply hostile to the effects of industrialization. It was this situation that gave rise to the seeming paradox that at the very time when a veritable cult of technology was developing in German cultural life, the engineering profession was complaining that public antipathy towards technology had never been greater (Hortleder, 85; Wege, 307 f.). Among the range of intellectual responses to the impact of technology in the mid-1920s we find the philosopher Friedrich Dessauer arguing, sensibly but naively, that technology was essentially just the application of human invention to the satisfaction of a humanly defined purpose in a manner which was implicit in the laws of nature, and thus consistent with the notion of a divine plan;[1] and we find the anthropologist Helmuth Plessner imagining that the impetus of technological progress will impose an inhibiting "apparatus" upon future generations unless it is taken in hand by a heroic social élite—an idea which was taken up with enthusiasm by right-wing thinkers

---

[1] Friedrich Dessauer, *Philosophie der Technik: Das Problem der Realisierung* (Bonn: Cohen, 1927); see also Klaus Tuchel, *Die Philosophie der Technik bei Friedrich Dessauer: Ihre Entwicklung, Motive und Grenzen* (Frankfurt: Josef Knecht, 1964), 27–43.

in the circumstances of political crisis around 1930.[2] Technology, in other words, was as much of a disputed territory between the adherents of old and new conceptions of authority as any other cultural theme of the period.

For an initial illustration of how technology came to figure so prominently in public awareness, we need look no further than the famous radio-room scene of *Hoppla, wir leben!*, the production with which the Piscatorbühne opened in 1927. On the one hand the scene is an opportunity for Piscator to deploy all the technical devices available to him in order to give the audience the illusion that they have been transported into a future world where exciting new technical possibilities have become a reality. It is a world in which telegraphists can receive not only sound, but visual images of events in distant places; a world in which not only has transatlantic air travel become commonplace, but the heartbeat of a sick passenger can be relayed to the ground with a request for medical advice; and the illusion of that world as a reality is enhanced by the inclusion of a supposedly live broadcast from Cairo of the hit-song from the very show the audience are watching—"Hoppla, wir leben!" (Toller, *GW* 3, 81–3). On the other hand the scene also provides Toller's protagonist Karl Thomas with the opportunity to ask about the uses to which humanity is putting its own inventiveness, and the response he gets from the telegraphist is far from encouraging. Beneficial inventions are being suppressed in the interests of big business, he is told, and the interest of governments in technological development appears limited to acquiring ever more refined methods of killing (there is talk of a new type of bomber which will devastate European cities in an instant). It is a scene, in other words, which is designed to highlight both the exhilaration and the anxieties associated with rapid technological advance.

In most cases, the authors discussed in this chapter had no specialized knowledge of the technological developments occur-

---

[2] Helmuth Plessner, "Die Utopie in der Maschine" (1924), in *Gesammelte Schriften*, vol. x (Frankfurt: Suhrkamp, 1985), 31–40. Hermann Graf von Keyserling similarly calls for a new breed of masters to rule over the mass culture to which technology is giving rise in *Die neuentstehende Welt* (Darmstadt: Reichl, 1926).

ring at the time. What they did bring to the subject was an ability to extrapolate from the experiences of their own lifetime and imagine the purposes to which technical capabilities might be put in the future. And in so far as they looked beyond the power of imagination in its turn, they were able to present ethical questions about those purposes. What interests me above all in this chapter are the terms in which the implications of technological development were presented, and what they show us about the relationship between the representation of technology and the inherited discourse of German intellectual culture.

The ambivalence we notice in the 1920s had precedents, of course, in the literary writing of earlier decades. It had accompanied the rise of the railways in the middle of the nineteenth century.[3] Wilhelm Raabe, in his novel *Pfisters Mühle* (Pfister's Mill, 1884), had written of the pollution, and the disruption of traditional lifestyles, brought about by the concentration of production in large factories; and Max Kretzer had depicted the decline of the traditional craftsman in *Meister Timpe* (Master Timpe, 1888). Neither author was condemning technological development as such, rather they were drawing attention to the social consequences of unrestrained industrialization. Responses became more starkly polarized after the turn of the century, however. On the one hand there were expressions of exhilaration at the new possibilities for personal fulfilment apparently offered by the motor car and the aeroplane, which paralleled the highly publicized enthusiasms of the Italian Futurists; on the other hand industry was demonized as a devouring Moloch in forms which have become familiar to us particularly through the poetry of Georg Heym (Daniels, 352–63). On the one hand the detailed experiences of industrial labour were celebrated in a new tradition of worker poetry; on the other hand the dominant intellectual culture remained disdainful towards industry as a subject for literary treatment, and expressions of hostility for the world of the factory and the machine became more

---

[3] The classic account of the impact of the railways on human perceptions in the German context is Wolfgang Schivelbusch, *Geschichte der Eisenbahnreise* (Munich: Hanser, 1977).

intense as Expressionist poetry entered its agitatory phase between 1916 and 1918.[4] The experiences of the First World War had brought not only a sustained demonstration of the destructive power of technological warfare, but also an enhanced awareness of how society as a whole was being organized in order to meet the demands of industrial processes. A particularly clear example of the literary response to these developments is the climactic eleventh scene of Toller's first play, *Die Wandlung* (Transfiguration, 1918), in which it is the awful prospect of humanity being reduced to a merely mechanical existence that motivates the young hero Friedrich in his call to the people to put spiritual reflection before material action (*GW* 2, 50).

It is a similar horror at the notion of humanity in thrall to mechanistic *thinking* that is dramatized in the most ambitious of the Expressionist attempts to deal with the issue of technology, Georg Kaiser's *Gas* trilogy (1916–19). At the heart of Kaiser's treatment of the theme there lie two lines of dramatic development: one concerns the tragedy of a society committed to inexorable technological progress, the other concerns the tragedy of the individual who seeks to oppose that commitment. The first of the three plays, *Die Koralle* (The Coral), sets itself somewhat apart from the other two by focusing on the psychology of class relations in industrial society. The billionaire figure who is placed at the centre of the dramatic action here is presented as someone driven to acquire wealth and power by his fear of falling back into the impoverished and squalid circumstances of his childhood background. When he finds his offspring taking the part of the exploited underclass against the heritage he would have wished to see them preserve, he opts for a course of action which leads first to the symbolic obliteration of his personal identity, and ultimately to the embracing of death

---

[4] The contrast is well captured in R. Samuel and R. Hinton Thomas, *Expressionism in German Life, Literature and the Theatre* (Cambridge: W. Heffer & Sons, 1939), 112 f. Explicit condemnation of the factory world is particularly to be found in the poetry of Karl Otten (*Menschheitsdämmerung*, 227 f., 241) and Albert Ehrenstein (*Gedichte und Prosa* (Neuwied: Luchterhand, 1961), 178). Intimations of the demise of the factory are also to be found in poems by Franz Werfel ("Geistige Freude"), Ludwig Rubiner ("Die Stimme"), and Johannes R. Becher ("An die Dichter"). On the Worker Poets, see Günter Heintz (ed.), *Deutsche Arbeiterdichtung 1910–1933* (Stuttgart: Reclam, 1974).

as the only means of eliminating the pain of living. (In this respect Kaiser may be said to be turning nineteenth-century pessimistic philosophy against the nineteenth-century faith in historical progress: the piece of coral which has been used throughout the play to distinguish the character of the billionaire from the look-alike whom he employs as a secretary is invoked on the final page as an emblem of the principle of individuation, the breaking-off of individuality from the organic "stock" of life, which brings us all into life with a "wound".[5]) It is around the legacy of the billionaire's son that the two *Gas* plays themselves are organized.

Gas as an energy source provided Kaiser with a potent central symbol for his dramatic themes in three ways. It could be plausibly presented to audiences of his day as the driving force behind industrial development which had come to supplant coal and water power; it was commonly known to entail the danger of catastrophic explosions; and with the battlefield experiments of the First World War a recent memory, the mental leap from gas as a fuel to poison gas as a weapon was not a large one for audiences to take. But these points in themselves provide only moments of anticipation and climax in the dramatic action. What actually drives that action is Kaiser's concern with the logical implications of a particular human caste of mind which appears to characterize the industrial age. *Gas I* in particular is so constructed as to reveal the operation of essentially the same mechanistic rationality in the industrial, economic, and political institutions of society, and to present humanity at large as standing in need of redemption from that caste of thought. The explosion which overtakes the gas production plant in Act I— despite the assiduously correct calculations on which production is based, and despite the disciplined observation of safety procedures—is not a consequence of technological advance in itself; it is a peril which lies in wait, like a predatory beast indeed, *beyond the bounds* of what human calculation can encompass (*Werke* II, 16 f.). The billionaire's son, who interprets this explosion as a warning sign that humanity should retreat from its dependence on ever more powerful technical solutions

---

[5] This is presumably what the critic Bernhard Diebold had in mind when he wrote of the ending of *Die Koralle*, "Man erhoffte Karl Marx, aber es wurde Schopenhauer" (Rühle 1967, 125).

and content itself with the modest life-goals of a low-density, low-tech community faces three kinds of opposition in addition to the professional commitment of his engineer to the path of technological refinement. There are the representatives of capitalism—the "men in black" in Act III—whose interests are circumscribed by the balance sheets of their particular firms and by the trends of economic growth which will sustain their profits, and who view the prospect of adapting to a less efficient energy source as ruinous. There is the representative of government in Act V, who glosses the catastrophic explosion as a "regrettable incident" which has to be treated as subsidiary to the potential effects of economic dislocation on the power of the state and the military. And finally there is the general populace, as represented by the workforce, who have suffered most directly as a result of the explosion and who are capable— in the highly stylized strike meeting of Act IV—of recognizing the transformation that comes over their personal relationships when the industrial routine is broken, but whose habits, expectations, and material interests lock them into the continuation of the industrial regime. What all these parties share is a devotion to immediate ends, regardless of the long-term consequences. Theirs is a mentality which the billionaire's son compares with that of someone who reaches the end of a blind alley, beats his head against the wall, and proclaims that he has reached his goal (*Werke* II, 22). In *Gas II*, Kaiser shows us a military leadership which enjoys a state monopoly of energy supplies consciously choosing to enter a "tunnel with no exit" (*Werke* II, 65) which will culminate in general annihilation.

As Harro Segeberg has recently argued, Kaiser is not saying that the necessary outcome of historical progress is annihilation, he is showing us in a particularly concentrated dramatic form what *would* happen if all social development *were* to be utterly subordinated to the goal of unleashing an ever-increasing technological potential (Segeberg 1989, 299). That is perhaps as fair a summary as it is possible to give of Kaiser's humane purpose. Two points should be made, however, about the dramatic technique with which he presents that purpose. For one thing, by constructing his plot around the figure of an individual who has purportedly glimpsed a higher truth but fails in his mission to persuade others of its validity, Kaiser casts a pessimistic pall over the prospect of humanity finding reasonable solutions to its social and economic problems. For another thing, he presents the plight from which humanity needs to be saved in terms of an antiquated image of industrial production. It is antiquated because management techniques had already begun to reflect the need for quality, as well as quantity, of effort in mass production processes (cf. Segeberg 1987a, 239 f.). That image—which is evoked by the billionaire's son in his efforts to persuade the workers' delegates of the need for radical change, by the workers' families at the strike meeting, and again by the *Großingenieur* in *Gas II* when he is explaining the loss of productive capacity—is the image of the worker as the "hand" that is constantly required to service the levers of the industrial machine. It is an unreliable image of actual production processes, and it conveniently ignores the tendency of technology to develop machines which depend less and less on human labour. But for a generation which had experienced the subordination of all productive labour to the war effort, it served as a potent metaphor of the subjugation of humanity to the demands of technological production.

That image, which remains a rhetorical figure of thought within Kaiser's text, was to give rise to the most commonly remembered visual representation of industrial labour from the 1920s, namely the power-house sequences of Fritz Lang's film *Metropolis* (1927). Several motifs in Lang's film bear a strong resemblance to Kaiser's trilogy.[6] The son of the industrial overlord descends to the world of labour that is hidden from the sight of the social elite. There he experiences a form of work which consists in utter subservience to the apparatus of the power generator: he works a shift on the regulating mechanism which prevents the electrical system from overcharging. That mechanism is presented as a monstrous dial with arms that have persistently to be moved into position by means of full body movements. In technological terms it is a grotesquely inefficient

---

[6] On the notoriously eclectic nature of the screenplay by Thea von Harbou, see Reinhold Keiner, *Thea von Harbou und der deutsche Film bis 1933* (Hildesheim: Georg Ohms, 1984), 93 f.

use of human labour; but in the language of the film it is an eloquent image of the enslavement of human effort to the demands
of technological production. The futuristic world that Lang
depicts is one that is serviced by armies of dispirited labourers,
and the apocalyptic culmination towards which it is tending is
expressed in the visionary sequence of the machine as a Moloch
devouring streams of human beings. Lang's film, in other words,
converted the intellectually perceived threat of technological
dominance into the ostensible reality of the visual image. But
by this time the visual presentation of the machine as a devouring menace already had a precedent on the German stage
in a production which purported to come much closer to the
historical reality of the industrial world. When Ernst Toller's
play *Die Maschinenstürmer* (The Machine Wreckers) was
first staged in Berlin in 1922, the set designers, John Heartfield
and Franz Dworsky, took full advantage of the potential that
industrial machinery has as an image of the dehumanization
of labour. As a contemporary reviewer described it, they constructed a colossal mechanical monster with iron shafts, pis-
tons, fly-wheels, driving belts and steam vents, which towered
over the human figures operating the looms to either side of it.
When the weavers intent on destroying the machine arrived on
stage, the first to attack it was seized by the mechanism and
crushed.[7]

The scene in question comes at the very end of the play, as
part of the violent climax to an action in which Toller drama-
tizes the conflict between impulsive rejection of technological
innovation and long-term political vision. By developing that
theme on the basis of motifs associated with the Luddite movement in early nineteenth-century England, Toller was allowing
himself a great deal of poetic licence: actual documentation of
the movement is sparse, but it appears that the breaking of
machines was historically a tactic of last resort, and a deliberate one, used by groups of workers against factory-owners who
reneged on agreed terms of employment or who were under-
cutting the market by producing shoddy goods (Segeberg 1987*a*,
214–17).[8] As a text, *Die Maschinenstürmer* is also overbur-

---

[7] Max Osborn in *Berliner Morgenpost*, 13 July 1922; quoted in Rühle 1967, 386.
[8] Criticism of the historical veracity of Toller's play has been based on the
reconstruction of the activities of machine breakers by E. P. Thompson in *The*

dened by rhetorical bravura, and stronger on momentary pathos than on consistent thematic development.[9] Like Kaiser's *Gas* plays it focuses on the martyrdom of one far-sighted individual at the hands of the misguided mass of humanity. Jimmy Cobbett (the choice of name is evidently a tribute to the nineteenth-century campaigner for parliamentary reform, William Cobbett) is the political visionary of Toller's play, who sees the need to accept the deleterious consequences of mechanical production in the short term so that a workers' movement can be built as a national organization strong enough to "conquer" the machine and put it to work to the labourer's advantage in the long term. And yet the set designers of 1922 were not going against the spirit of Toller's script by constructing their machine as an awe-inspiring colossus. The dialogue of Acts I and II anticipates the appearance of the machine as a devouring demon and a hundred-headed monster, and in more rational terms as an instrument of enslavement. One worker who has experienced machine labour describes it indeed in terms of the worker being "chained" to a mechanical operation which effectively dis-members him by requiring only repetitive movements of hand or foot (*GW* 2, 140). The intellectual thrust of the play may be towards the achievement of a form of society capable of bringing fulfilment to the 'whole man', as it was in the case of Kaiser's *Gas I*; but what dominates the emotional and visual experience of the play is the image of the machine—and an antiquated form of machine, at that—as the emblem of human-ity's subjugation to the mechanical pursuit of material purposes, to "Zweckdienst" for Mammon, as Jimmy Cobbett puts it (*GW* 2, 143).

Several motifs in Toller's drama appear to have been derived directly from the chapter of *Das Kapital* in which Karl Marx describes the impact of industrial machinery on manufacturing processes (cf. Segeberg 1987*a*, 219). Among those motifs is the image of the Luddites as opponents of mechanized production as

---

Making of the English Working Class (Harmondsworth: Victor Gollancz, 1963), and M. I. Thomis, *The Luddites: Machine Breaking in Regency England* (Newton Abbot: David and Charles Archon, 1970). For a summary of historical inaccuracies in Toller's play, see M. Pittock, *Ernst Toller* (Boston: Twayne's World Authors, 1979), 83.

[9] Among contemporary reviewers, it was Alfred Döblin who identified the play's weaknesses most clearly: see *Kleine Schriften* II, 103.

such, who have yet to learn the distinction between the mechanical means of production and the capitalist mode of production.[10] Toller's evocation of the reduction of human labour to the status of a machine part in the production process, and of the need to achieve a form of society in which the whole productive potential of human beings once more comes into play, is also a faithful reflection of portions of Marx's argument about the condition of labour under capitalism. Marx even provides the description of the industrial machine as a "mechanical monster" whose body fills whole factories and whose "demonic force" manifests itself in the feverish dancing of its myriad working parts.[11] But on this point there is a crucial distinction between Marx's metaphor and the use to which Toller puts it. Marx is evoking the revolutionizing impact of mechanized production on an inherited system of manufacture, whereas in Toller's play the demonic machine itself becomes the manifest symbol and thus the immediate representation of an exploitative system of production. Toller even gives a speech to the engineer in his final scene which evokes the century of environmental disruption and devastation that is to follow upon the introduction of industrial machinery, whereas for Marx the advent of mechanical production in itself carries a positive revolutionary potential in that it entails a constant revision of production processes and thus provides a source of dynamic forces which challenge the entrenched power of capital.[12] Marx sees the fragmentation of the production process into specific mechanical operations as a form of the division of labour which has been artificially preserved under capitalism, and mechanical production as contradicting that preservation because of the flexibility and adaptability it

---

[10] In this connection Marx comments, "Es bedarf Zeit und Erfahrung, bevor der Arbeiter die Maschinerie von ihrer kapitalistischen Anwendung unterscheiden und daher seine Angriffe vom materiellen Produktionsmittel selbst auf dessen gesellschaftliche Exploitationsform übertragen lernt." Marx/Engels, *Werke*, vol. xxiii (Berlin: Dietz Verlag, 1962), 452.

[11] Ibid. 402: "An die Stelle der einzelnen Maschine tritt hier ein mechanisches Ungeheuer, dessen Leib ganze Fabrikgebäude füllt und dessen dämonische Kraft, erst versteckt durch die fast feierlich gemeßne Bewegung seiner Riesenglieder, im fieberhaft tollen Wirbeltanz seiner zahllosen eigentlichen Arbeitsorgane ausbricht."

[12] Ibid. 511: "Die moderne Industrie betrachtet und behandelt die vorhandene Form eines Produktionsprozesses nie als definitiv. Ihre technische Basis ist daher revolutionär, während die aller früheren Produktionsweisen wesentlich konservativ war."

demands of the workforce.[13] Marx's argument about the inherent potential of technology as a vehicle of human emancipation invites the question about the economic purpose, and thus the economic system, which technological innovation is designed to serve, particularly in the light of mass production processes as they have been experienced in the twentieth century (cf. Wulf, 55 f., 157). But his optimism in that respect nevertheless had a decisive influence on the way the organized working class of Germany actually responded to technological innovation in the 1920s.

A particular drive for industrial efficiency made itself felt in the post-war years, as Germany emerged from its wartime isolation and recognized the need to catch up with technical developments that had been taking place elsewhere, especially in America, if it was to retain its place among the world's leading industrial nations (P. Berg, 97 f.). 'Scientific management' of labour had been pioneered in the United States by Frederick W. Taylor, whose approach was indeed to evaluate human effort in terms of mechanical laws, and to regard the worker as a functional unit from which the maximum effort was to be extracted for the minimum reward. 'Taylorism' as a postulated extreme form of the regulation of labour by management thus offered itself as a natural target for trade union opposition in the 1920s, and as the butt of inventive caricature—of which John Heartfield's cartoon "Die Rationalisierung marschiert" of 1927 (Fig. 8) is a striking example. It pictures a human figure assembled from mechanical parts on the one hand and emblems of the regulation of time and motion on the other, arranged in a posture suggestive of the fierce pace of rationalized production, while its choice of texts hints strongly at the collusion of Social Democracy in the subordination of human effort to the criteria of industrial efficiency. Taylor's methods were promoted in Germany by the main representative organization of the engineering profession, the Verein Deutscher Ingenieure, but they were slow to make an impact in practice. Only a few concerns in Berlin and Stuttgart had adopted elements of Taylor's approach before 1914, and even in the more favourable circumstances of the post-war years time-and-motion studies only

---

[13] Ibid.

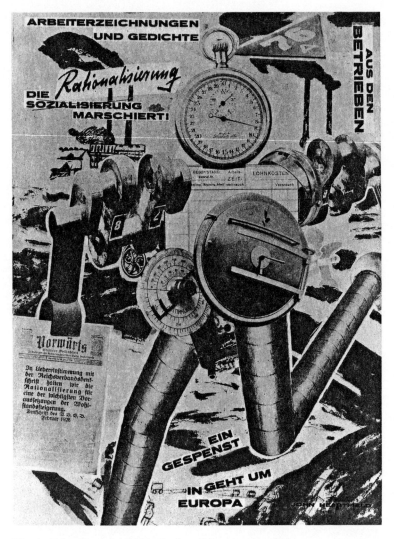

Fig. 8. John Heartfield, *Die Rationalisierung marschiert*, 1927

gradually made their impact on the shopfloor because of managerial misgivings about the cost of adaptation and bureaucratic supervision, about the possible loss of personal power and influence under a rationalized system, and about exciting resistance from the workforce to the more patently demoralizing aspects of Taylor's system (Wulf, 71–80). Rationalization as a principle nevertheless received strong support from workers' organizations connected to the SPD, who were eager to encourage developments likely to assist Germany's economic recovery; and Taylor's theories of scientific management also attracted intense interest among the leadership of the Soviet Union in the post-war years, when they too were anxious to boost industrial activity and expansion (Wulf, 81–93). In addition to practical considerations, the theoretical Marxism to which both Communists and Social Democrats subscribed led them to expect the development of technological potential to contribute directly to the emancipation of the working class, and to view productivity in itself as a criterion of progress (Wulf, 57f., 114f.). The constellation of ideological and economic circumstances around the time when Toller's play was being performed was leading the opponents as well as the proponents of specific technical innovations to profess that, whatever their priorities were, they were definitely "not machine wreckers" (Wulf, 26, 34, 103).

With the stabilization of the currency at the end of 1923 and the implementation of the Dawes Plan in 1924, general interest in technological modernization intensified. Even if the primary purpose of the Dawes Plan was to settle the political dispute over the reparation payments Germany was required to make under the Treaty of Versailles, it had the effect of injecting a large international loan and substantial American investments into the German economy. Apart from anything else, this was a spectacular demonstration of the superior productivity of the American economy, and it prompted a wave of visits to the USA by engineers, scientists, economists, and trade union delegations, all eager to identify those aspects of American technical, economic, and social organization which might serve as a positive model for the future.[14] At the centre of their interest was the achievement of Henry Ford, whose autobiography *My Life and Work* sold well when it appeared in German translation at the end of 1923. Ford's commercial success was based on the fact that he had identified a particular commodity—the motor

[14] For a recent account of these developments in English, see Mary Nolan, *Visions of Modernity* (New York: Oxford University Press, 1994).

car—for which rapid growth in demand could be foreseen, had concentrated production on a single design type, and had rationalized the production process in ways which enabled his factories to turn out large numbers of high-quality cars cheaply and at the same time to pay high wages. He presented his experiences in terms of an economic philosophy which emphasized the community of interests between employers and workers: wherever goods could be produced cheaply and efficiently they would find a ready market, which enabled both profits and wage levels to remain high, and high wages in turn boosted consumption. A further ingredient in the popular appeal of Ford's writings was the emphasis he placed on the positive contribution of the entrepreneur, as opposed to the financier, to the good of the community. (This emphasis was a consequence of Ford's personal experience, and helps to account for his anti-Semitism (P. Berg, 101); his tract *The International Jew* had been translated into German as early as 1919.) Although Ford's high-wages policy was used as an argument *against* introducing his methods into Germany (because of Germany's dependence on exports), 'Fordism' became a watchword that appealed to liberals and nationalists alike because it appeared to offer a recipe for resolving social conflicts through prosperity rather than political change, and because it pointed the way to a harmonious and economically strong nation. In broad terms, Ford's ethic of service to the community also appealed to the Catholic tradition, which had its own influential trade union organization at the time (P. Berg, 101–7). By contrast with 'Taylorism', which carried the implication of ruthless exploitation of the individual labourer, Ford's macroeconomic conception of mutually enhancing interests made his thinking attractive to many socialists, too, not least because it appeared consistent with the Marxist notion of 'technical reason' as a motor of historical and social progress (Wulf, 118–25, 152).[15] Against that background, it is less surprising than it might appear to find a writer such as Brecht around 1930 linking the names of Henry Ford and Lenin (together with Einstein) as representatives of the "progressive attitude" to which his conception of epic theatre corresponds,

[15] Amongst Communists there were differences of opinion over whether Ford's policies were positively contributing to the process of world revolution or serving to hold it up: P. Berg, 113 f.

or speaking of Ford's style of assembly plant as a "bolshevistic" operation (*BFA* 21, 274, 383).

I shall turn to the question of how literary authors negotiated these changes in the climate of opinion shortly. But before I do that it is worth noting that alongside the intellectual tradition of antipathy to technology there was also a vigorous popular tradition of futuristic science fiction throughout the early twentieth century, which has only recently begun to attract the critical attention it possibly deserves. This was a genre which thrived on the excited anticipation of technological development and, because it was based on fantasies about how the world of the future might look, also provided a ready outlet for political wish-fulfilment following the humiliation of Versailles.

An early example of this genre is Bernhard Kellermann's novel *Der Tunnel* (1913), which imagines a gigantic project to link the continents of North America and Europe by means of a tunnel under the Atlantic Ocean. Such a notion evidently seemed less far-fetched at the time than it probably does now: in the light of the Tay Bridge disaster of 1879 and the sinking of the *Titanic* in 1912, plans to link land masses in various parts of the world by under-sea tunnels were being seriously discussed before the First World War as safe and viable alternatives to surface travel. Kellermann's novel was received with intellectual disdain in 1913 (the reviewer of *Die Aktion* dismissed it as a "literary bluff"), but it enjoyed steady commercial success throughout the period between the wars,[16] and it stands out from the common run of pre-1918 novels about industrialists— which tended to focus on their patriarchal role in Germany's hierarchical society, and which also had a loyal readership in the 1920s[17]—in that it constructs a heroic model of the technical innovator as a benefactor of mankind (Segeberg 1987*a*, 173–207). Mac Allan, the American protagonist, has made his fortune by inventing a cheap substitute for diamonds as the standard material for drill heads; he has mastered the

[16] Donald Ray Richards, *The German Bestseller in the 20th Century* (Berne: Herbert Lang, 1968), 164, estimates sales of 358,000 by 1940.
[17] Both Hanns von Zobeltitz's *Arbeit* (1905), which gives a nationalistic account of the rise of an ordinary worker to become the owner of a weapons factory, and Rudolf Herzog's story of an entrepreneurial dynasty, *Die Stoltenkamps und ihre Frauen* (1917), continued to sell well after 1918: see Schneider et al., 162–6.

optimization of the use of time as well as materials; and he commands a team of managers and technicians who share his single-minded dedication to the realization of his project, regardless of the human cost in the short term. As a figure in whom technical and economic calculation are seen to come together, Allan can be seen as an embodiment of Fordist principles *avant la lettre*, and like Henry Ford he presents a positive image of the industrial overlord as servant of the community, while finance capital is negatively portrayed through the profit-seeking and decadent figure of Samuel Woolf, whose attitudes are motivated by resentments associated with his humble East European Jewish background (Segeberg 1987a, 191-7).

Fantasy fictions of a technologized future world came more fully into vogue in the wake of the First World War, and the way they characterized human figures and situations often reflected the post-war political situation of Germany. Reinhold Eichacker, in *Der Kampf ums Gold* (The Battle for Gold, 1922), imagined the invention of a machine for fabricating gold, which would solve Germany's reparation problems overnight. Other authors of the mid-1920s imagined the rediscovery of Atlantis by bathyscope and its colonization for Germany, or the construction of a German mechanized city in the Australian desert which was to be powered by nuclear energy and would stand as a spiritual, peaceful rival to Canberra—supposedly an emblem of violent imperial might. As Peter S. Fisher observes in his recent study of such technological fantasies (p. 110), a common impulse among them is to expunge the notion of 'war guilt' while also exacting a kind of mental revenge on the victorious enemy. Even where they were not overtly anti-Semitic these novels tended to work with racial stereotypes. The most successful exponent of the new formula fiction was Hans Dominik, an electrical engineer who had turned to journalism and the popularization of science. In his *Die Macht der drei* (The Power of the Three, 1922), an American dictator is seeking to gain control of a German invention which is capable of concentrating huge amounts of energy and thus functioning as a ray gun; he is successfully resisted by the German and his Aryan allies, an Indian and a Swede, who together combine the learning of Buddhism and Nordic mysticism which equips them with telepathic powers that have become lost to Western rationalists.[18] In later novels, *Der Brand der Cheopspyramide* (The Burning of the Pyramid of Cheops, 1926) and *Das Erbe der Uraniden* (The Legacy of the Uranids, 1928), nuclear energy becomes the focus of a struggle between Germany and North African or Anglo-American villains, while in *König Laurins Mantel* (The Cloak of King Laurin, 1928), a German inventor and his English companion use a flying submarine powered by a new energy source to help Mexico defeat the United States. In works of this kind the engineer-as-messiah has become a potent figure of national salvation (Fisher, 104–22).

Thea von Harbou was working a similar vein of popular fantasy with the novels which provided screenplays for Fritz Lang, even if she initially retained the negative image of technological potential that was carried over from Expressionism. Rotwang, the inventor figure in *Metropolis* (1927), is again characterized as one who commands arcane and mystical powers, an heir to medieval alchemy crouched at the heart of a mechanized world, master of the bewildering catacombs beneath the city, and capable of controlling the destiny of society by creating a mechanical witch to supplant the madonna figure of Maria as the focal point for the emotional lives of the working class. These arcane powers are placed in the service of the autocrat Fredersen, a representation of total commitment to the dominance of technological potential over frail human material, but shown as softening, in the face of disaster, into an acceptance of "the heart" as mediator between "the head" and "the hand". The resolution towards which Harbou's plot moves is one which endorses an authoritarian order precisely by presenting itself as pursuing interests that are "above politics", as she puts it herself in the prefatory statement to her novel.[19] The plot of *Frau im Mond* (Woman in the Moon, 1929) comes closer still to the stock formulae of the nationalistic technological

[18] On the occult dimension of the nationalistic technology novel, see also William B. Fischer, *The Empire Strikes Out* (Bowling Green: Bowling Green State University Popular Press, 1984).

[19] The senses in which the restoration of authority in Metropolis is achieved through the projection of a mystified (female) sexuality onto a mystified technology are explored by Andreas Huyssen in his article "The Vamp and the Machine: Technology and Sexuality in Fritz Lang's *Metropolis*", *New German Critique* (Fall/Winter 1981–82), 221–37. For the close affinity between the imagery of social relations in *Metropolis* and the ideology of National Socialism, see Siegfried Kracauer, *From Caligari to Hitler* (London: Dennis Dobson, 1947), 164 f.

novel: it hinges on the defence of a romantically idealistic German moon project against the subversive efforts and the mean material interests of a foreign financial syndicate (Fisher, 137–40).

There is one particularly ambitious literary work of the early 1920s which took the inherent impulses of the futuristic technology novel and developed them far beyond the parameters of the standard formula fiction. Alfred Döblin's *Berge Meere und Giganten* (Mountains Oceans and Giants, 1924) has been seen as an attempt to outdo the technomania of the Italian Futurists, and the mechanical fantasies of Marinetti's *Mafarka* novel in particular (A. Arnold, 99), but Döblin's text also exceeds Marinetti's in its exploration of the heights and the depths to which human inventiveness can aspire. It extends the timeframe for the contemplation of future technological development to a period of several centuries; it pushes speculation about the destructive potential of technology to greater extremes than the works of Harbou or the Expressionists; and it invites readers to reflect on more fundamental aspects of human nature in its exploitation of the natural world than any other work of the period.

Berge Meere und Giganten begins with an evocation of the First World War as a distant memory. The generations who lived through that war, and who subsequently went about their daily business as if nothing had happened, have long since passed away. The nations of the western world have bequeathed to their descendants the enormous power of modern machinery and the calculated harnessing of natural energies, and that power has been exploited in the colonial subjugation of Asian and African peoples. After a period in which mechanization brings enhanced wealth, the decreased need for labour leads to increased social disparities, the concentration of power in the hands of a privileged few, and a relentless economic dynamism driven by the need to keep the restless masses in check. Political organization becomes concentrated in the form of huge city-states, each with its own, technocratically dominated senate. The conflict between the rulers and the excluded masses—which gathers momentum over a period of centuries, and acquires an increasingly ruthless character as humanity becomes gradually conditioned to altered social circumstances—is resolved in the twenty-sixth century in favour of the senates by means of the secret development of synthetic foodstuffs, which make agriculture redundant and bring about a total concentration of populations in the cities. When that process in its turn makes the masses moody and disconsolate, an alliance of European leaders resorts to fomenting war as a means of maintaining political control, and a full-scale confrontation between western and eastern hemispheres—the "Uralic War"—leaves the plains of Russia devastated and the participating states in a condition of exhausted trepidation.

Thus far, it is easy to see how Döblin has extrapolated from the experiences of the recent past. The devastation of landscapes by fighting from entrenched positions with modern weaponry, the development of substitute foodstuffs under the conditions of blockade, Germany's experience of autocratic rule under the military Supreme Command, the growth of urban populations in the period of industrialization before 1914, and the intimation of cynical motives on the part of the ruling class in precipitating war in 1914[20]—all these find echoes in Döblin's account of the centuries to come. The very conduct of the Uralic War combines elements of science fiction with images drawn from recent experience: it is fought with horses and vast numbers of troops, as well as involving walls of flame, aircraft, ray-guns, and artificial gales. Another feature of the early twentieth-century world, the intellectual and emotional revolt against technology, is also reflected in Döblin's narrative in the way central state power is repeatedly challenged, whether by individuals or by mass movemements. In the period before the Uralic War, such challenges provide a pretext for the tightening of technocratic control; in the aftermath of the war it is precisely in the city-state of Berlin that the ruling caste itself makes a determined effort to roll back the tide of technology. Under the leadership of Marduk—a name probably suggested by the ancient Babylonian deity who was associated with fertility and vegetation—a sustained campaign is conducted to destroy

---

[20] Among the satirical articles that Döblin published under the pseudonym Linke Poot in 1919–20, there is a passage which ruminates on various dishonourable motives for going to war, and concludes with the remark that wars in general are not brought about by peoples, but by their "bell-wethers and their retinues" (*Maskenball*, 79).

factories and drive the population out of the cities and back onto the land. But what then follows in Central Europe is a period which resembles the Thirty Years War (which had been the subject of Döblin's previous novel): warring groups and itinerant hordes vie for dominance, and exact vengeance on each other with sadistic brutality. Part of Döblin's purpose in this work, plainly, is to demonstrate the auto-destructive potential of the lust for power, and of sexuality, on a mass scale as well as in the individual; and he develops that theme through his depiction of various other political leaders, both male and female, as well as through Marduk (cf. Müller-Salget, 216–18; Denlinger, 38–44, 55–60). But what is of particular interest in our present context is the capacity for combinative fantasy he brings to bear on the issue of technological development in the ensuing phases of his narrative.

London—which has retained its reputation for shrewd political management in the face of the most varying historical circumstances, and has demonstrated it most notably in the covert development and controlled introduction of the synthetic food—becomes the main power-base for the next phase of technological megalomania, which begins as a project to focus the energies of, and thus regain control over the volatile masses of the western world, but which ends as a cataclysmic confrontation between the will of western leaders and the forces of nature itself. This project, too, bears echoes of earlier historical ventures, namely the efforts of European states to transport elements of their 'surplus population' to distant and thinly populated lands. It is a project in which European expertise is coordinated with a view to thawing out and colonizing Greenland. The heat supply is achieved by cracking open the volcanoes of Iceland, and the energy thus obtained is transferred by means of nets made of tourmaline, a silicon compound known for its pyro-electric properties. But as Döblin describes it, what results from this melting of Greenland's ice-cap is an immediate eruption of ecological profusion which unleashes, not just primeval creatures, but hybrid monsters—malformations, as they are explicitly called in the text (p. 403)—which migrate to northern Europe and threaten all known life-forms. The merest contact with these monsters destroys animal organisms by causing them to be absorbed into the hypertrophied growth of the particular limb or organ touched. Europe's leaders respond by constructing biological fortifications, towers in which animal, vegetable, and mineral components have been amalgamated with human beings. The most power-hungry amongst them then apply the secret technique to themselves, transforming their bodies into protean monsters (the "giants" of the title), laying waste the human societies out of which they have emerged, and pursuing their power-struggles amongst themselves in their new guise.

By contrast with Marinetti, whose Mafarka seeks to transcend the human by dispensing with sexual reproduction and begetting a son by purely mechanical means, Döblin imagines a future technology which is centred on biological knowledge, and on the manipulation of the life-force. The preparation of synthetic food involves the use of live human beings—or at least, their body parts. Marduk, who spearheads the "post-Uralic" anti-technological movement, uses his advanced knowledge about plant-life in order to destroy his rivals, imprisoning them overnight among the trunks of fast-growing trees. And the transformation of human beings into "giants" is still ostensibly based on man's application of his own understanding about the natural world, even if it is more and more clearly driven by his desire to triumph over nature (cf. Kort, 54; Müller-Salget, 209 f.). But the manner in which Döblin deploys his imagery of the natural world is also syncretic: it aims at dissolving the boundaries between scientific concepts. The 'family' relationships between chemical elements are presented in organic, rather than inorganic terms (p. 331); the eruption of organic forms from Greenland is intimately connected with the chemical composition of the earth (p. 396 f.); and the energy that is derived from volcanoes and stored electrostatically in the tourmaline nets is referred to as the "soul" of life itself (pp. 413 f.). In the explanatory note he published at the same time as *Berge Meere und Giganten*, Döblin described the work as a representation of "telluric adventure" and a hymn to the "maternal powers" (*Leben*, 52–4). As the visionary character of his narrative grows more and more apocalyptic, it does indeed seem that he is combining his knowledge of modern biology, chemistry, and geophysics with a mythic awareness of the world derived from his classical education. While it is difficult (and possibly futile) to seek precise connections between particular figures or motifs in this text and ancient deities (cf. Denlinger, 81–93), the way Döblin deploys his references to elements of the natural world certainly carries echoes of the cult of Cybele (and her tamer Roman counterpart, Tellus), which involved the worship of such pre-organic features of 'mother earth' as mountains, rocks, water-sources, and fire.[21]

Two things stand out about the way Döblin resolves the conflict between man and nature at the end of this work. One is his resort to the imagery of a bountiful nature, which is exemplified in the soft and verdant landscape of France, and in the idealized femininity of Venaska, an exotic and unfadingly erotic figure who neutralizes the power and the hatred of the giants. In these motifs, Döblin brings his narrative back to the familiar habits of mind—or prejudices, as some would doubtless argue—of contemporary readers. The other is a narrative strand which by its very nature resists the impression that humanity is simply returning to an idyllic harmony with nature once the giants have become absorbed into the landscape. This strand focuses on the figure of Kylin, the Scandinavian engineer who masterminded the splitting of the Icelandic volcanoes, and who has survived the terrors of the Greenland expedition with a much reduced band of followers. When Kylin commits these survivors to a bond of fellowship in the sign of the sundered mountain and the flame, then what is symbolized in that act is the determination to preserve the knowledge of cataclysmic potential, of inflicted devastation, and of personal suffering and remorse, which the group carries with it as it disperses amongst a revived humanity in a regenerating natural world (cf. Kort, 54–8; Müller-Salget, 219 f.).

It would be foolish to attempt to summarize in a few words the wealth of suggested meaning in Döblin's text. Like no other work of the Weimar period, it sustains a powerful sense of the ambivalent relationship between modern man and his natural

---

[21] Erich Neumann, in his book *Die große Mutter* (Olten: Walter Verlag, 1974), 246, gives all these examples of cult worship associated with Cybele, citing references in Bachofen—a likely source for Döblin—as well as other texts. For historical and archaeological details of the cult (upon which the Romans imposed restrictions when they imported it at the time of the Hannibalic war), see Maarten J. Vermaseren, *Cybele and Attis: The Myth and the Cult* (London: Thames & Hudson, 1977).

environment, between the hubristic application of technical know-how to nature and the knowledge of the ultimate oneness of the natural realm of which mankind is a part. But the key to the narrative technique with which Döblin encourages his readers to reflect on the implications of technological ambition surely lies in that syncretic fusion of perceptual categories in the imagery of the text. His human protagonists become aware of themselves as the custodians of both the spark of life and the flame of destruction. It is with this duality in mind that Döblin invites his readers to contemplate the potential of human technology to shape a future world in much the same way that the ancients conceived their world as the product of titanic struggle.

In 1932, Döblin published a revised version of *Berge Meere und Giganten* under the title *Giganten*. At that time he evidently felt compelled to make it plain where he stood in the intellectual debates about the future of European culture, and decided, as he put it in his afterword, to "side with the giants". Many of the more extravagant passages are stripped out of the 1932 version of the text, and the mission of Kylin's group at the end becomes one of restoring the culture of the city and the machine as an instrument of humanity at large, as opposed to a property of the technocratic élite, and to preserve it in balance with the demands of nature by subjecting it to the sense of a higher law. Döblin, in other words, was adjusting the terms of his narrative towards a vindication of the human capacity for technological invention, albeit in pallid terms by comparison with the 1924 text. What is intriguing about the manner in which German literary discourse generally becomes adapted to the affirmation of technology in the period between 1924 and 1932 is the way the imagery of mechanization becomes accommodated within other, pre-existing strands of cultural thought.

A feuilleton article of 1924 by Joseph Roth gives a clear example of how this transition initially came about. Just as an earlier generation—Rilke and the Expressionist poets—had used vitalistic and sacral imagery to evoke the values they felt to be threatened by the mechanization of the modern world, Roth now applied such imagery in a profession of enthusiasm for a mechanized environment. He was writing about the area of the railheads which served the South of Berlin, commonly referred to by the name of the nearby underground station, "Gleisdreieck".[22] Walter Mehring had evoked the Gleisdreieck in the opening number of his *Ketzerbrevier* (1921) as a symbol of the new pace of city life (*Chronik*, 117f.). In Roth's article this industrial landscape becomes anthropomorphized: it is the "heart" of a world which sends vital energies coursing down "iron arteries". Even the factory chimneys round about acquire a libidinous potency (Roth describes the smoke emerging from them as "zeugungsträchtig"). The sacral vocabulary with which the Expressionists had demonized industrial culture—as Baal, as Moloch—comes into play as Roth evokes a sense of awe for the scale and the power of this mechanized landscape: it is a "temple of technology" and a "playground of the machine" characterized by "cruel" operational rhythms and "shrieking sirens". Roth even invokes a "godhead of the machine", to which one has to submit in order to experience the pride and enhancement it can confer. "My Gleisdreieck," he writes, is dominated by "the will of a logical brain which, in order to be assured of success, eschewed the unreliability of the human form, and entered a body of unequivocal reliability, the body of a machine." (*Werke* 2, 218–21) What we are seeing here, in other words, is an attempt to employ a familiar vocabulary in voicing the acceptance of something new and unfamiliar which appears to traditional forms of literary understanding as a higher destiny, as "ananke" (cf. Wege, 320f.).

Expressionist habits of mind died hard. The authors who aligned themselves with the radical left in 1918–19 continued to evoke the processes of social transformation in abstract and apocalyptic terms in their agitatory writing of the early 1920s, not least when they were addressing the issue of technology. The case of Toller has already been discussed; Franz Jung, who takes up Toller's theme of the need to "conquer" the machine in his prose work *Die Eroberung der Maschinen* (1923), offers little more than a distant prospect of the atmosphere of political struggle in an industrial context; and Johannes R. Becher continues to write poetry which is strong on fulmination against

---

[22] For an explanation of the development of this complex railway junction, and of its emblematic value in the landscape of Berlin, see Bienert, 21f.

the ruling classes and the instruments of oppression, but has
nothing to say about the processes of mechanized production,
even where he is evoking the startling effects of electrical energy
and the collective strength of labour in the machine age.[23]
Against that background, Hannes Küpper emerges as something of a pioneer in the literary expression of enthusiasm for
technology—long before Brecht asked for his "Iron Man" poem
to be printed in *Die Literarische Welt*—although his chosen
mode of representation reveals again how deeply rooted in vitalistic categories the intellectual culture of the early 1920s was.

By 1923 Küpper was already involved in a project which
shows Expressionist pathos being adapted to the celebration of
technology as a dynamic historical force. Together with Maxim
Vallentin (who was to become a leading exponent of agitprop
theatre, but who did not join the Communist Party until 1926),
Küpper put together a sequence of texts entitled *Die Sache ist
die* (The Thing is This, 1923), which range in character from
hymnic incantation to pantomime scenario, but which consistently despiritualize such Expressionist motifs as sacrifice, regeneration, and moral transformation. A recurrent motto in the text
is "In the beginning was breath! Then movement! and so on!"
The good and the beautiful are defined in terms of "brains with
logical, dynamic, perfectly functioning thoughts" and "bodies
with disciplined, obedient limbs". The factory is proclaimed as
the church of today, and the "man of the machine" as the new
Messiah. In the final section, which is presented as a scenario
for dumb show or for a choreographed film, "Dynamo" takes
"Material" by the hand, conducts it across the iron bridge that
leads to the future, and compels it to "dance to its rhythm".
Elements of an assertive Nietzschean vitalism are being put to
work here, in other words, in the pantomimic evocation of the
impact of mechanization.

The problem of adapting an inherited intellectual culture to
an as yet undefined new world is equally apparent in Alfred
Döblin's essay "Der Geist des naturalistischen Zeitalters" (The

[23] Becher's collection *Maschinenrhythmen* contains items which date from 1922
to 1924, although it was not published until 1926; these evoke electrical power in
association with the name of Lenin (an allusion to the USSR's drive for industrialization), but allude to factory production only in the context of images of oppression and of the power of labour to *halt* production: GW 2, 281–7, 318–30.

Spirit of the Naturalist Age), which again dates from 1924. Döblin argues that the theological ideas and humanist categories which had characterized an earlier age are being supplanted by an emphasis on the bodily senses and the musculature in the modern age of scientific understanding; but when his argument extends into the realm of social and political organization he himself falls back on theological vocabulary, describing trade and industry as the *"ecclesia militans"* of technological power, and Soviet Russia as its Messiah (*Ästhetik*, 169–74, 181–3). In line with the thinking we have seen to be implicit in his novel *Berge Meere und Giganten*, Döblin's essay interprets the force for change in the contemporary world, embodied in techno-logical development, as a "will to power" which exceeds the designs of particular industries or political systems.

In the period after 1924, technology became a prominent theme in the rhetorical battle between old and new world-views. The notion of America as a model for the future called forth expressions of abhorrence from conservatives. Stefan Zweig, writing in a Berlin newspaper in 1925, complained that the age of mechanical production was making the world monotonous. When he visited Europe's great cities he was finding distinctive local traditions being eroded and life being levelled down to a "uniform cultural schema". Everywhere people were listening to the same radio broadcasts, watching the same films, dancing the same stereotyped dance. The perception outlined before the First World War by Georg Simmel that modern society was also giving individuals an unprecedented level of choice in how to organize their lives is evidently lost on Zweig.[24] He sees only the tendency of mass markets to pursue patterns of standardization; he argues that inner personality and individuality are being eroded by the influence of a "mass soul"; and he blames America (together with Soviet Russia) for a process of cultural subjugation which he attributes to Europe's economic decline (Kaes et al., 397–400). The publisher Samuel Fischer and the essayist Max Rychner bemoan the shallowness of contemporary cultural trends, and see spiritual interests disappearing in a society that is becoming anonymous and "inorganic" (Kaes,

[24] Georg Simmel, "Die Großstädte und das Geistesleben", in *Das Individuum und die Freiheit* (Frankfurt: Fischer, 1993), 198 ff.

273, 277). Friedrich Sieburg, who was then becoming influential as a foreign correspondent of the *Frankfurter Zeitung*, complains in 1926 that a facile idealization of engineering is sweeping over Germany as America comes to take the place formerly occupied in German intellectual culture by Hölderlin's idealization of ancient Greece (*LW* 2, 30, 8; Kaes et al., 402–4). Adolf Halfeld's book *Amerika und der Amerikanismus* (1927), which presents European culture and communal identity as threatened by a crass materialism and the mechanization of life in all its aspects, found ready echoes in *völkisch* circles (Kaes, 278–80; P. Berg, 136–44). Laments about the subordination of intellectual values to the mechanized and the technicized became commonplace among the academic élite (Ringer, 247–50). Anxieties about the dissolution of individuality in a functionally orientated society are at the heart of the thoughts that Karl Jaspers, perhaps the most respected academic philosopher of the time, devotes to the subject of technology in his work *Die geistige Situation der Zeit* (translated as *Man and the Modern Age*) of 1931.[25]

This list could easily be extended into the welter of texts which appeared around 1930, at the time of deepening political crisis, and which sought to diagnose the condition of an old culture in decay. In addition to publications by Oswald Spengler and Ernst Jünger, to which I shall give closer consideration later in this section, the best known—because the most intellectually rigorous as well as the most august—are Ortega y Gasset's *Revolt of the Masses*, which attracted much attention when it was translated into German in 1930, and Ernst Robert Curtius's *Deutscher Geist in Gefahr* (German Spirit in Danger) of 1932. Even Rudolf Kayser, who had struck a sane and balanced note in his analysis of the processes of cultural modernization in 1925 (Kaes et al., 395–7), was writing in June 1932 that humanity was "dying of its own works" because it was elevating assembly-line production to the status of a new religion and entrusting moral and metaphysical values to technology (*NR* 43, 860). It is in documents of this kind, rather than necessarily in literary texts, that we find the most direct evidence

---

[25] Karl Jaspers, *Die geistige Situation der Zeit* (Berlin: de Gruyter, 1931), 28–31.

of that "dethroning of ideocracy" which the novelist Robert Musil describes in 1930 as a defining experience of the age (*GW* I, 408).

When Brecht decided to publicize Hannes Küpper's "Iron Man" poem as a positive model for lyric poetry in the *Literarische Welt* competition of 1926–7 (cf. above, pp. 82 f.), then by implication he was endorsing the change of public atmosphere which had come about in the mid-1920s, with technology no longer seen as a threat to human society, but as the way of the future. The champion racing cyclist Reggie MacNamara, who is the subject of Küpper's poem, was a popular object of veneration, and thus of collective identification, at the time; and by celebrating MacNamara's prowess in the language of mechanical production—his limbs are wrought iron, his heart is a steel spring, and his brain is a switchboard—Küpper was reflecting the popular esteem for technological products as superior in power and potential to mere human effort. In his own play *Mann ist Mann*—in the form in which it was performed and published in 1926—Brecht was in any case making use of technological imagery in a direct repudiation of those voices which were decrying the tendency towards standardization and anonymity in the new mass society. The "transformation" of the complaisant packer Galy Gay into a "fighting machine" is explicitly presented to the audience as a demonstration of the need to adapt to the ways of the world, inconstant and "dangerous" as they may be (*BFA* 2, 123). The "reassembly" of Galy Gay's personality, which is enacted in a notoriously burlesque sequence of cabaret-style "numbers",[26] entails the progressive obliteration of his social identity until, in the guise of "the man who did not want to be named", he refuses to be recognized by his own wife, is court-martialled and condemned to death for misappropriating an imaginary item of army property, and is ultimately obliged to deliver a funeral oration upon himself as the "last individual" (*der letzte Charakterkopf*) in history (*BFA* 2, 140). By showing the adaptation of a human being to the demands of his social environment (in this instance a Kiplingesque fantasy imperial army) in the manner of the con-

---

[26] See Marianne Kesting, "Die Groteske vom Verlust der Identität", in H. Steffen (ed.), *Das deutsche Lustspiel*, vol. ii (Göttingen: Vandenhoeck & Ruprecht, 1969), 180–99.

version of a motor car from one customized purpose to another, Brecht was playing provocatively upon the sense that the demands industrial society was making for the subordination of individual needs and individual identity to the exigencies of collective endeavour were cutting the ground from under a traditional conception of personality.

It was still the traditional antipathy towards technology that the journalist Heinrich Hauser saw himself as combatting when he published a series of studies in 1928 under the title *Friede mit Maschinen* (Peace with Machines). In order to counter the prejudices of the conventionally educated (p. 3)—and of a general public misled by such "silly fantasies" as the *Metropolis* film (p. 79)—he found it necessary to emphasize that mechanized production was, after all, a phenomenon of the natural (as opposed to the supernatural) world. What makes Hauser's text interesting as a historical document is the manner in which he builds bridges for his anticipated readers into an unfamiliar domain. He opens with a discussion of the way in which the inherent properties of materials can be applied to specific purposes—for example, a particular variety of steel might be needed for railway lines in a curve, where they are subject to particular kinds of stress—but then goes on to illustrate his point by describing a technique of bell-casting which has remained virtually unchanged for centuries: what brings about the most "rational" result (in the language of modern production techniques) is, he suggests, a subtle human judgement about the interaction of molten metal with an earthen mould (pp. 7 f.). In other ways, too, it soon becomes apparent that Hauser is trying to break down suspicions about the world of mechanized work by presenting it, again, in anthropomorphic terms. He presents machines as if they were natural creatures with a life-cycle of their own, visits the hall where obsolete machines are laid out as "corpses", describes the "personality" of individual motor cars, and speaks of a lorry as a trusty "companion" (pp. 22–4, 54 f.). The perfected technical performance of a machine becomes the virtuosity of a Rubinstein, and a crankshaft becomes an object for awed contemplation like the musculature of a champion boxer's arm (pp. 58–61). In his section on driving—which, apart from anything else, serves to remind us that driving any kind of motor vehicle was still an unfamiliar experience for most readers of the time—he emphasizes that machines are after all so designed as to be well attuned to the movements of the human body, and that the movements required to operate them easily become instinctive (pp. 38–46). That prepares the ground for his defence of the Taylor system of automated labour, in which he insists that "mechanical" work need not be debilitating or exhausting because the regular rhythm of bodily labour leaves the mind free to think its own thoughts (pp. 49 f.).[27] The rhetorical structure of Hauser's text aims, in other words, not just to reconcile the reader to the precept that mechanization is a natural adjunct of human work, but also to invite acquiescence in the managerial control of the production process via the machine. To that extent, Helmut Lethen's critique (1970, 68–71) of *Friede mit Maschinen* as a contribution to the defence of technocratic order is perfectly justified.

An effective antidote to Hauser's naive enthusiasm for technology can be found in the writings of Erik Reger. Having worked as a press officer for Krupps until 1927, Reger was perfectly placed to demonstrate quite how superficial and inventively "literary" the reporting of Hauser and others was when the Ruhrgebiet became a popular destination for journalists in the late 1920s (*Kleine Schriften*, vol. i, 130–7, 146–54). He was quick to point out how the social reality behind the processes of industrial manufacture was composed of many more—and more mundane—elements than the spectacular technical operations which were catching the attention of the national press. His novel *Union der festen Hand* (Union of the Firm Hand, 1931) gives a sardonic account of the way relations between major industrialists and their workforce had developed between the First World War and the Great Depression. It is a work which dispenses with any elaborate attempt to entwine personal destinies into a symbolic representation of a society, and its manner of composition can therefore leave the impression of a combination of anecdote and documentary reportage.[28] But its

---

[27] Hauser polemicizes in particular against the description of the Taylor system as a dehumanized mode of labour in Arthur Holitscher, *Amerika heute und morgen* (Berlin: S. Fischer, 1912).

[28] On the formal aspect of Reger's novel, see Jost Hermand, "Erik Regers *Union der festen Hand* (1931), Roman oder Reportage?" *Monatshefte für den deutschen Unterricht*, 57/3 (Mar. 1965), 113–33.

most powerful writing goes into the depiction of a huge system of entrepreneurial patronage and control, in which the lives of thousands are shown to be locked into the interests of the firm. Using pseudonyms, Reger exposes the machinations of leading German industrialists, in their competition amongst themselves, in their dealings with their employees, and in their covert support for anti-republican political parties (cf. Lethen 1970, 73 f.). But his depiction of working-class figures is, if anything, still more unflattering: for the most part they are disdainfully presented as victims of their own servile attitudes and base appetites, as is clearly brought out in the discussion of this novel by Erhard Schütz (1986, 141–6). In Reger's account of the situation, the employers have a more reliable grasp of the banal nature of the workers' aspirations than any left-wing politician. Technology, in this context, appears on the one hand as the mundane apparatus of everyday labour, and on the other hand as an equally mundane instrument of economic competition.

Brecht made an attempt to approach this world of work in the summer of 1927, teaming up with the composer Kurt Weill and the film director Carl Koch in the hope of producing a multi-media show for the city of Essen. The intention behind this project, commonly referred to as the "Ruhrepos", appears to have been to commemorate the unprecedented heights which technological achievement had reached in the twentieth century (*BFA* 21, 205), but the idea was never realized because the city authorities, nervous about Brecht's radical reputation, withdrew their support.[29] What is of interest in our present context, however, is the technique Brecht devises for presenting machinery as an integral component of social life. In the verses he composed for the "Ruhrepos", the cranes of Ruhrort are not only named (as they may well have been by the workforce), they are presented as participants in the manufacture of products for both military and domestic purposes, as workers who need to acquire the discipline that brings financial reward, and as comrades with a stake in the socialization of the means of production. One of them, Milchsack No. 4, is made to speak in the manner of a woman who has seen her men come and go—

---

[29] See Eckhardt Köhn, "Das *Ruhrepos*: Dokumentation eines gescheiterten Projekts", *Brecht-Jahrbuch* (1977), 52–80.

victims of war, disease, industrial injury and political violence—
and who has outlived them all, an emblem of the continuity of
proletarian fellowship (*BFA* 13, 374–8). Brecht also draws on
the idiom of popular American jazz revues, and presents industrial machines collectively as the "black stars" who are singing
for Europe. Theirs is no romantic song to a lone star, nor the
sound of the wind in the tree-tops, but the savage droning of
daily labour, the language of the cities that is soon to be the language of the whole world (*BFA* 13, 378 f.). At this stage of his
career, then, Brecht was seeking to harness the contemporary
public fascination for mechanical power and use it to draw
attention to the social connections between technological potential and shared human interests.

By contrast with this attempted socialization of technology in
the "Ruhrepos", Arnolt Bronnen—whose name had been linked
with Brecht's as an *enfant terrible* of the early 1920s, but
whose allegiances had subsequently moved to the political right,
as Brecht's had moved to the left—succeeds only in conjuring
up a horror vision of a world in which machines are running
free of human control when he addresses the theme in 1927.
Bronnen evokes the towering dock cranes of Hamburg as
primeval monsters which are not even begotten by men, but by
a race of other machines.[30] There are signs elsewhere, too, that
anxieties about the apparently increasing domination of technology over humanity continued to haunt right-wing thinkers
at the end of the decade.[31] But by then the nationalist right, no
less than the liberals and the socialists, had found their own
ways of laying that particular spectre to rest.

It is in the writings of the radical right that we can trace most
precisely the manner in which an inherited discourse adapts
to the impact of technology in the 1920s, because here a fundamentally anti-modern ideology, which had formerly viewed

---

[30] Arnolt Bronnen, "Das Wiederauftauchen der Mammute", in *Sabotage*, 141:
"Wie die Dinosaurier an den Flüssen, so stehen Rudel von gigantischen Kränen im
Hamburger Hafen, neigen ihre Hälse ins Meer und beschnuppern die Schiffe. [. . .]
Diese Lebendigkeit hätten Menschen geschaffen? Hier liegen schon Generationen
von Maschinen zwischen dem Erfinder und dem Produkt. Schon sind die wahren
Väter dieser Lebenwesen die Maschinen."

[31] Ernst Niekisch, for example, was still speaking of technology as a "man-eater"
in 1931. See S. Breuer, *Anatomie der konservativen Revolution* (Darmstadt: Wissenschaftliche Buchgesellschaft, 1995), 73.

technology as an instrument of the industrialization and urbanization that was eroding traditional social structures, found itself compelled in the wake of the First World War to absorb the self-evident truth that any future assertion of national interests by military means was going to be dependent on technological strength. This was the situation that gave rise to a body of thought which the historian Jeffrey Herf has aptly labelled "reactionary modernism". There were many figures on the anti-democratic right during the 1920s engaged in the harnessing of technology to the values of conservative nationalism; their activities were focused on such organizations as the *Tat* journal, the industrialists' June Club, and the Stahlhelm association of war veterans (Herf, 25; Mohler, 539–54).[32] But among them, the two figures who illustrate the development of attitudes most clearly are also the two whose writings—together with those of Carl Schmitt—probably exerted the greatest intellectual influence during the Weimar years: Oswald Spengler and Ernst Jünger.

In certain obvious senses, Spengler's *Der Untergang des Abendlandes* (The Decline of the West), the first half of which appeared as the First World War was coming to an end in 1918, is a prime example of that anti-modernism which saw industrialization and the increasingly rationalized organization of life as inimical to the "soul" of a culture, to its organically conceived integral identity. The particular spin that Spengler put on that brand of cultural pessimism was to present all human cultures as developing according to an organic pattern or life-cycle, and to label as "civilization" the phase of decline and decadence at the end of any such cycle. But that did not prevent him from interpreting technology as an instrument for the self-preservation and self-assertion of a culture. At the end of Part I of *Der Untergang des Abendlandes*, Spengler is already distinguishing between "theoretical" development, which represents for him the intellectualization and thus the disintegration of the intrinsic symbolic system of a culture, and "technical" development, which he interprets as a manifestation of the organic impetus of a culture (*Untergang*, 538 ff.). At the end of

---

[32] For the current state of research on the anti-democratic right, see Breuer, op. cit.; R. Woods, *The Conservative Revolution in the Weimar Republic* (Basingstoke: Macmillan, 1996).

Part II, which he published in 1923, he is more insistent still that technology is an expression of "life itself", and he presents the crisis of contemporary Europe as a struggle for hegemony between (organic) culture on the one hand and the forces of the money economy, with their tendency towards abstraction and their enervating effect on culture, on the other. In this context, Spengler identifies the cause of culture at one moment with "the blood" and at another moment with "technical thought". With the model of classical antiquity in mind, he anticipates a new "caesarism" which will arise to break the dominance of capital; and in that connection he proclaims the engineer to be the "knowing priest" of the "Faustian" culture of modern Europe and the embodiment of its true resilience (*Untergang*, 1191 ff.).

The synthesis that Spengler contrived between conservative politics and the endorsement of technological strength, and which he promoted through direct contacts with German industrialists, was to earn him the description "philosopher of heavy industry" in the left-liberal press (*WB* 27, 36, 369–72).[33] In 1931 he published a simplified version of his historical vision, and one which focused still more squarely on the interpretation of technology, in *Der Mensch und die Technik* (Man and Technology). The definition of technology he gives here is one which distances it emphatically from any association with rational or intellectual problem-solving. It is, he states, the tactical expression of a given life-form in the Darwinian struggle for life; fundamentally it is a weapon with which a particular biological type seeks to dominate others. On this basis he can present the industrial technology of modern Europe both as an organic feature of its "Faustian" culture, and as the necessary means of its defence against alien cultures. Towards the end of the text it becomes apparent how Spengler has modified the terms of his argument in order to stiffen the sinews of German nationalism in its political struggles, both external and internal. He acknowledges the mechanization of life and the alienation of labour that industrialization has brought in its train, arguing that these are inevitable features of the advanced stage that "Faustian culture" has reached; but he does so in order to condemn those whose responses to these developments take the form of social revolt

---

[33] On Spengler's contacts with industrialists, see W. Struve, *Elites against Democracy* (Princeton: Princeton University Press, 1973), 232–73.

against mechanization on the one hand or romantic flight from mechanization on the other. He deplores the dissemination of technical know-how, whether to wider sections of the population at home or to colonially subjugated peoples abroad, and when he concludes his text with an injunction to endure, stoically, in the face of cataclysms to come, then—in addition to confirming his pessimistic vision of cyclical progressions in history—he is implicitly urging the German intelligentsia to guard its "Faustian" knowledge from those political forces in the contemporary world who would seek to apply it for ends inimical to German conservatism. It is by this intellectual route that the "caesarism" foreseen by Spengler becomes strongly linked with the principle of technocracy.

Ernst Jünger's contribution to the assimilation of technology to anti-liberal thought took the form of integrating it into the model of community he had derived from his wartime experiences at the front. His early post-war writings—*In Stahlgewittern* (1920) and *Der Kampf als inneres Erlebnis* (1922)—still bear the traces of an antipathy towards industrial culture which is similar to that of the Expressionists, but by the mid-1920s we find him, too, adapting his system of thinking in order to accommodate technology (cf. Prümm 1974, 210ff.). Like Spengler, he was having to confront the fact that an advanced industrial technology had become indispensable to the conduct of wars, but that it was also gaining dominion over the creative—or in Jünger's context, the heroic—potential of the individual human being. Whereas his earlier publications had focused on the capacity of the individual to withstand the terrors of the modern infantry war (as we saw in chapter 6), in *Feuer und Blut* (Fire and Blood, 1925) he addressed the subject of the increasing importance of mechanized warfare in the closing stages of the First World War. "Material", in this context, carries the meaning of "the vital energy of the industrialized nations" unleashing itself in the heavy artillery bombardments on the Western front (*Feuer*, 21–5). Jünger's narrative perspective is still that of the front-line fighter, but into that perspective he now admits a vision of the production and supply of armaments as a perfected industrial mechanism, the competitive advantage of which depends on its productive efficiency (*Feuer*, 25 f.). The imagery of industrial manufacture becomes still more explicitly linked to Jünger's sense of military purpose in *Das Wäldchen 125* (Copse 125, 1925), where he imagines "a machine that is simply and practically conceived, without embellishment and with optimal efficiency, which could be sent into war with the same confidence with which an automobile firm sends its best car to a road rally" (*Wäldchen*, 118). The aims of human endeavour which Jünger expresses in these texts remain those of a Nietzschean passion for intensity of experience, in accordance with which the banal utilitarian satisfaction of material needs is explicitly rejected; but the machine has acquired a function in the pursuit of those aims which, as Jünger notes, Nietzsche never anticipated. It is not just that the fighting machine has become a natural metaphor for the battle-hardened infantry company, the very notion of machinery takes on a special beauty for "him who loves life in its fullness and violence" (*Feuer*, 66 f.).

In an early section of *Das Wäldchen 125*, Jünger describes a visit to a military air squadron in the summer of 1918. He stylizes these flyers as an élite drawn from the front-line fighters, and as the representatives of a new human type forged by the war and destined to become the future leaders of Europe, whether they hail from the landed aristocracy or the industrial bourgeoisie. In their manner of fighting he recognizes the need for a combination of instinctive rage with cold-blooded precision, for "an ice-cold brain above a fiery heart" (*Wäldchen*, 76–80). In peacetime, too, the glimpse of a smooth-running machine-room as Jünger describes it a few years later in *Das abenteuerliche Herz* (The Adventurous Heart, 1929) conjures up the excitement of sitting at the controls of an aircraft at the moment before take-off, an excitement which he associates in turn with the "cold and insatiable rage", and the lure of "more dangerous games", that is aroused by the act of engaging with physical materials. Machinery, here, is stylized into the instrument of a self-consciously "modern" rupture with all that is civil, ordered, and staid.[34]

---

[34] "Hier empfand ich wieder, was man hinter dem Triebwerk des Flugzeugs empfindet, wenn die Faust den Gashebel nach vorn stößt und das schreckliche Gebrüll der Kraft, die der Erde entfliehen will, sich erhebt [...]. Es ist die kalte, niemals zu sättigende Wut, ein sehr modernes Gefühl, das im Spiel mit der Materie schon den Reiz gefährlicherer Spiele ahnt und der ich wünsche, daß sie noch recht lange nach ihren eigentlichen Symbolen auf der Suche sei. Denn sie als die

At the end of that passage from *Das abenteuerliche Herz*, Jünger speaks of wishing that this pursuit of "dangerous games" might eventually find its own form of symbolic expression, but that the supplanting of the old order by a new one should take a long time in order that it might be all the more thorough. The political crisis of the early 1930s evidently prompted him to formulate the new values more urgently, however, because in *Der Arbeiter* (The Worker, 1932) he attempted to set out his vision of the new symbolic order in theoretical terms. *Der Arbeiter* is a project for the historical transcendence of bourgeois liberalism, which Jünger rejects as unheroic (the bourgeois does not know the meaning of danger), disunited (characterized by individual freedom, and lacking in "bonding"), inorganic (subject to "mechanical thinking"), and therefore un-German. The "worker" as Jünger conceives him is not the representative of a labouring class within the "mechanistic" system of liberal capitalism, but the embodiment of the characteristics which will transform civil society (as conventionally understood) into a new state where the employee will become a warrior, the masses will be forged into an army, and contractual relations between individuals will be replaced by a command structure (p. 25). In a long section dedicated to technology (pp. 149 ff.), Jünger describes how its role will be that of an instrument for mobilizing material, and productive effort, in the service of this new state. Imagining that technology is nearing a state of technical perfection, Jünger envisages that it will bring about the dissolution of archaic social distinctions (estates), as it erodes the differences between life in the country and life in the town; that it will overcome the division of knowledge into specialisms and provide the language for a system of social relations which will transcend the factionalism of parliamentary democracy; that its fundamental character will be recognized, as it had been in time of war, as a manifestation of power; and that it will become the "space" inhabited by a world of "total work". Here, then, the definition of technology has become assimilated to a vision of

sicherste Zerstörerin der Idylle, der Landschaften alten Stils, der Gemütlichkeit und der historischen Biedermeierei wird diese Aufgabe um so gründlicher erfüllen, je später sie sich von einer neuen Welt der Werte auffangen und in sie einbauen läßt." (*Werke* VII, 153 f.). The violent escapism of this passage is significantly attenuated in the 1938 version of *Das abenteuerliche Herz*: see Ernst Jünger, *Sämtliche Werke* (Stuttgart: Klett, 1979), vol. ix, 223–5.

the total mobilization of society within a framework of authority which has only ever been approached under the conditions of a war economy.[35]

We ought perhaps to remind ourselves at this point that we are dealing here with ideological pipe-dreams rather than political realities. In the light of what we all know about the relentless and murderous uses that the Nazi regime made of technological know-how after it had come to power in 1933, it is common to associate its brand of political control with the application of technological expertise. It is on this mental association that the writer Günter de Bruyn plays, for example, when he recalls that on the day of his birth, 1 November 1926, the German railways introduced the 24-hour clock and Josef Goebbels became Gauleiter for Berlin: the refinement of technology, he openly implies, accompanied the disintegration of ethics.[36] But this way of linking the two processes is very much a conflation in retrospect. The visions of a technologized future outlined by Spengler and Jünger may be said to anticipate certain features of the way the Nazis liked to conceive Germany. Spengler offers them the image of technology as a weapon with which a particular biological type seeks to dominate others, and Jünger constructs a vision of the total mobilization of society for war-like purposes. But Spengler and Jünger are contributing to an adjustment of intellectual thinking in which the Nazi leadership scarcely participated, because from their early days they took it for granted that German military strength needed to be based on industrial power, and that German technological expertise was an expression of racial superiority (cf. Herf, 194 ff.). As for the relationship between the engineering profession and the Nazi Party, the few engineers who joined the party before 1933 were primarily concerned, like other core party members, with political organization rather than the assertion

[35] For fuller critical accounts of Jünger's *Der Arbeiter*, see H. Segeberg, "Technikverwachsen: Zur Konstruktion des 'Arbeiter' bei Ernst Jünger", *Der Deutschunterricht*, 46 (1994), 3, 40–50; U.-K. Ketelsen, " 'Nun werden nicht nur die historischen Strukturen gesprengt, sondern auch deren mythische und kultische Voraussetzungen.' Zu Ernst Jünger's *Die totale Mobilmachung* (1930) und *Der Arbeiter* (1932)", in H.-H. Müller and H. Segeberg (eds.), *Ernst Jünger im 20. Jahrhundert* (Munich: Fink, 1995), 77–95.
[36] Günter de Bruyn, *Zwischenbilanz: Eine Jugend in Berlin* (Frankfurt: S. Fischer, 1992), 22 f.

of technological interests; and while the pressure to join
became irresistible for many after 1933, statistical evidence suggests that engineers were rather less inclined to do so than
lawyers and doctors. The professional organizations of engineers may well have sought to emphasize the community
of interest between strong technology and a strong state, but
the behaviour of the profession both before and after 1933
showed it to be pragmatic and opportunistic, rather than
ideologically motivated, in its cooperation with the government
of the day.[37]

In the concluding section of this chapter I shall focus specifically
on Brecht's treatment of technological themes, not least because,
of all the literary writers of the Weimar period, he goes furthest
in shaking off the lure of fantasy and idealization, and instead
explores the implications of technology as a natural human
activity. The sense of purpose with which he invests technology
is plainly locked into a specific ethical discourse of the time,
namely that of the Communist movement. But whatever
the historical limitations of his perspectives on the subject in
that respect, the approach he was taking around 1930 at least
provides a practical framework for considering the nature of
technological development as an interaction between humanity
and the natural world, and for relating it to social and ethical
issues.

We have already noted the way that Brecht adopted technological motifs in the mid-1920s as an instrument for challenging old assumptions about human identity and the literary
expression of it. When he presented the modification of Galy
Gay's personality in *Mann ist Mann* as a process of mechanical
reassembly (*Ummontierung*), it was in order to repudiate the
conception of human character which had traditionally under-
pinned the writing of drama, namely that it was organically
determined and—for the purpose of devising dramatic
conflicts—immutable. The fact that Galy Gay was being converted into a ruthless fighting machine was not, at this stage,

[37] See Karl-Heinz Ludwig, *Technik und Ingenieure im Dritten Reich* (Düsseldorf:
Droste, 1974); Herf, 152 ff.; Hortleder, 93 ff.; M. Renneberg and M. Walker (eds.),
Science, Technology and National Socialism (Cambridge: Cambridge University
Press, 1995).

presented as anything sinister or alarming; in fact, as late as the
Berlin production of January 1928, the script of *Mann ist Mann*
was emphasizing the positive advantage of the strength that
Galy Gay has acquired as a result of his conversion, and presenting him at the end of the process as an embodiment of the
collective will to accomplish what a Joshua or a Napoleon had
achieved before—the new man was the better man (*BFA* 2, 411).
In similar vein, Brecht presented Küpper's "Iron Man" poem
to the world in January 1927 as a model of how to write lyric
poetry in the contemporary world, and showed no sign of distancing himself from Küpper's description of his technologically
enhanced sports champion as a potential "new Caesar"—an
echo of Spengler's historical prophecy which at least one reader
of *Die literarische Welt* picked up and endorsed (*LW* 3, 7, 8).
But very soon after this episode Brecht was taking a more circumspect line on the relationship between technological power
and human substance. In a talk which accompanied a radio
broadcast of *Mann ist Mann* in March 1927, Brecht reaffirmed
that the play was directed against the interests of the older generation, but also explicitly distanced himself from the view that
technology might itself be shaping the future nature of humanity, concluding that, whatever the 'new man' was going to look
like, he would above all look like a human being (*BFA* 24,
40–2). He repeated these sentiments in the programme note
he supplied for the opening night of the Piscatorbühne later the
same year (*BFA* 21, 208 f.). In the crane songs he wrote for
the *Ruhrepos* in the summer of 1927, as we saw earlier, he
emphasized the aspect of social interaction between industrial
machinery and the workforce. In February 1928 he satirized the
contemporary fascination for technology in his poem about a
crowd of intellectuals worshipping an oil tank (*BFA* 11, 174–6).
And by the time we arrive at the second Berlin production of
Mann ist Mann, which was in rehearsal at the end of 1930 and
the beginning of 1931, Brecht was reversing the message associated with the conversion of Galy Gay by deleting the scenes
which had shown him in action as a fighting machine, and by
adding to Widow Begbick's commentary—which now *prefaced*
the whole play—the well-known lines about the need to watch
out in case the likes of Galy Gay are turned overnight into
butchers (*BFA* 2, 203, 412 f.). It is in the development of another

group of texts between 1928 and 1930 that the ramifications of Brecht's engagement with technological themes can be most usefully observed.

Kurt Weill had been working with Brecht since 1927, on the abortive *Ruhrepos* and on the musical settings which were to grow into the *Mahagonny* opera. At the end of 1928 he approached him again when he needed material for a contribution to the Baden-Baden Music Festival of 1929, the focus of which was to be music specifically composed for radio. The subject-matter on which they agreed was Charles Lindbergh's single-handed flight from New York to Paris of May 1927, which had made Lindbergh the object of extraordinary public veneration.[38] Early in 1929, Brecht was also approached by Paul Hindemith, who was similarly looking to prepare a composition for the Baden-Baden Festival, and whose special interest lay in communal music-making. This was how the text we know as the *Badener Lehrstück* came to be written in close association with the Lindbergh text; and as the date of the Festival approached, Weill and Hindemith even joined forces in setting the Lindbergh text to music (Krabiel, 39 ff.). The versions of the two texts performed at Baden-Baden in July 1929 were fragmentary and provisional, and were acknowledged to be so in the programme notes. Revised versions, on which Brecht worked with Elisabeth Hauptmann, and later also with Slatan Dudow, were published in early volumes of the *Versuche* in 1930, and it is primarily on these versions that I shall focus here. After the Second World War, in the knowledge of the solidarity that Lindbergh had shown with fascist regimes in the meantime, Brecht produced a new version of the first text under the title *Der Ozeanflug* (The Ocean Flight), from which the name of Lindbergh was expunged (*BFA* 3, 404)—but that is of no relevance to the present discussion.

In line with the investigative approach Brecht was taking to the political dimension of performance media in this period, each text contained a reflection on the communicative context for which it was intended. The performance of the Lindbergh piece at Baden-Baden—as a radio play set to music—involved

---

[38] The public response in Europe to Lindbergh's achievement is vividly described in Eksteins, 242 ff. Sadly, Eksteins' book as a whole is organized around suggestive associations between the evidence he collects rather than argued connections.

a simulation of the relationship between the radio broadcast and the listener, with the part of Lindbergh sung by the "listener", whose spatial separation from the source of the broadcast was symbolized by the arrangement of the performers on the podium. In this way, Brecht tried to incorporate into the presentation the idea that the social isolation of the radio listener might be countered by the broadcast of performances in which the listener was encouraged to take an active part (cf. *BFA* 24, 87–9). However quixotic that notion might appear, the principle of active participation remained fundamental to the conception of later versions of the piece, which reflect Kurt Weill's interest in school opera, as well as Brecht's concern with the medium of radio (Krabiel, 46 f., 86 f.). In the 1930 version—the title of which pointedly refers to the protagonist as a collective phenomenon: *Der Flug der Lindberghs* (The Flight of the Lindberghs)—participants are invited by the voice of the community, i.e. the radio, to join together in the re-enactment of Lindbergh's experience, a re-enactment which also puts them in the position of reflecting upon what it takes to carry technological progress forward.

In the case of the *Lehrstück* prepared for Hindemith, the idea that mattered to the composer—communal participation in music-making—was developed into a manifest theme of the work. The case that Brecht chose to focus on here was that of a pilot who has come to grief in the attempt to achieve what Lindbergh had accomplished; it is based, in fact, on the disappearance of the Frenchman Charles Nungesser (who had a high public profile in the 1920s as a former fighter ace and a glamorous dare-devil) together with his co-pilot François Coli, while trying to fly from Paris to New York only a few days before Lindbergh's successful crossing (Krabiel, 57). In the 1930 version, the Nungesser figure is accompanied by three mechanics, and Brecht uses their situation to pose the question about the relationship between individual achievement and the interests of the community, and about the nature of the society in which that question is being put. The differences of opinion that arose between Brecht and Hindemith were related to this difference of conception. When the musical edition of the *Lehrstück* appeared in late 1929, Hindemith prefaced it with a statement to the effect that its main purpose was simply communal participation, and that it was of little importance which portions of the text were used, or omitted, or replaced with other material. Brecht's response—apart from taking measures to ensure that his freedom to determine the future shape of the work was protected in contract—was to insist all the more strongly on the pedagogic purpose of the text as he had devised it, and to reflect on the frailty of existing artistic media in providing an educative counter-thrust to the powerful collective forces which were pulling contemporary society apart (*BFA* 24, 90 f.; Krabiel, 71 f.). Newspaper reviews of the Baden-Baden performance give some clear indications of the type of collective forces with which Hindemith's conception of communal singing was associated in public awareness: in quarters where communal singing was associated with the romantic and nationalistic youth movement the *Badener Lehrstück* was denounced as a barbaric act of "cultural bolshevism" (Krabiel, 67–9). It was precisely the expectations of such listeners as these that the analytical, investigative, and indeed provocative character of Brecht's text was designed to disrupt.

In a number of ways, the text of the *Badener Lehrstück* presents the reader or spectator with puzzles to resolve. Some of these are deliberately contrived: the notorious "clowns number", for example, in which the actions performed bizarrely contradict the sentiments of the dialogue, and the series of intricate paradoxes which are built into the commentaries on the airmen's situation.[39] Others appear to have resulted from the combination of circumstances in which the text came into being. The ending of *Der Flug der Lindberghs* had placed the technical attainment of flight in a wider perspective by speaking of the need to remember "the unattainable", a reference which reviewers of the Baden-Baden performance had interpreted as introducing a Romantic note (Krabiel, 35). As Brecht acknowledged when reworking the same material for the opening of the *Badener Lehrstück*, in order to be consistent with the general

---

[39] It is this aspect of the *Badener Lehrstück* that gives it a certain in-built resistance to critics who seek to read out of it a straightforward endorsement of the Communist collective (whether they regard such a notion with favour or with hostility), or indeed who take their cue from the term "Einverständnis" in the title of the 1930 version, and present the text as a logically coherent illustration of the need to adjust one's thoughts to the objective realities of both the natural and the social world (cf. Knopf, vol. i, 77–80).

thrust of the Lindbergh text, that line ought to have been amended to read "that which has not yet been attained" (*BFA* 3, 27). In the prefatory note to the *Lehrstück*, Brecht also voices concern about the way this text dwells on the subject of dying, wryly observing that there is not a great deal of use value in dying. There is nevertheless a constructive purpose to this theme of death which is essentially similar to the role it plays in Döblin's *Berlin Alexanderplatz*:[40] just as Franz Biberkopf has to be brought low and surrender his old identity in order to be reborn as an integrated member of society, so too must the stranded airmen of the *Lehrstück* die a metaphorical death, letting go of the attributes which have singled them out as exceptional individuals, in order to be accepted into the community to which they have appealed for help. Of more direct relevance to our present concerns, however, are the traces of an intellectual development in this pair of texts which point beyond the terms in which technology had been discussed and represented by authors in the preceding decade.

The experiences with which "the Lindberghs" are confronted include the conquering of the elements. They are required to do battle with the fog which disorientates the senses, with snow-storms which load the plane with ice, and with the threat of falling into the waters below. These are the episodes which highlight the risk involved in the transatlantic flight, instil a sense of the frailty and mortality of anyone who undertakes such a venture, and account for the reference to the elements as "enemies" at a later stage of the flight (*BFA* 3, 15). But there are three other aspects of the way the flight is presented which place this struggle against nature in a wider context. One is the reference, at the start of the flight, to Lindbergh's precise calculation of what would be needed in order to fly 3,000 kilometres single-handed, to the paring down of equipment and rations to just what is required for this specific task. This aspect of calculation extends to the assessment of weather conditions: there has been an element of risk in taking off when the weather is known to be not entirely favourable, but when

---

[40] Although he does not refer to this particular theme, Fritz Sternberg recalls in his memoir of Brecht, *Der Dichter und die Ratio* (Göttingen: Sachse & Pohl, 1963, 17), that he and Brecht read and discussed *Berlin Alexanderplatz* intensively in 1929.

the plane runs into fog, the Lindbergh role speaks of being willing to turn back if necessary, rather than play the hero (*BFA* 3, 12). Another additional aspect is that of teamwork which, like the details of the equipment and conditions, was a feature of Lindbergh's own account of the flight (*BFA* 3, 402). The mechanics who built the engine and the aircraft are explicitly commemorated; the example of their labouring for twenty-four hours at a stretch in order to finish the job is invoked at the point where "the Lindberghs" are having to fight against tiredness; and the message they send back to America at the end of the flight is to tell the team that "our engine" stood the test and that "their work" was sound (*BFA* 3, 12 f., 15, 23). Similarly, in the dialogue the Lindberghs have with the engine towards the end of the flight, the emphasis is on the "work" that each of them—the pilot and the engine—has to do, and on what they need to do it.

The third aspect takes us to the question of how Lindbergh's undertaking contributes to the technological advance of mankind as a whole. As a dramatic construct, *Der Flug der Lindberghs* may be said to be structured towards this inquiry, but the relationship is made explicit in scene 8, which is pointedly entitled "Ideologie". Here the text written for "the Lindberghs" speaks with unqualified confidence of the arrival of "new times", and carries unmistakable echoes of the early writings of Karl Marx in the references to the rolling back of religious beliefs by the progressive advance of scientific understanding.[41] But what is particularly interesting in this passage is the poetic development of the notion of "the primitive" in ways which link the term both to the notion of superstitious faith and to the current state of technology. Lindbergh's flight across the Atlantic, it is suggested, will soon appear laughable because— even if it represents an advance over the steamship—the apparatus in which he did it left enormous room for improvement. The technology was still primitive, as the general condition of human awareness is still primitive. The aim, according to the text, should not be to overcome nature, but to make that which is primitive—both ourselves and our technology—more like

---

[41] I am thinking particularly of Marx's emphasis on religion as a product of social circumstances in the *Kritik der Hegelschen Rechtsphilosophie* and in *Die deutsche Ideologie*.

nature: "Laßt uns bekämpfen die Natur I Bis wir selber natürlich geworden sind" (Let us struggle against nature until we
have ourselves become natural—*BFA* 3, 16). It is through the
refinement of technique, the text is suggesting, through the
adaptation of human understanding to the precise nature of
the material world we inhabit, that historical progress is to be
brought about.

The aspect of human struggle that is taken up at the beginning of the *Badener Lehrstück* is that *between* individuals. The
stranded airmen speak of having been involved in the fervid
competition to fly higher and faster; in their haste to get ahead,
they have forgotten the purpose behind their flight: "über
den geschwinderen Aufbruch I Vergaßen wir unseres Aufbruchs
Ziel" (*BFA* 3, 28). When this line is echoed by the chorus at the
end of the piece, the implication is clearly that what ultimately
provides the sense of purpose for technical endeavour is communal interest. But by implication, too, these airmen have come
to grief because, in their pursuit of competitive advantage, they
have failed to take precise account of what will be needed to
achieve their end, they have not made that careful assessment
of needs and conditions which had made Lindbergh's successful flight possible. The attitude to technology that is being
offered for scrutiny here is one of disdain towards the material
conditions which make human achievement possible. That attitude is underscored at a later point in the text when the egoistic pilot asks, "what is an aircraft without its pilot?" (*BFA* 3,
42). He is characterized, indeed, as the very embodiment of a
hubris which treats technology as a vehicle for the pursuit of
personal prestige. The context for his remark is his refusal to
comply with the advice to give up material possessions and the
attributes of personal renown, insisting on retaining his identity
as the man who flew "incredibly high" and who has set himself
apart from the multitude. That refusal leads to his exclusion
from the community and to the expunging of his identity from
the collective memory, whereas the mechanics, who accept the
need for humility and anonymity, are welcomed back in order
to participate in the forward march of history.

There are several senses in which these texts are working
against tendencies that manifest themselves elsewhere in the
writing of the Weimar period. By emphasizing the importance

of mundane work and collective endeavour, they construct an image of technological achievement which runs counter to any tendency to identify it with a heroic individual, or indeed with the domination of a technocrat. By emphasizing the element of rational calculation that is necessary to achieve a technical success, they also work against the conception of technology as an expression of instinct and the evolutionary life-force, as it was developed by Spengler in particular. By emphasizing the role of understanding in bringing about historical change, and of technology as the instrument of that change, they counter both the crude notion that technology should help man to dominate nature and the anxiety that technology might be gaining dominion over mankind. Moreover, by representing the refinement of technology as a process which will bring it closer to nature, these texts provide a strong antidote to the image of technological sophistication as something mysterious and arcane. In these particular ways, *Der Flug der Lindberghs* and the *Badener Lehrstück vom Einverständnis* establish perspectives which counter the mystification of technology we find on the nationalist right, as well as in popular fiction and film. This is not to deny that the *Badener Lehrstück* in particular is also shaped by a Communist dogmatism which demands the suppression of individuality in favour of a collectivist ethos.[42] But it does highlight the senses in which Brecht's treatment of technology is based on the very premises from which the empirical investigations of the young Karl Marx took off, namely that the social world is the product of an interaction between the work of specific human beings and the conditions of their material environment.[43]

---

[42] Willy Haas, in his *Bert Brecht* (New York: Frederick Ungar, 1970), 70 f., noted the formal similarities between the ritual expulsion of the pilot in the *Badener Lehrstück* and the counter-reformation drama of the baroque period, and commented that here Brecht had "appropriated the entire doctrine of grace and put it to work for the Party". For a discussion of how the collectivism of the *Lehrstücke* compares with that of Ernst Jünger's *Der Arbeiter*, see David Roberts, "Individuum und Kollektiv: Jünger und Brecht zu Ausgang der Weimarer Republik", *Orbis Litterarum*, 41 (1986), 157–75.

[43] See *Die deutsche Ideologie* (Marx/Engels, *Werke* (Berlin: Dietz, 1962), vol. iii, 20 f.): "Die erste Voraussetzung aller Menschengeschichte ist natürlich die Existenz lebendiger menschlicher Individuen. Der erste zu konstatierende Tatbestand ist also die körperliche Organisation dieser Individuen und ihr dadurch gegebenes Verhältnis zur übrigen Natur. [. . .] Indem die Menschen ihre Lebensmittel produzieren, produzieren sie indirekt ihr materielles Leben selbst."

There is a certain irony in the fact that a pair of texts written around 1930 can appear to transcend the literary treatment of technology over the previous decade by adopting the tenets of a philosophical position established eighty-five years earlier. But perhaps that is itself an indication of the strength of the anti-technological tradition which Brecht and his associates were trying to overcome. The horror of mechanization (rather than of the machine as such) as a threat to inherited conceptions of humanity, which provides a dominant theme of Expressionist drama around 1920, is carried forward into various elements of the discussion of technology in the latter half of the Weimar period, at the same time as the potential advantages of technological refinement are being acknowledged and debated in a practical sense by workers and industrialists alike. The self-consciously modernizing impetus behind Brecht's projects takes them through the banalization of technological motifs in the mid-1920s, and on to an experimental framework in which technological endeavour can be examined as a product of human aspiration, and what it means to be human can be examined in relation to the social demands of collective endeavour.

Epilogue
Interpreting Weimar Culture

> The notion of the 'necessity' of a given historical process
> feeds on the supposition that for any historical event there
> must be sufficient reasons which bring it about. In reality,
> however, there were contradictory tendencies which were
> resolved by conflict, and that amounts to a good deal less.
>
> Brecht[1]

I set out to write a book which would distinguish among the trends and factors at work in the literary culture of the Weimar Republic, and I hope that the book I have written provides specialists and non-specialists alike with an accessible guide to the dominant issues and developments. What we are dealing with in the Weimar period is not a straightforward paradigm shift from one literary style to another nor a straightforward collapse into authoritarian attitudes, as was suggested by the models of interpretation presented thirty years ago by Horst Denkler and Peter Gay respectively. Rather we are dealing with a contest among writers and artists over the appropriate attitudes to adopt towards the post-war situation of the German-speaking world, over the interpretation of major cultural issues which present themselves in that situation, and over the techniques of representation appropriate to that task of interpretation.

The innovative developments we see taking place in the period are concerned with adaptations of a more or less radical nature to that sense of an altered situation. In lyric poetry they take the form of reflective responses to the functions of language as a medium of social communication, as well as to the experience of cultural disintegration and reorientation. In the theatre

---

[1] Bertolt Brecht, "Notizen über Dialektik", *Gesammelte Werke* (Frankfurt: Suhrkamp, 1967), vol. viii, 712.

they relate to the problem of how to nurture critical insight under particular social circumstances, as well as to the cultivation of a heightened sense of epochal change. Narrative writers, too, in addition to developing intellectually ambitious techniques for representing and reflecting on the historical character of the times, also adopt new popular styles in an effort to influence the way the social trends of the period are perceived. The political crisis of 1929–33 brings a sharpening of conflicts which is reflected in the social novel as well as in the theatre, and which manifests itself particularly clearly in the contest over how to interpret the experience of the First World War. While those conflicts also make themselves felt in discussions of the relationship between Berlin and the provinces, it becomes apparent on closer inspection that the life of the city provides authors with a vocabulary for expressing their sense of the general character of modern times, and that provincial life provides them with opportunities to reflect on the contribution of subjective human factors to the political and social trends of the times. The most obvious evidence of the adaptation of a literary culture to processes of change arises in the responses of writers to technological development. Here we find clear expressions of anxiety and horror on the one hand, and attempts to commandeer the issue for particular political ideologies on the other. But we also see how the antipathy of a vitalistic intellectual culture towards technology, which dominates at the start of the Weimar period, gives way not only to unthinking enthusiasm, but also to a self-critical awareness of technological change as an outcome of the interaction between humanity and the natural environment in a social context.

In the course of writing my account of these developments, I have naturally become aware of aspects which warrant further investigation. For a start, there are particular authors who are relatively little known outside the German-speaking world, and whose works would undoubtedly repay attention in relation to the broad cultural developments I have presented. There is Walter Mehring and Max Herrmann-Neiße among the poets, and among the novelists there is Ernst Weiß, whom I was unable to include in the present volume. It would also be helpful to have a more precise picture of the way the policies of cultural institutions affected the character of literary writing in the period, and thus helped to determine the public perception of what Weimar culture meant at the time. A great deal is known about the contribution of the Berlin theatres to this process, but the precise position of provincial theatres in relation to the dominant trends of the time could do with fuller investigation. Equally important is the role of the publishing houses in encouraging public taste to move in particular directions during the 1920s, although this may be more difficult to piece together, since the archival material appears to be more scattered. In addition to the larger houses such as Ullstein and Rowohlt, the Kiepenheuer Verlag is of particular interest because of the role it played in the promotion of young writers of the time.

Beyond that, there are questions of social and psychological perspective. While some attention has recently been given to the influence of filmic representation on the narrative style of Weimar writers, it would also be useful to have a more precise account of narrative stance in the fiction of the period. In relation both to the experience of social crisis and to the depiction of provincial life, a systematic analysis of the social points of view from which narrative accounts are constructed could be very instructive. The attitudes which come to be attached stereotypically to the generations at the end of the 1920s are to some extent mutually defining, but we could do with a clearer sense of the part the distinctive conditioning experiences of each generation plays in establishing those attitudes. And alongside the investigation of women's experiences and women's perspectives, it would be worth developing a clearer sense of what 'manliness' signified in the discourse of the time, for in addition to its obvious connotations of heroism, dominance, and aggression, it is clearly also used as an indicator of adulthood, responsibility, and citizenship. We could also do with a full investigation of the preoccupation with death, which might help us to distinguish the reflective and constructive treatments from the destructive and the downright morbid. That in turn might help us develop a reliable sense of how the retrospective narratives of wartime experience really relate to the literary modernism which developed around the time of the First World War.

The bigger tasks, finally, relate to the senses in which the literary writing of the Weimar period can be placed in a longer-term perspective. I am thinking here not so much of the attempts to recover or restore the legacy of Weimar culture in the period after the Second World War, of the fact that one of the first post-war cultural events in Berlin in 1945 was a revival of *The Three-penny Opera*, or that the 1960s and 1970s were the heyday of the reception of such writers as Brecht, Horváth, and Fleißer. I am thinking rather of the cultural impulses out of which the 'high modernism' of the Weimar period was generated, and of what became of those impulses under subsequent historical conditions. The question of 'Sachlichkeit' as a form of aesthetic awareness is linked to issues in the sphere of design and technology which reach back to the turn of the century and forward to the present day.[2] The terms in which the life of the city is presented similarly relate back to discussions about the abstractness of the modern economy at the turn of the century, and forward to the universalization of urban culture that we are experiencing in our own time. And literary responses to technology link back on the one hand to Nietzsche's critique of the mechanized character of modern society in the late nineteenth century, and forward to present-day anxieties about the application and control of human inventiveness on the other. The disillusionment and despair expressed in certain of the novels of around 1930 suggest a still wider time-frame: they relate to the disappointment of hopes and assumptions which had been articulated and nurtured by the Enlightenment, and which have been subjected to sustained philosophical critique in the period since the Second World War. What is less clear is how the anxieties communicated by the social novels of the period relate to changing perceptions of the character of modern society. A recent study has shown how the intellectual utopianism of both left and right under the Weimar Republic is characterized by a revolt against the conception of modernity entailed in Max Weber's description of modern knowledge as inescapably "disenchanted" and fragmented (Bolz). It would be worth establishing precisely how the novels of the period relate to the same issue.

---

[2] For a stimulating brief account of the heritage of the Werkbund in contemporary aesthetic awareness, see Albrecht Wellmer, "Art and Industrial Production: The Dialectics of Modernism and Postmodernism", in *The Persistence of Modernity* (Cambridge: Polity, 1991), 95–112.

In his novel *Doktor Faustus*, which he was writing as the Second World War came to an end, Thomas Mann strongly suggested that a whole national culture was being destroyed along with the National Socialist regime. Through the figure of his humanist narrator he voiced the fear that a valuable cultural heritage had been dragged into war and ignominy, and through the fate of his composer protagonist he hinted that the historical development of that cultural heritage made it somehow complicit in its own demise. Such thinking has been taken seriously in a recent contribution to the study of Weimar literature, which seeks to map out a pattern of development and decline in the literary culture of the period around the two world wars (Lindner). According to this line of reasoning, there appears to be an inherent impetus in German cultural thinking which runs its course in the early twentieth century, and which can be distinguished from the political consequences of the period of National Socialist rule and of defeat in the Second World War, which obviously have a profound effect on cultural activity in the German-speaking world after 1945. That impetus begins with a utopian and vitalistic revolt against social constraints before the First World War, experiences progressive disillusionment and introversion in the wake of the revolutionary upheavals of 1918–19 and under the impact of the Great Depression, and peters out in ontological introspection around 1960. Lindner's arguments are couched in terms which make it possible to interpret this development as the transmission of cultural assumptions from one generation to another and the modification of those assumptions in the light of social experience. The effect of his thesis is to direct our attention to the precise manner in which the inherited cultural thinking of the early twentieth century was transmitted, questioned, challenged, and modified by successive generations of writers in that period up to 1960, and to the question of what was significantly different about the cultural orientation of writers who came after them.

The role of cultural institutions, the social perspectives of writers (in terms of generation, class, and gender), and the long-term fate of modernist culture: these are the lines of inquiry which I believe are most likely to contribute further to our understanding of the significance of that explosive phase in German history which we think of as Weimar culture.

Bibliography

A. PRIMARY LITERATURE FROM THE PERIOD OF THE WEIMAR REPUBLIC

BECHER, JOHANNES R., *Gesammelte Werke*, Berlin: Aufbau, 1966 ff.

BENJAMIN, WALTER, *Gesammelte Schriften*, Frankfurt: Suhrkamp, 1974 ff.

BENN, GOTTFRIED, *Gesammelte Werke*, Wiesbaden: Limes, 1959 ff.

—— *Gedichte in der Fassung der Erstdrucke*, Frankfurt: Fischer, 1982.

BEUMELBURG, WERNER, *Gruppe Bosemüller*, Oldenburg: Gerhard Stalling, 1930.

BINDING, RUDOLF, *Gesammelte Werke*, vol. iii: *Aus dem Krieg*, Potsdam: Rütten und Loening, 1937 [1925].

BRECHT, BERTOLT, *Werke: Große kommentierte Berliner und Frankfurter Ausgabe*, Berlin: Aufbau/Frankfurt: Suhrkamp, 1988 ff.

BRENTANO, BERNARD VON, *Wo in Europa ist Berlin? Bilder aus den zwanziger Jahren*, Frankfurt: Suhrkamp, 1987.

BROCH, HERMANN, *Kommentierte Werkausgabe*, Frankfurt: Suhrkamp, 1976 ff.

BRONNEN, ARNOLT, *Werke*, Klagenfurt: Ritter, 1989.

—— *Sabotage der Jugend: Kleine Arbeiten 1922–1934*, Innsbruck: Institut für Germanistik, 1989.

CAROSSA, HANS, *Rumänisches Tagebuch*, Leipzig: Insel Verlag, 1924.

DIESEL, EUGEN, *Der Weg durch den Wirrsal*, Stuttgart: Cotta, 1926.

DÖBLIN, ALFRED, *Berge Meere und Giganten*, Olten: Walter-Verlag 1977 [1924].

—— *Berlin Alexanderplatz*, Olten: Walter-Verlag 1961 [1929].

—— *Giganten*, Berlin: S. Fischer, 1932.

—— *Der deutsche Maskenball: Wissen und Verändern!*, Olten: Walter-Verlag, 1972.

—— *Schriften zu Ästhetik, Poetik und Literatur*, Olten: Walter-Verlag, 1989.

—— *Schriften zu Leben und Werk*, Olten: Walter-Verlag, 1986.

FALLADA, HANS, *Bauern, Bonzen und Bomben*, Reinbek: Rowohlt, 1964 [1931].

—— *Kleiner Mann—was nun?*, Berlin: Rowohlt, 1932.

FEUCHTWANGER, LION, *Jud Süß*, Munich: Drei Masken-Verlag, 1925.

—— *Erfolg*, Berlin: Gustav Kiepenheuer, 1930.

FLEIßER, MARIELUISE, *Gesammelte Werke*, Frankfurt: Suhrkamp, 1972.

FRANK, LEONHARD, *Das Ochsenfurter Männerquartett*, Leipzig: Insel Verlag, 1927.

——*Von drei Millionen drei*, Berlin: S. Fischer, 1932.

GLAESER, ERNST, *Jahrgang 1902*, Berlin: Gustav Kiepenheuer, 1928.

——(ed.), *Fazit*, Kronberg: Scriptor, 1977 [1929].

GRAF, OSKAR MARIA, *Ausgewählte Werke*, Munich: Süddeutscher Verlag, 1975 ff.

GURK, PAUL, *Berlin*, Berlin: Agora Verlag, 1980 [1934].

HARBOU, THEA VON, *Metropolis*, Frankfurt: Ullstein, 1978.

HAUSER, HEINRICH, *Friede mit Maschinen*, Leipzig: Reclam, 1928.

——*Schwarzes Revier*, Berlin: S. Fischer, 1930.

HERRMANN-NEIßE, MAX, *Gesammelte Werke*, Frankfurt: Zweitausendeins, 1987.

HORVÁTH, ÖDÖN VON, *Gesammelte Werke*, Frankfurt: Suhrkamp, 1970.

IHERING, HERBERT, *Der Kampf ums Theater und andere Streitschriften 1918 bis 1933*, Berlin: Henschelverlag, 1974.

——*Theater in Aktion: Kritiken aus drei Jahrzehnten 1913 bis 1933*, Berlin: Henschelverlag, 1986.

JUNG, FRANZ, *Die Eroberung der Maschinen*, Hamburg: Nautilus, 1989 [1923].

JÜNGER, ERNST, *In Stahlgewittern*, Berlin: E. S. Mittler & Sohn, 1920.

——*Der Kampf als inneres Erlebnis*, Berlin: E. S. Mittler & Sohn, 1922.

——*Feuer und Blut*, Magdeburg: Frundsberg-Verlag, 1925.

——*Das Wäldchen 125*, Berlin: E. S. Mittler & Sohn, 1925.

——*Der Arbeiter*, Hamburg: Hanseatische Verlagsanstalt, 1932.

——*Werke*, Stuttgart: Klett, 1960 ff.

KAISER, GEORG, *Werke*, Frankfurt: Propyläen Verlag, 1971 ff.

KÄSTNER, ERICH, *Gesammelte Schriften für Erwachsene*, Munich: Droemer Knaur, 1969.

KELLERMANN, BERNHARD, *Der Tunnel*, Berlin: S. Fischer, 1913.

KESSEL, MARTIN, *Herrn Brechers Fiasko*, Stuttgart: Deutsche Verlags-Anstalt, 1932.

KESTEN, HERMANN, *Josef sucht die Freiheit*, Berlin: Gustav Kiepenheuer, 1927.

——*Ein ausschweifender Mensch*, Berlin: Gustav Kiepenheuer, 1929.

——*Glückliche Menschen*, Berlin: Gustav Kiepenheuer, 1931.

——*Der Scharlatan*, Berlin: Gustav Kiepenheuer, 1932.

——(ed.), *24 neue deutsche Erzähler*, Berlin: Gustav Kiepenheuer, 1930.

KEUN, IRMGARD, *Gilgi—eine von uns*, Düsseldorf: Claassen, 1979 [1931].

——*Das kunstseidene Mädchen*, Düsseldorf: Claassen, 1979 [1932].

KINDERMANN, HEINZ, *Das literarische Antlitz der Zeit*, Halle: Max Niemeyer 1930.

——"Vom Wesen der 'Neuen Sachlichkeit'", *Jahrbuch des freien deutschen Hochstifts* (1930), 354–86.

KISCH, EGON ERWIN, *Gesammelte Werke*, vol. v (*Der rasende Reporter; Hetzjagd durch die Zeit; Wagnisse in aller Welt; Kriminalistisches Reisebuch*), Berlin: Aufbau, 1983.

KLABUND [ALFRED HENSCHKE], *Gesammelte Gedichte*, Vienna: Phaidon-Verlag, 1930.

KOEPPEN, EDLEF, *Heeresbericht*, Berlin: Horen-Verlag, 1930.

KRACAUER, SIEGFRIED, *Das Ornament der Masse*, Frankfurt: Suhrkamp, 1963.

——*Schriften*, Frankfurt: Suhrkamp, 1971 ff.

KRAUS, KARL, *Die letzten Tage der Menschheit*, Vienna: Verlag 'Die Fackel', 1922.

KRELL, MAX (ed.), *Das deutsche Theater der Gegenwart*, Munich: Rösl & Co., 1923.

KÜPPER, HANNES and VALLENTIN, MAXIM, *Die Sache ist die*, Potsdam: Gustav Kiepenheuer, 1923.

LEHMANN, WILHELM, *Sämtliche Werke*, Gütersloh: Sigbert Mohn, 1962.

LOERKE, OSKAR, *Gedichte und Prosa*, 2 vols., Frankfurt: Suhrkamp, 1958.

LUKÁCS, GEORG, *Die Theorie des Romans*, Darmstadt: Luchterhand, 1971 [1920].

——*The Theory of the Novel*, London: Merlin Press, 1971.

MANN, HEINRICH, *Gesammelte Werke*, Berlin: Aufbau, 1974 ff.

——*Essays*, Berlin: Aufbau, 1960.

——*Sieben Jahre*, Berlin: Paul Zsolnay, 1929.

MANN, KLAUS and FEHSE, WILLI R. (eds.), *Anthologie jüngster Lyrik*, Hamburg: Gebr. Enoch, 1927.

MANN, THOMAS, *Gesammelte Werke*, Frankfurt: S. Fischer, 1974.

MEHRING, WALTER, *Chronik der Lustbarkeiten*, Düsseldorf: Claassen, 1981.

MUSIL, ROBERT, *Gesammelte Werke*, Reinbek: Rowohlt, 1978.

——*Briefe*, Reinbek: Rowohlt, 1981.

OTTWALT, ERNST, *Denn sie wissen, was sie tun*, Berlin: Klaus Guhl, 1978 [1931].

PINTHUS, KURT (ed.), *Menschheitsdämmerung*, Hamburg: Rowohlt, 1959 [1920].

PISCATOR, ERWIN, *Das politische Theater*, Berlin: Adalbert Schütz, 1929 [English version: *The Political Theatre*, trans. Hugh Rorrison, London: Eyre Methuen 1980].

——*Schriften*, 2 vols., Berlin: Henschelverlag, 1968.

PLIEVIER, THEODOR, *Des Kaisers Kulis*, Berlin: Malik, 1929.

——*Der Kaiser ging, die Generäle blieben*, Hamburg: Konkret Literatur Verlag, 1979 [1932].

REGER, ERIK, *Union der festen Hand*, Berlin: Rowohlt, 1931.

——*Kleine Schriften*, 2 vols., Berlin: Argon, 1993.

REMARQUE, ERICH MARIA, *Im Westen nichts Neues*, Cologne: Kiepenheuer & Witsch, 1959 [1929].

RENN, LUDWIG, *Krieg*, Frankfurt: Societäts-Verlag, 1928.

RILKE, RAINER MARIA, *Sämtliche Werke*, Frankfurt: Insel Verlag, 1955 ff.

ROTH, JOSEPH, *Werke*, Cologne: Kiepenheuer & Witsch, 1989 ff.

SCHARRER, ADAM, *Vaterlandslose Gesellen*, Vienna: Agis-Verlag, 1930.

SCHAUWECKER, FRANZ, *Aufbruch der Nation*, Berlin: Frundsberg-Verlag, 1929.

SCHICKELE, RENÉ, *Werke*, Cologne: Kiepenheuer & Witsch, 1959.

SEGHERS, ANNA, *Der Kopflohn*, Amsterdam: Querido, 1933.

SPENGLER, OSWALD, *Der Untergang des Abendlandes*, Munich: Beck, 1981 [1918/1923].

——*Der Mensch und die Technik: Beitrag zu einer Philosophie des Lebens*, Munich: Beck, 1971 [1931].

STERNHEIM, CARL, *Die Schule von Uznach oder Neue Sachlichkeit*, Berlin: Paul Zsolnay, 1926.

TERGIT, GABRIELE, *Käsebier erobert den Kurfürstendamm*, Berlin: Rowohlt, 1931.

TOLLER, ERNST, *Gesammelte Werke*, Munich: Hanser, 1978.

TUCHOLSKY, KURT, *Gesammelte Werke*, Reinbek: Rowohlt, 1975.

UTITZ, EMIL, *Die Überwindung des Expressionismus*, Stuttgart: Ferdinand Enke, 1927.

VON DER VRING, GEORG, *Soldat Suhren*, Berlin: J. M. Spaeth, 1927.

WEHNER, JOSEF MAGNUS, *Sieben vor Verdun*, Munich: Georg Müller, 1930.

WERFEL, FRANZ, *Barbara oder Die Frömmigkeit*, Berlin: Paul Zsolnay, 1929.

WOLF, FRIEDRICH, *Gesammelte Werke*, Berlin: Aufbau, 1960 ff.

ZÖBERLEIN, HANS, *Der Glaube an Deutschland*, Munich: Zentralverlag der NSDAP, 1930.

ZUCKMAYER, CARL, *Gesammelte Werke*, Frankfurt: S. Fischer, 1948 ff.

ZWEIG, ARNOLD, *Der Streit um den Sergeanten Grischa*, Potsdam: Gustav Kiepenheuer, 1927.

ZWEIG, ARNOLD, *Junge Frau von 1914*, Berlin: Gustav Kiepenheuer, 1931.

——*De Vriendt kehrt heim*, Berlin: Gustav Kiepenheuer, 1932.

——*Erziehung vor Verdun*, Amsterdam: Querido, 1935.

B. SECONDARY LITERATURE

ALKER, E. (1977), *Profile und Gestalten der deutschen Literatur nach 1914*, Stuttgart: Kröner.

ALT, P. A. (1985), *Ironie und Krise: Ironisches Erzählen als Form ästhetischer Wahrnehmung in Thomas Manns "Der Zauberberg" und Robert Musils "Der Mann ohne Eigenschaften"*, Frankfurt: Peter Lang.

ALTER, R. (1980), "Alfred Döblin's 'Republicanism' 1918–1933", *German Life and Letters*, 35, 47–57.

ANZ, T. and STARK, M. (eds.) (1982), *Expressionismus: Manifeste und Dokumente zur deutschen Literatur 1910–1920*, Stuttgart: Metzler.

ARNOLD, A. (1966), *Die Literatur des Expressionismus: Sprachliche und thematische Quellen*, Stuttgart: Kohlhammer.

ARNOLD, H. L. (ed.) (1982), *Joseph Roth*, Munich: Text und Kritik.

BALME, C. B. (1985), *The Reformation of Comedy: Genre Critique in the Comedies of Ödön von Horváth* (Otago German Studies, 3), Dunedin: University of Otago.

BANCE, A. F. (ed.) (1982), *Weimar Germany: Writers and Politics*, Edinburgh: Scottish Academic Press.

BARNOUW, D. (1985), "Zeitbürtige Eigenschaften: Musils Rathenaukritik" in J. and J. Strutz (eds.), *Musil-Studien* 13 (*Robert Musil—Theater, Bildung, Kritik*), Munich: Fink, 166–84.

——(1988), *Weimar Intellectuals and the Threat of Modernity*, Bloomington: Indiana University Press.

BAUER, G. (1987), *Gefangenschaft und Lebenslust: Oskar Maria Graf in seiner Zeit*, Munich: Süddeutscher Verlag.

BAUR, U. and CASTEX, E. (eds.) (1980), *Robert Musil: Untersuchungen*, Königstein: Athenäum.

BAYERDÖRFER, H.-P. (1983), "Weimarer Republik", in W. Hinderer (ed.), *Geschichte der deutschen Lyrik vom Mittelalter bis zur Gegenwart*, Stuttgart: Reclam, 439–76.

BECKER, S. and WEISS, C. (eds.) (1995), *Neue Sachlichkeit im Roman: Neue Interpretationen zum Roman der Weimarer Republik*, Stuttgart: Metzler.

BENSON, T. O. (1987), *Raoul Hausmann and Berlin Dada*, Ann Arbor: UMI Research Press.

BERG, J. (ed.) (1981), *Sozialgeschichte der deutschen Literatur von 1918 bis zur Gegenwart*, Frankfurt: Fischer.

BERG, P. (1963), *Deutschland und Amerika 1918–1929: Über das deutsche Amerikabild der zwanziger Jahre* (Historische Studien, 385), Lübeck/Hamburg: Matthiesen.

BERGMANN, K. (1970), *Agrarromantik und Großstadtfeindschaft*, Meisenheim am Glan: Hain.

BERLE, W. (1983), *Heinrich Mann und die Weimarer Republik: Zur Entwicklung eines politischen Schriftstellers in Deutschland*, Bonn: Bouvier.

BERTONATI, E. (1974), *Die Neue Sachlichkeit*, Munich: Schuler.

BESSEL, R. (1988), "The Great War in German Memory: The Soldiers of the First World War, Demobilization, and Weimar Political Culture", *German History*, 6/1, 20–34.

——(1993), *Germany after the First World War*, Oxford: Clarendon Press.

BEST, O. F. (ed.) (1976), *Theorie des Expressionismus*, Stuttgart: Reclam.

BIENERT, M. (1992), *Die eingebildete Metropole: Berlin im Feuilleton der Weimarer Republik*, Stuttgart: Metzler.

BITHELL, J. (1959), *Modern German Literature 1880–1950*, London: Methuen.

BLUDAU, B., HEFTRICH, E., and KOOPMANN, H. (eds.) (1977), *Thomas Mann (1875–1975). Vorträge in Munich—Zürich—Lübeck*, Frankfurt: Fischer.

BOBERG, J., FICHTER, T., and GILLEN, E. (eds.) (1986), *Die Metropole: Industriekultur in Berlin im 20. Jahrhundert*, Munich: Beck.

BÖHME, H. (1974), *Anomie und Entfremdung: Literatursoziologische Untersuchung zu den Essays Robert Musils und seinem Roman "Der Mann ohne Eigenschaften"*, Kronberg: Scriptor.

BOHRER, K. H. (1978), *Die Ästhetik des Schreckens: Die pessimistische Romantik und Ernst Jüngers Frühwerk*, Munich: Hanser.

BOLZ, N. W. (1989), *Auszug aus der entzauberten Welt*, Munich: Fink.

BORMANN, A. VON (1974), "Vom Traum zur Tat: Über völkische Literatur", in W. Rothe (ed.), *Die deutsche Literatur der Weimarer Republik*, Stuttgart: Reclam, 304–33.

——(1978), "Weimarer Republik", in W. Hinderer (ed.), *Geschichte der politischen Lyrik in Deutschland*, Stuttgart: Reclam, 261–90.

BORNEBUSCH, H. (1985), *Gegen-Erinnerung: eine formsemantische Analyse des demokratischen Kriegsromans der Weimarer Republik*, Frankfurt: Peter Lang.

BRACHER, K. D. (1955), *Die Auflösung der Weimarer Republik*, Villingen: Ring-Verlag.

BRADY, P. V. (1972), "*Aus einem Lesebuch für Städtebewohner*: On a Brecht Essay in Obliqueness", *German Life & Letters* 26, 160–72.

BRAUNECK, M. (1973), *Die Rote Fahne: Kritik, Theorie, Feuilleton 1918–1933*, Munich: Fink.

——(1982), *Theater im 20. Jahrhundert, Programmschriften, Stilperioden, Reformmodelle*, Reinbek: Rowohlt.

——(1988), *Klassiker der Schauspielregie, Positionen und Kommentare zum Theater im 20. Jahrhundert*, Reinbek: Rowohlt.

BRINKMANN, R. (1980), *Expressionismus: Internationale Forschung zu einem internationalen Phänomen*, Stuttgart: Metzler.

BROKOPH-MAUCH, G. (ed.) (1983), *Beiträge zur Musil-Kritik*, Berne: Peter Lang.

BRONSEN, D. (1974), *Joseph Roth: Eine Biographie*, Cologne: Kiepenheuer & Witsch.

——(ed.) (1975), *Joseph Roth und die Tradition*, Darmstadt: Agora.

BROOKER, P. (1988), *Bertolt Brecht: Dialectics, Poetry, Politics*, London: Croom Helm.

BULLIVANT, K. (ed.) (1977), *Culture and Society in the Weimar Republic*, Manchester: Manchester University Press.

CASPAR, G. (1988), *Fallada-Studien*, Berlin: Aufbau.

CEPL-KAUFMANN, G. (1990), "Hannes Küpper—Der Zeittyp", in G. Cepl-Kaufmann et al., *Stets wird die Wahrheit hadern mit dem Schönen: Festschrift für Manfred Windfuhr zum 60. Geburtstag*, Cologne: Böhlau, 395–420.

CHAMBERS, H. (ed.) (1991), *Co-existent Contradictions: Joseph Roth in Retrospect*, Riverside, Calif.: Ariadne Press.

CORINO, K. (1988), *Robert Musil: Leben und Werk in Bildern und Texten*, Reinbek: Rowohlt.

DANIELS, K. (1969), "Expressionismus und Technik", in H. Segeberg (ed.), *Technik in der Literatur*, 351–86 [orig. in W. Rothe (ed.), *Expressionismus als Literatur. Gesammelte Studien*, Berne: Francke, 171–93].

DAVIES, C. W. (1977), *Theatre for the People: The story of the Volksbühne*, Manchester: Manchester University Press.

DENKLER, H. (1967), "Die Literaturtheorie der zwanziger Jahre: Zum Selbstverständnis des literarischen Nachexpressionismus", *Monatshefte*, 4, 305–19.

——(1968), "Sache und Stil: Die Theorie der 'Neuen Sachlichkeit' und ihre Auswirkungen auf Kunst und Dichtung", *Wirkendes Wort*, 3, 167–85.

DENLINGER, A. (1977), *Alfred Döblins 'Berge Meere und Giganten': Epos und Ideologie*, Amsterdam: B. R. Grüner.

Deutsche Akademie der Künste zu Berlin (1967), *Zur Tradition der deutschen sozialistischen Literatur: Eine Auswahl von Dokumenten*, Berlin (East): Aufbau.

DONAT, H. and HOLL, K. (eds.) (1983), *Die Friedensbewegung: Organisierter Pazifismus in Deutschland, Österreich und der Schweiz*, Düsseldorf: Econ Taschenbuch Verlag.

DOVE, R. (1990), *He Was a German: A Biography of Ernst Toller*, London: Libris.

DURZAK, M. (1970a), "Der moderne Roman: Bemerkungen zu Georg Lukács' *Theorie des Romans*", *Basis: Jahrbuch für deutsche Gegenwartsliteratur*, 1, 26–48.

——(1970b), "Flake und Döblin: Ein Kapitel in der Geschichte des polyhistorischen Romans", *Germanisch-romanische Monatshefte*, 20/3, 286–305.

DUYTSCHAEVER, J. (1975), "Joyce—Dos Passos—Döblin: Einfluß oder Analogie?" in M. Prangel (ed.), *Materialien zu Alfred Döblin: "Berlin Alexanderplatz"*, Frankfurt: Suhrkamp, 136–49.

EKSTEINS, M. (1989), *Rites of Spring: The Great War and the Birth of the Modern Age*, London: Bantam.

ERMEN, R. (1977), "Amerikanismus und Exotismus—Flucht aus der Realität", in D. Ruckhaberle et al. (eds.), *Weimarer Republik*, 825–34.

FÄHNDERS, W. and RECTOR, M. (eds.) (1974a), *Literatur im Klassenkampf: Zur proletarisch-revolutionären Literaturtheorie 1919–1923*, Frankfurt: Fischer.

——(1974b), *Linksradikalismus und Literatur: Untersuchungen zur Geschichte der sozialistischen Literatur in der Weimarer Republik*, Reinbek: Rowohlt.

FERBER, C. (ed.) (1981), *Der Querschnitt*, Berlin: Ullstein.

FETTING, H. (ed.) (1987), *Von der Freien Bühne zum Politischen Theater*, Leipzig: Reclam.

FEUCHTWANGER, E. J. (1994), *From Weimar to Hitler. Germany, 1918–1933*, London: Macmillan.

FISHER, P. S. (1991), *Fantasy and Politics: Visions of the Future in the Weimar Republic*, Madison: University of Wisconsin Press.

FREESE, W. (1980), *Robert Musil und seine Epoche*, Munich: Fink.

FRÜHWALD, W. and SPALEK, J. M. (eds.) (1979), *Der Fall Toller: Kommentar und Materialien*, Munich: Hanser.

FUSSELL, P. (1975), *The Great War and Modern Memory*, New York: Oxford University Press.

GALLAS, H. (1971), *Marxistische Literaturtheorie: Kontroversen im Bund proletarisch-revolutionärer Schriftsteller*, Neuwied: Luchterhand.

GAY, P. (1974), *Weimar Culture: The Outsider as Insider*, Harmondsworth: Penguin.

GEISLER, M. (1982), *Die literarische Reportage in Deutschland: Möglichkeiten und Grenzen eines operativen Genres*, Königstein: Scriptor.

GLASER, H. A. (1983), *Deutsche Literatur: Eine Sozialgeschichte*, vol. ix: *Weimarer Republik—Drittes Reich: Avantgardismus, Parteilichkeit, Exil 1918–1945*, Reinbek: Rowohlt.

GLASS, D., RÖSLER, D., and WHITE, J. J. (eds.) (1989), *Berlin: Literary Images of a City*, Berlin: Erich Schmidt.

GNETTNER, I. (1993), *Vorkriegszeit im Roman einer Nachkriegszeit*, Würzburg: Königshausen & Neumann.

GOLLBACH, M. (1978), *Die Wiederkehr des Weltkrieges in der Literatur: Zu den Frontromanen der späten zwanziger Jahre*, Kronberg: Scriptor.

GRIMM, R. (1961), "Nichts—aber darüber Glasur", in H. O. Burger and R. Grimm, *Evokation und Montage*, Göttingen: Sachse & Pohl, 28–69.

——(ed.) (1968), *Deutsche Romantheorien*, Frankfurt: Athenäum/Fischer.

——and HERMAND, J. (eds.) (1970), *Die sogenannten Zwanziger Jahre*, Bad Homburg: Gehlen.

GROSSKLAUS, G. and LÄMMERT, E. (eds.) (1989), *Literatur in einer industriellen Kultur*, Stuttgart: J. G. Cotta.

GUTTSMANN, W. L. (1990), *Workers' Culture in Weimar Germany: Between Tradition and Government*, New York: Berg.

HAMBURGER, M. (1969), *The Truth of Poetry: Tensions in Modern Poetry from Baudelaire to the 1960s*, London: Weidenfeld & Nicolson.

HANNOVER, H. and HANNOVER-DRÜCK, E. (1966), *Politische Justiz 1918–1933*, Frankfurt: Lamuv.

HASSLER-RÜTTI, R. (1990), *Wirklichkeit und Leben in Robert Musils "Der Mann ohne Eigenschaften"*, Berne: Peter Lang.

HEIMANN, B. (1976), "Die Konvergenz der Einzelgänger: Literatur als Integration des problematischen Individuums in die Volksgemeinschaft: Hermann Stehr—Emil Strauß—Erwin Guido Kolbenheyer", in H. Denkler and K. Prümm (eds.), *Die deutsche Literatur im Dritten Reich*, Stuttgart: Reclam, 118–37.

HEIZMANN, J. (1990), *Joseph Roth und die Ästhetik der Neuen Sachlichkeit*, Heidelberg: Mattes.

HELLER, E. (1981), *Thomas Mann: The Ironic German*, Cambridge: Cambridge University Press [1958].

HENZE, V. (1988), *Jüdischer Kulturpessimismus und das Bild des alten*

Österreich im Werk Stefan Zweigs und Joseph Roths, Heidelberg: Carl Winter.

HERF, J. (1984), *Reactionary Modernism: Technology, Culture and Politics in Weimar and the Third Reich*, Cambridge: Cambridge University Press.

HERMAND, J. and TROMMLER, F. (1978), *Die Kultur der Weimarer Republik*, Munich: Nymphenburger Verlagshandlung.

HIRDINA, K. (1981), *Pathos der Sachlichkeit: Funktionalismus und Fortschritt ästhetischer Kultur*, Munich: Dietz.

HITCHCOCK, H. R. (1970), *Modern Architecture: Romanticism and Reintegration*, New York: Hacker [1929].

HOLDERNESS, G. (1992), *The Politics of Theatre and Drama*, London: Macmillan.

HOLL, K. and WETTE, W. (eds.) (1981), *Pazifismus in der Weimarer Republik*, Paderborn: Schöningh.

HONNEF-BECKER, I. (1991), *"Ulrich lächelte". Techniken der Relativierung in Robert Musils Roman "Der Mann ohne Eigenschaften"*, Frankfurt: Peter Lang.

HORTLEDER, G., (1970), *Das Gesellschaftsbild des Ingenieurs: Zum politischen Verhalten der technischen Intelligenz in Deutschland*, Frankfurt: Suhrkamp.

HOWIND, A. (1988), "Ein Antikriegsroman als Bestseller: Die Vermarktung von *Im Westen nichts Neues* 1928–1930", in T. Westphalen (ed.), *Erich Maria Remarque 1898–1970*, Bramsche: Rasch, 55–64.

HUBER, L. (ed.) (1989), *Franz Werfel: An Austrian Writer Revisited*, Oxford: Berg.

HÜPPAUF, B. (ed.) (1983), *Expressionismus und Kulturkrise*, Heidelberg: Winter.

——(1984), *Ansichten vom Krieg*, Königstein: Athenäum.

INNES, C. D. (1972), *Erwin Piscator's Political Theatre: The development of Modern German Drama*, Cambridge: Cambridge University Press.

JÄGER, C. and SCHÜTZ, E. (1994), *Glänzender Asphalt: Berlin im Feuilleton der Weimarer Republik*, Berlin: Fannei & Walz.

JENS, I. (1971), *Dichter zwischen rechts und links*, Munich: Piper.

JUST, K. G. (1973), *Von der Gründerzeit bis zur Gegenwart*, Berne: Francke.

KAES, A. (ed.) (1983), *Weimarer Republik: Manifeste und Dokumente zur deutschen Literatur 1918–1933*, Stuttgart: Metzler.

KAES, A., JAY, M., and DIMENDBERG, E. (eds.) (1994), *The Weimar Republic Sourcebook*, Berkeley and Los Angeles: University of California Press.

KELLER, O. (1980), *Döblins Montageroman als Epos der Moderne*, Munich: Fink.

KESSLER, M. and HACKERT, F. (eds.) (1990), *Joseph Roth: Interpretation—Rezeption—Kritik*, Tübingen: Stauffenburg.

——and LÜTZELER, P. M. (eds.) (1987), *Hermann Broch: Das dichterische Werk. Neue Interpretationen*, Tübingen: Stauffenburg.

KIESEL, H. (1981), *Erich Kästner*, Nordlingen: C. H. Beck.

KIRSCH, K. (1987), *Die Weißenhofsiedlung: Werkbund-Ausstellung "Die Wohnung"—Stuttgart 1927*, Stuttgart: Deutsche Verlags-Anstalt.

KLEIN, A. (ed.) (1966), *Aktionen, Bekenntnisse, Perspektiven: Berichte und Dokumente vom Kampf um die Freiheit des literarischen Schaffens in der Weimarer Republik*, Berlin (East): Aufbau.

KNIESCHE, T. W., and BROCKMANN, S. (eds.) (1994), *Dancing on the Volcano: Essays on the Culture of the Weimar Republic*, Columbia, SC: Camden House.

KNOBLOCH, H. J. (1975), *Das Ende des Expressionismus: Von der Tragödie zur Komödie*, Berne: Herbert Lang.

KNOPF, J. (1980), *Brecht-Handbuch*, 2 vols., Stuttgart: Metzler.

KOEBNER, T. (ed.) (1982), *Weimars Ende: Prognosen und Diagnosen in der deutschen Literatur und politischen Publizistik 1930–1933*, Frankfurt: Suhrkamp.

KÖHN, L. (1974), "Überwindung des Historismus: Zu Problemen einer Geschichte der deutschen Literatur zwischen 1918 und 1933", *Deutsche Vierteljahrsschrift*, 48, 704–66 and 49, 95–165.

KOLINSKY, E. (1970), *Engagierter Expressionismus: Politik und Literatur zwischen Weltkrieg und Weimarer Republik*, Stuttgart: Metzler.

KÖNIG, H. (1972), *Heinrich Mann: Dichter und Moralist*, Tübingen: Niemeyer.

KOOPMANN, H. and SCHNEIDER, P.-P. M. (eds.) (1983), *Heinrich Mann: Sein Werk in der Weimarer Republik*, Frankfurt: Klostermann.

KORT, W. (1970), *Alfred Döblin: Das Bild des Menschen in seinen Romanen*, Bonn: Bouvier.

KRABIEL, K.-D. (1993), *Brechts Lehrstücke: Entstehung und Entwicklung eines Spieltyps*, Stuttgart: Metzler.

KREUTZER, L. (1970), *Alfred Döblin: Sein Werk bis 1933*, Stuttgart: Kohlhammer.

KREUZER, H. (1971), "Zur Periodisierung der modernen deutschen Literatur", *Basis: Jahrbuch für deutsche Gegenwartsliteratur*, 2, 7–32.

KRISCHKE, T. (1980), *Ödön von Horváth: Kind seiner Zeit*, Munich: Wilhelm Heyne.

LAMPING, D. (1989), *Das lyrische Gedicht: Definitionen zu Theorie und Geschichte der Gattung*, Göttingen: Vandenhoeck & Ruprecht.

——(1991), *Moderne Lyrik: Eine Einführung*, Göttingen: Vandenhoeck & Ruprecht.

LANE, B. M. (1968), *Architecture and Politics in Germany, 1918–1945*, Cambridge, Mass.: Harvard University Press.

LAQUEUR, W. (1976), *Weimar: A Cultural History 1918–1933*, London: Weidenfeld & Nicolson.

LAST, R. W. (1974), *Erich Kästner*, London: Oswald Wolff.

LEED, E. (1979), *No Man's Land: Combat and Identity in World War I*, Cambridge: Cambridge University Press.

LETHEN, H. (1970), *Neue Sachlichkeit 1924–1933. Studien zur Literatur des "Weißen Sozialismus"*, Stuttgart: Metzler.

——(1983), "Neue Sachlichkeit", in H. A. Glaser (ed.), *Deutsche Literatur: Eine Sozialgeschichte*, vol. ix: *Weimarer Republik— Drittes Reich: Avantgardismus, Parteilichkeit, Exil 1918–1945*, Reinbek: Rowohlt, 168–79.

——(1989), "Freiheit von Angst: Über einen entlastenden Aspekt der Technik-Moden in den Jahrzehnten der historischen Avantgarde 1910–1930", in G. Großklaus and E. Lämmert (eds.), *Literatur in einer industriellen Kultur*, Stuttgart: J. G. Cotta, 72–98.

——(1990), "Kältemaschinen der Intelligenz: Attitüden der Sachlichkeit", in E. Wichner and H. Wiesner (eds.), *Industriegebiet der Intelligenz*, 119–53.

——(1994), *Verhaltenslehren der Kälte: Lebensversuche zwischen den Kriegen*, Frankfurt: Suhrkamp.

LINDER, A. P. (1996), *Princes of the Trenches: Narrating the German Experience of the First World War*, Columbia, SC: Camden House.

LINDNER, M. (1994), *Leben in der Krise: Zeitromane der neuen Sachlichkeit und die intellektuelle Mentalität der klassischen Moderne*, Stuttgart: Metzler.

LOHNER, E. (1961), *Passion und Intellekt: Die Lyrik Gottfried Benns*, Neuwied: Luchterhand.

LUFT, D. S. (1980), *Robert Musil and the Crisis of European Culture 1880–1942*, Berkeley and Los Angeles: University of California Press.

LÜTZELER, P. M. (1973), *Hermann Broch—Ethik und Politik: Studien zum Frühwerk und zur Romantrilogie "Die Schlafwandler"*, Munich: Winkler.

——(1980), "Lukacs' *Theorie des Romans* und Brochs *Schlafwandler*", in R. Thieberger (ed.), *Hermann Broch und seine Zeit*, 47–59.

——(ed.) (1983), *Deutsche Romane des 20. Jahrhunderts: Neue Interpretationen*, Königstein: Athenäum.

LÜTZELER, P. M. (1986*a*), *Zeitgeschichte in Geschichten der Zeit*, Bonn: Bouvier.

—— (ed.) (1986*b*), *Hermann Broch*, Frankfurt: Suhrkamp.

McGOWAN, M. (1987), *Marieluise Fleißer*, Munich: Beck.

MAGRIS, C. (1966), *Der habsburgische Mythos*, Salzburg: Otto Müller.

MANDELKOW, K. R. (1966), "Orpheus und Maschine", in H. Segeberg (ed.), *Technik in der Literatur*, 387–410 [orig. in *Euphorion*, 61, 104–18].

MARCUS-TAR, J. (1982), *Thomas Mann und Georg Lukács: Beziehungen, Einfluß und "repräsentative Gegensätzlichkeit"*, Cologne: Böhlau.

MAYER, D. (1972), *Alfred Döblins "Wallenstein"*, Munich: Fink.

—— (1981), *Linksbürgerliches Denken: Untersuchungen zur Kunsttheorie, Gesellschaftsauffassung und Kulturpolitik in der Weimarer Republik (1919–1924)*, Munich: Fink.

—— (1984), *Die Epoche der Weimarer Republik* (= V. Zmegac (ed.), *Geschichte der deutschen Literatur vom 18. Jahrhundert bis zur Gegenwart*, vol. iii/1) Königstein: Athenäum.

MECKLENBURG, N. (1982), *Erzählte Provinz*, Königstein: Athenäum.

MENGES, K. (1970), *Kritische Studien zur Wertphilosophie Hermann Brochs*, Tübingen: Niemeyer.

MENNEMEIER, F. N. (1982), *Bertolt Brechts Lyrik: Aspekte Tendenzen*, Düsseldorf: Bagel.

MEYER, J. (1985), *Berlin—Provinz: Literarische Kontroversen um 1930 (Marbacher Magazin, 35)*, Marbach: Deutsche Schillergesellschaft.

MIDGLEY, D. (1980), *Arnold Zweig, Zu Werk und Wandlung 1927–1948*, Königstein: Athenäum.

—— (1981), "Entfremdete Erzählhaltung: Zur Funktion des fiktiven Erzählers in Hermann Brochs *Schlafwandler*-Trilogie", *Zeitschrift für deutsche Philologie*, 100, 204–19.

—— (1983), "Ödön von Horváth: The Strategies of Audience Enticement", *Oxford German Studies*, 14, 125–42.

—— (1988), "Aetiology of the Banal, Reflections on the textual singularities of *Der ewige Speißer*", *Sprachkunst*, 19/2, 23–32.

—— (1993), "The Dynamics of Consciousness: Alfred Döblin, *Berlin Alexanderplatz*", in D. Midgley (ed.), *The German Novel in the Twentieth Century: Beyond Realism*, Edinburgh: Edinburgh University Press, 95–109.

—— (1994), " 'Das hilflose Europa': Eine Aufforderung, die politischen Essays von Robert Musil neu zu lesen", *German Quarterly*, 67, 16–26.

MITCHELL, B. (1976), *James Joyce and the German Novel 1922–1933*, Athens, Oh.: Ohio University Press.

MODICK, K. (ed.) (1981), *Lion Feuchtwanger im Kontext der zwanziger Jahre: Autonomie und Sachlichkeit*, Königstein: Scriptor.

MOHLER, A. (ed.) (1972), *Die Konservative Revolution in Deutschland 1918–1932: Ein Handbuch*, Darmstadt: Wissenschaftliche Buchgesellschaft.

MOMBER, E. (1981), *'s ist Krieg! 's ist Krieg! Versuch zur Literatur über den Krieg 1914–1933*, Berlin: Das Arsenal.

MÖRCHEN, H. (1973), *Schriftsteller in der Massengesellschaft: Zur politischen Essayistik und Publizistik Heinrich und Thomas Manns, Kurt Tucholskys und Ernst Jüngers während der zwanziger Jahre*, Stuttgart: Metzler.

MOSER, W. (1980), "Diskursexperimente im Romantext zu Musils *Der Mann ohne Eigenschaften*", in U. Baur and E. Castex (eds.), *Robert Musil*, 170–97.

MÜLLER, G. (1972), *Ideologiekritik und Metasprache in Robert Musils Roman "Der Mann ohne Eigenschaften"* (Musil-Studien, 2), Munich: Fink.

MÜLLER, H.-H. (1986), *Der Krieg und die Schriftsteller*, Stuttgart: Metzler.

MÜLLER-FUNK, W. (1981), *Literatur als geschichtliches Argument: Zur ästhetischen Konzeption und Geschichtsverarbeitung in Lion Feuchtwangers Romantrilogie 'Der Wartesaal'*, Frankfurt: Peter Lang.

——(ed.) (1987), *Jahrmarkt der Gerechtigkeit: Studien zu Lion Feuchtwangers zeitgeschichtlichem Werk*, Tübingen: Stauffenburg.

——(1989), *Joseph Roth*, Munich: Beck.

MÜLLER-SALGET, K. (1972), *Alfred Döblin: Werk und Entwicklung*, Bonn: Bouvier.

MÜLLER-SEIDEL, W. (1987), "Literarische Moderne und Weimarer Republik", in K. D. Bracher, M. Funke, and H.-A. Jacobsen (eds.), *Die Weimarer Republik 1918–1933. Politik, Wirtschaft, Gesellschaft* (Schriftenreihe der Bundeszentrale für politische Bildung, 251), Düsseldorf: Droste, 429–53.

MURDOCH, B. (1993), "Narrative Strategies in Remarque's *Im Westen nichts Neues*", *New German Studies*, 17/3, 175–201.

NÖSSIG, L., ROSENBERG, J., and SCHRADER, B. (eds.) (1980), *Literaturdebatten in der Weimarer Republik: Zur Entwicklung des marxistischen literaturtheoretischen Denkens 1918–1933*, Berlin (East): Aufbau.

OBERMEIER, O. P. (1988), "Das Konstruktionsprinzip in der Wertphilosophie" in P. M. Lützeler and M. Kessler (eds.), *Brochs theoretisches Werk*, Frankfurt: Suhrkamp, 98–108.

OSSOWSKI, M. (1994), *Der kritische Provinzroman in der Weimarer Republik*, Rzeszów: Wydawnictwo Wyzsej Skoly Pedagogicznej.

PASCAL, R. (1970), "Georg Lukács: The Concept of Totality", in G. H. R. Parkinson (ed.), *Georg Lukács: The Man, his Work and his Ideas*, London: Reading University Studies on Contemporary Europe, 147–71.

——(1973), *From Naturalism to Expressionism*, London: Weidenfeld & Nicolson.

PATTERSON, M. (1981), *The Revolution in German Theatre 1900–1933*, Boston and London: Routledge & Kegan Paul.

PAUCKER, H. R. (ed.) (1974), *Neue Sachlichkeit, Literatur im "Dritten Reich" und im Exil*, Stuttgart: Reclam.

PETERSEN, K. (1982), " 'Neue Sachlichkeit': Stilbegriff, Epochenbezeichnung oder Gruppenphänomen?", *Deutsche Vierteljahrsschrift*, 56, 463–77.

PEUKERT, D. J. K. (1987), *Die Weimarer Republik*, Frankfurt: Suhrkamp.

PHELAN, A. (ed.) (1985), *The Weimar Dilemma: Intellectuals in the Weimar Republic*, Manchester: Manchester University Press.

PHILIPP, E. (1980), *Dadaismus*, Munich: Fink.

PIETZCKER, C. (1974), *Die Lyrik des jungen Brecht: Vom anarchischen Nihilismus zum Marxismus*, Frankfurt: Suhrkamp.

PÖRTNER, P. (ed.) (1960), *Literaturrevolution 1910–1925: Dokumente, Manifeste, Programme*, 2 vols, Neuwied: Luchterhand.

PRANGEL, M. (1986), "Das Geschäft mit der Wahrheit: Zu einer zentralen Kategorie der Rezeption von Kriegsromanen der Weimarer Republik", in J. Hoogeveen and H. Würzner (eds.), *Ideologie und Literatur(wissenschaft)*, Amsterdam: Rodopi, 47–78.

PRÜMM, K. (1972), "Neue Sachlichkeit: Anmerkungen zum Gebrauch des Begriffs in neueren literaturwissenschaftlichen Publikationen", *Zeitschrift für deutsche Philologie*, 91, 606–16.

——(1974), *Die Literatur des Soldatischen Nationalismus der 20er Jahre (1918–1933): Gruppenideologie und Epochenproblematik*, Kronberg: Scriptor.

——(1988), "Die Stadt der Reporter und Kinogänger bei Roth, Brentano und Kracauer: Das Berlin der zwanziger Jahre im Feuilleton der Frankfurter Zeitung", in Klaus R. Scherpe (ed.), *Die Unwirklichkeit der Städte*, 80–105.

RAABE, P. (ed.) (1977), *Das Buch in den zwanziger Jahren*, Hamburg: Hauswedell.

——(ed.) (1984), *Expressionismus: Der Kampf um eine literarische Bewegung*. Munich: Deutscher Taschenbuchverlag.

RASCH, W. (1967), *Über Robert Musils "Der Mann ohne Eigenschaften"*, Göttingen: Vandenhoeck.

——(1974), "Krisenbewußtsein und Moralität: Zu Heinrich Manns

Roman der zwanziger Jahre", in W. Müller-Seidel (ed.), *Historizität in Sprach- und Literaturwissenschaft*, Munich: Fink, 467–77.

REED, T. J. (1974), *Thomas Mann, The Uses of Tradition*, London: Oxford University Press.

REINISCH, L. (ed.) (1961), *Die Zeit ohne Eigenschaften*, Stuttgart: Kohlhammer.

RIDLEY, H. (1990), *Gottfried Benn: Ein Schriftsteller zwischen Erneuerung und Reaktion*, Opladen: Westdeutscher Verlag.

RIHA, K. (1974), *Moritat, Bänkelsang, Protestballade: Kabarett-Lyrik und engagiertes Lied in Deutschland*, Königstein: Athenäum.

RINGER, F. K. (1969), *The Decline of the German Mandarins: The German Academic Community 1890–1933*, Cambridge, Mass: Harvard University Press.

RITZER, M. (1988), *Hermann Broch und die Kulturkrise des frühen 20. Jahrhunderts*, Stuttgart: Metzler.

ROBERTS, D. (1971), *Artistic Consciousness and Political Conscience: The Novels of Heinrich Mann 1900–1938*, Berne: Hubert Lang.

ROH, F. (1925), *Nach-Expressionismus: Magischer Realismus. Probleme der neuesten europäischen Malerei*, Leipzig: Klickhardt und Biermann.

ROHRWASSER, M. (1980), *Der Weg nach oben: Politik des Schreibers*, Basel: Stroemfeld.

ROSENBERG, A. (1961), *Geschichte der Weimarer Republik*, Frankfurt: Europäische Verlagsanstalt.

ROSENSTEIN, D. (1991), *Irmgard Keun: Das Erzählwerk der dreißiger Jahre*, Frankfurt: Peter Lang.

ROSSBACHER, K. (1975), *Heimatbewegung und Heimatroman: Zu einer Literatursoziologie der Jahrhundertwende*, Stuttgart: Klett.

ROTHE, W. (ed.) (1973), *Deutsche Großstadtlyrik vom Naturalismus bis zur Gegenwart*, Stuttgart: Reclam.

——(ed.) (1974), *Die deutsche Literatur der Weimarer Republik*, Stuttgart: Reclam.

——(ed.) (1977), *Der Expressionismus: Theologische, Soziologische und anthropologische Aspekte einer Literatur*, Frankfurt: Klostermann.

RUCKHABERLE, D. et al. (1977), *Weimarer Republik: Ausstellungskatalog vom Kunstamt Kreuzberg, Berlin und dem Institut für Theaterwissenschaft der Universität Köln*, Berlin (West): Elefanten Press.

RUDOLPH, H. (1971), *Kulturkritik und konservative Revolution: Zum kulturpolitischen Denken Hofmannsthals und seinem problemgeschichtlichen Kontext*, Tübingen: Niemeyer.

RÜHLE, G. (1967), *Theater für die Republik 1917–1933 im Spiegel der Kritik*, Frankfurt: S. Fischer.

374   *Bibliography*

RÜHLE, G. (1972 ff.), *Zeit und Theater*, 6 vols., Frankfurt: Ullstein.
RUF, K.-U. (1987), "Autonomie, Kausalität und Politik: Oskar Maria Grafs Dorfroman *Die Chronik von Flechting* und die Tradition der Heimatkunst- und Heimatliteraturbewegung", in T. Kraft and D.-R. Moser (eds.), *Anpassung und Utopie: Beiträge zum literarischen Werk Oskar Maria Grafs, Lion Feuchtwangers, Franz C. Weiskopfs, Anna Seghers' und August Kühns*, Munich: Kommisionsverlag, 127–38.
RUPING, B. (1984), *Material und Methode: Zur Theorie und Praxis des Brechtschen Lehrstücks*, Münster: Litverlag.
RÜTER, H. (1980), *Erich Maria Remarques "Im Westen nichts Neues": Ein Bestseller der Kriegsliteratur im Kontext*, Paderborn: Schöningh.
SAMUELSON-KOENNEKER, M. (1982), *Oskar Loerke: Le défi d'une poésie cosmique au XXième siècle*, Lille: Université de Lille.
SAUTERMEISTER, G. (1982), "Thomas Mann: Der Ironiker als citoyen. Politische Rhetorik und kritische Diagnose in der Weimarer Republik", in T. Koebner (ed.), *Weimars Ende*, 271–302.
SCHÄFER, H. D. (1974), "Naturdichtung und Neue Sachlichkeit", in W. Rothe (ed.), *Die deutsche Literatur der Weimarer Republik*, 359–81.
——(1981), *Das gespaltene Bewußtsein: Deutsche Kultur und Lebenswirklichkeit 1933–1945*, Munich: Hanser.
——(1989), "Berlin—Modernität und Zivilisationslosigkeit", in D. Glass et al., *Berlin: Literary Images of a City*, 107–23.
SCHARRER, A. (1977), *Intellektueller Linksradikalismus in der Weimarer Republik*, Kronberg: Scriptor.
SCHERPE, K. (ed.) (1988*a*), *Die Unwirklichkeit der Städte: Großstadtdarstellungen zwischen Moderne und Postmoderne*, Reinbek: Rowohlt.
——(1988*b*), "Von der erzählten Stadt zur Stadterzählung: Der Großstadtdiskurs in Alfred Döblins *Berlin Alexanderplatz*", in J. Fohrmann and H. Müller (eds.), *Diskurstheorien und Literaturwissenschaft*, Frankfurt: Suhrkamp, 418–37 [English version: "The City as Narrator: The Modern Text in Alfred Döblin's *Berlin Alexanderplatz*", in A. Huyssen and D. Bathrick (eds.), *Modernity and the Text*, New York: Columbia University Press 1989, 162–79].
SCHEUNEMANN, D. (1978), *Romankrise: Die Entwicklung der modernen Romanpoetik in Deutschland*, Heidelberg: Quelle & Meyer.
SCHLAWE, F. (1962), *Literarische Zeitschriften*, vol. ii: 1910–1933, Stuttgart: Metzler.
SCHMELING, C. (1989), *Leonhard Frank und die Weimarer Zeit*, Frankfurt: Lang.

SCHMIDT, D. (1964), *Manifeste, Manifeste 1905–1933*, Dresden: VEB Verlag der Kunst.

SCHMIED, W. (1969), *Neue Sachlichkeit und Magischer Realismus in Deutschland 1918–1933*, Hanover: Fackelträger.

——(1985), "Points of Departure and Transformation in German Art 1905–1985", in C. M. Joachimides, N. Rosenthal, and W. Schmied (eds.), *German Art in the 20th Century*, London and Munich: Royal Academy of Arts and Prestel, 21–74.

SCHMITT, H. J. (ed.) (1973), *Die Expressionismusdebatte: Materialien zu einer marxistischen Realismuskonzeption*, Frankfurt: Suhrkamp.

SCHNEIDER, P. P. et al. (1987), *Literatur im Industriezeitalter* (Marbacher Kataloge, 42), 2 vols., Marbach: Deutsche Schillergesellschaft.

SCHONAUER, F. (1974), "Die Partei und die Schöne Literatur: Kommunistische Literaturpolitik in der Weimarer Republik", in W. Rothe (ed.), *Die deutsche Literatur der Weimarer Republik*, 114–42.

SCHRADER, B. and SCHEBERA, J. (1987), *Kunstmetropole Berlin 1918–1933*, Berlin: Aufbau.

SCHRÖTER, K. (1983), "Zwischen Autobiographie und Zeitgeschichte: Zu Heinrich Mann's Roman *Der Kopf*", in H. Koopmann and P.-P. M. Schneider (eds.), *Heinrich Mann: Sein Werk in der Weimar Republik*, Frankfurt: Klostermann, 169–81.

SCHÜRER, E. (1971), *Georg Kaiser and Bertolt Brecht*, Frankfurt: Athenäum.

SCHÜTZ, E. (1986), *Romane der Weimarer Republik*, Munich: UTB/Fink.

——and VOGT, J. (eds.) (1986), *Der Scheinwerfer: Ein Forum der Neuen Sachlichkeit 1927–1933*, Essen: Klartext.

SCHWARZ, E. (1970), "Die strampelnde Seele: Erich Kästner in seiner Zeit", in R. Grimm and J. Hermand (eds.), *Die sogenannten Zwanziger Jahre*, 109–42.

SCHWARZ, P. P. (1971), *Brechts frühe Lyrik, 1914–1922: Nihilismus als Werkzusammenhang der frühen Lyrik Brechts*, Bonn: Bouvier.

SEBALD, W. G. (1980), *Der Mythus der Zerstörung im Werk Döblins*, Stuttgart: Klett.

SEGEBERG, H. (1987*a*), *Literarische Technik-Bilder*, Tübingen: Niemeyer.

——(ed.) (1987*b*), *Technik in der Literatur*, Frankfurt: Suhrkamp.

——(1989), "Simulierte Apokalypsen: Georg Kaisers 'Gas'-Dramen im Kontext expressionistischer Technik-Debatten", in G. Großklaus and E. Lämmert (eds.), *Literatur in einer industriellen Kultur*, 294–313.

SLOTERDIJK, P. (1983), *Kritik der zynischen Vernunft*, Frankfurt: Suhrkamp.

SOERGEL, A. and HOHOFF, C. (1963), *Dichtung und Dichter der Zeit*, Düsseldorf: Reclam.

SONTHEIMER, K. (1961), *Thomas Mann und die Deutschen*, Munich: Nymphenburger Verlagshandlung.

——(1962), *Antidemokratisches Denken in der Weimarer Republik: Die politischen Ideen des deutschen Nationalismus zwischen 1918 und 1933*, Munich: Nymphenburger Verlagshandlung.

SPALEK, J. M. (ed.) (1972), *Lion Feuchtwanger: The Man his Ideas, his Work*, Los Angeles: Hennessey & Ingalls.

SPRENGEL, P. (1990), "Von der Baukunst zur Wortkunst: Sachlichkeit und Expressionismus im *Sturm*", *Deutsche Vierteljahrsschrift*, 64, 680–706.

STANZEL, F. K. and LÖSCHNIGG, M. (1993), *Intimate Enemies: English and German Literary Reactions to the Great War 1914–1918*, Heidelberg: Winter.

STARK, M. (1984), *Deutsche Intellektuelle 1910–1933: Aufrufe, Pamphlete, Betrachtungen*, Heidelberg: Lambert Schneider.

STEFFENSEN, S. (1972), *Bertolt Brechts Gedichte*, Copenhagen: Akademisk Forlag.

STEINECKE, H. (1968), *Hermann Broch und der polyhistorische Roman: Studien zur Theorie und Technik eines Romantyps der Moderne*, Bonn: Bouvier.

——(ed.) (1972), *Theorie und Technik des Romans im 20. Jahrhundert*, Tübingen: Niemeyer.

STEINWEG, R. (1972), *Das Lehrstück: Brechts Theorie einer ästhetischen Erziehung*, Stuttgart: Metzler.

STRUTZ, J. (1980), "Gesellschaftspolitische Implikationen bei Musil: zum Begriff des Eigentums im *Mann ohne Eigenschaften* und im Nachlaß", in U. Baur and E. Castex (eds.), *Robert Musil: Untersuchungen*, 67–84.

——(1981), *Politik und Literatur in Musils "Mann ohne Eigenschaften": Am Beispiel des Dichters Feuermaul*, Königstein: Hain.

STYAN, J. L. (1982), *Max Reinhardt*, Cambridge: Cambridge University Press.

TAYLOR, R. (1980), *Literature and Society in Germany, 1918–1945*, Hassocks: Harvester.

THIEBERGER, R. (ed.) (1980), *Hermann Broch und seine Zeit* (Akten des Internationalen Broch-Symposiums, Nice, 1979), Berne: Peter Lang.

THOMSON, P. (1989), *The Poetry of Brecht*, Chapelhill: University of North Carolina Press.

TIMMS, E. (1986), *Karl Kraus: Apocalyptic Satirist*, New Haven: Yale.

TRAVERS, M. P. A. (1982), *German Novels on the First World War and Their Ideological Implications, 1918–1933*, Stuttgart: H.-D. Heinz.

TROMMLER, F. (1966), *Roman und Wirklichkeit: Eine Ortsbestimmung am Beispiel von Musil, Broch, Roth, Doderer und Gütersloh*, Stuttgart: Kohlhammer.

——(1989), "Technik, Avantgarde, Sachlichkeit: Versuch einer historischen Zuordnung", in G. Großklaus and E. Lämmert (eds.), *Literatur in einer industriellen Kultur*, 46–71.

VOGT, G. (1986), "Robert Musil: Politik als Methode", in J. Strutz (ed.), *Kunst, Wissenschaft und Politik von Robert Musil bis Ingeborg Bachmann*, Munich: Fink, 146–64.

VOGT-PRACLIK, K. (1987), *Bestseller in der Weimarer Republik*, Herzberg: Bautz.

VOIGTS, M. (1977), *Brechts Theaterkonzeptionen: Entstehung und Entwicklung bis 1931*, Munich: Fink.

VOLLHARDT, F. (1986), *Hermann Brochs geschichtliche Stellung: Studien zum philosophischen Frühwerk und zur Romantrilogie "Die Schlafwandler" (1914–1932)*, Tübingen: Niemeyer.

VONDUNG, K. (ed.) (1980), *Kreigserlebnis: Der Erste Weltkrieg in der literarischen Gestaltung und symbolischen Deutung der Nationen*, Göttingen: Vandenhoeck & Ruprecht.

WAGENER, H. (ed.) (1975), *Zeitkritische Romane des 20. Jahrhunderts*, Stuttgart: Reclam.

WEGE, C. (1994), "Gleisdreieck, Tank und Motor: Figuren und Denkfiguren aus der Technosphäre der Neuen Sachlichkeit", *Deutsche Vierteljahrsschrift*, 68, 307–32.

WEIGAND, H. J. (1933), *The Magic Mountain: A Study of Thomas Mann's Novel "Der Zauberberg"*, New York: D. Appleton-Century.

WEISSENBERGER, K., (1975), "Leonhard Frank: Zwischen sozialem Aktivismus und persönlicher Identitätssuche", in H. Wagener (ed.), *Zeitkritische Romane des 20. Jahrhunderts*, 54–75.

WEISSTEIN, U. (1962), *Heinrich Mann: Eine historisch-kritische Einführung in sein dichterisches Werk*, Tübingen: Niemeyer.

WERNER, R. (1977), *Heinrich Mann: Texte aus seiner Wirkungsgeschichte in Deutschland*, Tübingen: Niemeyer.

WHALEN, R. W. (1984), *Bitter Wounds: German Victims of the Great War*, Ithaca: Cornell University Press.

WHITAKER, P. (1985), *Brecht's Poetry*, Oxford: Oxford University Press.

WHITFORD, F. (1984), *Bauhaus*, London: Thames & Hudson.

WICHNER, E. and WIESNER, H. (eds.) (1990), *Industriegebiet der Intel-*

ligenz: Literatur im neuen Berliner Westen der 20er und 30er Jahre, Berlin: Literaturhaus.

WILLETT, J. (1978a), *The New Sobriety: Art and Politics in the Weimar Period 1917–1933*, London: Thames & Hudson.

——(1978b), *The Theatre of Erwin Piscator: Half a Century of Politics in the Theatre*, London: Eyre Methuen.

——(1984), *Brecht in Context*, London: Methuen.

——(1988), *The Theatre of the Weimar Republic*, New York: Holmes & Meier.

WINTER, L. (1965), *Heinrich Mann und sein Publikum*, Cologne: Westdeutscher Verlag.

WISSKIRCHEN, H. (1986), *Zeitgeschichte im Roman* (Thomas-Mann-Studien, 6), Berne: Francke.

WRIGHT, E. E. (1989), *Postmodern Brecht: A Re-Presentation*, London: Routledge.

WULF, H. A. (1988), *"Maschinenstürmer sind wir keine": Technischer Fortschritt und sozialdemokratische Arbeiterbewegung*, Frankfurt: Campus.

ZACHAU, R. (1990), *Hans Fallada als politischer Schriftsteller*, New York: Peter Lang.

ZIMMERMANN, P. (1975), *Der Bauernroman: Antifeudalismus—Konservatismus—Faschismus*, Stuttgart: Metzler.

——(1976), "Kampf um den Lebensraum: Ein Mythos der Kolonial- und der Blut-und-Boden-Literatur", in H. Denkler and K. Prümm (eds.), *Die deutsche Literatur im Dritten Reich*, Stuttgart: Reclam, 165–82.

ZIOLKOWSKI, T. (1970), "Der Hunger nach dem Mythos: Zur seelischen Gastronomie der Deutschen in den Zwanziger Jahren", in R. Grimm and J. Hermand (eds.), *Die sogenannten Zwanziger Jahre*, 169–201.

Index

Academy of the Arts (Prussian) 170, 266 f.
Adorno, Theodor Wiesengrund 50
Aeschylus 246
aestheticism 67
agitprop 107 f., 109, 329
aircraft 29, 40, 306, 307, 323, 340, 347–50
Aktion, Die 76, 319
America 218, 290, 315, 317, 319, 320 f., 330 f., 336
'Americanism' 21 f., 44, 83, 331
anarchism 18, 38, 70, 99, 165, 250, 290
'Angestellte' 209–12, 273
Anthologie jüngster Lyrik (ed. Willi R. Fehse and Klaus Mann) 57 f., 83 f.
anti-Semitism 148, 161, 181, 217, 264, 265, 292, 296, 318
Anzengruber, Ludwig 134
architecture 30–2, 40, 166, 269, 304
'Asphaltkultur' 263
Auden, Wystan Hugh 59
Austria 12 f., 48, 126, 180 f., 183–5, 231
authoritarianism 147, 156, 194, 204, 225, 233, 288, 321, 353
autonomy, artistic 38, 61
avant-garde 10, 15 f., 37, 42, 62, 73, 103, 167, 169, 171 f.

Baader, Johannes 16
Bachofen, Johann Jakob 326
Baden-Baden 85, 128, 345, 347
Balázs, Béla 43, 46
Balfour Declaration 254
Balzac, Honoré de 49 f.
Bance, Alan Frederick 4
Barbusse, Henri 233
Barlach, Ernst 12, 24
Barnouw, Dagmar 169
Baudelaire, Charles 60, 242
Bauhaus 31 f.
Bayerdörfer, Hans-Peter 58, 78, 93
Bayreuth 97

Becher, Johannes Robert 36 f., 58, 61–4, 68, 76, 233, 235, 308, 328 f.;
Die hungrige Stadt 63; (CHCl = CH)₃As (Levisite) oder Der einzig gerechte Krieg 233
Beckmann, Max 25
Benjamin, Walter 6, 21, 29, 50–2, 55, 74, 92, 131, 177, 191 f., 205, 228, 273, 279; "Linke Melancholie" 50–2, 74, 191 f.
Benn, Gottfried 61, 63–8, 76, 93 f., 197; Morgue 63 f.; "Schutt" 65–7
Berlin 11, 12 f., 15 f., 29, 31, 43, 54, 65, 73, 76, 85, 93, 97, 98, 99, 102, 103–9, 112, 118, 129 f., 134 f., 173–8, 179, 198, 205, 207 f., 209, 211 f., 215, 217, 260, 263–76, 280, 282–7, 293, 294, 312, 315, 323, 328, 330, 342, 344, 354, 355
Berliner Zeitung 81
Bethmann-Hollweg, Theobald 150 f.
Beumelburg, Werner 244 f., 246; Gruppe Bosemüller 244 f.
Binding, Rudolf 230
Bloch, Ernst 6, 50, 52, 166, 286; Erbschaft dieser Zeit 52, 286
Blunck, Hans 262
Blunden, Edmund 226
'Blut-und-Boden-Literatur' 261 f.
Bohrer, Karl Heinz 241 f.
Bölsche, Wilhelm 170
Bolz, Norbert W. 248, 356
Borchardt, Rudolf 48
Bornebusch, Herbert 236, 252 f.
Brady, Philip V. 90 f.
Brahm, Otto 106
Brecht, Bertolt 3, 10, 14, 17 f., 19, 21, 22, 24, 26 f., 41, 42, 43 f., 49 f., 55, 57, 60 f., 67–73, 82–94, 95, 96 f., 101, 103, 112, 117–25, 127, 134 f., 137 f., 139 f., 172, 196, 278–82, 291, 294, 318, 332, 335 f., 343–52, 353, 356; Aufstieg und Fall der Stadt Mahagonny 22, 55, 87, 94, 121, 281, 345; Aus einem Lesebuch

Brecht, Bertolt (*cont*):
für Städtebewohner 88–94, 279–81;
Baal 17 f., 19; *Das Badener Lehrstück vom Einverständnis* 128 f., 345–8, 350 f.; *Die Dreigroschenoper* 41, 68, 124, 356; *Der Flug der Lindberghs* 129, 346–50, 351; *Die Hauspostille* 44, 68 f., 86 f.; *Im Dickicht der Städte* 118, 281; *Der Jasager* 129 f.; *Mann ist Mann* 332, 343 f.; *Die Maßnahme* 130–3; *Die Mutter* 132 f.; *Der Neinsager* 129; *Der Ozeanflug* 345; "Ruhrepos" 87, 94, 103, 335 f., 344; *Trommeln in der Nacht* 17 f., 42, 119, 122
Brenner, Hans Georg 47
Brentano, Bernard von 36, 272 f.
Breton, André 242
Brno 179
Broch, Hermann 13, 42, 142, 145, 163–9, 172, 262, 277, 278; *Die Schlafwandler* 164–9, 278
Brod, Max 38
Bronnen, Arnolt 12, 24, 42, 101, 299, 336; *O.S.* 299; *Vatermord* 42
Bruckner, Ferdinand 125; *Die Verbecher* 125
Büchner, Georg 106
Bullivant, Keith 4, 157
Bülow, Prince Bernhard 150, 153
Bund proletarisch-revolutionärer Schriftsteller 36, 48
Burri, Emil 132

cabaret 10, 61, 69 f., 73 f., 76 f., 94, 109, 270, 332
Carossa, Hans 77, 230
Carrà, Carlo 26
Caspar, Günter 297
censorship 101
Chirico, Giorgio de 26
chorus girls 21, 22
Christ, Lena 300; *Madam Bäurin* 300
cinema 21, 22, 105, 200, 211
class struggle 33, 120, 259, 308 f.
classicism 59 f., 61–8, 106
Cobbett, William 313
coldness 8 f., 29, 89, 272, 278 f., 340
Coli, François 346
collage 26, 93, 174
collectivism 43 f., 59 f., 80, 88, 89 f., 95, 122, 128 f., 138, 161, 193, 209,

247 f., 256, 273, 286 f., 329, 332, 344, 346 f., 350 f., 352
Cologne 215
comedy 14, 115, 133–6, 139, 183, 197 f., 203 f., 213, 216, 300
commercialism 42, 46, 47, 52, 54, 55, 73, 98, 104 f., 159, 193, 199, 224, 260, 281
commodification 41–3, 46
communism 33 f., 36, 48 f., 52, 60, 62, 76, 99, 107–12, 126 f., 130–3, 137 f., 140, 159, 181, 199, 209, 214, 239, 294, 296, 317, 329, 343, 347, 351
community 11, 96–101, 130–3, 138–40, 238, 262, 267, 268 f., 284, 295, 297 f., 310, 318, 320, 339, 346, 348, 350
consumerism 22, 23, 41 f., 55, 273, 275
Courts-Mahler, Hedwig 296
Credé, Carl 125; *Paragraph* 218 125 f.
Cummings, E. E. 233
Curtius, Ernst Robert 331
cynicism 8, 33, 64, 73, 76, 100, 115, 153, 200, 203, 231, 234 f., 298, 323

Dada 10, 15 f., 22, 26, 73, 174
Dame, Die 215
Darwinism 242, 337
Däubler, Theodor 58
Daumier, Honoré 199
Davies, Cecil W. 103 f.
Dawes Plan 31 f., 317
De Bruyn, Günter 342
death 63 f., 66, 70–2, 73 f., 175 f., 235 f., 241, 284 f., 289, 308 f., 348, 355
Denkler, Horst 353
design 30–32, 356
Dessau 31
Dessauer, Friedrich 305
deutsche Theater der Gegenwart, Das (ed. Max Krell) 100
Deutsches Volkstum 264
'Dichtung' 37, 156, 266
Diebold, Bernhard 19 f., 33, 42, 45, 48, 81, 119 f., 309
Diesel, Eugen 54; *Der Weg durch den Wirrsal* 54
Dinter, Arthur 296
disillusionment 11, 34, 44, 74, 99,

105, 153 f., 189–225, 226, 252,
273 f., 356
Ditzen, Rudolf, *see* Fallada, Hans
Dix, Otto 25 f., 270
Döblin, Alfred 37, 42, 45 f., 48, 55,
142, 146, 169–79, 187 f., 207, 229,
242, 260, 266, 277, 282, 284–7,
313, 322–7, 329 f., 348; *Berge
Meere und Giganten* 322–7, 330;
Berlin Alexanderplatz 169, 173–8,
187, 229, 282, 284–7, 348; "Der
Geist des naturalistischen Zeitalters"
169, 277, 329 f.; *Giganten* 327;
Manas 173; *Pardon wird nicht
gegeben* 207; *Wissen und
Verändern!* 170 f.
documentary writing 33, 35–7, 47–50,
52, 86, 116, 214, 220, 232, 235,
249, 251 f., 297, 334
Dominik, Hans 320 f.
Dorgelès, Roland 233
Dos Passos, John 174, 233
Dove, Richard 115
Dreieck, Das 85
Dresden 268
Dudow, Slatan 132, 345
Durieux, Tilla 112
Durzak, Manfred 145 f., 172
Duwe, Wilhelm 24
Dworsky, Franz 312

Eggebrecht, Axel 113, 174, 288
Ehrenstein, Albert 59, 308
Eich, Günter 81
Eichacker, Reinhold 320
Einstein, Albert 318
Einstein, Carl 172
Eisler, Hans 113, 130, 132
Eisner, Kurt 98 f., 153
Eksteins, Modris 235, 345
electricity 40 f., 51, 85
empiricism 181
Engel, Erich 118, 121
Engel, Fritz 106
engineers 179, 195 f., 305, 310 f., 314,
315, 317, 320 f., 326, 331, 337,
342 f.
Enlightenment 152, 155, 158, 199,
202 f., 204 f., 205 f., 223, 242, 356
epic 143 f., 172 f., 177, 284
'epic theatre' 96 f., 109, 117–24, 127,
131–3, 137, 172, 281, 318
Es liegt in der Luft (revue) 40–2

Essen 23, 84 f., 87, 103, 335
Expressionism 3, 5, 14 f., 16–19, 24,
26, 32, 36, 45 f., 52, 53, 55, 57, 59,
62, 67, 96, 101 f., 106, 115, 120,
134, 139, 152, 172, 230, 254, 272,
283, 290, 291, 308, 321, 322,
327 f., 329, 339, 352

Faktor, Emil 106
Falkenhayn, Erich von 245
Fallada, Hans 42, 210–13, 224 f.,
296–8, 299; *Bauern, Bonzen und
Bomben* 296–8; *Kleiner Mann—was
nun?* 210–13
Fazit (ed. Ernst Glaeser) 35 f., 46, 57,
274
Fechter, Paul 33, 107
Federal Republic of Germany 8
Federn, Karl 249
Fehling, Jürgen 114
Fehse, Willi R. 57, 83 f.
'Festspiel' 98
Feuchtwanger, Lion 22, 36, 42, 44,
55, 117, 125, 199–202, 204 f., 219,
223, 225, 294 f., 299; *Erfolg* 55,
199–202, 294 f.; *Der falsche Nero*
200; *Jud Süß* 201; *PEP* 22; *Die
Petroleuminseln* 125
feuilleton 35, 47, 191, 270–3, 274,
327
Fichte, Johann Gottlieb 155, 264
film 33, 40, 110–14, 116, 117, 120–2,
139, 196, 201, 208, 272, 311 f.,
329, 330, 335, 351, 355
Fischer, Samuel 229, 330
Fisher, Peter S. 320
Flake, Otto 172, 272, 282; *Stadt des
Hirns* 172
Flaubert, Gustave 145
Flechtheim, Alfred 20
Fleißer, Marieluise 85, 135 f., 291–4,
299, 356; *Fegefeuer in Ingolstadt*
135 f., 291; *Mehlreisende Frieda
Geier* 292–4; *Pioniere in Ingolstadt*
135, 291 f.; *Eine Zierde für den
Verein* 292
Fontane, Theodor 164, 194, 288
Ford, Ford Madox 233 f.
Ford, Henry 23, 317–19, 320
Frank, Bruno 38
Frank, Leonhard 231, 288–91, 299;
Das Ochsenfurter Männerquartett
288–91

Frankfurter Zeitung 47, 53, 119, 191, 210, 234, 239, 272 f., 331
Franz Joseph I 183, 221 f.
Frenssen, Gustav 261 f.
Freud, Sigmund 9
Frey, Alexander Moritz 249
Friedrich, Ernst 232, 235
functionalism 2, 7, 8, 31 f., 37, 39–41, 58, 60 f., 81 f., 86 f., 193, 220, 275 f., 286, 331, 340, 348 f.
Fussell, Paul 226–8
Futurism (Italian) 171, 307, 322

Gasbarra, Felix 109, 112
Gay, Peter 4 f., 353
'Gebrauchslyrik' 61, 74 f., 82, 86 f., 89 f.
George, Stefan 21, 57 f., 82
German Democratic Republic 62
'Gestaltung' 48–50, 144
Gide, André 167
Giehse, Fritz 22
'Girlkultur' 22
Glaeser, Ernst 35 f., 46, 53, 57, 191, 221, 249, 273, 274 f.; *Jahrgang 1902* 191, 221, 249
Goebbels, Josef 342
Goering, Reinhard 230
Goethe, Johann Wolfgang 69, 75, 172
Goll, Yvan 14, 59
Gorky, Maxim 108, 132
Gotthelf, Jeremias 300
Graf, Oskar Maria 18 f., 35, 37, 48, 300–3; *Die Chronik von Flechting* 300 f.; *Kalender-Geschichten* 302 f.
Granach, Alexander 115
Graves, Robert 226
Great Depression 23, 31, 108, 136, 211 f., 214, 334, 357
Greenwood, Walter 212
Grenville, Anthony 159
Grimm, Hans 261
Grimm, Reinhold 41
Grimmelshausen, Hans Jakob Christoffel von 240
Gropius, Walter 31
Großes Schauspielhaus 98, 105–7, 110, 114
Grossberg, Carl 29
Grosz, George 16, 25, 38, 73, 107, 113 f., 121, 189 f., 270
Gruppe Junger Schauspieler 125, 132
Gumbel, Emil Julius 231 f.
Günther, Hans 52 f.

Gurk, Paul 282–5; *Berlin* 282–4
Gutzkow, Karl 86

Haas, Willy 20, 45, 52, 265, 351
Habermas, Jürgen 133
Halfeld, Adolf 21, 331
Hamburg 250, 267, 336
Hamburger, Michael 59 f., 70, 89, 94
Handke, Peter 137
Hapsburg Empire 12 f., 48, 114, 126, 180, 183 f., 222 f.
'Hapsburg myth' 222
Harbou, Thea von 311, 321 f.; *Frau im Mond* 321 f.; *Metropolis* 311 f., 321, 333
Harden, Maximilian 151
Hart, Julius 106
Hartlaub, Georg Friedrich 24–6, 32
Hašek, Jaroslav 113
Hasenclever, Walter 59, 134
Hatvani, Paul 1, 14
Hauptmann, Elisabeth 85, 89, 129, 132, 279, 281, 345
Hauptmann, Gerhart 98, 127, 161
Hauser, Heinrich 53, 333 f.; *Friede mit Maschinen* 333 f.
Hausmann, Raoul 16
Heartfield, John 16, 26, 73, 107, 113, 127, 312, 315 f.
Hegel, Georg Wilhelm Freidrich 143
Hegemann, Werner 268
Heidelberg 232
'Heimatkunst' 262
Heine, Heinrich 70
Heller, Erich 163
Henschke, Alfred, *see* Klabund
Herald, Heinz 98
Herf, Jeffrey 337
Hermand, Jost 6
Hermann, Rudolf 39 f.
Herrmann, Klaus 44, 47
Herrmann-Neiße, Max 38, 76 f., 354
Herzog, Rudolf 319
Herzog, Wilhelm 155
Hesse, Hermann 10, 58
Hessel, Franz 273
Heym, Georg 307
Hilbeseimer, Ludwig 32
Hindemith, Paul 129, 345, 346 f.
Hindenburg, Paul von 4, 115, 233
Hitchcock, Henry Russell 31
Hitler, Adolf 3, 6, 7, 56, 200, 229, 246, 294

Höch, Hannah 26
Hoffmann, Ernst Theodor Amadeus
242
Hofmannsthal, Hugo von 12, 134
Hölderlin, Johann Christian Friedrich
331
holism 4, 26, 185
Holitscher, Arthur 334
Holl, Karl 24
Hollaender, Felix 105
Homer 143, 229
Horrocks, David 278
Horváth, Ödön von 43, 46, 55, 95,
96 f., 133–40, 189, 202–4, 213,
216, 224 f., 356; *Der ewige Spießer*
46, 202–4; "Gebrauchsanweisung"
137–9; *Geschichten aus dem Wiener
Wald* 134, 136, 138; *Italienische
Nacht* 139; *Kasimir und Karoline*
136, 138
housing estates 31 f.
Howind, Angelika 235
Huchel, Peter 81
Huelsenbeck, Richard 22, 288
humanism 1, 17, 22, 161, 169 f.,
268 f., 357
Huxley, Aldous 167

idealism, literary 55
idealism, philosophical 1, 54, 167,
181, 256
idealism, political 15, 18, 30, 34, 52,
72, 76, 99, 105, 115, 181, 191, 205,
260
Ihering, Herbert 20, 33, 36, 105–7,
116, 117, 123
individualism 16, 22, 53, 60, 64, 119,
123, 214, 242–4, 332 f., 350 f.
industrialists 153, 193, 255, 319,
334 f., 337 f., 352
industrialization 8, 11, 81, 96, 231,
260, 267, 287 f., 300 f., 305, 307,
314, 323, 337, 338 f.
Ingolstadt 135, 291, 293
'inner emigration' 80
Innes, Christopher D. 107
internationalism 60, 204
irrationalism 55, 97, 137, 320 f.

Jacobs, Monty 116
Jahnn, Hans Henny 12
Jaspers, Karl 331
jazz 22 f., 37, 63, 73, 87, 272, 336

Jessner, Leopold 102 f.
Jews 12, 103, 148, 159, 219, 221,
222, 254, 256, 273, 294 f., 320
Jirgal, Ernst 234, 238, 253
Johnson, Uwe 262
journalism 35–8, 107, 210, 264, 275,
297, 320, 333 f.
Joyce, James 167, 174
Jung, Franz 12, 107, 328; *Die
Eroberung der Maschinen* 328
Jünger, Ernst 230, 234, 240–4, 331,
337, 339–42; *Das abenteuerliche
Herz* 340 f.; *Der Arbeiter* 341 f.;
Feuer und Blut 241, 339 f.; *In
Stahlgewittern* 230, 240, 243 f., 339;
Der Kampf als inneres Erlebnis
242 f., 339; *Das Wäldchen 125* 340
Jünger, Friedrich Georg 77

Kaes, Anton 263
Kafka, Franz 146, 220
Kaiser, Georg 17 f., 67, 99, 101, 123,
134, 231, 308–11, 313; *Gas* 231,
308–11, 313; *Hölle Weg Erde* 17
Kandinsky, Vassily 24
Kant, Immanuel 49, 54, 202, 242
Kantorowicz, Alfred 265, 274
Kästner, Erich 45, 51 f., 55, 74–6, 84,
93, 189–91, 198 f., 204 f., 207–9,
215, 219, 223–5, 274; *Fabian*
198 f., 201, 205, 207–9, 215, 224 f.,
274; *Herz auf Taille* 189–91; *Lärm
im Spiegel* 51
Kaufmann, Hans 6
Kayser, Rudolf 16 f., 19, 22 f., 331
Keller, Otto 175 f.
Kellermann, Bernhard 231, 319 f.; *Der
Tunnel* 319 f.
Kerr, Alfred 111, 116
Kessel, Martin 205, 209 f., 224 f.,
274; *Herrn Brechers Fiasko* 209 f.,
274
Kesser, Hermann 275 f.
Kesten, Hermann 42, 45 f., 55, 57,
191, 205–7, 224; *Ein
ausschweifender Mensch* 205–7;
Glückliche Menschen 205; *Josef
sucht die Freiheit* 205–7; *Der
Scharlatan* 205
Keun, Irmgard 42, 55, 213–16, 224 f.;
Gilgi—eine von uns 213–15, 224;
Das kunstseidene Mädchen 215 f.,
224

Keyserling, Hermann Graf von 21, 305
Kiepenheuer (publishing house) 249, 355
Kindermann, Heinz 53 f., 74
Kipling, Rudyard 70, 282, 332
Kisch, Egon Erwin 13, 28 f., 35 f., 52, 181, 275; *Der rasende Reporter* 35
Klabund 38, 70, 77; *Die Harfenjule* 70
Klages, Ludwig 170, 184
Klammer, Karl 68
Knopf, Jan 83
Koch, Carl 335
Koeppen, Edlef 35, 59, 251–3, 256; *Heeresbericht* 251–3
Kolbenheyer, Erwin Guido 24, 262, 266 f.
Kolmar, Gertrud 81
Kolonne, Die 74, 81
Königsberg 107
Kortner, Fritz 102, 117
Kracauer, Siegfried 22, 35 f., 45, 47, 191 f., 210 f., 234, 248 f., 273; *Die Angestellten* 210 f., 248 f.; *Ginster* 47, 191, 234; *Das Ornament der Masse* 22
Kraus, Karl 184, 231, 251; *Die letzten Tage der Menschheit* 184, 231
Krechel, Ursula 213
Krell, Max 100
Křenek, Ernst 21 f.; *Jonny spielt auf* 21 f.
Kretzer, Max 307
Kroetz, Franz Xaver 137
Kunstwart, Der 264 f.
Küpper, Hannes 43 f., 82–5, 329, 332, 344; *Die Sache ist die* 329

Lagarde, Paul de 155, 181 f., 260
Lampel, Peter Martin 125; *Revolte im Erziehungshaus* 125
Lamping, Dieter 77, 79, 89 f.
Landauer, Gustav 98 f.
Landry, Harald 19, 35
Lang, Fritz 311 f., 321
Langbehn, Julius 261
Lania, Leo 33, 37, 112, 114, 117, 125; *Konjunktur* 33, 114, 125
Lasker-Schüler, Else 59, 76
Latzko, Andreas 231
Leed, Eric 238
Léger, Fernand 26

Lehmann, Wilhelm 79 f.
'Lehrstück' 117, 127–33
Leipzig 295
Lenin, Vladimir Ilich 111, 318, 329
Leonhard, Rudolf 59
Lessing, Theodor 142; *Geschichte als Sinngebung des Sinnlosen* 142
Lethen, Helmut 5 f., 8 f., 211 f., 334
Lewis, Sinclair 38
liberalism 10, 17, 19, 22, 52 f., 148 f., 181, 183, 204, 223–5, 242, 250, 275, 318, 336, 341
Lichtenstein, Alfred 70
Liebknecht, Karl 109 f.
Lindbergh, Charles 345–9
Lindner, Martin 357
Linkskurve, Die 48 f., 53, 76, 214, 239, 249 f.
literarische Welt, Die 20, 22, 37, 43–5, 46, 52, 82–8, 93, 113, 212, 265, 296, 302, 329, 332, 344
Lloyd George, David 110
Loerke, Oskar 24, 77–80; *Die heimliche Stadt* 78; *Der längste Tag* 78
London 269, 324
Loos, Anita 215
Ludendorff, Erich 229 f., 253
Ludwig II 301
Ludwig, Emil 38
Ludwig, Paula 84
Luft, David S. 180
Lukács, Georg 48–50, 52, 53, 143–6, 162 f., 164; *The Meaning of Contemporary Realism* 2, 146; "Reportage oder Gestaltung" 49 f.; *Die Theorie des Romans* 49, 143–5, 164
Luther, Hans 197
Lützeler, Paul Michael 163
lyric poetry 2, 10 f., 15, 24, 53, 57–94, 230, 332, 344, 353

Mach, Ernst 179 f.
machinery 29, 37, 87, 215, 304 f., 307 f., 311–14, 322, 327–9, 332–6, 339 f., 343 f., 349, 352
Magris, Claudio 222
Mallarmé, Stéphane 60
Mandelkow, Karl Robert 305
'manliness' 36, 43, 243, 247, 257, 292 f., 355
Mann, Heinrich 38, 44–6, 55, 142,

146–54, 155f., 163, 165, 192–8, 217, 224f., 267, 271f., 282; *Die Armen* 149f.; *Ein ernstes Leben* 198; *Eugénie oder Die Bürgerzeit* 194f.; "Geist und Tat" 152f.; *Die große Sache* 195–8, 224f.; *Henri IV* 154; *Der Kopf* 150–4, 194; *Mutter Marie* 194; *Der Untertan* 147–50, 217

Mann, Klaus 57, 83f.

Mann, Thomas 42, 111, 141f., 146, 151f., 154–64, 167, 173, 197, 228f., 266f., 277, 288, 357; *Betrachtungen eines Unpolitischen* 155f.; *Buddenbrooks* 154, 194; *Doktor Faustus* 357; "Gedanken im Krieg" 154f.; *Der Tod in Venedig* 154, 157; *Der Zauberberg* 42, 146, 157–63

Mannheim 24, 29

Marcuse, Ludwig 14

Marinetti, Filippo Tommaso 171f., 322, 325

Martin, Karlheinz 99, 107, 114

Marx, Karl 281, 309, 313–15, 349, 351f.

Marxism 6, 37, 43, 48–52, 64, 89, 99, 122, 130f., 140, 159, 181, 210, 254, 283, 296, 317, 318

mass culture 11, 22, 104, 193, 279

mass production 23, 31, 51, 283, 311, 315, 330f.

mechanization 11, 15, 22, 43, 52, 53, 99, 193, 220, 264, 275, 283, 287, 308–15, 321, 322, 327–31, 338–40, 352, 356

Mecklenburg, Norbert 261f.

Mehring, Walter 52, 72–4, 76f., 93, 107, 112, 270, 328, 354; *Der Ketzerbrevier* 73, 328

Meisel, Edmund 113

Mennemeier, Franz Norbert 67, 95

Menschheitsdämmerung (ed. Kurt Pinthus) 14, 15, 36, 57–9, 61

militarism 184, 191, 250

Mitterer, Erika 84

modernism 7, 10, 49f., 60, 79, 96, 241f., 248, 263, 266, 302, 340f., 355–7

modernism, 'reactionary' 337

modernity 143f., 167f., 182, 248, 276, 287, 290, 356

Moholy-Nagy, Laszlo 112

Mombert, Alfred 24

montage 10, 49, 65, 93, 173–5, 177f., 231, 285, 291

Moritat 69, 71

Mottram, Ralph Hale 233f.

Mühsam, Erich 38, 70, 112

Müller, Hans-Harald 249

Müller, Robert 22

Müller, Traugott 113f.

Münchner Neueste Nachrichten 221

Munich 18, 118, 136, 153, 200f., 204, 229, 268, 272, 294

Murdoch, Brian 228

music hall 70

Musil, Robert 13, 42, 141f., 146, 167, 169, 172, 173, 178–88, 220, 223, 228f., 242, 276, 277, 331; *Der Mann ohne Eigenschaften* 178f., 183–8, 223, 276

Mussolini, Benito 20

Muthesius, Hermann 30

mysticism 68, 79

Nägele, Rainer 128, 133

Napoleon III 195

narrative representation 2, 11, 45, 49f., 141–88, 206f., 212f., 215f., 226–8, 239ff., 285f., 293, 353, 355

National Socialism 4, 5f., 7, 32, 54, 64f., 74, 80, 104, 157, 199, 200, 232, 246, 248, 261f., 264, 267, 287, 294–7, 321, 342f., 357

nationalism 10, 53f., 60, 97f., 103, 134, 147, 149, 157, 162, 181, 184, 229, 231f., 236f., 239, 243–8, 256, 257, 263, 265–7, 298f., 318, 321f., 336f., 338f., 347, 351

Natonek, Hans 47

Naturalism 29, 45f., 53, 97, 102, 106, 108, 120, 123, 127, 132, 134, 170, 206

nature poetry 79–81

Neher, Caspar 121, 129

Nestroy, Johann Nepomuk 134

neue Bücherschau, Die 36, 44, 47, 76, 84

neue Literatur, Die 265

neue Merkur, Der 16

neue Rundschau, Die 17, 22, 42, 155, 275

'Neue Sachlichkeit' 5–7, 9f., 12, 14–56, 166, 192, 220f., 225, 253, 270, 274, 290, 293, 305, 356

Neue Sachlichkeit (art exhibition)
24–6
Neumann, Erich 326
'new age' 39, 141, 167, 169, 272,
341, 349
'new man' 340, 344
New York 345, 346
newspapers 17, 19, 21, 33, 35, 37,
47 f., 52, 80, 199, 250, 263, 265,
268, 270–3, 278, 297 f., 330, 334
Nicolson, Harold 273
Niekisch, Ernst 336
Nietzsche, Friedrich 64, 99, 142, 155,
158, 162, 201 f., 242, 329, 340,
356
nihilism 2, 64, 68, 72, 218, 265, 278
Nordau, Max 261
Nungesser, Charles 346

office workers, *see* 'Angestellte'
Ortega y Gasset, José 331
Ossietzsky, Carl von 36
Ossowski, Miroslav 299
Otten, Karl 59, 308
Ottwalt, Ernst 49 f.; *Denn sie wissen,
was sie tun* 49 f.

pacifism 53, 232, 239, 283
Pallenberg, Max 114
pan-Europeanism 204
Paquet, Alfons 33, 35 f., 109 f., 117;
Fahnen 109, 117; *Sturmflut* 33, 110
Paris 16, 269, 345, 346
Paucker, Henri R. 6
peasants 261, 289, 295 f., 298, 299,
300 f.
Phelan, Anthony 4
photography 47, 110, 232, 297
Picasso, Pablo 26
Pinthus, Kurt 14, 15, 36, 43, 47,
57–9, 61
Piscator, Erwin 32 f., 97, 107–22,
125–7, 133, 139 f., 172, 174, 228,
306; *Das politische Theater* 108,
110 f., 113, 115 f., 117; *Revue Roter
Rummel* 109; *Trotz alledem* 109 f.
Piscatorbühne 34, 111–17, 119, 121,
125, 306, 344
Plato 185
Plessner, Helmut 305 f.
Plievier, Theodor 35, 126, 249 f.; *Des
Kaisers Kulis* 126, 249 f.
Poe, Edgar Allan 242

Poelzig, Hans 100
Pohl, Gerhart 84
Ponten, Joseph 226, 229, 245
press, *see* newspapers
production line, *see* mass production
proletariat, *see* Bund proletarisch-
revolutionärer Schriftsteller; worker;
working class
provincial life 11, 39, 81, 147, 201–3,
261 f., 263, 265, 267, 274, 276,
287–303, 341, 354, 355
Prümm, Karl 211
Prussia 183 f., 195, 254, 263, 264,
266, 298
psychoanalysis 166
Puccini, Giacomo 136

Querschnitt, Der 20 f.

Raabe, Wilhelm 307
racialism 10, 12, 54, 149, 246, 320,
342
Räderscheidt, Anton 29
radio 40, 90, 137, 139, 306, 330,
344–6
Radziwill, Franz 29
Raimund, Ferdinand Jakob 134
Rasch, Wolfdietrich 184, 195
Raschke, Martin 81
Rasputin, Grigoriy 20, 113
Räterepublik 18
Rathenau, Walter 141, 185
rationalism 54, 64, 97, 137, 158, 199,
202, 242, 320 f.
rationalization 4, 23, 43, 54, 167,
182, 197, 210, 212, 224, 269,
315–18, 337
realism, critical 2 f., 42 f., 55, 97,
137–40, 192, 263
realism, magical 24
realism, nineteenth-century 49, 253
Realism, Socialist 49
Reed, Terence James 152, 156, 163
Reger, Erik 23, 35, 216, 241, 334 f.;
Union der festen Hand 23, 216,
334 f.
regression 4, 53, 208 f.
Rehfisch, Hans-José 108
Reich, Bernhard 21
'reification' 43
Reinhardt, Hartmut 163
Reinhardt, Max 97 f., 100, 103,
104–7, 139

Remarque, Erich Maria 47, 227, 234–9, 240, 244, 248, 249, 251, 256; *Im Westen nichts Neues* 47, 227, 234–9, 244, 248, 249
Renn, Ludwig 229, 234, 239 f., 248, 256; *Krieg* 234, 239 f., 248; *Nachkrieg* 239
reportage 3, 33, 34–8, 44 f., 47 f., 49 f., 53, 81, 175, 220, 253, 334
resignation 43, 48, 154, 219 f., 223
revolution 18, 34, 37, 52, 56, 70, 98 f., 107, 111, 114 f., 119–21, 122, 126 f., 131 f., 153, 159, 170, 205, 216, 218 f., 228, 246, 250 f., 302, 314 f., 357
Revolution, Bolshevik 62, 110, 126, 132, 254
Revolution, French 152
revue 10, 21, 40–2, 105, 336
Richter, Otto 113
Ridley, Hugh 64
Rilke, Rainer Maria 57, 82, 304 f., 327; *Duineser Elegien* 57, 304; *Sonette an Orpheus* 57, 304
Rimbaud, Arthur 68
Ringelnatz, Joachim 70
Ringer, Fritz K. 168
Roberts, David 150 f., 153
Roh, Franz 24
Rolland, Romain 106, 108, 155
romance 39, 74, 292, 296, 300
Romantic irony 144 f.
Romanticism 1, 31, 39, 58 f., 78, 110, 116, 136, 145, 155, 161 f., 164, 171, 179, 264, 267, 282, 290, 322, 336, 339, 347
romanticization 42
Rorrison, Hugh 116 f.
Rosenberg, Alfred 261
Rosenstein, Doris 213
rote Fahne, Die 33 f., 116
Roth, Joseph 13, 35 f., 37, 45, 46–8, 55, 216–25, 272, 327; *Die Flucht ohne Ende* 47, 220, 224; *Hiob* 48, 221; *Hotel Savoy* 218 f.; *Radetzkymarsch* 48, 221–3; *Die Rebellion* 217 f.; "Schluß mit der 'Neuen Sachlichkeit'" 46–8; *Das Spinnennetz* 217; *Zipper und sein Vater* 220
Rotter, Alfred 108
Rotter, Fritz 108
Rousseau, Henri 26

Rousseau, Jean-Jacques 152
Rowohlt (publishing house) 20, 355
Rubiner, Ludwig 308
Ruf, Kai-Uwe 301
Rühle, Günther 101, 114
Ruhrgebiet 23, 87, 103, 335 f.
Rychner, Max 22, 330

Saalfeld, Martha 84
Sachlichkeit, *see* Neue Sachlichkeit
Salzburg 12, 98
Samuelson-Koenneker, Marguerite 80
Sassoon, Siegfried 226
satire 7, 44, 51 f., 60 f., 70, 72, 135, 147–9, 185, 191, 200, 231, 249, 251, 275, 294, 344
Schad, Christian 28 f.
Schäfer, Wilhelm 266 f.
Scharoun, Hans 32
Scharrer, Adam 250 f.; *Vaterlandslose Gesellen* 250 f.
Schauwecker, Franz 247 f.; *Aufbruch der Nation* 247 f.
Scheffler, Karl 268–70
Scheinwerfer, Der 23, 84 f.
Scherpe, Klaus 286
Schickele, René 59, 298 f.; *Das Erbe am Rhein* 298 f.
Schiffer, Marcellus 40 f.
Schiller, Friedrich 54, 100 f., 102 f., 104, 110, 242; *Wilhelm Tell* 102 f.
Schlichter, Rudolf 26
Schmeling, Christian 289
Schmied, Wieland 26, 30
Schmitt, Carl 337
Schneckenburger, Max 75
Schnitzler, Arthur 101
Scholti, August 299; *Ostwind* 299
Schopenhauer, Arthur 38, 309
Schrimpf, Georg 26
Schröder, Rudolf Alexander 77
Schubert, Franz 161 f.
Schütz, Erhard 335
Schwitters, Kurt 26
science fiction 319–27
Segeberg, Harro 310
Seghers, Anna 45, 295 f., 299; *Der Kopflohn* 295 f.; "Die Wellblech-Hütte" 45
self-cultivation 10
self-improvement 104, 199, 203
self-irony 41 f., 209, 242, 284
Sengle, Friedrich 287 f., 300

Shakespeare, William 102, 106, 118, 122
Sieburg, Friedrich 331
Simmel, Georg 276f., 330
Sinclair, Upton 38
Sloterdijk, Peter 8, 189
sobriety 5, 19, 23, 29f., 33, 37, 42f., 54
social democracy 149, 157, 165, 170, 200, 214, 250, 297f., 315, 317
socialism 10, 221, 250, 318, 336
Sophocles 124
Soviet Union 49, 107f., 169, 221, 233, 317, 329f.
Speirs, Ronald Cowan 18
Spengler, Oswald 21, 141, 166, 170, 181, 184, 219, 242, 277f., 286, 331, 337–9, 342, 344, 351; *Der Mensch und die Technik* 338f.; *Der Untergang des Abendlandes* 141, 166, 242, 277, 337f.
Spoliansky, Mischa 40f.
sport 21, 272, 275, 292
'stabilization phase' 7, 21, 52, 54, 108, 193, 197, 224, 233, 264, 317
Stadler, Ernst 58
Stalin, Josef 130
Stapel, Wilhelm 260, 264f.
Stehr, Hermann 262
Steinecke, Helmut 143
Steinweg, Reiner 128
Sternberg, Fritz 122, 348
Sternheim, Carl 38f., 101, 134; *Die Schule von Uznach oder Neue Sachlichkeit* 38f.
Stinnes, Hugo 255
Stramm, August 73
Strasbourg 256
Strauß, Emil 262
Strauß, Johann 136
Stresemann, Gustav 153, 193, 197
Sturm, Der 76, 171
Stuttgart 31f., 179, 315
Styan, John Louis 106
Subiotto, Arrigo 212
Süddeutsche Monatshefte 264f.
surrealism 242
symbolism 68
Swales, Martin 157

Tage-Buch, Das 35, 47, 265
Tat, Die 21

Taut, Bruno 32
Taut, Max 32
Taylor, Frederick Winslow 315–17, 318, 334
technocracy 44, 257, 320f., 322f., 327, 334, 339, 351
technology 7, 8, 10, 11, 21, 23, 29, 31, 32–4, 37, 39f., 42, 54, 55, 64, 94, 105, 110–14, 117, 118–21, 129, 169f., 245, 276, 304–52, 354, 356
telephone 40, 51
Tergit, Gabriele 273; *Käsebier erobert den Kurfürstendamm* 273f.
theatre 2, 11, 21, 32–4, 37, 42–4, 88, 95–140, 155, 264, 353f., 355
Third Reich, *see* National Socialism
Thoma, Ludwig 134, 300
Tirpitz, Alfred von 150, 229
Toller, Ernst 17, 34, 37f., 45, 48, 55, 99, 113–16, 134, 231, 306, 308, 312–14, 328; *Feuer aus den Kesseln* 126; *Hoppla, wir leben!* 34, 113–16, 125, 306; *Die Maschinenstürmer* 114, 312–14; *Masse Mensch* 114; *Die Wandlung* 17, 99, 231, 308
Tolstoy, Alexei 113
Tolstoy, Leo 49f., 108, 300
Trakl, Georg 58
transience 78
travel writing 12, 109
Travers, Martin 229f.
Troeltsch, Ernst 161
Trommler, Frank 6
Trotsky, Leon 49
Tucholsky, Kurt 48, 52, 72, 74, 76, 253, 265, 275
Tzara, Tristan 16

Ullstein (publishing house) 235, 238f., 355
Unruh, Fritz von 41, 57, 134, 230; *Phaea* 41, 57
unsentimentality 39–41, 44, 54, 120, 215, 299
urban life 11, 41, 73f., 75, 78, 81, 89–92, 98, 125, 173f., 260f., 262–5, 267–87, 302f., 322f., 341, 354, 356
utilitarianism, *see* functionalism
Utitz, Emil 53f.; *Die Überwindung des Expressionismus* 53f.

utopianism 2, 62, 185 f., 231, 260, 270, 356 f.

Vallentin, Maxim 108, 329
van der Rohe, Mies 31
Verdun 244–7, 257 f.
verism 29
Versailles, Treaty of 228, 261, 293, 317, 319
Vidor, King 234
Vienna 134, 268 f., 294
24 neue deutsche Erzähler (ed. Hermann Kesten) 45 f., 57
Vieth von Golssenau, Arnold Friedrich, *see* Renn, Ludwig
Villon, François 70, 72
vitalism 7, 9, 18 f., 54, 155, 161, 242–4, 247 f., 277, 286 f., 325 f., 327 f., 329, 337–9, 351, 354, 357
Vogel, Bruno 232 f.
Vogt-Praclik, Kornelia 248
Völker, Karl 29, 30
Volksbühne 33, 103–5, 108–11, 114, 117, 118, 126, 132
Volksstück 133–9
von der Vring, Georg 229, 234, 249; *Soldat Suhren* 234, 249
Vossische Zeitung 22, 80, 234 f., 267, 272

Wagener, Hans 205 f.
Wagner, Martin 269
Wagner, Richard 97
Wandt, Heinrich 232
war novels 2, 11, 35, 47, 226–59
Wassermann, Jakob 10, 277, 278
Weber, Max 167, 248, 356
Wedderkop, Hermann von 20 f.
Wedekind, Frank 69 f., 71, 93, 101, 152
Wehner, Josef Magnus 245 f.; *Sieben vor Verdun* 245 f.
Weigel, Helene 124, 132
Weill, Kurt 87, 103, 121, 124, 129, 335, 345 f.
Weimar 31
Weinheber, Josef 77
Weininger, Otto 165
Weiskopf, Franz Carl 45
Weiß, Ernst 38, 354
Weiß, Konrad 78
Weißenhofsiedlung 32

Welk, Ehm 110 f.
Weltbühne, Die 35, 43, 51, 59, 265
Werfel, Franz 12, 58 f., 82, 181, 216, 308; *Barbara oder Die Frömmigkeit* 216
Werkbund 30 f., 356
Westheim, Paul 270
white-collar workers, *see* 'Angestellte'
Wild, Rainer 220
Wilde, Oscar 242
Wilhelm II 147–50, 151, 156, 164, 183, 232, 250
Wilhelm, Crown Prince 246
Wilhelmine Germany 9, 15, 56, 97, 102, 147–54, 163 f., 195, 253 f.
Willett, John 5, 41, 95
Winckelmann, Johann Joachim 143
Wittgenstein, Ludwig 167
Wolf, Friedrich 125, 127; *Cyankali* 125; *Die Matrosen von Cattaro* 126 f.; *Tai Yang erwacht* 127
Wolfenstein, Alfred 59
Wolfskehl, Karl 21
women writers 12, 213–16, 355
workers 87, 107, 130, 165, 210, 212, 214, 250 f., 255, 258, 307, 310 f., 313, 315, 317, 334–6, 341 f., 352
working class 7, 11, 34, 70, 103 f., 107–12, 115 f., 132, 138, 148, 150, 210, 212, 250, 258, 315, 317, 321
worker correspondents 34
World War I 2, 5, 8, 9, 12 f., 15, 18, 21, 22, 31, 35, 46, 47, 56, 59, 68, 73, 93, 99, 102, 104, 107, 116, 126, 141, 147 f., 150 f., 153, 154–6, 160, 163, 168, 181, 183, 186, 189, 191, 205, 207, 220 f., 223, 226–59, 261, 263, 269, 277, 296, 302, 305, 308, 309 f., 320, 322 f., 334, 337, 339 f., 353, 355
World War II 3, 126, 249, 345, 355, 356 f.
Wright, Elizabeth 128, 131
Wunberg, Gotthart 219 f.
Wunderwald, Gustav 29, 270 f.
Würzburg 288–90, 299

Zech, Paul 24, 59
Zimmermann, Peter 263
Zobeltitz, Hanns von 319
Zöberlein, Hans 246 f.; *Der Glaube an Deutschland* 246 f.

Zola, Émile 38, 45
Zollikofer, Fred von 84
Zuckmayer, Carl 118, 134–6; *Der fröhliche Weinberg* 134–6; *Der Hauptmann von Köpenick* 135; *Katharina Knie* 135; *Schinderhannes* 135

Zweig, Arnold 36, 47, 100, 216, 226, 234 f., 249, 253–9; *De Vriendt kehrt heim* 216; *Erziehung vor Verdun* 257–9; *Junge Frau von 1914* 256 f.; *Der Streit um den Sergeanten Grischa* 47, 234 f., 249, 253–6
Zweig, Stefan 57 f., 221, 330